# Citizens and Paupers

# Citizens and Paupers

*Relief, Rights, and Race, from the Freedmen's Bureau to Workfare*

CHAD ALAN GOLDBERG

THE UNIVERSITY OF CHICAGO PRESS    CHICAGO AND LONDON

CHAD ALAN GOLDBERG is associate professor of sociology at the University of Wisconsin–Madison. This is his first book.

The University of Chicago Press, Chicago 60637
The University of Chicago Press, Ltd., London
© 2007 by The University of Chicago
All rights reserved. Published 2007
Printed in the United States of America
16 15 14 13 12 11 10 09 08 07      1 2 3 4 5

ISBN-13: 978-0-226-30076-4 (cloth)
ISBN-13: 978-0-226-30077-1 (paper)
ISBN-10: 0-226-30076-5 (cloth)
ISBN-10: 0-226-30077-3 (paper)

Library of Congress Cataloging-in-Publication Data

Goldberg, Chad Alan.
    Citizens and paupers : relief, rights, and race from the Freedmen's Bureau to workfare / Chad Alan Goldberg.
        p.   cm.
    Includes bibliographical references and index.
    ISBN-13: 978-0-226-30076-4 (cloth : alk. paper)
    ISBN-10: 0-226-30076-5 (cloth : alk. paper)
    ISBN-13: 978-0-226-30077-1 (pbk. : alk. paper)
    ISBN-10: 0-226-30077-3 (alk. paper)
    1. Public welfare—United States—History.   2. Welfare state—United States—History.
I. Title.
    HV91.G56   2007
    361.5'560973—dc22
                                                          2007014108

Among American citizens there should be no forgotten men and no forgotten races.

*Franklin Delano Roosevelt,*
*Howard University, Washington, DC, October 26, 1936*

# Contents

TO MY TEACHERS

# Abbreviations

| | |
|---|---|
| ACORN | Association of Community Organizations for Reform Now |
| ADC | Aid to Dependent Children |
| AFDC | Aid to Families with Dependent Children |
| AFL | American Federation of Labor |
| AFSCME | American Federation of State, County, and Municipal Employees |
| CCC | Civilian Conservation Corps |
| CETA | Comprehensive Employment and Training Act |
| CGO | New York City Council Committee on Governmental Operations |
| CGW/CHE | New York City Council Committee on General Welfare and Committee on Higher Education |
| CIO | Congress of Industrial Organizations |
| EITC | Earned Income Tax Credit |
| FLSA | Fair Labor Standards Act |
| GAR | Grand Army of the Republic |
| HRA | Human Resources Administration |
| IRS | Internal Revenue Service |
| MTA | Metropolitan Transportation Authority |
| NAACP | National Association for the Advancement of Colored People |
| NELP | National Employment Law Project |
| NLRB | National Labor Relations Board |
| NNC | National Negro Congress |
| NUL | National Urban League |
| NYSEC | New York State Economic Council |
| NYWRB | New York Workers' Rights Board |

| OAA | Old Age Assistance |
| OAI | Old Age Insurance |
| OASDI | Old Age and Survivors Disability Insurance |
| OASI | Old Age and Survivors Insurance |
| PRWOA | Personal Responsibility and Work Opportunity Act |
| PWA | Public Works Administration |
| SSB | Social Security Board |
| SNA | Safety Net Assistance |
| TANF | Temporary Assistance to Needy Families |
| UNITE | Union of Needle Trades, Industrial, and Textile Employees |
| WEP | Work Experience Program |
| WIN | Work Incentive Program |
| WPA | Works Progress Administration |

# Acknowledgments

Science, as John Dewey pointed out, is a collaborative enterprise. Nothing makes this so apparent as the experience of researching and writing a book. I am grateful to everyone who offered assistance, encouragement, and advice for improving earlier versions and pieces of this manuscript.

This book is loosely based upon the doctoral dissertation I wrote at the New School for Social Research. I owe a special debt of gratitude to Mustafa Emirbayer, my committee chair, who has also been my teacher, mentor, colleague, and friend. More than anyone else, he has influenced how I think about and practice sociology. He has given me ceaseless encouragement and has guided me with unfailingly good advice. Without him, I would never have undertaken the project of transforming my dissertation into the ambitious book it has become. I am also grateful to Frances Fox Piven for the warm and generous support, advice, and encouragement she has given me since I was a graduate student. Although she will no doubt disagree with some things in this book, it would not have been possible without everything I have learned from her and her work over the years, starting in college, when I read *Poor People's Movements* for the first time. Thanks also to Claus Offe, whose brilliant and insightful work stimulated my interest in the welfare state, and who generously shared his time and expertise; Nancy Fraser, whose work on women, welfare, and the "politics of need interpretation" inspired my research; and Charles Tilly, who kindly gave me the benefit of his advice, despite his initial skepticism about the project.

While at the New School for Social Research, I benefited from the support and advice of many people. Thanks to my New College friends, including Kevin Arlyck, Danielle Chynoweth, Daphne Gabrieli, Emily and

John Heath, Paul Kennedy, Stan Kranc, Amy Laitinen, Dana Lockwood, Mike Palmer, Tracy Rahn, Mike Rothbaum, and Mark Sanders, who kept me grounded; the friends I made in graduate school, including Sada Aksartova, Hubertus Buchstein, Victoria Johnson, Adam Lupel, Lyn Macgregor, Stacy McGoldrick, Joyce Robbins, Julie Stewart, and Roberta Ziemba; my New School teachers, including Andrew Arato, Jeffrey Goldfarb, and Vera Zolberg; critics and commentators at the New York University sociology department's "Power, Politics, and Protest" workshop, including Chris Bonastia, Craig Calhoun, Brian Gifford, Jeff Goodwin, Drew Halfmann, and Steven Lukes; the participants in Charles Tilly's "Contentious Politics" workshop at Columbia University, including Brenda Coughlin, Michael Hanagan, and Francesca Polletta; and the kindred spirits I met along the way, including Jeanette Gabriel, John Krinsky, Ellen Reese, and Brian Steensland. I am also grateful to Millie Silva, Nate, Juanita, and the other ACORN organizers and workfare workers whose struggle I was privileged to participate in and observe. Thanks to my parents (my first teachers), for their love and support, and my brother Jarrod, who persuaded me to finish graduate school when a personal crisis caused me to seriously consider dropping out. Finally, Anna Paretskaya deserves special mention. She has seen this project develop from dissertation to book, and in countless conversations has helped me to clarify and develop my ideas. She has been a wonderful partner to whom I am deeply indebted for her good counsel, brilliant insights, and unstinting encouragement and support.

When I came to the University of Wisconsin in 2001, I incurred a new set of debts. I am especially grateful to Phil Gorski and Erik Wright, who have been outstanding faculty mentors. I thank all of the colleagues, students, and friends who gave me advice, suggestions, or encouragement, including Bert Adams, Rob Asen, Richard Aviles, J. P. and Elyce Bader, Ian Beilin, Jenny Belcher (who taught me long before I came to Wisconsin to be nobody but myself), Uri Ben-Eliezer, Matt Boxer, Michelle Bright, Peter Brinson (a fellow Novocollegian), Kenny Burruss (also a Novocollegian), Chas Camic, Jane Collins, Matt Desmond, Mitch Duneier, Nina Eliasoph, Ivan Ermakoff, Myra Marx Ferree, Anna Fishzon, Bob Freeland, Joan Fujimura, Adam Gamoran, Anne Genereux, Jess Gilbert, Hanna Grol-Prokopczyk, Harry Hanbury (another Novocollegian), Ben Herzog, Ellen and Richard Jacobson, Adriana Kemp, Shamus Khan, Paul Lichterman, Mara Loveman, Cameron Macdonald, John Levi Martin, Jerry Marwell, Tony Michels, Camilla Mortensen (also a Novocollegian),

Matt Nichter, Taly Noam, Jesse Norris, Dan O'Brien (another fellow
Novocollegian), Pam Oliver, Jamie Peck, Kerstin Schaars, Carly Schall,
Gay Seidman (who generously read and commented on the entire first
draft), Joe Soss, Mark Suchman, Ruth López Turley, Franklin Wilson,
and Jonathan Zeitlin. Thanks also to the Politics, Culture, and Society
brownbag; the Race & Ethnicity brownbag; the "Flying Culture" discussion group; and the crack staff of the University of Wisconsin sociology
department. I was fortunate to receive helpful comments and suggestions from Eileen Boris, Elisabeth Clemens, Janet Irons, Jason Kaufman,
James Lorence, Robin Stryker, Jeff Weintraub, and Viviana Zelizer. I am
grateful to Peter Bearman and Jeff Goodwin for helping to arrange visit-
ing scholar status at Columbia University and New York University. I am
also grateful for the assistance of archivists, librarians, and staff at Columbia University; the Franklin D. Roosevelt Presidential Library; the
John W. Kluge Center at the Library of Congress; the National Archives
and Records Administration; the New York Public Library, including the
Schomburg Center for Research in Black Culture; New York University,
including the Tamiment Library and Robert F. Wagner Labor Archives;
the University of Wisconsin; and the Wisconsin Historical Society. The
research for *Citizens and Paupers* was funded by generous grants from
the University of Wisconsin Graduate School; the 2005–2006 J. Franklin
Jameson Fellowship in American History from the Library of Congress
and the American Historical Association; and a 2006 summer research
fellowship from New York University's Center for the Study of the Impact of the Cold War on the United States.

Last but not least are the debts I incurred during the publication of
*Citizens and Paupers*. I am grateful to the legendary Doug Mitchell, Tim
McGovern, Mary Gehl, and the rest of the outstanding team at University of Chicago Press, with whom I have been privileged to work. Many
thanks to Edwin Amenta and Robert Lieberman, who reviewed my manuscript. Not only did I learn a great deal from their own work, but I also
benefited immensely from their careful reading of my manuscript and
their thoughtful recommendations. Thanks to Blackwell Publishing for
permission to reprint material from "Welfare Recipients or Workers?
Contesting the Workfare State in New York City," *Sociological Theory* 19,
no. 2 (July 2001): 187–218. Thanks to Springer Science and Business
Media for permission to reprint material from "Haunted by the Specter of Communism: Collective Identity and Resource Mobilization in the
Demise of the Workers Alliance of America," *Theory and Society* 32,

no. 5–6 (December 2003): 725–773. Thanks to Duke University Press for permission to reprint material from "Contesting the Status of Relief Workers during the New Deal: The Workers Alliance of America and the Works Progress Administration, 1935–1941," *Social Science History* 29, no. 3 (Fall 2005): 337–371.

I close with a few words of modesty from T. H. Marshall, a man whose work inspired this book. What Marshall said about his now famous lecture "Citizenship and Social Class" ([1949] 1964, 65) applies to this work as well.

> It may be . . . that sociology is on trial here in my person. If so, I am sure I can rely on you to be scrupulously fair in your judgment, and to regard any merit you may find in my lectures as evidence of the academic value of the subject I profess, while treating everything in them that appears to you paltry, common or ill-conceived as the product of qualities peculiar to myself and not to be found in any of my colleagues.

Chad Alan Goldberg
December 12, 2006
Madison, Wisconsin

## CHAPTER ONE

# Paupers or Citizens?

## Struggles over the Status and Rights of Welfare State Claimants

What happens in politics depends upon the way in which people are divided.—E. E. Schatt-schneider, *The Semisovereign People: A Realist's View of Democracy in America*

The stigma which clung to poor relief expressed the deep feelings of a people who understood that those who accepted relief must cross the road that separated the community of citizens from the outcast community of the destitute. . . . The stigma which attached to the Poor Law made 'pauper' a derogatory term defining a class.—T. H. Marshall, *Class, Citizenship and Social Development*

The central thesis of this book is that social welfare policies have been preeminent sites for political struggles over the meaning and boundaries of citizenship in the United States. These struggles are easier to grasp if we understand citizenship as an instrument of social closure through which people monopolize valuable material and symbolic goods while excluding others. As Brubaker (1992, chap. 1) has shown, the modern state distinguishes members from foreigners, conferring rights upon the former while excluding the latter. In the nineteenth century, for example, states restricted and regulated the immigration of the foreign poor in order to exclude them from national systems of poor relief (Brubaker 1992, 64–71; R. Smith 1997, 225–27). This form of social closure, which may be termed external, excludes noncitizens from rights and benefits that are available only to citizens. In addition, if citizenship is understood to be a gradational category rather than a status that one either wholly possesses or completely lacks, then citizenship may also be seen as a means of internal social closure, an "instrument of social stratification" in the words of T. H. Marshall ([1949] 1964, 110), which operates within the boundaries of the polity. This is readily apparent from the common-place distinction between second-class and full citizenship. From this perspective, stripping a person of citizenship or barring her from acquiring it are the most extreme forms of civic exclusion—but they are not the only ones. People who are nominally citizens (i.e., members of the polity) but whose citizenship rights are circumscribed or curtailed also experience a form of civic exclusion: They are excluded from some (though generally not all) of the benefits associated with citizenship. Again, poor relief provides a case in point, for states not only barred the immigration of foreign paupers in the nineteenth century but also curtailed the citizenship rights of native-born or naturalized paupers.[1]

The internal social closure to which paupers were subjected may be better understood if, following Marshall ([1949] 1964, 71–72), we distinguish civil rights necessary for individual freedom, political rights to participate in the exercise of political power, and social rights to at least "a modicum of economic welfare and security." Although Marshall associated social rights with the twentieth-century welfare state, he did not claim that social rights were a creation of the welfare state. In fact, Marshall noted, social rights were established well before the modern welfare state, but they were "detached from the status of citizenship" (80). In other words, paupers forfeited their civil and political rights in exchange for relief. Traditional poor relief thus "treated the claims of the poor, not as an integral part of the rights of the citizen, but as an alternative to them—as claims which could be met only if the claimants ceased to be citizens in any true sense of the word" (80). Furthermore, "this divorce of social rights from the status of citizenship" (81) was a gendered phenomenon that extended beyond relief to the regulation of labor markets. Legislators and judges, Marshall observed, initially refused to apply protective labor laws "to the adult male—the citizen *par excellence*. And they did so out of respect for his status as a citizen, on the grounds that enforced protective measures curtailed the civil right to conclude a free contract of employment. Protection was confined to women and children, and champions of women's rights were quick to detect the implied insult. Women were protected because they were not citizens. If they wished to enjoy full and responsible citizenship, they must forgo protection" (81). Hence, in the nineteenth century, citizenship was equated with manly independence and liberty of contract, while relief and protective labor laws were defined as paternalistic and demasculinizing. In Marshall's view, the modern welfare state broke with this legacy, not by establishing social rights, but by incorporating social rights into the status of citizenship.[2]

This book builds on Marshall's insights, particularly his suggestion that civil and political rights could be and often were treated as an alternative to social rights rather than a foundation for them. At the same time, I challenge Marshall's claim that the twentieth-century welfare state broke definitively with traditional poor relief; I suggest that the transition from poor relief to the welfare state was instead quite a bit messier.[3] As shown in the chapters that follow, major policy innovations in the United States that expanded state involvement in social provision often generated intense struggles over whether to model the new policy on or sharply distinguish it from traditional poor relief. What Heclo (1974, 317) observes about Britain and Sweden was, thus, true in America as well: new policies were shaped by the "reaction against the poor law" and the search for "an alternative to poor relief" for those deemed deserving. Yet Heclo's observation captures only half of the truth, for reformers were constrained again and again by conservatives (in the literal sense of the word) who drew different lessons from the past and sought to preserve or reproduce many of the features of traditional poor relief. At stake in these struggles were the citizenship status and rights of the policies' clients, who struggled not only to acquire new social rights but also to avoid losing their civil and political rights in the process.[4] These struggles continued to emerge well into the twentieth century, reflecting broader and more enduring conflicts over the meaning of citizenship and its relationship to labor, gender, nationality, and race in the United States.[5]

Along with recurring pressures to limit the rights of welfare state claimants, there is another reason why social welfare policies have so often been the site of political struggles over the meaning and boundaries of citizenship. Traditional poor relief tended to conflate poverty with deviance and criminality, and the poorhouse consequently provided care to the needy on condition that they "agreed to reform their characters" (Wagner 2005, 40–41). New social welfare policies often assumed this rehabilitative function. Such policies continued to operate on the assumption that poverty was a consequence (or, alternatively, a cause) of poor morals and poor habits, and they aimed, implicitly or explicitly, to mold the habits, behavior, or dispositions of their clients and thereby turn them into (or preserve their character as) good and virtuous citizens. Thus, these policies were not merely exclusionary—even when they stripped recipients of citizenship rights—but were also formative and constitutive. This rehabilitative function ensured that new social policies had the potential to be as paternalistic and authoritarian as traditional poor relief. When policymakers agreed that recipients' vices or deficiencies made them unworthy of full citizenship, and when they viewed the recipients as suitable objects for civic improvement, new policies usually became not so much a means of helping the recipients as they were, but a means of making them what they ought to be. The purpose of the policy, in other words, became the creation of a new person upon whom policymakers could write something acceptable to themselves. As in the poorhouse, the rights of the recipient became conditional upon his or her transformation. Under these circumstances, conflicts frequently arose over the nature of the transformation required, the degree to which it had been or could be successfully completed, and the fairness of the demands placed upon recipients. Of course, attempts by policymakers to foster good citizenship need not be so sinister. Indeed, when autonomy and participation are deemed essential to citizenship, such efforts may even empower recipients. Yet even the most benign efforts are likely to turn social welfare policies into sites of political struggle, because policymakers, recipients, and other interested groups rarely agree about what it means to be a good citizen. In this way, too, social welfare policies provide a window into larger conflicts over the content and meaning of citizenship.[6]

## Research Design and Overview

The chapters that follow examine the contested status and rights of welfare state claimants in the United States through a comparison of three major policy innovations from the nineteenth century onward: the Freedmen's Bureau (1865–1872), the Works Progress Administration (WPA, later renamed Work Projects Administration, 1935–1942), and the dramatic expansion of workfare after the 1996 federal welfare reform. These cases were selected for several reasons. All of them involved important changes in social welfare policy that postdated traditional poor relief. In addition, each of these policy innovations created a new group of clients whose status and rights were initially uncertain and subsequently contested. Finally, in all three cases, the policy innovations coincided with moments of crisis and reform: the Civil War and Reconstruction; the

Great Depression and the New Deal; and the protracted unraveling of Fordism, the New Deal political order, and the Keynesian welfare state. In at least the first two cases, the policy innovations did not merely affect the citizenship status and rights of their newly defined clients, but were part of larger processes of political and constitutional change that transformed American citizenship more generally.

Drawing on a combination of archival and secondary sources, chapter 2 focuses on the Freedmen's Bureau. In the aftermath of the Civil War, four million freed slaves-turned-citizens sought economic independence in the form of land redistribution. What they received instead were limited and grudging forms of government assistance from the U.S. Bureau of Refugees, Freedmen, and Abandoned Lands, America's first federal welfare and regulatory agency. The Freedmen's Bureau, as it was popularly known, positioned its clients in contradictory ways. The agency strove to assist freedpeople's transition from slavery to freedom, worked to establish and protect new citizenship rights for them, and conditioned public relief on work in keeping with the prevailing ideology of free labor. Nevertheless, the bureau's relief and regulatory efforts made freedpeople vulnerable to stigmatizing charges of dependence, idleness, and pauperism, all of which were understood to be incompatible with full citizenship. Consequently, from 1865 until Congress terminated the Freedmen's Bureau in 1872, the agency's supporters and opponents, including freedpeople themselves, clashed over the civic status and rights of its clients.

Sixty years later, when millions of Americans found themselves unemployed as a result of a new and different kind of crisis, the unemployed demanded jobs. What they received instead were new forms of federal assistance, including work relief from the WPA, a federal program that provided temporary employment at a substandard security wage for millions of Americans certified as needy by their local relief agencies. This policy innovation, also investigated through archival and secondary sources, is the focus of chapter 4. Like the Freedmen's Bureau, the WPA positioned its clients inconsistently. Neither the policymakers who designed the program nor the officials who administered it ever resolved whether the WPA should operate as a work program or a relief program. Although supporters praised the WPA for allowing the unemployed to preserve their dignity and self-respect as workers and citizens, it was never completely divorced from local relief. Consequently, as one administrator ruefully admitted, the program forced workers to "submit to the equivalent of a pauper's oath" (quoted in D. Howard 1943, 413).

These conflicting tendencies gave rise to an intense struggle from 1935 until Congress terminated the WPA in 1942 concerning the civic status and rights of WPA workers. While WPA workers mobilized to protect and expand their citizenship rights, conservative countermovements sought to disenfranchise federal relief recipients and curtail their political activities.

In 1996, Congress passed the Personal Responsibility and Work Opportunity Reconciliation Act, which radically reshaped the social policies established by the New Deal. Fulfilling President Clinton's promise to "end welfare as we know it" (Clinton 1993), the legislation repealed the Aid to Families with Dependent Children (AFDC) program, which had been the primary form of public assistance for poor, single mothers in the United States for sixty years. Like unemployed workers in the 1930s, welfare recipients had demanded jobs, not welfare. What they received instead were decentralized, locally administered workfare programs that required most adult public-assistance recipients to work within two years of receiving aid. Using participant observation of a workfare organizing campaign; documents and reports from government, labor unions, and community organizing groups; newspaper accounts; and secondary sources, chapter 6 focuses on the largest of these workfare programs, which was in New York City. There, tens of thousands of welfare recipients labored in municipal agencies in exchange for their meager benefits. Like the Freedmen's Bureau and the WPA, New York's workfare program positioned its clients in ambiguous ways. Welfare recipients found themselves doing the same work as unionized municipal employees and often working alongside them, but receiving only a fraction of union pay and little protection from existing labor laws. In the 1990s, New York City workfare workers denounced the program as a new form of slavery, echoing earlier struggles that had arisen with the Freedmen's Bureau and the WPA, and demanded the same rights and protections as unionized municipal employees.

Through a comparison of these three primary cases, this book seeks to explain why struggles over the citizenship status and rights of welfare state claimants emerge, when they are most likely to erupt, and why these struggles are a recurring feature of American welfare state development. To be sure, these cases are dissimilar in many respects; the struggles of freedpeople, WPA workers, and workfare workers took place in very different economic, social, political, and historical contexts. Yet it is precisely these differences that make comparison fruitful. These comparisons reveal that similar mechanisms and processes generated similar struggles over the citizenship status and rights of welfare state claimants in all three cases, despite the many other differences between the cases that might have seemed causally relevant. As Charles Tilly (1995, 1602) describes it, this explanatory strategy involves "breaking down big events into causally connected sequences of events, and examining each link in the chain" in order to "identify deep causal analogies across detailed features of ostensibly different historical sequences." In other words, my comparisons do not aim to show that these cases are equivalent or that they conform to a single invariant model; rather, it is to demonstrate that historically specific struggles over the citizenship status and rights of welfare state claimants can be accounted for in terms of more general social mechanisms or combinations of mechanisms. Some of these mechanisms, such as social closure, have already been noted. Others, including policy competition, moral entrepreneurship, and criteria shifting, are described more fully below.[7]

This book also seeks to explain variation in the outcomes of these struggles. Why are some welfare state claimants classed as paupers who must forfeit their civil and political rights while others successfully obtain recognition as full rights–bearing citizens who have earned and deserve public aid? Because freedpeople, WPA workers, and workfare workers largely failed to obtain recognition as full citizens, it is necessary to contrast their struggles with those of others who were more successful. To gain analytical leverage, these secondary cases should be as similar as possible to the primary cases except for the outcomes. Comparison of the failed struggles with those that were more successful can then help to reveal the crucial set of mechanisms and processes that account for this difference in outcomes. To this end, the book contrasts the failed struggles of freedpeople, WPA workers, and workfare workers with the more-successful struggles over the status and rights of Civil War pensioners in the postbellum nineteenth century (described in chapter 3), Old Age Insurance (OAI) recipients in the 1930s and 1940s (covered in chapter 5), and Earned Income Tax Credit (EITC) recipients in the 1990s (the focus of chapter 7). Since these cases are less central to the book, they are treated more briefly and described in less detail, and my discussion of them relies more heavily on secondary sources.

The primary and secondary cases are comparable in a number of respects. Struggles over the Freedmen's Bureau and Civil War veterans' pensions were roughly contemporary, as were struggles over the WPA and OAI and struggles over workfare and the EITC. By contrasting the struggles of freedpeople, WPA workers, and workfare workers against contemporaneous struggles, I aim to control as much as possible for differences in the historical contexts that might possibly account for the success or failure of these struggles. Furthermore, in each paired comparison of a primary case and a secondary case, the policies in question shared important structural features, and Americans used similar language and invoked the same civic ideals to contest the status and rights of policy clients. All of the policies examined here tied benefits to work or public service of some kind, and their supporters tried to distinguish the policies from traditional poor relief or public assistance on that basis. Yet in spite of these similarities, the secondary cases were more successful. Unlike freedpeople, Civil War pensioners were lauded as morally worthy citizen-soldiers whose virtuous service entitled them to "all the public provision necessary to live honorable and decent lives free from want" (Skocpol 1992, 149). The Civil War pension system, "like subsequent provision for 'deserving' Americans," was thus "defined in opposition to charity or public programs for paupers at state and local levels" (149). Likewise, OAI recipients obtained recognition as self-supporting individuals who earned their benefits rather than as dependent paupers in need of discipline and supervision. Similarly, policymakers and the public defined EITC recipients as the working rather than the idle poor—and thus, morally worthy. In summary, the book's logic of comparison mainly stresses how the struggles of freedpeople, WPA workers, and workfare workers were similar, but these similarities are underscored through the secondary and contrasting cases of Civil War veterans' pensions, OAI, and the EITC.

## Theoretical Framework and Contributions

To understand the origins and outcomes of America's recurring conflicts regarding the citizenship status and rights of welfare state claimants, this book builds upon and extends three broad lines of sociological research. First, it aims to deepen our understanding of the relationships among social policy, gender, and race. Previous studies have shown how a gendered and racialized division between citizens and paupers was reproduced in the federal structure of the New Deal welfare state (Fraser 1989; Quadagno 1994; Lieberman 1998; Brown 1999; Kessler-Harris 2001; Williams 2003). In the 1930s, nationally administered social insurance and labor policies positioned their predominantly white, male clients as "rights-bearing individuals" and "members of a liberal regime. . . . To New Dealers, these persons qualified as 'independent' citizens, and thus as free and equal bearers of rights, strictly because they were long-term, full-time wage earners" (Mettler 1998, xi, 23). In contrast, women and minority men were more likely to be relegated to state-administered public assistance programs and protective labor laws, which treated their clients "in a nonliberal manner" as "dependent persons who required supervision and protection rather than as bearers of rights" (Mettler 1998, xi–xii, 24). Building on these insights, I show how freedpeople, WPA workers, and workfare workers all struggled to avoid being classed as dependent paupers in need of discipline and supervision while demanding recognition as independent, rights-bearing citizens. They did so not by eschewing government assistance or protection but by trying to renegotiate their relationship with the state. At the same time, this book extends the insights of feminist scholarship beyond the New Deal, looking backward toward America's "precocious social spending regime" (Skocpol 1992, 63) in the nineteenth century and forward to its emerging workfare state in the twenty-first century. Furthermore, rather than contrasting the liberal and illiberal tiers of the American welfare state, it focuses on contradictory policies that combined both liberal and illiberal features. These hybrid policies comprise an understudied third tier of the American welfare state.[8]

Second, this book draws upon and contributes to historical-institutionalist studies of the welfare state. As previous studies have shown, institutions structure political struggles and their outcomes in a variety of ways. Institutions influence the formation of groups and their political capacities, ideas, and demands; they shape how individuals and groups define their interests and goals; and they provide models, schemas, or scripts for behavior (Skocpol 1985; Steinmo, Thelen, and Longstreth 1992; Clemens and Cook 1999). From this perspective, "policies themselves must be seen as politically consequential structures" that restructure politics (Pierson 1994, 46). In other words, policies are not merely an outcome or consequence of past political struggles; they also influence subsequent struggles through their material and symbolic effects on political elites, interest groups, and mass publics (Pierson 1993; Mettler and Soss 2004). Historical institutionalists have described these effects as "policy feedbacks" (Skocpol and Amenta 1986, 149–51; Quadagno 1987, 118–19; Weir, Orloff, and Skocpol 1988a, 25–27; Skocpol 1992, 57–60; Pierson

1994, 39–50). Following Orloff (1993a, 304–5), two broad perspectives on policy feedbacks can be distinguished: on the one hand, the social citizenship perspective "emphasizes the potential of social provision in democratic states, secured at least partially through the political struggles of citizens and others, to counter domination." On the other hand, the social control perspective emphasizes how "social policies reflect and reinforce relations of dominance and exploitation." As Soss (2002, 15) points out, scholars frequently link these theories to the different tiers of the U.S. welfare state, suggesting that "social insurance recipients are treated as something akin to social citizens—they are 'rights-bearing beneficiaries and purchasing consumers of services'—while public assistance recipients are treated as dependent objects of social control." This book suggests the need for a more complex view that transcends the social citizenship/social control dichotomy, at least when it comes to the kinds of hybrid policies examined here. Without denying the disciplinary and regulatory functions of the Freedmen's Bureau, the WPA, and workfare, I question whether these policies always conformed to a coherent functionalist logic. Instead, I draw attention to the internal contradictions of the welfare state and the opportunities for resistance and social change those contradictions open up (cf. Habermas 1975; Offe 1984).

Finally, drawing upon and extending the cultural sociology of Pierre Bourdieu, this book treats conflicts over the citizenship status and rights of welfare state claimants as classification struggles. To be more precise, they are struggles to classify clients as citizens or paupers. While struggles over names and labels may appear trivial, they can in fact have far-reaching consequences. At stake in classification struggles is "the power to make people see and believe, to get them to know and recognize, to impose the legitimate definition of the divisions of the social world and, thereby, to make and unmake groups" (Bourdieu 1991, 221). The last point is perhaps the most important: classification struggles are not merely struggles between already existing groups over how to interpret the social world, but struggles that help form groups in the first place. Because classificatory schemes are "the basis of the representations of the groups and therefore of their mobilization and demobilization," struggles over classificatory schemes help "bring into existence the thing named" and *"contribute to producing* what they apparently describe or designate" (Bourdieu [1979] 1984, 479; Bourdieu 1991, 220, 223; original emphasis). In these struggles, stratifying factors, such as gender, race, or ethnicity, may be constitutive of the groups formed, or they may constitute competing sources of social division (Swartz 1997, 153–58). Regardless of how and where people draw group boundaries, they include some in the group and exclude others, thereby defining the group's identity. In Bourdieu's writings, the concept of classification struggles serves primarily to explain the formation, reproduction, and mobilization of social classes. In the chapters that follow, I extend Bourdieu's insights about symbolic classification in new directions, drawing on his cultural sociology to show how historical struggles over the boundary between citizens and paupers have shaped both the meaning of citizenship and access to the corresponding material and symbolic profits. (Thus, one might say that the book is concerned more with "citizenship struggles" than class struggles, though classification is an essential dimension of both.) In so doing, I demonstrate that Bourdieu's concept of classification struggles not only deepens our understanding of class formation, but also provides a flexible and useful tool for analyzing the intersection of citizenship, class, race, gender, and nation.[9]

## Why are Classification Struggles a Recurring Feature of American Welfare State Development?

Having outlined the research design and theoretical contributions of *Citizens and Paupers,* I now elaborate upon the two main substantive questions that the book addresses. This section and the one that follows take up the preparatory work needed to resolve these questions more fully in subsequent chapters. Here, as in later chapters, I begin with the origin of the classification struggles that I examine. Fraser and Gordon (1992) provide a useful starting point. Their work suggests that the recurrence of classification struggles in U.S. welfare state development was in part a product of American political culture. Civil and political rights may have provided the foundation for social rights in Britain, they argue, but in the United States, "the cultural mythology of civil citizenship . . . stunt[ed] the capacity to envision social citizenship" (Fraser and Gordon 1992, 50). American political culture therefore "combines a richly elaborated discourse of 'civil citizenship' with a near total silence about 'social citizenship.'" Consequently, Fraser and Gordon conclude, "U.S. thinking about social provision has been shaped largely by images drawn from civil citizenship, especially images of contract." This "hegemony of contract," in turn, "helped to generate a specifically modern conception of 'charity' as its complementary other." They argue that "most debates over welfare state policy [in the United States] have been framed in terms of this contract-versus-charity opposition. . . . It is understandable therefore that reformers seeking to win social rights tried to move 'welfare' from the charity to the property side of the line" (Fraser and Gordon 1992, 47, 59, 63). In short, without a language of social citizenship to legitimize claims to government assistance, Americans have been forced to rely on the language of civil citizenship. Supporters of government assistance try to define it as a form of civil exchange that resembles private contracts, thereby preserving recipients' standing as independent citizens, while opponents attack it as a form of charity that is incompatible with freedom, independence, and citizenship.

Fraser and Gordon (1992) do not explain why civil citizenship provided a foundation for social citizenship in Britain but stunted the development of social citizenship in the United States. A full answer to this question is beyond the scope of this book as well. However, I tentatively suggest that the timing of *political* citizenship provides at least part of the answer. It has frequently been argued that prolonged working-class struggles for suffrage sharpened class divisions in Britain and other European countries, while early manhood suffrage blurred class divisions and weakened class consciousness among workers in the United States. "Because the suffrage was extended to white males [in the United States] before industrialization, the lower classes were never melded into a cohesive, class-conscious block by their shared exclusion from the rights of political citizenship" (Lipset and Marks 2000, 58). As a corollary to this thesis, I suggest that as early manhood suffrage incorporated white workingmen into the polity and reduced the salience of class divisions in the United States, it *sharpened* divisions between white workingmen and those who remained politically excluded, including paupers. (These divisions were of course gendered and racialized. Like paupers, women continued to be excluded from full citizenship, and Native Americans and slaves continued to be excluded from citizenship altogether [Fraser and Gordon 1992, 1994; R. Smith 1993, 1997; Roediger [1991] 1999; Glenn 2002].) Indeed, "states adopted 'pauper' exclusions as they moved to eliminate formal property qualifications for the vote. . . . Far from being anachronisms, pauper exclusions were integral to a new, nineteenth century way of defining full membership in a republican polity" (Steinfeld 1989, 335, 337; cf. Montgomery 1993, 21–22; R. Smith 1997, 126, 214–15; Keyssar 2000, 61–65). Although economic independence remained an important prerequisite for full citizenship within this new definition, propertyless white workingmen successfully challenged their classification as dependents by 1850, relocating themselves on the more-privileged side of the boundary (Keyssar 2000, chap. 2).[10] Where wage earners and recipients of poor relief had once occupied the same political status, the enfranchisement of the former and the exclusion of the latter now divided "the undifferentiated propertyless of the colonial era . . . into two distinct categories" (Steinfeld 1989, 337). This division was enormously consequential, for "in America, the ballot did more than identify who could vote—it defined a collective national identity (as women's suffrage advocates so tirelessly pointed out)" (Foner 1988, 278). To summarize, if the division between citizens and noncitizens divided the working class from the bourgeoisie in Europe, it divided white workingmen from paupers and other groups that remained politically excluded in the United States. In the American context, political rights therefore failed to provide a bridge from civil to social citizenship.[11]

Fraser's and Gordon's (1992) argument must be extended in a second way as well. A stunted discourse of social citizenship may well have forced Americans to legitimize government assistance in terms of civil citizenship, but the liberal language of contractual exchange was not the only idiom available to them. Americans also drew upon a variety of other political traditions to redefine and legitimize government assistance in ways that preserved the standing of claimants as citizens. However, just as the language of contractual exchange helped to generate a modern conception of charity as its antithesis, these other idioms generated their own symbolic foils that opponents could exploit to delegitimize government assistance as incompatible with American citizenship (cf. Alexander and Smith 1993). For example, Americans drew on the civic republican tradition to justify government assistance as a reward to virtuous citizens for their public (frequently military) service. At the same time, the republican language of civic virtue generated complementary notions of civic vice and incompetence that could only be rectified through discipline and supervision. Likewise, Americans have sometimes justified government assistance by drawing on a political tradition that Rogers Smith (1993, 563n4) calls ascriptive Americanism: "Adherents of . . . ascriptive Americanist traditions believe true Americans are in some way 'chosen' by God, history, or nature to possess superior moral and intellectual traits, often associated with race and gender." This idiom also generated its complementary other: all those allegedly inferior human beings who were not born with the ascribed characteristics that presumably defined "true Americans." As Americans struggled over the civic classification of welfare state claimants, they often resorted to what I call criteria shifting: dropping one idiom or criterion of civic worthiness for another. In the 1930s, for example, conservatives gained the upper hand in public debate over the status and rights of WPA workers by steering debate away from liberal-contractual considerations about work toward civic republican considerations about Americanism, anti-Communism, and loyalty to the nation.[12] Alternatively, Americans have sometimes combined different idioms and criteria of civic worthiness, mapping them on to one another to reinforce political claims. In the early twentieth century, for example, maternalist reformers justified mothers' pensions both as compensation for public service and as measures to preserve and protect the white race. Similarly, in the 1930s, many Americans associated racial equality with Communism, allowing civic republican attacks on Communist disloyalty to serve as a proxy for ascriptive Americanism. These complex and shifting uses of different idioms alert us to the need to consider not only how Americans have mapped class, race, and gender divisions onto the division between citizens and paupers, but also how Americans have related these categories to the "imagined community" of the nation (B. Anderson 1991).

Fraser's and Gordon's (1992) argument must be extended in a third way as well. Although the recurrence of classification struggles in American welfare state development can partly be traced to the nation's political culture, a more complete explanation must also take into account institutions, resources, and the historical social relations (labor relations, political coalitions, and the like) in which these struggles were rooted and which they sometimes threatened to disrupt or reconfigure. Here again, Bourdieu's cultural sociology proves helpful. Classification struggles, he suggests, cannot be understood apart from the social arenas or "fields" in which people struggle to accumulate and monopolize different kinds of resources (economic, cultural, social, and symbolic), which he describes as forms of capital. These fields are in turn structured by the amount and type of capital that people possess. The dominant groups within the field struggle over the relative value of different types of capital, while dominated groups control little capital of any kind. This insight has been usefully extended to the sociology of the welfare state by Michel Peillon (1998, 2001), who postulates the existence of a "welfare field" wherein state officials, service providers, employers, clients, unions, and social movements struggle to convert the resources they possess (economic, political, cultural, or symbolic) into the kinds of capital they seek to accumulate (greater legitimacy, better services and benefits, lower taxes, influence over policy administration, and so forth). Social movements from below are thus only one manifestation of the struggles over the classification of welfare state claimants, whose mobilization is often shaped by their relationships with elites or other actors in the field. Citizenship itself may be seen as a form of political capital that constitutes both a stake of these classification struggles and a resource that people may use to appropriate other goods.

The concepts of field and capital encourage us to think about social welfare policy in relational terms, which helps to explain when and why policies generate classification struggles. As shown in subsequent chapters, these struggles tend to emerge soon after the introduction of new policies, suggesting that policy innovations provide a window of opportunity (an expanding "political opportunity structure" in the language of social movement theory) to define the status and rights of the policy's clients *relative to other clients in the field.*[13] Because the standing of clients is relational, preexisting policies serve as important benchmarks in these classification struggles, providing models to be avoided (e.g., traditional poor relief) or standards of treatment to which clients can aspire (e.g., the National Labor Relations Act). Furthermore, policies and their elite patrons frequently stand in a *competitive relationship,* which may contribute to classification struggles as well. The officials who administer a policy, for example, are usually invested in it and therefore have institutional, organizational, and professional interests in raising it to a dominant position (in terms of prestige and resources) within the welfare field. As in other fields, this is generally achieved through social distinction; administrators seek to distinguish their policy sharply from others, emphasizing its merits and, conversely, the flaws of its competitors. Such efforts need not be merely symbolic, but may also involve efforts to incorporate and monopolize valued policy features. (These policy features may therefore be seen as another form of capital over which agents struggle in the welfare field.) The classification of clients as honorable, rights-bearing citizens may result in part as a by-product of these competitive struggles among policymakers and administrators. Finally, classification struggles are more likely to emerge when clients occupy an *intermediate position within the welfare field.* Although "the objects of the social world" always include a degree of indeterminacy, vagueness, and "semantic elasticity"

that make classification struggles possible, "it is in the intermediate positions of social space . . . that the indeterminacy and objective uncertainty
of relations between practices and positions is at a maximum, and also,
consequently, the intensity of symbolic strategies" (Bourdieu 1989, 20).
Within the welfare field, it is the clients of hybrid policies, positioned in
some respects as rights-bearing citizens but in other respects as dependent paupers in need of discipline and supervision, who occupy these intermediate positions.[14] Their indeterminate status is not merely a product
of muddled minds or linguistic confusion; it also reflects how government
assistance is organized, which in turn reflects how classificatory schemes
are institutionalized. When inconsistent or contradictory classificatory
schemes are objectified in policies, the policies are likely to encourage
classification struggles.

As these remarks suggest, Bourdieu's claims that the state is the "supreme tribunal" in classification struggles and the "holder of the monopoly of legitimate symbolic violence" must not be exaggerated (Bourdieu
1985, 732; Bourdieu 1989, 21–22). The state may not possess the necessary bureaucratic and administrative capacity to play this role, particularly at the early stages of historical development. Moreover, contrary
to the "pessimistic functionalism" of social control theories, the state itself must be seen as an arena of struggle—not as a unified apparatus—
especially in countries like the United States where political authority is
divided among various branches and levels of government (Bourdieu and
Wacquant 1992, 102, 111–15; Bourdieu 1994). Classification struggles are
thus fought not only *against* the state but also *within* the state. These internal struggles may lead the state to engage in inconsistent and contradictory classificatory practices that inadvertently increase indeterminacy
and undermine the state's symbolic authority. Under these conditions,
when the state fails to exercise symbolic power in a coherent and authoritative way, when its capacity to codify, delegate, and guarantee symbolic
capital is constrained by internal conflicts among elites, symbolic capital
must rest more heavily on collective recognition (Bourdieu 1994). This,
too, creates opportunities for dominated groups to contest their classification. Finally, even when the state does act in a unified way, "the hold-
ers of bureaucratic authority never establish an absolute monopoly. . . .
In fact, *there are always, in any society, conflicts between symbolic powers
that aim at imposing the vision of legitimate divisions,* that is, at construct-
ing groups" (Bourdieu 1989, 22; original emphasis). These conflicts create
additional opportunities to contest the dominant classificatory schemes.

## What Explains the Outcome of Classification Struggles?

In addition to explaining why classification struggles have been a recurring feature of American welfare state development, this book also seeks to explain variations in the outcome of these struggles. Why were the clients of some policies classed as dependent paupers in need of discipline and supervision while others successfully obtained recognition as independent, deserving, rights-bearing citizens? Each of the classification struggles examined in this book was historically contingent and shaped by specific circumstances. Nevertheless, comparison of the struggles suggests that several important generalizations can be drawn about their outcomes. Although economic factors were important, the outcomes were not simply determined by an underlying economic foundation. Instead, the outcomes of these struggles depended heavily on institutional factors and racial politics. To be more precise, in each of the book's three primary cases, the structure of the policy and the mobilization of a racial backlash against the policy or the policy's clients contributed crucially to clients' failure to obtain recognition as full citizens. These proximate causes were, in turn, rooted in previous classification struggles, which shaped the structure of subsequent policies and facilitated the mobilization of social agents along racial lines. In other words, the institutions and racial divisions that structured classification struggles were themselves socially and historically constructed through past struggles.

### Beyond epiphenomenalism

Since the 1970s, neo-Marxism has shaped much of the sociological thought regarding the welfare state. While building upon the insights of this theoretical tradition, I also seek to move beyond its limitations. In particular, I argue that the outcomes of classification struggles cannot adequately be explained by epiphenomenalist accounts that minimize the causal significance of symbolic work and collective identity. These accounts, which rely on the Marxian distinction between an economic base and its superstructure, suggest that the mode of production, class interests, and class power ultimately determine classification struggles. From this perspective, the recurring classification struggles in American welfare state development are merely a secondary and derivative phenomenon. They are strategic battles between already constituted groups (labor and capital) driven by conflicting interests that are objectively determined by the socioeconomic position of group members. Classification struggles are thus seen as a means to purportedly noncultural ends, such as profits, power, and so forth. As a corollary, epiphenomenalist accounts suggest that a successful outcome is most likely to be achieved when it is consistent with the interests of dominant groups or when dominated groups have enough power to force concessions.

What's wrong with this kind of explanation? As Bourdieu has shown, the base/superstructure distinction reflects a longstanding but problematic dichotomy in the social sciences between materialism and idealism. Like Bourdieu, I reject this dichotomy and seek to transcend it (Swartz 1997, 39–40, 65–94).[15] First, consider the relationship between classification struggles and power resources. To be sure, resource mobilization influences the capacity of agents to impose and legitimize their preferred vision and division of the social world. However, as noted above, our conception of resources must be expanded to include not only economic capital but also cultural, social, and symbolic power. Moreover, classification struggles do not merely reflect resource mobilization; they also shape the capacity of agents to mobilize resources. Research on social movements has shown that dominated groups typically acquire resources in two ways: relying on the funding and sponsorship of elite allies or appropriating an "indigenous" organizational base (McAdam 1982, 20–59; McAdam, Tarrow, and Tilly 2001, 44, 47–48). By shaping the formation and collective identity of groups, classification struggles affect both their alliances and their capacity to hang on to indigenous organizational resources (Goldberg 2003).

Second, consider the relationship between classification struggles and material interests. Of course, material interests do partly determine "the play of ideas within which different groups figure out the world and their role and *allegiances* in it" (Hall 1988, 45, emphasis in the original). However, by focusing exclusively on the strategic use of classificatory schemes by preexisting collective actors, epiphenomenalist accounts neglect the important question of how naming and categorizing serve to constitute collective actors in the first place. Moreover, "social collectivities have more than one set of interests." In addition to class interests, agents may have gender, race, and national interests that are equally "real, or (for the epistemologically squeamish) real enough" (Hall 1988, 45–46). Furthermore, if we extend the idea of interest to cultural goods, it becomes apparent that agents have symbolic as well as material interests (Swartz 1997, 66–73; M. Weber 1946, 1958). Because these diverse "interests can be and frequently are contradictory, even mutually exclusive," they may be articulated according to "alternative inferential logics," leading to quite different lines of political action (Hall 1988, 45–46; cf. Omi and Winant 1986, 33, 65). Symbolic work is therefore necessary to "provide a concrete definition of interests to guide strategic choices" (Plotke 1992, 176). Thus, rather than being "given as an objective feature of a structure of positions in a social system," the interests and identities of actors are "constructed, *constituted,* in and through the ideological process" (Hall 1988, 45, emphasis in the original; cf. Emirbayer 1992).[16]

Finally, consider the relationship between classification struggles and coercion. Although symbolic work is more effective when it is backed by political and police violence, the converse is also true: political and police power rests partly on symbolic work. As Durkheim's ([1893] 1984) discussion of the forced division of labor, Max Weber's (1946) notion of legitimacy, and Gramsci's (1971) concept of consent all make clear, political and police violence typically requires some form of justification. Even Marx recognized that in order to rule, a social class must "represent its interest as the common interest of all the members of society" (Tucker 1978, 174). Bourdieu, even more than his predecessors, has shown the importance of symbolic work in developing and maintaining power relations. Symbolic power, he stresses, legitimizes economic and political power without reducing to them: "Every power . . . to impose meanings and to impose them as legitimate by concealing the power relations which are the basis of its force, adds its own specifically symbolic force to those power relations" (Bourdieu and Passeron 1977, 4). Symbolic work is especially important during periods of social change and upheaval (like Reconstruction or the New Deal) when an historical bloc has disintegrated and social agents are struggling to construct a new one. At such times, political actors must "enter into struggle and win space *in civil society itself*" using "the trenches and fortifications of civil society as the means of forging a considerable ideological and intellectual *authority* outside the realm of the state proper and indeed *before*—as a necessary condition to—taking formal power *in* the state" (Hall 1988, 47) Just as symbolic work is necessary to constitute the identities and interests of groups, it is also needed for brokerage purposes, to disarticulate old political formations, rework their elements into new ones, construct alliances between different groups and social forces, and transform coercion into the "authority of a leading bloc" (Hall 1988, 53; cf. Emirbayer 1992).

To sum up, I have argued that the outcomes of classification struggles cannot adequately be explained from a Marxian perspective that minimizes the causal significance of symbolic work and collective identity. The problem with this approach is not that it points to material determinants of classification struggles, but rather that it separates what is in fact unified in practice—the material and symbolic dimensions of social life—and that it privileges one over the other. Consequently, the Marxian approach misconstrues the relationship of classification struggles to power resources, material interests, and coercion. But if the outcomes of classification struggles cannot be fully explained in terms of an underlying economic base, how else might we seek to explain them? Just as a social fact can only be explained by another social fact (Durkheim [1895] 1982), so must one look to past classification struggles in order to understand the outcome of subsequent struggles. While this view breaks with the base/ superstructure model, it is consistent with other aspects of Marx's thinking, particularly his insistence that "men make their own history, but they do not make it just as they please; they do not make it under circumstances chosen by themselves, but under circumstances directly found, given and transmitted from the past" (Tucker 1978, 595). Just as classification struggles over the meaning and boundaries of citizenship during Reconstruction constrained the struggles of the New Deal era, so the outcome of classification struggles in the New Deal era constrained struggles over the status and rights of workfare workers in the 1990s. Hence, in the outcome of classification struggles, as in their emergence, timing matters.

The outcome of earlier classification struggles influences later struggles on two levels—as "incorporated history" internalized by social agents and as historical practice objectified in institutions: in minds and in things, inside and outside of agents (Bourdieu and Wacquant 1992, 127–28). The internalization of particular classificatory schemes generates habits and dispositions that impede subsequent attempts to realign agents in new ways, particularly when a close correspondence between dispositions and institutions renders habitual categories of thought self-evident and taken for granted. The history of agents is thus embodied in categories of thought that structure their preferences and mediate their strategic choices. Therefore, rather than treat classification struggles as merely an expression of preexisting, underlying interests, I suggest, as in the Indian myth about the world resting on elephants, that the social world is classification struggles "all the way down." To put it differently, because classification struggles and interests are mutually constitutive, there are no interests that exist prior to classification struggles.[17]

At the same time, the objectification of symbolic boundaries in institutions generates "unequal access to and unequal distribution of resources (material and nonmaterial) and social opportunities" (Lamont and Molnar 2002, 168). Indeed, classification struggles frequently result in the kind of social closure described at the beginning of this chapter, as agents seek to monopolize the material and symbolic profits of privileged names, titles, or categories while excluding others. As noted above, citizenship itself may be understood in these terms. The objectification of classificatory schemes thereby alters the proximity or distance of agents in social space—making future alliances more or less likely—and erodes the power resources of some agents while it enables other agents to appropriate more resources.[18] To recapitulate, past classification struggles influence subsequent struggles by shaping how groups define themselves and their interests, the available resources they can mobilize to protect those interests, the alliances and coalitions they form, and even the constitution and dissolution of the groups themselves. What epiphenomenalist accounts take to be the real, underlying determinants of classification struggles are in fact internalized or objectified praxis, the dead trace of previous classification struggles.

## Classification struggles and social welfare policy

As the previous discussion suggests, classification struggles and policy structure are related in two ways. First, the outcomes of classification struggles are institutionalized in policies (among other things). The structure of a policy reflects past classification struggles and embodies particular classificatory schemes. A successful classification struggle therefore results not only in the internalization of new classificatory schemes in the minds of social agents but also in the objectification of those schemes in institutions. Consequently, recognition of clients as independent, rights-bearing citizens entails more than a change in discourse or categories of thought; it requires institutional changes as well. Second, as research on policy feedbacks suggests, the institutional structure of a policy shapes subsequent classification struggles. The form of public provision (in other words, how the provision of benefits is organized) communicates something about the status of the recipients and thus serves an important symbolic function. The more isomorphic a new policy is with traditional poor relief (i.e., the more policy features they share) the more likely it is that clients of the new policy will be classed as paupers. To put it differently, when two policies are isomorphic, their clients occupy proximate social positions within the welfare field, making it easier to group them together. Clients are also more likely to be classed as paupers when the new policy is linked to or dependent upon traditional poor relief for distributing benefits, determining eligibility, and so forth. Conversely, policies confer dignity and independence to the extent that they are separated and differentiated from traditional poor relief. A variety of policy features have been used to accomplish this end. In the 1930s and 1940s, for example, policymakers financed OAI through payroll taxes rather than general revenue in order to avoid any resemblance to relief. For similar reasons, policymakers rejected dependents' allowances for unemployment insurance and restricted eligibility to persons who were "ordinarily" and regularly employed (Mettler 1998, 126, 150; J. Zelizer 1998, chap. 2). Though the particular means may vary, the ability of public officials, pressure groups, and social movements to successfully separate and distinguish a new social welfare policy from traditional poor relief is crucial for the classification of the policy's clients.[19]

Classification struggles are related to the legitimacy of policies in a similarly twofold way. On the one hand, the classification of a policy's clients influences the legitimacy of the policy. When policymakers treat the clients of a new policy as paupers, for example, they erode the policy's legitimacy and reduce public support for it. On the other hand, policy legitimacy also affects the classification of its clients. Whether intended or not, attacks on the legitimacy of a policy typically have important spillover effects that shape public attitudes toward the policy's clients. In summary, the relationships among policy legitimacy, policy structure, and the classification of a policy's clients may be diagrammed as seen in figure 1.1.

*Classification struggles and racial politics*

In the cases examined below, whether welfare state claimants were classed as paupers or rights-bearing citizens depended not only on the institutional structure of social welfare policies but also on racial politics. Simply put, my research suggests that the clients of a new policy were more likely to be classed as paupers when the policy's opponents successfully mobilized a significant racial backlash against it. To be sure, racial politics was not altogether independent of policy structure. Indeed, as the historical institutionalist perspective would suggest, the structure of certain policies made it easier for opponents to set off a racial backlash. First, the

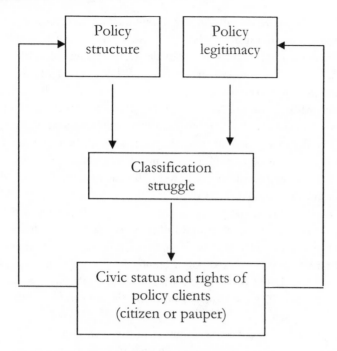

FIGURE I.I. Classification struggles and social policies.

racial composition of the policy's clients obviously mattered. As shown in the chapters below, African Americans were repeatedly shunted to policies that were structured like traditional poor relief, which in effect racialized the stigma of pauperism (and thus struggles over the classification of welfare state claimants). Even so, a high proportion of black clients was generally not sufficient to produce a racial backlash. Second, the policy was more likely to generate a racial backlash when it became a vehicle for the advancement of black citizenship rights (civil, political, or industrial; cf. Quadagno 1994). While the Freedmen's Bureau, the WPA, and New York City's workfare program shared a variety of policy features with traditional poor relief, the hybrid and contradictory nature of the policies also provided a basis for countervailing rights claims. When these claims challenged racialized patterns of social closure, the policy swiftly became a target of racial hostility. Third, a racial backlash was also more likely when the policy included regulatory or redistributive features, particularly when those features could have potentially expanded the political or other forms of capital available to black workers. Fourth, federalism also mattered. The more decentralized the policy's administration, the more vulnerable it was to racial backlash, because federal authorities tended to be more committed than local authorities to racial fairness. Still, the racial backlashes that thwarted freedpeople, WPA workers, and workfare workers were not *determined* by their respective policies. In each case, the backlash was the product of agency as well as structure. (Nor was agency confined to policy opponents. While policy opponents called attention to the race of the clients and sought to limit the reach of federal authority, black workers used the new policies to advance their claims to full citizenship and constrain the power of hostile local officials.) By itself, policy structure cannot easily explain the timing of racial backlash. Moreover, racial politics shape policy as much as policy shapes racial politics. As I will show in the chapters that follow, racial politics sometimes influenced the structure of new social welfare policies, encouraged changes in policy structure, or mediated policy feedback effects. For these reasons, racial politics should be seen as having a distinct influence on the outcome of the classification struggles that is partly independent of the influence of policy structure.

While this argument is consistent with previous findings about race and the welfare state, I extend these findings in several ways. Most importantly, rather than taking racial divisions as a given, I examine how and why agents mobilized along racial lines. As the previous remarks about agency suggest, political and symbolic work was crucial to this process. Of course, political entrepreneurs did not create racial divisions or racist sentiment *de novo,* but symbolic work was required to make racial divisions salient (and more so than competing sources of social division), mobilize racial antagonism, and turn potential racial groupings (what Bourdieu might call "racial-groupings-on-paper") into real, mobilized racial groups. "If the legitimate mode of perception is such an important prize at stake in social struggles," as Bourdieu (1985, 730) points out, "this is partly because the shift from the implicit to the explicit is in no way automatic. . . . [S]ocially known and recognized differences only exist for a subject capable not only of perceiving differences but of recognizing them as significant." Furthermore, attempts to mobilize agents along racial lines were enabled or constrained by the legacy of previous classification struggles. Thus, racial divisions not only contributed to the failure of the classification struggles examined in this book but also were, at least in part, a product of past struggles. As suggested above, the failure to overcome racial divisions and the reinscription of those divisions in social policies at key historical junctures were not inevitable, but they did make it harder for agents to overcome those divisions of the social world in the next round of classification struggles. Internalized in the minds of social agents, racial divisions shaped their identities and structured their preferences in ways that constrained subsequent efforts to regroup them along alternative lines.[20] Objectified in social welfare policies and other political institutions, racial divisions generated unequal access to economic, cultural, social, and symbolic capital, widening the social distance between agents categorized as white or black and thereby making biracial coalitions less stable.

While race and class crucially shaped the classification struggles examined here and are therefore central to answering the book's two main questions, it should be emphasized again in closing that gender and nation also played significant roles. The importance of these categories is evident in several respects already indicated in the preceding pages. To begin with, recall that the book's principal categories of citizen and pauper were themselves gendered. Although male paupers were common, many Americans regarded relief and protective labor laws as paternalistic and demasculinizing. Hybrid policies, such as the Freedmen's Bureau, the WPA, or New York's workfare program therefore gendered their clients in ambiguous ways. For male clients, this ambiguity was especially threatening. If their political claims invoked standards of citizenship that were largely masculine, their fear of pauperization partly reflected a fear of losing their manly independence. Similarly, the category of pauper was also "nationalized" whenever pauperism was associated with foreign-born immigrants or un-American elements. Thus, when clients made claims to the status and rights of citizenship, their claims were often as much about nationality and allegiance as they were about masculinity. Moreover, recall that clients had gender and national interests as well as racial and class interests, which allowed them to be grouped and divided, mobilized and demobilized in different ways. The process I term criteria shifting (rejecting one criterion of civic worthiness in favor of another) often indicated attempts to realign agents in precisely this way. These attempts did not merely pit clients against others but also sometimes precipitated struggles among clients themselves over how to define their own collective identity. Finally, recall that clients' gendered and nationalized political claims and collective identities influenced the alliances they were likely to form, orienting them toward some movements and groups rather than others. In summary, *Citizens and Paupers* maintains its primary focus on race and class (like several other important studies of the American welfare state), but it also investigates the intersection of these categories with gender and nation.

## Conclusion

Citizenship is the central point from which all of my observations derive and to which they constantly return; it is the dominant theme that binds the book together. Above all, *Citizens and Paupers* is intended to be a contribution to the political, cultural, and historical sociology of citizenship, envisioned as a field of study that investigates the development of citizenship rights over time, changing levels and forms of civic engagement and political participation, and shifting patterns of civic inclusion and exclusion. One of the advantages of placing the welfare state in this broader context is that it reorients how we understand and assess social policies. Existing studies of contemporary welfare reform tend to evaluate it narrowly in terms of its economic consequences. However, if policies make citizens as much as citizens make policies (Campbell 2003), then the most important outcome of welfare reform may instead lie in the way it affects civic inclusion and democratic participation. As Soss (1999, 376) puts it, "political debates over how welfare programs affect incorporation in the market (i.e., employment) should be joined by discussions of how they affect incorporation in the polity."

Citizenship is central to this book in another way as well. As my previous remarks suggest, the book does not merely take citizenship as its object of study; it also aims to influence citizenship practices and foster greater civic inclusion. Historical sociology, I believe, can play a modest but useful role in this kind of social reconstruction. To present history "from the sociological standpoint," as John Dewey (1993, 100) once noted, is to treat history "as a matter of analysis of existing social relations—that is to say as affording insight into what makes up the structure and working of society. . . . Only a mind trained to grasp social situations . . . can get sufficient hold on the realities of this life to see what sort of action, critical and constructive, it really demands." In pragmatist fashion, my research began in the mid-1990s with the practical problem of organizing thousands of workers—most of them women and people of color—who were toiling in New York City's workfare program. Although I opposed workfare, I hoped it would inadvertently encourage the mobilization of welfare recipients, foster an alliance between welfare recipients and organized labor, and expand welfare recipients' political opportunities. In other words, as Charles Tilly once quipped, I hoped that welfare reform would turn out to be a "mitigated" rather than an "unmitigated disaster." Though I did not know it then, similar aspirations to improve the lot of welfare recipients led centrist New Democrats like President Clinton to endorse the very policies that I opposed. "Blending the causes of the left and the right in ways that unsettled both," the Clinton administration supported work requirements for welfare recipients in order to "attract public support" for its antipoverty strategy and "avoid the racial backlash that had burdened previous programs for the poor."[21] In retrospect, neither my aspirations nor those of the Clinton administration were fully realized. Nevertheless, even failure can be instructive. My hope is that activists and academics alike will read this book, and that by studying past struggles to deepen and extend the promise of American democracy, they will learn how to conduct subsequent struggles more effectively. If so, this book may help to ensure that there are fewer forgotten men and women among American citizens—today and in the future.

# PART I

# Claiming Rights as Citizen-Soldiers

*Struggles during Reconstruction*

## CHAPTER TWO

# "The 'pauper slavery' of the poorhouse"

## *The Freedmen's Bureau, 1865–1872*

### Between Slavery and Citizenship: Freed Slaves after the Civil War

*The Civil War and the transformation of American citizenship*

The Civil War was a war of liberation. It did not begin as one, but it became one, first as an unintended consequence of wartime disruption, and later as a policy that the Union, driven by military necessity, intentionally adopted to weaken the Confederacy. When the carnage ended at Appomattox on April 9, 1865, four million slaves were—or would soon become—slaves no more; the bloodshed, unprecedented in its enormity for Americans, had indeed created "a new birth of freedom" (Lincoln 1991, 104). But what status and rights would the former slaves have in the new postwar social and economic order? Before the war, in the infamous Dred Scott decision of 1857, the Supreme Court had ruled that blacks— even free blacks—were not American citizens. Roger Taney, chief justice of the United States, declared that they were a third class of "subject nationals," between citizens and aliens, or, if the Constitution offered only the alternatives of citizenship or alienage, they were "citizens without full rights" (Belz 1976, xiii, 20). Although the war obliterated slavery and "unsettled ingrained ideas about who was rightfully a citizen" (N. Cohen 2002, 27), Americans "failed to agree on answers to the questions raised by emancipation." Even among the freed slaves' "most ardent champions," there was no consensus. "Were Negroes to be protected only in such elementary rights as the security of their persons and property, or were they to be allowed to vote, hold office, and enjoy all the privileges accorded other citizens?" (White 1970, 134; cf. Nieman 1979, xv–xvi; Regosin 2002, 3–4). These questions would only be resolved after years of political struggle.[1]

The legacy of the Civil War was not confined to the emancipation of the slaves. The war brought additional changes in its wake that fundamentally shaped the ensuing struggles over the freed slaves' postwar status and rights. Perhaps the most important of these changes was a general transformation of citizenship that affected all Americans, black and white alike. Before the war, national citizenship derived from and depended upon state citizenship. Consequently, "the states alone could determine the condition, status, and rights of persons within their jurisdictions. . . . It was as state citizens that persons enjoyed the multitude of civil rights that characterized a republican political order." As a result, the power of state legislatures over civil rights was far reaching, limited only by voters and judicial review under state constitutions. With few exceptions, the federal government was largely uninvolved in the citizenship rights of most Americans (Belz 1976, x, 26). However, Congress effectively nationalized citizenship during the war, giving the federal government unprecedented power and responsibility over the rights and liberties of Americans. This shift did not eliminate dual citizenship, but it reversed the relationship of national and state citizenship, making the former primary and the latter secondary: "An American citizen was first of all a citizen of the United States and then a citizen of the state in which he resided" (Belz 1976, ix, 29–30, 162–63). In addition, Congress expanded the scope and content of national citizenship, particularly in regard to political rights. After the war, political rights became an integral part of national citizenship—a change from having been "privileges conferred by those who already possessed them—the political community—upon those deemed qualified to assume them . . . on grounds of expediency and the public good" (Belz 1976, xiii, 27; cf. Foner 1988, 231). These changes in the structure of American citizenship encouraged former slaves to claim new rights and expanded their access to federal authorities upon whom they could make such claims. At the same time, postwar struggles to incorporate former slaves into the polity reinforced this general transformation of American citizenship and pushed it further.

The war also cleared the way for the construction of a free-labor society in the former slave states, which had equally important implications for the citizenship status and rights of the freed slaves. As Marshall ([1949] 1964, 71, 75) points out, the civil element of citizenship includes the right to own property, the right to conclude valid contracts, and "the right to work, that is to say the right to follow the occupation of one's choice in the place of one's choice." These rights were central to the free-labor ideology championed by the Republican Party, which sharply distinguished free labor from slavery, stressed the economic and social superiority of the former, and sought to contain and ultimately eradicate the latter. One of the principal virtues of a free-labor society, Republicans argued, was that it afforded wage earners opportunities to become property-owning farmers or craftsmen and thereby achieve independence. They identified free labor with democracy, progress, and prosperity while equating slavery with social stagnation (Foner [1970] 1995, ix). For free-labor advocates, the North's victory over the rebellious Southern states opened the prospect of "an affluent, democratic, free labor South, with small farms replacing the great plantations and Northern capital and migrants energizing the society" (Foner 1988, 28–29).

Complicating this project, however, was the ambiguous and contested meaning of free labor, even in the North. For starters, the category of free labor lumped together "two distinct economic conditions—the wage laborer seeking employment in the marketplace, and the property-owning small producer enjoying a modicum of economic independence." Although these two definitions of free labor were "partly reconciled by the insistence that free society offered every industrious wage earner the opportunity to achieve economic independence," some free-labor enthusiasts stressed "freedom of contract in the labor market" while others emphasized "ownership of productive property" (Foner [1970] 1995, x–xi, xxv–xxvi, xxxvi; Foner 1988, 54, 164; N. Cohen 2002, 29). Moreover, freedom of contract was itself an ambiguous and contested concept. Between 1815 and 1860, Northern courts generated two competing models of contractual freedom.

> On the one hand, the majority of judges and other legal commentators . . . supported what might be called a right to security. For them, a promise to deliver a set amount of labor had to be performed in full before the state could obligate the recipient [i.e., the employer] to accept the exchange and pay. Practically speaking, this reasoning meant that workers could not quit before their contracts expired, unless they wanted to forgo all payment. At the same time, these jurists believed that an employer who discharged a worker before the

end of a contract could be penalized by being forced to pay for the whole term, as if the labor had been performed. On the other hand, a minority of judges believed that accepting labor on an ongoing basis raised a promise to pay for it. This conception implied a right to quit, and concomitantly a right to fire, for it reduced the exchange to a daily act that could be terminated at any time. (Schmidt 1998, 16–17)[2]

Lastly, the enactment of modern vagrancy laws after the Civil War in both Northern and Southern states raised still more questions about the meaning of free labor (Schmidt 1998, 5; Stanley 1992). Did free labor merely entail a right to leave individual employers or did it also entail a right to exit the labor market altogether? While an expansive interpretation of free labor could empower black laborers, a narrow understanding pointed to a more compulsory employment regime. During the reconstruction of North Carolina, for example, Provisional Governor William Holden argued that "the State had always had laws to compel white vagrants to work, and it must now coerce the blacks in the same way" (Owens 1943, 91). In summary, the South was reconstructed at a time when free labor had more than one meaning, and "the rights available to workers under labor contracts were in flux" (Schmidt 1998, 7–8, 163; cf. Steinfeld 2001). Black agricultural workers, their former masters turned employers, and Northern occupiers could thus draw on multiple and competing notions of free labor to advance their material and symbolic interests (Schmidt 1998, 6–8, 163, 237).

Finally, the Civil War resulted not only in the emancipation of the slaves, the nationalization of American citizenship, and the construction of a free-labor society in the Southern states, but also in the creation of the nation's first federal welfare and regulatory agency, the U.S. Bureau of Refugees, Freedmen, and Abandoned Lands, popularly known as the Freedmen's Bureau. Congress passed the original Freedmen's Bureau bill in March 1865, shortly before the end of the war. This may in part explain why the bureau was established as a military agency operating under the U.S. Department of War. The decision also likely stemmed from the military's prior experience managing the large numbers of slaves who fled their masters and gathered near Union military encampments during the war. In addition, in 1865, only the military could provide the administrative and bureaucratic capacity the federal government needed to carry out the tasks that Congress envisioned.[3] The bureau was headed by Major General Oliver Otis Howard, who served as its commissioner. Ten assistant commissioners served under Howard, appointed, as he was, by the president of the United States with the consent of the Senate. Below the assistant commissioners were the bureau's staff, composed mainly of soldiers who never numbered more than 901, dwindling to 159 by the end of 1868 (McFeely 1968, 23, 65, 289, 302).

After Abraham Lincoln's assassination in April 1865, the Freedmen's Bureau was subsumed by President Andrew Johnson's lenient reconstruction policies. As the bureau's full name suggests, its programs were open to both freedpeople and white refugees, and many of the latter were initially dependent on the bureau for relief. However, "with the passage of time . . . freedmen became the predominant beneficiaries" (Colby 1985, 219–20, 226). By the end of 1865, with the fighting over, "most of the refugees had returned to their homes," and in February 1866, General Joseph Fullerton reported to President Johnson that there were no more refugees (Bentley 1955, 103, 118). In July 1866, Congress enacted a second Freedmen's Bureau Act over Johnson's presidential veto, revealing an emerging conflict between Congress and the president over Reconstruction policy. The 1866 legislation expanded the bureau's powers and extended its operations for two more years. Along with the 1866 Civil Rights Act (also passed over Johnson's veto), the 1866 Freedmen's Bureau Act was intended as a forceful response to outbreaks of violence against blacks and the enactment of "black codes" (new laws to preserve white supremacy) in the defeated Southern states. After the 1866 midterm election strengthened the hand of the Radical Republicans in Congress, Johnson lost control of Reconstruction policy, Congress passed the 1867 Military Reconstruction Acts (again over Johnson's vetoes), and the Freedmen's Bureau was now subsumed by Radical Reconstruction. The new arrangements placed the South under military control and the bureau's activities under the authority of military district commanders. By taking "the command of the Bureau at the state level away from the Commissioner in Washington" (McFeely 1968, 296), the military in effect absorbed the bureau and usurped its independence. Furthermore, in 1868, Congress began to readmit Southern states that met its requirements into the Union, releasing them from the mandates of the Freedmen's Bureau. However, in order to protect blacks from an upsurge in Ku Klux Klan violence and assure the election of Republican candidate and former Union Army general Ulysses S. Grant as President in 1868, Congress enacted a third Freedmen's Bureau bill in July 1868. This legislation again extended the bureau's life, but directed Commissioner Howard to discontinue most of the bureau's activities on January 1, 1869, with the exception of its educational work and the collection and payment of black veterans' bounties. By 1870, all of the former Confederate states had been readmitted to the Union under new and generally Republican-controlled governments based on black suffrage, and in July 1872, Congress terminated the Freedmen's Bureau altogether.

During its several years of operation, the bureau was involved in the civil, political, and social rights of its clients. First, in the field of civil rights, the bureau sought to protect freedpeople's right to justice by establishing special courts that tried minor cases involving blacks wherever civil courts were not functioning or did not allow black testimony; it referred more serious cases to military commissions. Furthermore, to ensure basic civil rights in the economic field, the bureau established a system of labor contracts and regulated labor relations between Southern planters and black agricultural workers. Trattner (1984, 83) goes so far as to call the Freedmen's Bureau an "employment agency," but the bureau mainly put blacks to work in the private sector rather than provide public employment for them. Second, the Bureau worked to establish and protect political rights for blacks by registering black voters in their reconstructed states. Although this task was not initially part of the Bureau's mission, it became an important part of the Bureau's work following passage of the 1867 Military Reconstruction Acts, which authorized blacks to vote. Third, the Freedmen's Bureau was also active in the field of social rights. "It served as a relief agency on an unprecedented scale, distributing twenty-two million rations" from the Army's Commissary Department, clothing and blankets from the Army Quartermaster, transportation, and fuel "to needy persons in the devastated South." The Freedmen's Bureau also "employed doctors and maintained hospitals," providing medical assistance to more than a million freedpeople and white war refugees (Trattner 1984, 83). These efforts required what were at the time enormous federal expenditures. Pierce (1904, 93, 99) estimates that the bureau spent a total of $2,000,000 for medical purposes and another $4,500,000 for food and clothing. The bureau also promoted education—"the first decisive step on the road to the reestablishment of the social rights of citizenship in the twentieth [century]" (Marshall [1949] 1964, 82)—by establishing more than a thousand black schools and colleges and assisting and coordinating the work of private freedmen's aid and benevolent associations. Although Congress charged the bureau with redistributing abandoned and confiscated lands—arguably the soundest way to furnish freed slaves "a modicum of economic welfare and security" (Marshall [1949] 1964, 72)—President Johnson's restoration policies prevented it from doing so.

## The Freedmen's Bureau and the rights of freed slaves

Because the Freedmen's Bureau was responsible for the freed slaves and because it was involved in all three types of citizenship rights, it provides a privileged site for investigating the classification struggles that emerged during Reconstruction over the citizenship status and rights of Southern blacks. Indeed, the bureau contributed to these struggles and influenced them in important ways. As noted in the previous chapter, policies shape the formation of groups and their political capacities, ideas, and demands, thereby restructuring politics and influencing subsequent political struggles (Skocpol 1985, 21; Pierson 1994). The Freedmen's Bureau was no exception. First, the creation of the bureau added to the ambiguity and uncertainty surrounding the postwar status and rights of the former slaves. Since the bureau was a major policy innovation, it was not immediately clear how its clients stood relative to those assisted under existing policies. Would the bureau's assistance be modeled on or sharply distinguished from traditional poor relief? Would it provide social welfare and protective labor regulations as an alternative to freedpeople's newly acquired citizenship rights or as an integral part of them? While traditional poor relief served as a model for freed slaves to avoid, other policies set standards to which they could aspire and against which they could measure injustices. For example, "between 1862 and 1872, the government awarded over 100 million acres of land and millions of dollars in direct aid to support railroad construction. . . . Blacks could not help noting the contrast between such largesse and the failure to provide the freedmen with land. Why, asked Texas freedman Anthony Wayne, 'whilst Congress appropriated land by the million acres to pet railroad schemes . . . did they not aid poor Anthony and his people starving and in rags?'" . . . (Foner 1988, 467; cf. McFeely 1968, 230). Similarly, generous pensions and land grants for military veterans prior to the Civil War also provided positive policy precedents for freedpeople (Freund 1969; Oberly 1990; Jensen 2003). In brief, existing policies provided competing organizational models for the Freedmen's Bureau, and this indeterminacy fueled political contention over the citizenship status and rights of the bureau's clients.

Furthermore, the bureau positioned its clients in ambiguous or contradictory ways. These ambiguities and inconsistencies are reflected in conflicting interpretations of the bureau's work. Beginning in the mid-1950s, a revisionist school of thought portrayed the Freedmen's Bureau as a well-intentioned and partly successful attempt to assist the former slaves and integrate them socially and politically into American society (Bentley 1955; Stampp 1965). This view of the bureau dovetails with social citizenship theories of the welfare state, which emphasize the potential of social policies to empower dominated groups. In contrast, the post-revisionist studies of Reconstruction that began to emerge in the 1970s painted a very different picture. From this perspective, the Bureau was paternalistic and even reactionary, more concerned with reestablishing order and reviving agricultural production in the South than promoting racial equality or protecting the rights of freed slaves (McFeely 1968; Gerteis 1973; Litwack 1979). This view of the Freedmen's Bureau has a clear affinity with social control theories of the welfare state, which stress the regulatory and disciplinary functions of social policy. Rather than view these as competing or mutually exclusive interpretations, I suggest that each perspective selectively emphasizes certain features of the bureau, thereby capturing some truth, albeit partial, about the bureau's activities. Scholarly disputes between revisionists and post-revisionists thus reveal the inconsistencies and contradictions of the bureau itself. These contradictions are evident in at least three major aspects of the bureau's work: its social policies, its labor policies, and its regulation of black family relations.[4]

SOCIAL POLICIES.   In contrast to traditional poor relief, the Freedmen's Bureau generally did not incarcerate relief recipients in poorhouses or workhouses as a condition of public aid, nor did it deprive relief recipients of their political rights. On the contrary, the bureau provided relief while simultaneously seeking to establish and protect freedpeople's civil and political rights. Indeed, in some cases, the bureau provided relief *in order to* secure their rights. When employers dismissed freedmen who voted for Republican candidates, bureau officials sometimes sought to counter this economic coercion by providing them with relief (Owens 1943, 62–63, 173–74, 294, 312–13, 356). In this way, the bureau at least temporarily rendered freedmen less dependent on their employers and enabled them to use their political rights more freely. (Of course, as the bureau's critics pointed out, this practice also rendered freedpeople more dependent on the bureau and thereby increased its influence over them.) Furthermore, according to Colby (1985), the bureau's relief work was structurally separated from traditional poor relief. He argues that the bureau operated alongside "existing public and private community services," resulting in the creation of a "dual welfare system" (219–20, 226, 228). In principle, this separation of the bureau's relief work from existing institutions should have made it easier for freedpeople to escape the stigma of traditional poor relief. In practice, however, freedpeople found it difficult to avoid this stigma for three reasons.

First, the dual welfare system established by the Freedmen's Bureau was based on racial segregation. Although Colby (1985, 228) faults bureau officials for not forcing "the integration of existing programs and services," segregation was probably due more to resistance on the part of local authorities than lack of effort on the part of the bureau (Office of the Commissioner, Annual Reports, 1866–68, Boxes 1, 3, 4; Records of the Commissioner, Correspondence, Synopses of Letters and Reports Relating to Conditions of Freedmen and Bureau Activities in the States, January 1866–March 1869; Cimbala 1997, chap. 4). In any case, segregation reflected exclusion and discrimination by whites, not preferential treatment for blacks. Rather than privileging blacks, the dual welfare system set them apart as a socially impure and polluting class.[5]

Second, while Colby (1985) is correct about the stigmatizing effects of segregation, he overstates the degree to which the bureau's programs were actually separated from local and state institutions. In fact, the bureau's relief efforts were never entirely divorced from local and conventional forms of poor relief. For example, the bureau distributed relief through the local "overseers of the poor" in Alabama, and it relied on local civil authorities ("members of the Parish Police Juries") in Louisiana (Office of the Commissioner, Annual Reports, 1866–1868, Boxes 1, 3). At other times, the bureau "furnished planters with food for their laborers," thereby reinforcing, rather than undercutting, the economic dependency of black workers on their employers (Bentley 1955, 143–44). Furthermore, Bureau officials regarded their relief efforts as temporary emergency measures; they saw long-term relief as more properly the responsibility of local civil authorities, upon whom they sought to shift their relief burdens over time (Office of the Commissioner, Annual Reports, 1866–1868, Boxes 1, 3, 4; Bentley 1955, 79; Bremner 1980, 120–22; Foner 1988, 152; Cimbala 1997, chap. 4). Freedpeople were thus trapped between the humiliating Scylla of segregation and the stigmatizing Charybdis of traditional poor relief.

Third, the bureau incorporated many of the same degrading policy features that made traditional poor relief undesirable. To begin with, the bureau generally provided in-kind rather than cash assistance. In-kind assistance is more paternalistic and easier for authorities to earmark for activities they condone and approve, and it restricts recipients' autonomy as consumers (V. Zelizer 1994). Furthermore, bureau assistance was generally means tested and (like the workhouse) work tested. "Careful discrimination was to be exercised in administering relief, so as to include none who were not absolutely necessitous and destitute" (Pierce 1904, 95). In addition, "the Bureau was generally careful not to let able-bodied men and women subsist long on its charity and thus forget how to work. It kept its relief subordinated to its labor program and held down its issues of rations so that Negroes would have to earn their own livings" (Bentley 1955, 144). Bureau officials also tried to make freedpeople contribute to their own support in a variety of ways: taxing agricultural laborers and their employers for relief of the aged and infirm, putting the able-bodied to work on public works or poor farms, or compelling "those able to work . . . to pay for rations as issued or to give a lien upon their crops as security for such payment" (Bentley 1955, 85, 141; Pierce 1904, 95). Finally, although crop failures and other natural disasters required renewed relief efforts, bureau officials sought retrenchment of relief whenever possible. Retrenchment both reflected and reinforced the perception of freedpeople as undeserving. In these respects, the bureau's social policies resembled traditional poor relief and treated the agency's clients like paupers (Pierce 1904, chap. 6; Bentley 1955, 76–79, 84, 122, 139–44, 209; Bremner 1980, 116, 120–22; Foner 1988, 152–53).

LABOR POLICIES.    The bureau's labor policies also reveal the inconsistent manner in which it positioned its clients. On the one hand, the Freedmen's Bureau established a system of labor contracts that served to discipline black labor. This is evident in several ways. First, Bureau and military officials took temporary but stringent measures to remove unemployed blacks from towns and keep them on the plantations. They also pressured and even compelled reluctant freedmen to enter into written contracts with planters, though coercion generally ceased after 1866 (Office of the Commissioner, Annual Reports, 1866–68, Boxes 1, 3, 4; Nieman 1979, 61–62, 162–68, 209–10; Cimbala 1997, 139). Second, Bureau officials undermined the bargaining position of black workers and discouraged their use of collective action to extract more favorable terms of employment,

partly because the free-labor ideology denied any genuine conflict of interest between labor and capital, and partly because they believed that
"freedmen should seek protection from the Bureau rather than combine
to protect themselves" (Nieman 1979, 170; see also 168–69, 177–79, 210;
McFeely 1968, 311–12). The Bureau's stance also reflected a general wariness of labor organizations among Radical Republicans, who regarded
them as coercive and reactionary organizations that interfered with freedom of contract and "revived the spirit of special interest" (Montgomery [1967] 1981, 230–33, 247). Third, when black agricultural workers left
employers before their contract expired, some bureau officials compelled
specific performance of the labor contracts or allowed state officials to
do so; this usually entailed punishing workers or returning them to their
employers (Nieman 1979, 60, 173–76). This practice was less common after the first two years of the bureau's existence. After 1866, bureau officials continued to pressure freedpeople "to honor their contractual obligations," but "they generally refused to authorize agents to use force to
prevent freedmen from deserting their employers" (Nieman 1979, 212).
Fourth, bureau officials encouraged—or at least permitted—state officials
to enforce laws that punished employers who enticed workers from other
employers, thereby hindering black workers from leaving one employer
for a better one (Nieman 1979, 176–77). Fifth, bureau agents "protected
planters in their right to control the coming and going of their employees," "generally reinforced planters' authority to direct the work of employees," and "sought to compel freedmen to be punctual in their labor
and to work well" (Nieman 1979, 178–79, 211–12). As some of the bureau's contemporaries pointed out, these disciplinary practices left black
workers in the South less free in important respects than their white counterparts in the North (Litwack 1979, 413; Foner 1988, 166–67; Schmidt
1999, 250). Post-revisionist historians have even gone so far as to call the
bureau the "planter's guard" (Litwack 1979, 386).

On the other hand, bureau officials disciplined planters as well as laborers when they deemed it necessary to uphold or enforce the contract
system. First, bureau officials strongly recommended that planters and agricultural laborers have their contracts approved by the Freedman's Bureau, and they annulled or refused to recognize unjust contracts based on
coercion or deception (Nieman 1979, 162, 214). Second, bureau agents
"adjudicated black workers' grievances" and tried to compel planters and
black laborers alike to fulfill their contractual obligations (Nieman 1979,
65; Montgomery 1993, 119). Typically, this meant preventing planters

from violently assaulting workers, terminating contracts unilaterally, dismissing workers without pay, cheating workers out of pay after the crop was harvested, compelling workers to do tasks not stipulated in the labor contract, or denying workers their personal rights (Office of the Commissioner, Annual Reports, 1866–68, Boxes 1, 3, 4). The Freedmen's Bureau also "insisted that workers' claims to wages took precedence over landlords' claims for rent or merchants' claims for credit advances" (Montgomery 1993, 119). Although Bureau officials generally refused to establish a minimum wage, fearing it would sap freedmen's self-reliance, they sometimes regulated wages indirectly. In Alabama, for example, Assistant Commissioner Wager Swayne "considered [it] wrong . . . to prescribe the fixed rates of compensation," but nevertheless, he required labor contracts "to include the necessaries of life, *in kind,* and ample for their families and themselves" (Office of the Commissioner, 1866–68, Box 1 [original emphasis]; Bentley 1955, 80–81; Gerteis 1973, 190; Nieman 1979, 61). In other words, this requirement represented the penetration of the labor market by the principles of citizenship, the "invasion of contract by status, the subordination of market price to social justice, the replacement of the free bargain by the declaration of rights" (Marshall [1949] 1964, 111). Bureau officials also worked with civil authorities to compel planters to fulfill their contractual obligations, and they sometimes resorted to more coercive measures, such as seizing crops or arresting and incarcerating planters when it was deemed necessary (Office of the Commissioner, Annual Reports, 1866–68, Boxes 1, 3, 4; Bentley 1955, 148–51; Nieman 1979, 60, 65, 179–89, 214–22; Cimbala 1997, 138–52, 160). The system of labor contracts was thus double edged for planters as well as freedpeople. While the Freedman's Bureau may have served in some respects as the "planter's guard," planters nevertheless regarded it as dangerous, "arbitrary," and "despotic," because, as one planter put it, the bureau transferred "authority . . . in all questions of labor" from the planters' hands to "the agents of the Government" (quoted in Nieman 1979, 41; cf. Bentley 1955, 79–86, 105–07; Foner 1988, 167–168; Montgomery 1993, 119; Cimbala 1997, 142–44).

REGULATION OF FAMILY RELATIONS.    The bureau's regulation of family relations, like its provision of social welfare and regulation of labor relations, also positioned former slaves in ambiguous or inconsistent ways. After the Civil War, structural economic changes made it increasingly difficult to view wage labor as a temporary condition, eventually leading

Northern workers to shift from rejecting permanent wage labor to demanding a "family," or, "living" wage. "The ideal of the family wage, a wage sufficient to maintain a household and to support a nonemployed wife and children," gradually replaced self-employment as the "benchmark of freedom, independence, and citizenship" (Fraser and Gordon 1994, 318; Foner [1970] 1995, xxxvi; Glickman 1997, 1–7). Similar changes promoted this shift in the South under the guidance and supervision of the Freedmen's Bureau. Congress had directed the bureau to reduce freedpeople's dependency on the government and to transform them into "'a self-supporting class of free laborers'" (Farmer 1999, 161). However, the failure of Congress to redistribute land and the reluctance of whites to sell or rent land to black laborers foreclosed the option of self-employment for most blacks.[6] Consequently, the Freedmen's Bureau embraced the family-wage ideal early on, urging black men to take responsibility and provide for their wives and children (Cimbala 1997, 196; Schwalm 1997, 266–67; Farmer 1999, 174–75). In so doing, the Freedmen's Bureau signaled that even landless black men could achieve manly independence.

The bureau reinforced this ideal by supporting and enforcing freedmen's paternal authority. In Georgia, for example, bureau officials awarded a black father's children to him after his wife abandoned him, "gave permission to a planter to discharge a freedwoman if she failed to live with her legal husband," and jailed adulterous wives. In addition, the Georgia Freedmen's Bureau generally supported black men in their struggles with employers over control of their children's labor. "The [black] husband," Georgia Assistant Commissioner Davis Tillson insisted, "has the same right to control his wife and children that a white man has" (quoted in Cimbala 1997, 194–203). This support helped freedmen "establish greater control over their wives and children than slavery had permitted," despite resistance from planters (Nieman 1979, 123–24; see also Montgomery 1993, 121–22; Cimbala 1997, 203). In this way, the bureau not only limited employers' exploitation of black labor but also reinforced black men's "identity as free people." As Cimbala (1997, 198) points out, this gendered identity entailed black men's "right to determine the destinies of their families in the face of planters who were still trying to reassert their mastery by exploiting the most vulnerable segment of the freed population." In short, when freedmen's paternal authority was challenged from below by unruly dependents or from above by former masters, the bureau often stepped in to support and sustain it. The bureau thus affirmed freedmen's newfound independence in opposition to the dependence of women, children, and slaves.

However, even as the Freedmen's Bureau affirmed black men's independence in some ways, it simultaneously undermined it in other ways. Above all, the bureau failed to guarantee black men the family wage that bureau officials expected and repeatedly urged freedmen to earn. Consequently, "most black women could not afford to withdraw from outside labor after emancipation; many continued to work in the fields alongside their men, while others moved into the towns in the hope of obtaining more remunerative employment" (Litwack 1979, 246). Despite the bureau's best efforts to rationalize black women's labor as a temporary necessity, black men's inability to become reliable family breadwinners undercut their claims to manly independence. Moreover, the bureau sometimes eroded rather than reinforced freedmen's paternal authority. When black men failed to support their families, for example, the bureau stepped in to force them to fulfill their paternal obligations. Often acting on complaints from freedwomen, bureau officials compelled freedmen to support their wives and children, ordering those who had "deserted their families without 'good' cause" to return home to their spouses or to pay child support. In Virginia, the bureau used cases of family desertion to "educate, or perhaps remind, freedmen of their marital responsibilities." Bureau officials also interceded in family affairs to "resolve problems of [domestic] abuse and abandonment" and determine custody of children (Cimbala 1997, 194–203; Farmer 1999, 176). These interventions reduced the arbitrary discretion that black fathers and husbands could exercise in family affairs and limited the sanctions they could bring to bear upon other family members; these interventions also made wives and children less dependent on their goodwill. Even when the bureau sided with black husbands and fathers in these interventions, its efforts to prop up their paternal authority could be construed as protective measures that simultaneously revealed freedmen's weaknesses and their inability to exercise that authority unassisted.

In summary, the Freedmen's Bureau's involvement in black family relations—often on behalf of women—meant that the freedman was hardly king in his own home; he quickly discovered that the bureau's regulation of family relations was as double edged as its regulation of labor relations. Just as the bureau transferred "questions of labor" from the planters' hands to "the agents of the Government," so, too, did it take family questions out of the hands of the family's ostensible male head.

## Reasons for the bureau's contradictory policies

Why did the Freedmen's Bureau operate in such contradictory ways? One reason for the inconsistent treatment of freedpeople is that the bureau pursued multiple, often incompatible, policy goals (Foner 1988, 143–44, 153). Many of these goals fell under the heading of what O'Connor (1973) calls the "accumulation function" of the welfare state: reviving agricultural production in the South, promoting economic recovery in a region devastated by war, proletarianizing former slaves, pressuring them to go back to work on the plantations, and disciplining labor. Many Northern investors promoted these goals in hopes that "the bureau would help them make money in the South" (Bentley 1955, 49). Other goals fell under the heading of what O'Connor (1973) terms the "legitimation function" of the welfare state: guaranteeing the rights of former slaves, protecting black workers from violence and fraud, alleviating social unrest, and preventing civil disorders like the 1866 race riots in Memphis and New Orleans. Letters to Congress and the president advocating a continuation of the bureau's work frequently emphasized this function. Many argued that the bureau was indispensable, because local civil authorities did not adequately protect freedpeople. "What is wanted," wrote a delegate to Georgia's constitutional convention in 1867, "is a power to see that simple justice is done" (Office of the Commissioner, Letters from the Executive Mansion, Box 19).[7] Furthermore, insofar as the Republican-dominated Congress used the bureau to build support for the Grand Old Party in the South, the bureau also served partisan political objectives. Though not averse to other policy goals, Republicans used the bureau to ensure "their continuance in office" and increase "their political power in Washington" (Bentley 1955, 49).[8] Finally, for true-blue Radical Republicans and the most zealous advocates of free labor, the bureau was a means to reconstruct people as well as institutions. For them, the bureau's primary purpose was nothing less than the transformation of slaves into citizens. This project rested on two assumptions: first, that former slaves were not, in their present condition, fit for citizenship in a republican polity; and second, that the state could render them fit by inculcating the necessary virtues, habits, and dispositions. While there was little disagreement between supporters and opponents of Radical Reconstruction on the first point, they parted company on the second. Radicals assumed precisely what white supremacists denied: that fitness for citizenship could be acquired, even by nonwhites.[9] They sought therefore to

FIGURE 2.1. The bureau's legitimation function. ("The Freedmen's Bureau," *Harper's Weekly*, July 25, 1868, Library of Congress)

justify the extension of citizenship to freed slaves not on the basis of their existing qualities, but on the basis of what they would become if granted citizenship. The contradictions in the bureau's treatment of freedpeople arose in part because these multiple functions—reviving production, maintaining the peace, keeping Republicans in office, and molding slaves into citizens—were often difficult to reconcile, a situation exacerbated by the growing rift between Congress and President Johnson over how Reconstruction should proceed. As one historian has put it, Commissioner Howard was like a horseman struggling to head his various steeds in the same direction (McFeely 1968, 191).

The Freedmen's Bureau's inconsistent treatment of freedpeople also reflected institutional differences between the federal and state governments and between military and civil authorities. As Mettler (1998, 12–13) has shown, "social citizenship determined by the states, judging by its ability to incorporate citizens on a broad and equal basis, has generally tended to be inferior to social citizenship with national standards for eligibility and administration." Since the Freedmen's Bureau was a federal agency, one might expect it to have administered its policies in a "centralized, unitary manner through standardized, routinized procedures," and to govern its clients as rights-bearing "members of a liberal regime" (Mettler 1998, xi). In some respects, this was true. Despite the bureau's less savory policy goals, it positioned former slaves as rights bearers to a greater extent than they had ever been before. Bureau agents could and sometimes did mistreat blacks, but they were bound by a bureaucratic system of rules and regulations that reduced their discretionary power. A growing awareness of these rules may have made freedpeople less fearful that bureau officials would use their authority arbitrarily and more confident that officials would respond to legitimate requests. Moreover, because freedpeople associated the bureau with the government as a whole, their experiences with the bureau may have had important spillover effects that would have fostered a more assertive orientation toward government and political action (cf. Soss 1999).

Federal control over bureau activities was limited, however, by the discretion granted to state-level assistant commissioners and by the "legal and extra-legal pressures which white southerners might employ" to influence bureau officials (O. Howard 1907, 363; Oubre 1978, 192–193). These pressures included hostility, insults, threats, and even murder (Office of the Commissioner, Annual Reports, 1866–68, Boxes 1, 3, 4). Federal control was also limited by the bureau's need to cooperate with—at times rely on—and ultimately shift its responsibilities to local civil author-ities (Pierce 1904, 51–54; Cimbala 1997, chap. 4). As Alabama Assistant Commissioner Wager Swayne put it in his 1866 annual report, the bureau aimed "to mould existing institutions which are permanent, rather than to displace such by a temporary antagonism of military power."[10] "What-ever directives flowed out of the national office," concludes one historian, "the crucial power of the Freedmen's Bureau rested with the state and lo-cal officials" (Litwack 1979, 382–83).

Furthermore, many of the same institutional and economic factors that account for the inferiority of state-level citizenship also affected the Freedmen's Bureau. Until the late 1950s and 1960s, state governments, un-like the federal government, possessed broad police powers to "'provide for the public health, safety, and good order' of the community," largely unrestrained by the Bill of Rights and the Fourteenth Amendment. "Without liberal guarantees of rights, states tended to . . . preserve the social order . . . rather than to promote equality" (Mettler 1998, 13–14). As a military agency sometimes operating in a context of martial law, the Freedmen's Bureau also exercised relatively unrestrained police pow-ers. Moreover, state governments were more vulnerable to capital flight than the national government and therefore more reluctant to imple-ment redistributive policies that increased business costs (Mettler 1998, 14–15). Likewise, because bureau officials sought to revive agricultural production in their districts, they were reluctant to implement policies that might drive away Northern investments. As a result of these limita-tions, bureau policies partly resembled state-level social and labor pol-icies: discretion and variability seeped into the bureau's work (Bentley 1955, 131–32), and officials sometimes treated freedpeople in nonliberal ways as dependent persons in need of supervision and protection rather than as rights bearers.

Finally, the Freedmen's Bureau's contradictory treatment of freed-people also reflected its ties to religious institutions, which were major players in the nineteenth-century welfare field. Although the Freedmen's Bureau was a government agency, its work was not clearly differenti-ated from the humanitarian and relief work of private churches. Indeed, the bureau worked closely with church-based freedmen's aid societies as well as evangelical groups like the American Missionary Association, and Protestantism exercised a strong influence over the bureau's top of-ficers (Bremner 1980, 115; Shattuck 1987, 21; Richardson 1999). Commis-sioner Howard, known throughout the nation as the "Christian Soldier," organized the bureau in a manner that resembled the organization of the United States Christian Commission and believed that "bureau work was missionary work. . . . Christianity among the freedmen was to be encouraged through the example of Christian virtue of the assistant commissioners and the bureau agents" (McFeely 1968, 85–87; Shattuck 1987, 76).[11] Moreover, like Howard, almost all of the bureau's assistant commissioners were "Protestants belonging to the great denominations of the center who believed that man, stimulated in the emotional atmosphere of revivals, could find salvation by working to perfect the world" (McFeely 1968, 72, 177). This religious fervor even filtered down to some bureau agents. For example, South Carolina Freedmen's Bureau agent Willard Saxton (the brother of Assistant Commissioner Rufus Saxton) described his efforts on behalf of the freed slaves as "the Lord's work," adding that this knowledge made him "feel courage & strength to fight still harder" (quoted in McFeely 1968, 135). In brief, the Freedmen's Bureau practiced faith-based welfare *avant la lettre.*

How did these religious influences shape the bureau's treatment of freedpeople? On the one hand, the bureau's work dovetailed with the evangelically inspired perfectionist movement, which was "mature by 1865" and whose proponents were eager to "undertake a movement of social reform" (McFeely 1968, 72; see also T. Smith 1957; Shattuck 1987, 2; Woodworth 2001, 11–15). This perfectionist movement converged with a liberationist interpretation of the Civil War that was popular among abolitionists and vividly expressed in Julia Ward Howe's "Battle Hymn of the Republic": as Christ "died to make men holy," Union soldiers died "to make men free" (Shattuck 1987, 15–16; Woodworth 2001, 107–08). These perfectionist and liberationist themes appealed to freedpeople, as well; they "took Moses and the Exodus as models for their millenarian aspirations" (Magdol 1977, 9). When these aspects of American Protestantism guided the bureau's "missionary work," officials tended to place more emphasis on the protection of freedpeople's rights. On the other hand, Protestantism could also encourage bureau officials to impose stern discipline on their clients. In both the North and the South, mid-nineteenth-century American evangelicalism stressed individual moral accountability, self-control, and self-restraint; these virtues were understood to produce moral order and (as divine rewards) worldly success, power, and prosperity (Daly 2002). Prior to the Civil War, Protestants had racialized these moral categories in debates over slavery, defining the "evangelical model of character" in opposition to the presumed moral deficiencies of blacks

(Daly 2002, 83). They debated whether slavery was the cause of these deficiencies, as antislavery evangelicals argued, or the remedy, as proslavery evangelicals maintained. They also debated how best to build moral character and inculcate discipline—through slavery or free labor. However, antislavery and proslavery evangelicals both agreed on the need to instill discipline in those who lacked it. Many bureau officials shared this assumption; they adopted corrective policies to break the cultural legacy of slavery and extirpate the vices that antislavery evangelicals attributed to it (Nieman 1979, 40, 53–57).[12] Thus, under the influence of the Protestant ethic, they aimed to bring about not only a political and social revolution in the South, but a "disciplinary revolution" (Gorski 2003) as well.[13] In this respect, Protestant religious influences merged with the bureau's rehabilitative goals to encourage paternalistic, coercive, and even punitive treatment of the bureau's clients.

## From Contradiction to Contestation: The Struggle over the Civic Classification of Freedmen's Bureau Clients

The bureau's contradictory treatment of its clients reflected and exacerbated conflicts over the postwar status and rights of the freed slaves. Ironically, while the bureau strove to turn slaves into citizens, its relief efforts and regulatory activities made its clients vulnerable to stigmatizing charges of pauperism, which most Americans deemed incompatible with full citizenship. Resisting efforts that would class them as paupers, freedpeople sought recognition as honorable, rights-bearing citizens whose wartime services entitled them to state assistance. They demanded that the government furnish them with land or, failing that, safeguard their autonomy as laborers and protect them from coercive and abusive employers. In their view, these social rights were necessary and integral aspects of the citizenship they claimed, no less important than the civil and political rights they sought to acquire. The struggle over the civic classification of the bureau's clients was thus not merely a dispute over names and labels; it was also a struggle over the material and symbolic profits that citizenship conferred. As Americans contested what citizenship entailed and whether federal aid pauperized freedpeople, they tried to objectify their preferred classificatory schemes in political institutions. These classification struggles therefore had important policy implications. While critics of the Freedmen's Bureau advocated the kind of discipline and retrenchment typically meted out to paupers, freedpeople sought policy improvements that would establish and confirm their standing as independent, deserving, rights-bearing citizens.

## "Wards of the nation": Freedpeople as undeserving paupers

ASCRIPTIVE AMERICANISM.   From its inception, the Freedmen's Bureau generated staunch opposition, not only among white Southerners, but also among Northern Democrats and even some Republicans. The bureau's critics attacked it on a variety of grounds, all of which implicitly or explicitly questioned freedpeople's fitness for full and equal citizenship. Perhaps the most obvious source of opposition was the political tradition that Rogers Smith (1993, 1997) calls ascriptive Americanism, which advocated exclusion on explicitly racial grounds. Ascriptive Americanism was widespread in the North as well as the South. Indeed, while Radical Republicans pushed their party toward a cautious, sometimes reluctant, and partly self-interested commitment to the civic inclusion of African Americans, the Democrats used overt appeals to white supremacy to help unite the political coalition that supported their party (Stampp 1965, 196–97; Belz 1976, 70, 92; Foner 1988, 31). These appeals castigated blacks as inherently unfit for citizenship—so different from whites, in the words of Indiana Senator Thomas Hendricks, that "we ought not to compose one political community" (quoted in Foner 1988, 278).

LAISSEZ-FAIRE.   A second source of opposition to the Freedmen's Bureau was the fear that it would stifle independence and self-reliance among blacks. According to this view, the bureau was a dangerously paternalistic institution, the very incarnation of the "immense and tutelary power" about which Tocqueville ([1840] 1972, 319–21) had warned Americans. While the bureau's supporters described it as exercising a temporary, necessary, and benevolent guardianship over childlike wards, many of its critics agreed with Thomas Wentworth Higginson, who rejected such guardianship as harmful and best avoided (Belz 1976, 72, 77, 97–98; Cimbala 1997, 18). Higginson, one of the "Secret Six" who helped finance John Brown's 1859 raid on Harpers Ferry and a Union Army officer who commanded black troops in the Civil War, declared that for their own sake freedpeople "should not continue to be kept wards of the nation" (quoted in Foner 1988, 448–49). Instead, critics like Higginson favored a laissez-faire approach to freedpeople that "questioned the wisdom of government supervision of the former slaves" and sought to leave them alone "to make their own labor arrangements and provide for themselves" (Belz 1976, 70, 92; Foner 1988, 67–68). This laissez-faire approach was shared by many abolitionists, some Republicans, and even some African Americans, most notably the former slave and prominent black abolitionist Frederick Douglass (Belz 1976, 70, 92, 99, 152; Magdol 1977, 53, 79–82; Litwack 1979, 403, 521–22; Foner 1988, 448–49). In response to "the persistent question 'What shall we do with the Negro?'" Douglass "had only one answer: 'Do nothing. . . . Give him the chance to stand on his own legs! Let him alone!'" (Oubre 1978, 76; Foner 1988, 67–68).

Unlike white supremacists, proponents of the laissez-faire approach did not seek to deny civil and political rights to freedpeople. On the contrary, they regarded these rights as "essential attributes of autonomous citizenship in a competitive society" (Foner 1988, 277). However, they rejected government assistance and protection as deeply incompatible with such rights. Even land reform was considered "government paternalism" that would have a "blighting influence on the initiative of those who received it" (Stampp 1965, 130). Instead, the bureau's laissez-faire critics urged freedpeople "to take their place as citizens and participants in the competitive marketplace. . . . With their civil and political equality assured, blacks no longer possessed a claim upon the federal government; the competitive rules of the free market would determine their station in society" (Foner 1988, 67, 449). As Marshall ([1949] 1964, 87) put it, civil rights "gave to each man, as part of his individual status, the power to engage as an independent unit in the economic struggle and made it possible to deny to him social protection on the ground that he was equipped with the means to protect himself." This attitude became especially pronounced during struggles over black voting rights, which culminated in the Fifteenth Amendment. Many Republicans clearly envisioned voting rights as an *alternative* to continued government assistance in the form of the Freedmen's Bureau. "'The Fifteenth Amendment,' declared Congressman James A. Garfield, 'confers upon the African race the care of its own destiny. It places their fortunes in their own hands. 'The negro is now a voter and a citizen,' echoed an Illinois newspaper. 'Let him hereafter take his chances in the battle of life'" (Foner 1988, 448–49). From this perspective, freedpeople's demands to be recognized as citizens undercut their claims to government protection and assistance; their social rights vanished to the extent that they acquired civil and political rights.

This view quickly became apparent in debates over the Freedmen's Bureau. Many Americans feared that the bureau's relief efforts would foster pauperism, dependence, idleness, and vice among blacks (Bentley 1955, 76–79; Abbott 1967, 121; McFeely 1968, 208–09, 279; Foner 1988, 247–48; Berlin et al. 1990, 15–16). Even bureau officials shared these concerns and accordingly sought to cut back relief as much as possible (O. Howard 1907, 213–14, 226, 423; Bentley 1955, 76–79; Bremner 1980, 119, 125; Foner 1988, 152–53; Farmer 1999, 162–63, 167–68). This reaction against the Freedmen's Bureau's relief efforts reflected the division between citizens and paupers inherited from earlier classification struggles (see chapter 1), which made it difficult for freedpeople to square federal relief with their claims to citizenship. As a Tennessee bureau official put it, "a man can scarcely be called free who is the recipient of public charity" (quoted in Foner 1988, 152). Moreover, this same logic led the bureau's laissez-faire critics to oppose its regulation of labor relations. As noted in the previous chapter, protective labor laws initially excluded adult men out of respect for their status as citizens, "on the grounds that enforced protective measures curtailed the civil right to conclude a free contract of employment. Protection was confined to women and children . . . because they were not citizens. If they wished to enjoy full and responsible citizenship, they must forgo protection" (Marshall [1949] 1964, 81).[14] Critics of the Freedmen's Bureau drew similar conclusions about blacks. In 1864, as Congress debated the bill to create the Freedmen's Bureau, Kentucky congressman William Henry Wadsworth questioned its "authority to put overseers and clerks over *free* Negroes, to 'fix their wages, direct their labor, adjudicate their rights without a judge or jury,' and he asked, if Congress had these powers over free Negroes, did it not have them over free white men?" (Bentley 1955, 38, emphasis in the original). Wadsworth and likeminded detractors would likely have agreed with McFeely's (1968, 156) assessment: the freedman not only remained "the child of an ancient paternalism" exercised by his former master, "but he also had acquired a Yankee stepfather," the bureau agent who was "committed to seeing that the [labor] contracts were made and met." This reaction against the bureau's labor regulations subsequently discouraged the enactment of protective labor laws at the state level. When a South Carolina legislator proposed in 1869 that a state labor commission be created, even Republican legislators attacked the bill as paternalistic. "Disillusioned memories of the Freedmen's Bureau agents who supervised contracts between planters and their laborers . . . hung over the debates. Referring to the Bureau, [white Republican legislator Reuben] Tomlinson charged that the bill would put 'task masters' over the workers. He insisted that 'if these men were able to be citizens, they were able as well to manage their own affairs'" (Holt 1977, 159–61). Thus, in labor policy, as in relief policy, the Freedmen's Bureau's laissez-faire critics viewed social rights as an alternative to citizenship rights rather than as an integral part of them.

FEAR OF FEDERAL AND MILITARY DESPOTISM.   A third source of opposition to the Freedmen's Bureau lay in fears that a growing concentration of federal power, an extraordinary expansion of federal bureaucracy, and unprecedented military intrusion into civil affairs were rapidly resulting in centralized despotism. According to this view, a bloated and costly federal government was overstepping its authority, usurping responsibilities, such as relief, that properly belonged to local civil authorities, and jeopardizing states' rights and individual liberties (Pierce 1904, 35; Abbott 1967, 124; Belz 1976, 70, 92). These fears, though exaggerated for political purposes, reflected real and fundamental changes in the scope and powers of the federal government during the Civil War, including the creation of "a government-controlled currency," the introduction of military conscription, a dramatic rise in federal expenditures, and a growing reliance on direct taxation rather than tariffs or land sales to sustain the state's "bureaucratic and military machinery" (Montgomery [1967] 1981, 46–47). Furthermore, these changes at the federal level were mirrored by similar changes at the state and local levels, as Republican-led governments in both the North and South raised taxes and increased the public debt to subsidize railroad corporations and expand public health, public works, welfare, and schools (Foner 1988, 364–411, 469). These policies increased opportunities for graft and raised the cost of government, fueling a burgeoning tax revolt that was partly led and mobilized by the Democratic Party (Montgomery [1967] 1981, 265; Foner 1988, 364–65, 415–16). Democrats demanded "a return to rule by 'intelligent property-holders'" as the only way to lower taxes and shrink the government. Republicans, they argued, could neither lower taxes nor tighten state budgets "since 'the *negro vote* will always be unaffected by regard for economy in government'" (Foner 1988, 416, 424; original emphasis).

The Freedmen's Bureau became embroiled in these controversies early on. Leading congressional Democrats like S. S. Cox of Ohio objected that the bureau was "a measure too sweeping and revolutionary for a government of limited and express powers" (Pierce 1904, 38). President Johnson, voicing similar views in his veto of the 1866 Freedmen's

Bureau bill, criticized the bill for increasing the federal tax burden, denounced its expansion of federal bureaucracy and concentration of executive power as dangerous, and objected to federal relief, land redistribution, and the passing of the bill without Southern representation in Congress as unconstitutional (Bentley 1955, 119; Foner 1988, 247–48). "In appealing to fiscal conservatism, raising the specter of an immense federal bureaucracy trampling upon citizens' rights, and insisting [that] self-help, not dependence upon outside assistance, offered the surest road to economic advancement, Johnson voiced themes that to this day have sustained opposition to federal intervention on behalf of blacks" (Foner 1988, 248).

Public concerns about the expansion of military authority reinforced these fears of centralized despotism. For example, Sarah Whintesey, a resident of Virginia and a self-professed loyalist, complained to President Johnson about military authorities who "interfere with our civil authorities and trample upon state laws. . . . Shall our state laws be crushed under *military* heels, and our city authorities driven before *military* commands?" (Office of the Commissioner, Letters from the Executive Mansion, Box 19, emphasis in the original). Nor were these fears confined to Southerners. In the North, "wild rumors of violence" circulated during the 1866 congressional election as "each party accused the other of planning to seize the government by force with the soldiers' aid, and excitable individuals on both sides actually proposed such action" (Dearing 1952, 104). When President Johnson issued a proclamation in the spring of 1866 declaring that the Confederate insurrection was over, he warned darkly that "standing armies, military occupation, martial law, military tribunals and the suspension of the writ of *habeas corpus*" were opposed to American constitutionalism (quoted in Nieman 1979, 116). Consistent with this stand, Johnson denounced the 1866 Freedmen's Bureau bill for establishing military courts in peacetime (Bentley 1955, 119). The Supreme Court appeared to back Johnson's position in 1866 in *Ex parte Milligan*,[15] ruling that "military tribunals lacked authority to try civilians" when "civil courts were open and functioning" (Nieman 1979, 146). Because the Court's opinion overturned the conviction of a military commission in Indiana, a Northern state, its applicability to the unrestored states in the South was unclear. Nevertheless, when Congress passed the 1866 Freedmen's Bureau Act over Johnson's veto, it was mindful of the *Milligan* decision, ordering bureau courts continued only where conditions of rebellion still existed. A year later, the Military Reconstruction Acts "met the *Milligan* decision squarely and instructed the federal courts to sustain the use of army courts for civilians in the South" (McFeely 1968, 271, 273; Nieman 1979, 202–9). These military tribunals helped federal authorities counter an upsurge of terrorism against blacks and Southern Unionists. Nevertheless, *Ex parte Milligan* probably bolstered the perception that the bureau's use of military tribunals made it dangerously tyrannical (Bentley 1955, 162–68; McFeely 1968, chap. 13; Foner 1988, 272).

OPPOSITION TO SPECIAL PRIVILEGES.   A fourth source of opposition to the Freedmen's Bureau was the belief that it was a form of "class legislation," or, what Americans might now call preferential treatment or reverse discrimination. Advocates of this view held that the law should be impartial and uniform rather than favor particular groups or classes (Belz 1976, 148–49). They opposed protective labor laws on these grounds, which brought them into conflict with the labor movement's campaign for an eight-hour day in the 1860s and 1870s (Montgomery [1967] 1981). This aversion to protective labor laws also roused their hostility to the Freedmen's Bureau, and in this case racial prejudices reinforced class prejudices.[16] This is evident from congressional debates over the 1865 Freedmen's Bureau bill. Some Republican critics of the bill, fearing that "the freedmen might receive privileges and benefits not available to whites," objected to its "exclusive attention to blacks" and insisted on "equal rights for white southern war victims" (Belz 1976, 100). As Bentley (1955, 140) points out, "some Congressmen were more ready to support an institution that helped white people than one whose benefits went exclusively to Negroes." Accusations of special treatment also reflected concerns that the Freedmen's Bureau might serve as a precedent for further class legislation. When Massachusetts congressman Thomas Eliot first introduced his Freedmen's Bureau bill in 1863, the minority report of the Select Committee on Emancipation warned that it would obligate "the government to support similar agencies for other racial and ethnic groups," such as "a potential 'Irish Bureau'" (Colby 1985, 221). These concerns led Congress to broaden the bureau's target population in the final legislation. By including "Southern white refugees as well as freedmen," Congress "aimed to counteract the impression of preferential treatment for blacks" (Foner 1988, 69). These concerns also led the bureau's commissioner to limit the lifespan of its courts, hospitals, and charitable institutions; Howard was "convinced that blacks would benefit more by recognition as equal citizens than from being treated as a special class permanently dependent upon federal assistance and protection" (Foner 1988, 148).

Despite these precautionary measures, critics of the Freedmen's Bureau continued to attack it as class legislation, fostering an angry and divisive politics of resentment. Southern whites erroneously criticized the bureau for redistributing land and providing education to blacks but not whites (Abbott 1967, 116, 122). In his veto of the 1866 Freedmen's Bureau bill, President Johnson expressed similar views, objecting that the federal government "never deemed itself authorized to expend the public money for the rent or purchase of homes for . . . the white race who are honestly toiling from day to day for their subsistence." Federal relief, Johnson added, "was never contemplated by the authors of the Constitution; nor can any good reason be advanced why, as a permanent establishment, it should be founded for one class or color of our people more than another" (Fleming 1905, 12–15, chap. 6 and 7; Du Bois [1935] 1962, 276; McFeely 1968, 243; Foner 1988, 247). Some critics of the Freedmen's Bureau went further, contrasting the Republican Party's alleged generosity to freedpeople to its stingy disregard for Union veterans. In fact, many veterans did experience hardship at the war's end; provisions for disabled soldiers were initially inadequate, and rapid demobilization of the army flooded the labor market and increased unemployment. In this context, veterans' grievances provided fertile ground for a politics of resentment. While some veterans directed their anger at employers or politicians, others blamed blacks for diverting attention and resources that might otherwise have gone to them. Democrats stoked these resentments, charging that "so far as Congress was concerned, the Negroes were the 'favored class.' Not only did the blacks live in government quarters; they ate and drank at the taxpayers' expense, and their children received free education. 'We have not heard of the government supporting the wives or orphans of the white soldiers slain in battle'" (Dearing 1952, 52, 54–55, 62–63, 72–73, 77). Nor was opposition to class legislation confined to angry whites. Prominent African Americans like Frederick Douglass feared that "'special efforts' on the freedman's behalf might 'serve to keep up the very prejudices, which it is so desirable to banish,' by promoting an image of blacks as privileged wards of the state" (Foner 1988, 67–68; Oubre 1978, 76). For similar reasons, many black newspapers and political conventions advised freedpeople to become self-made yeomen

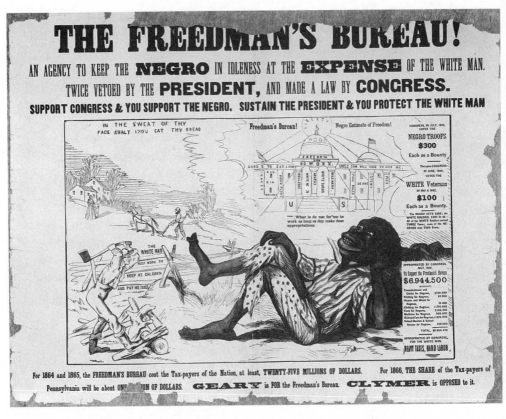

FIGURE 2.2. Freedpeople as dependent paupers and recipients of special privileges. (Democratic broadside from 1866 election, Pennsylvania, Library of Congress)

farmers by means of hard work and saving, demanding "even-handed justice" rather than "special privileges or favor" (Litwack 1979, 522).

REACTION AGAINST CORRUPTION AND PATRONAGE.   Corruption in the Freedmen's Bureau and its involvement in political patronage generated yet another source of opposition. Many of the bureau's critics accused it of "employing corrupt or incompetent administrators who wasted federal money" and "acting as a political agency for the Republican party" (Stampp 1965, 132). For example, "an editor of a rural weekly [in South Carolina], reckoning that the Bureau had cost taxpayers from fifteen to twenty million dollars, charged that the bulk of this amount had gone into the pockets of officers and agents, and not towards the welfare of the Negro. 'It is a very easy thing for a Radical to appear as the friend of the colored people when he is getting a good salary for it,' he concluded" (Abbott 1967, 124). Northern labor leaders like William Sylvis, president of the Iron Molders' International Union, echoed these charges, denouncing the Freedmen's Bureau as a "huge swindle upon the honest workingmen of the country" (quoted in Foner 1988, 480). Prominent congressional Democrats like S. S. Cox made similar accusations, declaring that the bureau "open[ed] up a vast field for corruption, tyranny, greed, and abuse" (Pierce 1904, 38). When President Johnson sent two generals, Joseph Fullerton and James Steedman, on a tour of inquiry in the South to assess the bureau's work, their well-publicized official reports seemed to confirm these allegations, accusing bureau agents of embezzlement, fraud, and corruption (Bentley 1955, 123–33; McFeely 1968, 247–58; Foner 1988, 248). Although the bureau's critics exaggerated the misconduct of bureau agents for political purposes, their concerns were not unfounded (Owens 1943, 86–88, 174–75; Bentley 1955, 132–33, 136–51; Stampp 1965, 132–34). In Louisiana, for example, "many [Freedmen's Bureau] agents were . . . guilty of such fraudulent practices as accepting bribes, charging fees for services that should have been free, diverting relief supplies, and embezzling funds" (White 1970, 35, 38; cf. Bentley 1955, 138–39). In his 1868 annual report, Louisiana's assistant commissioner declared that it was "mainly owing to the incompetency, inefficiency and misconduct in office that the Bureau has been so unpopular and the freedmen suffered so much in many Parishes of this State." He concluded that "many of its agents in this state are thoroughly dishonest."

Allegations that the Freedmen's Bureau provided patronage in return for Republican votes also aroused hostility, encouraging calls to curb or repeal black voting rights. As freedpeople became politically active in South Carolina, for example, "most whites became wholly convinced that Bureau officials were using their influence to organize them in support of the Radical Republican cause" (Abbott 1967, 123). "The mass of unemployed Negroes will constitute an army corp[s] of idle, reckless vagrants," declared the *Charleston Courier,* "who will plunder the country with an unsparing hand and with shameless impunity and from time to time be marched to the polls to carry the elections as the Radical orders are issued" (quoted in Owens 1943, 274). This view was widely shared among Southern whites. On the eve of the crucial 1868 presidential election, "conservative southern journals declared that the Radicals wanted the Freedmen's Bureau continued only because it was 'their most powerful electioneering machinery throughout the South,' and asserted that it was a 'vast engine of influence and patronage' that was going to 'barter soup for suffrage for another year'" (Bentley 1955, 200–01). Northern newspapers, particularly those aligned with the Democratic Party, made similar accusations. The *New York World,* for example, denounced the Bureau as "an electioneering machine of the radicals, through which millions of the people's money were spent to support negroes in idleness year after year in return for their votes for the radical party" (quoted in Pierce 1904, 169–70). Samuel Tilden, leader of New York's Democratic Party (and future Democratic nominee for President in 1876), declared in 1868 that the Freedmen's Bureau was "partly an eleemosynary establishment" and partly "a job for its dependants and their speculative associates. But in its principle character, it is a political machine to organize and manage the three millions of negroes" (quoted in Pierce 1904, 169). Two years later, Democratic congressman Fernando Wood of New York reiterated the charge, accusing Commissioner Howard and other bureau officials of favoring "the political machinery" of the Republican Party "in the southern states" and exercising "the official authority and power" of the bureau "for personal and political profit." The bureau's "main motive," Democratic congressman S. S. Cox bluntly concluded, "was to perpetuate the existence of the Republican party" (Pierce 1904, 170; O. Howard 1907, 436–44).

Like allegations of corruption, allegations of political patronage were exaggerated but not unfounded. Indeed, the bureau's involvement in patronage was probably inevitable given the fact that democratization preceded the bureaucratization of civil administration in the United States (Orloff 1988, 1993b; Skocpol 1992): "Because the 'state's power was rooted in the new Republican organization and its capacity to channel the actions of governing elites,' state officials did not develop as autonomous agents but remained first and foremost representatives of the party" (Orloff 1993b, 224, quoting Skowronek 1982, 30). This made the Freedmen's Bureau a useful tool for Radical Republicans. "[T]he patronage it could be made to control . . . [and] the strategic position it offered for influencing votes of the Negroes . . . were rich prizes" (Bentley 1955, 35–36).[17] Following passage of the 1867 Military Reconstruction Acts, which authorized blacks to vote, the Freedmen's Bureau not only registered black voters but also encouraged them to vote for the Republican Party. Under the leadership of the Congressional Union Republican Committee, "most of the Bureau's assistant commissioners and many of its other of-

ficers became active workers for the Republicans." Although the Freedmen's Bureau worked inconspicuously, "its contribution was great." As
noted above, congressional Republicans used the bureau to ensure that
Republicans would represent the ex-Confederate states in Congress and
guarantee the election of Ulysses S. Grant as president in 1868. At that
time, "Southern Democrats were eagerly wooing the colored vote," and
"there was no assurance that the Republican party could carry the South."
Under these circumstances, many Republicans concluded, "the continuation of the Freedmen's Bureau might make the difference between victory and defeat." These considerations undoubtedly influenced the enactment of the third Freedmen's Bureau Act in July 1868. The gambit
paid off: "Grant's popular majority was only 309,584, and he probably received the votes of 450,000 Negroes. That those votes were cast, and cast
for the Republican candidate, was very largely due to the efforts of the
Freedmen's Bureau. It had thoroughly accomplished one of its original
tasks, that of helping the Radical politicians keep their party in power"
(Bentley 1955, 186–87, 190, 199–200, 202).

In summary, opponents of the Freedmen's Bureau acted as "moral entrepreneurs" in Becker's (1963, 139, 147–63) meaning of the term. They
tried to "enlist the support of other interested organizations and develop, through the use of the press and other communications media,"
an unfavorable public attitude toward the bureau, which, whether intended or not, inevitably influenced public attitudes toward the bureau's
clients. Some critics, appealing to white supremacy, drew upon ascriptive Americanism. Others, advocating a laissez-faire approach or attacking class legislation, invoked the liberal political tradition. Still others
used the language of civic republicanism, stressing the bureau's corruption or its alleged threat to states' rights. Although each of these criticisms focused public attention on a different fault of the bureau, they all
shared one thing in common: they represented the Bureau's clients, implicitly or explicitly, as a source of moral contamination and contagion,
a class of anti-citizens whose civic inclusion and political participation
threatened to pollute the Republic in various ways.[18] In the discourse of
the bureau's critics, freedpeople were dependent and childlike and were
therefore easily manipulated by unscrupulous politicians. The bureau's
clients were lacking in necessary civic virtues, racially unfit to participate in the administration of justice or the exercise of political power, a
source of corruption and despotism, or selfishly demanding of preferential treatment and endangering the public good. Moreover, the bureau's

opponents frequently combined these criticisms, drawing on multiple political traditions and mapping different criteria of civic worthiness onto one another—identifying corruption with racial unfitness, for example— to reinforce their political claims. Ironically, many of the policies that bureau officials implemented to inoculate themselves from criticism served as "rituals of degradation" (Piven and Cloward [1971] 1993, 1977), symbolic means for representing cultural norms about work and relief to the bureau's clients that ultimately reinforced public hostility to their wards. Campaigns to purge the able-bodied and unworthy from relief rolls, for example, or disciplinary labor policies to put freedpeople back to work seemed to confirm the allegations of the bureau's harshest critics, who were not slow to present these rituals of degradation for public display. As with later welfare programs, "legislative investigations and newspaper exposés" branded the bureau's clients "as sexually immoral, as chiselers, and as malingerers" (Piven and Cloward [1971] 1993, 169). As Piven and Cloward further point out, "it is partly by such public spectacles that popular definitions of relief are formed" (169). Thus, the bureau's own practices reflected and reinforced "the deep feelings of a people who understood that those who accepted relief must cross the road that separated the community of citizens from the outcast community of the destitute" (Marshall [1949] 1964, 80–81).[19]

### "The power that saved the nation": Freedpeople as virtuous citizens

While those who opposed the civic inclusion of freedpeople mobilized primarily through the Democratic Party or terrorist organizations like the Ku Klux Klan, freedpeople mainly mobilized themselves through the Republican Party and the Union League. The Union League arose in the North during the Civil War as a patriotic club to support President Lincoln and the war effort. After the war, it spread to white Southern Unionists and then, under Radical Reconstruction, to thousands of newly enfranchised blacks. Although the hostile political climate of the South forced the Union League to become a secretive organization, it expanded rapidly under the sponsorship of the league's National Council and Republican congressional leaders, who provided funds and other necessary resources (Owens 1943; Fitzgerald 1989). As a result, the Union League quickly "became a major factor in the political situation. . . . For two years, longer in some areas, the League constituted the Republican party's southern organizational arm. It controlled nominations for office, influenced policy, and essentially functioned as a Radical machine within the party" (Fitzgerald 1989, 2). The Union League, however, was more than an arm of the Republican Party. Although the organization's moderate white leadership retained power at the state and national levels, "freedmen soon gained control of the leagues [at the local level] and increasingly turned them toward the critical issues for the black community: the agricultural labor system and self-defense" (Fitzgerald 1989, 38; cf. Gibson 1957, 535; Magdol 1977, 42; Hahn 2003, 187). The southern wing of the Union League thus became "one of the largest black social movements in American history," often functioning like "a nascent labor organization" (Fitzgerald 1989, 4, 6).

As freedpeople mobilized to claim new rights, they rallied round the Freedmen's Bureau as a valuable—though not always reliable—source of protection and support. The strongest evidence for this stance comes from the appeals, petitions, and declarations issued by black political conventions after the war. "Within a year after Appomattox, in nearly every ex-Confederate state," African Americans elected delegates to statewide conventions that they called, managed, and financed themselves, independently of whites, and that "brought together a remarkable cross section of the black population" (Litwack 1979, 507–8, see also 511). Although these conventions concerned themselves primarily with civil and political rather than social rights, "nearly every black convention endorsed the Freedmen's Bureau" (519, see also 521–22, 524–25). To be sure, "the praise was apt to be tempered with criticism of the actions and racial attitudes of various local agents," but "despite the Bureau's shortcomings, blacks recognized that even the minimal protection it provided was better than none at all" (519). Freedmen in North Carolina put it this way: "'As a few leaky places in the roof of a man's house would not be considered a sufficient ground for pulling it down and living out of doors neither can we see sufficient reason in these abuses for removing the Bureau but a greater reason why it should be perfected and maintained'" (519).

This stance toward the Freedmen's Bureau is also evidenced by the activities of the Union League. In some states, the league developed close ties to the Freedmen's Bureau, helping bureau officials register and recruit black voters for the Republican Party in exchange for the bureau's aid and patronage (Owens 1943; Bentley 1955, 186–87; Fitzgerald 1989, 38, 71). "League leaders . . . often acted as auxiliaries for Bureau personnel," and "military officials frequently utilized the League network to bolster their own efforts on behalf of the freedmen" (Fitzgerald 1989, 103). This

cooperative relationship did not mean that freedpeople were pliant dupes
of the bureau or uncritical in their support. As with the Republican Party,
black Union League activists maintained some independence from the
Freedmen's Bureau, and "relations between the League and Bureau
agents were not always . . . harmonious." Indeed, league "activists frequently harassed agents they thought insufficiently zealous" (Fitzgerald
1989, 104). Rather, the Union League's activities suggest that freedpeople
generally supported the Freedmen's Bureau while striving to improve it.

While the Republican Party, the Union League, and (to a limited extent) the Freedmen's Bureau itself provided organizational bases for
freedpeople to claim civil, political, and social rights, the liberal and republican traditions in American political culture furnished a language in
which to articulate these claims. Even as critics of the Freedmen's Bureau drew on these political idioms to delegitimize government assistance
and protection as deeply incompatible with American citizenship, the bureau's clients and their allies drew on these same idioms to redefine and
legitimize government assistance in ways that preserved and reinforced
their standing as citizens. Just as later American reformers would rework
liberalism to justify new welfare state measures (Orloff and Skocpol 1984,
735; Skocpol 1992, 21), freedpeople creatively appropriated liberal and
republican traditions to demand land reform or greater autonomy as laborers while distancing themselves from others whom treason or dependence disqualified from full citizenship.

LIBERALISM AND PROPERTY RIGHTS.    The liberal political tradition proved
surprisingly flexible for making bold, even radical political claims. Many
scholars have concluded that land redistribution was doomed to failure,
because it clashed with the liberal emphasis on property rights in American political culture. Yet freedpeople turned this argument on its head,
using liberal notions of property rights to demand land. As Rogers Smith
(1997, 299–300) points out, "liberal economic thought" since John Locke
"insisted that valid property rights originated only in rational, productive labor." This emphasis on labor as the source of all value became a
part of the free-labor ideology, which former slave laborers appropriated to "challenge the claims of largely idle slaveowners" to their lands.
"Consonant with Lockean concepts, African-Americans repeatedly argued . . . that they were seeking title to property they had earned as a
matter of right: as a Tennessee freedman said, 'We made what our Masters had.'" Acting on this premise, a group of Georgia freedmen report-

edly "divided up a farm among themselves" in 1865 and "explained to the irate owner, 'they had been working for massa [sic] all their lives, they had a right to the land in payment for their labor'" (Magdol 1977, 257n87). Union League activists reportedly encouraged such claims. "'The negroes were told of their sufferings in slavery,' an Alabama Democrat recalled of the [Union] League. 'They were told, All this property that you see here, these lands, were cleared by you; you made all these fences; you dug all these ditches; and you are the men they belong to'" (Fitzgerald 1989, 130). Freedpeople made similar claims to the lands of their former masters in speeches and public meetings in Alabama and Virginia, and these claims were endorsed by sympathetic Freedmen's Bureau officials, Treasury Department agents, and black newspapers (McFeely 1968, 5–6, 95–96; Magdol 1977, 172; Oubre 1978, 12; Foner 1988, 290; Berlin et al. 1990, 15, 57; Hahn 2003, 135). Freedpeople thus sought to renegotiate the meaning of land redistribution, defining it not as charity or government paternalism but rather as "fair compensation . . . for their many years of unrequited toil" (Stampp 1965, 124). Moreover, by underscoring the industriousness of black laborers in contrast to the idleness of their former masters, these claims helped to counter criticism that freedpeople preferred public relief to work. As a South Carolina freedman put it, "they take all our labor for their own use and get rich on it and then say we are lazy and can't take care of ourselves" (quoted in Litwack 1979, 388; cf. Litwack 1979, 389; Webster [1916] 1970, 29). In these ways, freedpeople sought to render their demands for economic security compatible with their newfound standing as independent citizens.

REWARDING CIVIC VIRTUE.    While freedpeople occasionally used the language of liberalism to make claims on civil and military authorities, they resorted far more often to the language of civic republicanism. This, too, required some ideological reworking. White supremacists frequently invoked republican language to subordinate and exclude those whom they deemed racially unfit for self-government (Saxton 1990; Jacobson 1998). However, contrary to the claims of some scholars that racial exclusion is inseparable from civic republicanism and fundamental "to the working of American democracy" (Williams 2003, 28–29), blacks frequently turned the language of republicanism against white supremacists to make inclusive and egalitarian political claims during Reconstruction. Of course, blacks invoked republican ideals in part for instrumental reasons; framing their grievances in this way was calculated to persuade white Americans in a wartime context that made republican virtues more salient. But civic republicanism was more than a frame cynically deployed to further preexisting goals; it also shaped freedpeople's identity, aspirations, and expectations. Thus, rather than merely serving as a tool of competing groups, republicanism helped to constitute them; it divided whites even as it provided the ideological glue for (admittedly fragile) biracial political coalitions. In this context, freedpeople sought to counter white supremacists' claims that they were racially unfit for self-government with clear evidence of their allegiance to the Union and their indispensable role in crushing the "Slaveholders' Rebellion" (Litwack 1979, 517, 532). These claims highlighted the civic virtue of blacks in sharp contrast to the treason of Confederate whites.

Two key themes emerged whenever freedpeople used the language of civic republicanism to make political claims on civil and military authorities. First, freedpeople demanded civil, political, and social rights as a reward for their virtuous wartime services. If, as Andrew Johnson insisted in 1864, "treason must be made odious, and the traitors must be punished and impoverished," (quoted in Foner 1988, 177) then rewarding loyalty was the other side of the coin. As a black delegate to Arkansas's 1868 constitutional convention put it, blacks did not "ask [for] charity," but claimed rights they had earned by coming to the aid of the Union. Equal citizenship, he explained, "is ours, because . . . we have stood unswervingly by our country and the flag. . . . The government owes the debt. . . . We are here, sir, to receive the amount due us" (quoted in Du Bois [1935] 1962, 548–49). Throughout the South—in Arkansas, the District of Columbia, Louisiana, Mississippi, North and South Carolina, Tennessee, and Virginia—freedpeople repeatedly made this kind of argument in newspapers, petitions to Congress, mass meetings, and political conventions. Whether they demanded suffrage or land, they linked their claims again and again to their services during the war (Du Bois [1935] 1962, 159, 230–31, 233, 457, 462, 530, 548–49; Litwack 1979, 517–18, 532, 534; Berlin, Reidy, and Rowland 1982, 811–18, 822–23).

Freedpeople's services were in fact extensive and crucial to the Union's war effort (Du Bois [1935] 1962, chap. 4). Persistent military labor shortages led the Union army and navy to employ former slaves as artisans, teamsters, nurses, laundresses, hospital attendants, personal servants, cooks, and common laborers (Bremner 1980, 99–100; Berlin et al. 1990). "By the fall of 1862, the Union war effort rested in large measure on the labor of former slaves," who, despite poor compensation, typically "performed the army's most taxing, tedious, and dangerous tasks," many of which were shunned by soldiers. This labor "represented a double gain" for the Union insofar as the labor was simultaneously "subtracted from the Confederacy" (Berlin et al. 1990, 20–21). In addition, large numbers of blacks served as soldiers in the Union army (Du Bois [1935] 1962, chap. 5; Belz 1976, chap. 2; Berlin, Reidy, and Rowland 1982). Congress began preliminary steps to enroll blacks into military service in 1862, in part because of opposition to conscription among Northern whites. Altogether, roughly 180,000 African Americans—over twenty percent of the nation's adult male black population under age 45—fought for the Union. Moreover, because white soldiers enlisted earlier and their terms of enlistment expired sooner, black soldiers formed a disproportionate share of the Union army at the end of the war (Berlin, Reidy, and Rowland 1982, 733).[20] These black soldiers, most of whom were former slaves, "contributed much to the saving of the Union" (Bentley 1955, 19). According to Secretary of the Navy Gideon Welles, all of the Union's "increased military strength" came "from the negroes," and President Lincoln believed that the recruitment of black troops would enable the Union to quickly "close this contest" (quoted in Bentley 1955, 19). Martin Delaney, a black officer in the Union army and later a Freedmen's Bureau agent, put it more bluntly: African Americans, he declared, were "the power that saved the nation from destruction" (quoted in Du Bois [1935] 1962, 233).

These developments provided an important basis for freedpeople to claim citizenship rights. Reflecting the centrality of the male citizen-soldier in the civic republican political tradition, military service has historically been one of the most important routes to full citizenship and political participation in the United States. By 1865, many African Americans had started upon this route (Keyssar 2000, xxi, 88). "Once let the black man get upon his person the brass letters U.S.; let him get an eagle on his button, and a musket on his shoulder and bullets in his pocket," wrote Frederick Douglass in 1861, "and there is no power on earth which can deny that he has earned the right to citizenship in the United States" (quoted in Du Bois [1935] 1962, 102; Belz 1976, 21; R. Smith 1997, 281). Although black military service "did not by itself change the law of citizenship, it began to alter the factual underpinning on which the law rested.... Although they exaggerated its effects, Democratic opponents of the Negro soldier policy were right in arguing that the logic of admitting blacks to the ranks of fighting men was to admit them eventually to a general civil equality with white persons" (Belz 1976, 17, 23–24).

African Americans were quick to grasp and apply this republican logic, frequently equating votes with bayonets, ballots with muskets, and the ballot box with the battlefield in their political claims. In contrast to critics of the Freedmen's Bureau, who depicted freedpeople as paupers unfit for self-government, freedmen represented themselves as virtuous citizen-soldiers. Shifting from one criterion of civic worthiness to another, they steered debate away from liberal-contractual considerations about work and relief toward civic republican considerations about loyalty and service to the nation. In 1865, for example, a petition from the "Colored Citizens of Nashville" to the Union Convention of Tennessee asked: "[W]hat higher order of citizen is there than the soldier? . . . If we are called on to do military duty against the rebel armies in the field, why should we be denied the privilege of voting against rebel citizens at the ballot-box? . . . This is not a Democratic Government if a numerous, law-abiding, industrious, and useful class of citizens, born and bred on the soil, are to be treated as aliens and enemies, as an inferior degraded class, who must have no voice in the Government which they support, protect and defend . . . both in peace and war" (quoted in Berlin, Reidy, and Rowland 1982, 811–16; cf. Litwack 1979, 538). Nor were blacks alone in linking their political claims to their military service. Congressmen, the Secretary of War, army generals, Freedmen's Bureau officials, and other elite allies endorsed the republican logic of these arguments (Gibson 1957, 526, 528; Du Bois [1935] 1962, 102, 162, 193; McFeely 1968, 127, 136; Belz 1976, 21, 24–25; Foner 1988, 8; Berlin et al. 1990, 35, 57; Keyssar 2000, 88). Union League activists even invoked the authority of Chief Justice Salmon P. Chase, who insisted that "the man who had borne the musket in defence [sic] of his Country, should be permitted to handle the ballot" (quoted in Gibson 1957, 526). Succinctly summing up this republican logic, the *New York Times* declared in 1865 that blacks "rendered an assistance to the government in times of danger that entitles them to its benign care" (quoted in Du Bois [1935] 1962, 201).

By rooting their political claims in their identity as citizen-soldiers, freedmen also reproduced a gendered conception of citizenship. Blacks and whites not only equated muskets with ballots, but also identified both with manliness. According to radical Missouri Unionist Charles Drake, for example, "the black race in America felt the power of a new manhood" when it took up arms on behalf of the Union (quoted in Belz 1976, 24). The creation of freedmen's militias by Union League activists may have reflected the same sentiment. To be sure, these militias served important practical purposes like self-defense (Fitzgerald 1989), but they may have fulfilled a dramaturgical function as well. In other words, freedmen may have participated in these militia companies not only out of self-interest but also as a symbolic expression of a gendered civic identity.[21] Extending the symbolism of manhood from bullets to ballots, U.S. senator from Massachusetts Charles Sumner declared in 1866 that "the ballot . . . teaches manhood." "Especially is it important," Sumner added, "to a race whose manhood has been denied" (quoted in Du Bois [1935] 1962, 194–95). As these remarks suggest, many Americans, black and white, perceived slavery as an emasculating condition that reduced black men to a state of childlike dependency. For Sumner and other proponents of black suffrage, the "partisan political participation" that had become "part of the very definition" of white manhood in the decades before the Civil War (Skocpol 1992, 323) would now serve to establish and confirm the manliness of blacks after the war. By emphasizing their manliness, freedmen not only distanced themselves from dependent women and children but also forcefully rejected white paternalism. The *New Orleans Tribune,* the nation's first black daily newspaper, put it this way in 1865: "We have asserted our manhood, and we will do it again. We need friends, it is true; but we do not need tutors. The age of guardianship is past forever. We now think for ourselves, and we shall act for ourselves" (quoted in Magdol 1977, 72). To assert manliness was therefore to assert independence, and in more ways than one. While these kinds of political claims undoubtedly resonated in a society that defined independence in gendered ways, they proved problematic in other respects. As noted above, the Freedmen's Bureau encouraged these sorts of gendered political claims by promoting ideals of manly independence, but it simultaneously undercut such claims by failing to guarantee black men a family wage and infringing upon their paternal authority. Moreover, claiming citizenship on the basis of manly independence excluded or subordinated freedwomen, dividing blacks along gender lines. In addition, linking citizenship to manly independence strained blacks' alliance with another disfranchised group that was mobilizing to demand suffrage: white women.[22] These strains would erupt into full-blown splits when the Fifteenth Amendment guaranteed political rights to black men but not white women (DuBois 1978; Foner 1988, 447–48).

CITIZENSHIP AND ECONOMIC INDEPENDENCE.    While many blacks demanded citizenship rights as a reward for virtuous and manly wartime services, a second theme also emerged when they used the language of civic republicanism to make political claims. Freed slaves frequently invoked the traditional republican assumption that citizenship required economic independence. Freedpeople interpreted this assumption not as a justification for disfranchising the landless, but rather as a justification for land redistribution. As Magdol (1977, 17–18) puts it, freedpeople tried to "acquire land in order to realize the American nineteenth-century dream: an independent homestead in their own version of the happy 'republican township.'" Indeed, many freedpeople "refused to resign themselves to the permanent status of a landless agricultural working class. Like most Americans, they aspired to . . . economic independence and self-employment. Without that independence, their freedom seemed incomplete, even precarious. 'Every colored man will be a slave, & feel himself a slave,' a black soldier insisted, 'until he can raise him own bale of cotton & put him own mark upon it & say dis [sic] is mine!'" (Litwack 1979, 399). Another freedman expressed his hopes and fears this way: "Gib [sic] us our own land and we take care ourselves; but widout [sic] land, de ole massas [sic] can hire us or starve us, as dey [sic] please" (quoted in Litwack 1979, 401). Black newspapers like the *New Orleans Tribune* were even more explicit: "There is . . . no republican government, unless the land and wealth in general, are distributed among the great mass of the inhabitants" (quoted in Hahn 2003, 142). The civil and military authorities upon whom these claims were made also grasped the republican logic underlying them. Freedpeople preferred to "complete their emancipation by setting up for themselves in a small way," observed a sympathetic Alabama Freedmen's Bureau agent in 1867. "Thus, they see clearly enough, they liberate themselves from the immediate control of shrewd and selfish employers." Such behavior, he added approvingly, would foster the "self-reliance" of these new citizens (Office of the Commissioner, Letters from the Executive Mansion, Box 19).

At the same time, the republican presumption that citizens must be economically independent generated anxieties about landless blacks. West Tennessee's federal military commander, suggesting an analogy between landless blacks in the South and the white laborers in the North who were bitterly denouncing wage slavery, described freedpeople's predicament this way: "Says the newly emancipated black, toil was the chief misery of my former condition. I am now free . . . And if I am compelled to work for wages to support me wherefore is my condition bettered?" (quoted in Hahn 2003, 135–36). This analogy between landless blacks in the South and white wage earners in the North usefully reveals the perils and problems of linking citizenship to economic independence. Property-less white workingmen were initially disfranchised in the United States on the grounds that they were economically dependent upon their employ-ers. As noted in chapter 1, white workingmen successfully challenged this division of the social and political world in the first half of the nineteenth century, redefining themselves as independent and thereby obtaining po-litical rights (Keyssar 2000, chap. 2). This achievement posed a dilemma for freedpeople. On the one hand, freedpeople's propertyless condition led them to deny that their wage labor and lack of property signified eco-nomic dependence and a corresponding incapacity for self-government. In this respect, they simply reiterated the claims made by white working-men decades earlier. On the other hand, freedpeople's demands for land led them to emphasize the economic independence conferred by land ownership as a precondition for full citizenship and effective political par-ticipation. In this respect, their political demands echoed contemporane-ous condemnations of wage slavery, questioned the free-labor ideology's lumping together of wage earners and property owners, and challenged the notion that wage laborers were truly economically independent. These implications, disturbing for propertyless whites, were inadver-tently driven home by Radical Republicans in the North, who warned Northern laborers that "if the South were allowed to take away the lib-erty and freedom of the Southern laborers they would in the near future do the same to them" (Owens 1943, 172). Such anxieties were especially salient for small farmers and urban workers during Reconstruction, who watched helplessly as their cherished independence was eroded by Civil War debts, crop failures, falling agricultural prices, rising taxes, railroad expansion, the growth of farm tenancy, growing concentrations of wealth, mechanization of industry, the increasing scale of production, economic depression, and proliferating vagrancy laws (Foner 1988, 393–94, 474, 477, 480, 519). Freedpeople's claims therefore had broader significance; they were potentially explosive, because they threatened to unsettle the classification of propertyless white workingmen (and declassed Ameri-cans on the verge of joining their ranks) as independent, a vision of the social world that was hard fought but increasingly difficult to sustain in the face of the massive economic changes that followed Reconstruction. In brief, while the freed slaves' propertyless condition encouraged them to sever the link between property ownership and citizenship, their aspi-rations encouraged them to strengthen the connection.

## Summary and Conclusion

Struggles over the Freedmen's Bureau and the status and rights of its clients reflected sharply opposed visions and divisions of the postwar social order. On the one hand, federal assistance to freedpeople, whether
in the form of land redistribution, protective labor regulations, or relief,
led many Americans to see them as paupers and therefore unfit for full
citizenship. This view reflected an enduring republican suspicion, stretch-
ing back at least as far as the eighteenth century, that the economically
dependent were a threat to property interests, easily manipulated, and
not to be trusted (Keyssar 2000, 5–6, 9–12, 46–49, 61–65). On the other
hand, freedpeople vigorously resisted attempts to class them as paupers.
Although some black leaders like Frederick Douglass urged them to pur-
sue civic inclusion by eschewing government assistance or protection,
many freedpeople sought to redefine and legitimize government assistance in ways that preserved their standing as independent, rights-bearing
citizens. Rejecting the notion that the Freedmen's Bureau dispensed "the
charity of the Government" (a description employed by the bureau's own
assistant commissioner for South Carolina in a report dated October 1,
1867), they drew upon the liberal and republican traditions in American
political culture to recast government assistance in terms of contractual
exchange or as a reward for loyalty and civic virtue. These disputes were
part of a larger historical struggle over the meaning and boundaries of
citizenship in the United States, the stakes of which were material as well
as symbolic: under what conditions, if any, were freedpeople entitled to
become full and equal citizens? Were citizenship rights to be extended
across gender as well as racial lines? What rights did citizenship entail?
Did it include a right to economic security in the form of land or a family wage, or were guarantees of economic welfare and security incompatible with full citizenship? As these questions suggest, more was at issue in
the conflicts over the Freedmen's Bureau than the fate of the four million
black laborers whom the Civil War had liberated from slavery. Struggles
over the citizenship status and rights of the freed slaves had broader implications for American citizenship more generally.

   The struggles described in this chapter were in part the product of
large-scale, historically specific social forces that unsettled the structure
of citizenship and dislocated millions of former slave laborers, leaving
their status and rights unclear and ambiguous. The Civil War uprooted
slavery and freed Southern blacks without clearly fixing their new sta-

tus or defining their rights in the postwar social, political, and economic order. In addition, Congress began to nationalize American citizenship during the war, which allowed it to strengthen political rights and extend them to freedpeople during Reconstruction. Although this transformation of citizenship was the result in part of struggles to incorporate the freed slaves into the American polity, it also encouraged those struggles, providing freedpeople with new rights to assert, raising their aspirations and expectations, and expanding their access to federal authorities upon whom they could make claims. Finally, in the context of Northern efforts to construct a free labor society in the South, the ambiguities and multiple meanings of free labor encouraged further conflict over the status and rights of freedpeople, providing competing models that employers, workers, and political authorities could embrace to advance their divergent symbolic and material interests.

The Freedmen's Bureau, I have argued, provides a window into the citizenship struggles of Reconstruction, in part because it became a focal point of those struggles, and in part because it contributed to those struggles through its policy feedback effects. First, as the nation's first federal welfare and regulatory agency, the Freedmen's Bureau was a dramatic policy innovation. By conferring governmental benefits on a disparate mass of former slaves, the bureau turned them into a new group of clients whose status and rights relative other clients in the welfare field were initially uncertain. In particular, it remained to be determined whether they would be treated like recipients of traditional poor relief or sharply distinguished from them. At the same time, the conferral of governmental benefits heightened the political relevance of the former slaves and made them ripe for political mobilization by the Republican Party and social movement organizations like the Union League. Second, because of conflicting policy goals and institutional features, the Freedmen's Bureau treated its clients in a contradictory fashion, placing them in an intermediate position within the welfare field. As shown by reference to the bureau's social, labor, and family policies, the agency sometimes treated its clients in a liberal manner as autonomous, rights-bearing individuals, while at other times treating them in a nonliberal manner as dependent persons who required protection, supervision, or discipline. These contradictory practices provided a plausible basis for competing classificatory claims. Third, as noted in chapter 1, policy competition is often a major impetus for struggles over the classification of welfare state clients. Like the administrators of subsequent policy innovations, Commissioner

Howard denied that his bureau was a "pauperizing agency" (quoted in Foner 1988, 152). However, he made little effort to define the bureau's provision of social welfare as an honorable alternative to traditional poor relief. Instead, he sought to avoid the stigma of pauperism by deemphasizing the Bureau's relief functions and transferring them to local officials. Policy competition was thus a relatively weak impetus for classification struggles in the case of the Freedmen's Bureau. This weakness was probably due to the manner in which the bureau was administered. Since the Freedmen's Bureau was a military agency staffed mainly by soldiers, its officers were less invested in the organization. Unlike civilian administrators, their professional and organizational interests lay with the army rather than the bureau itself, and they could return to their military careers when the bureau was dismantled. (Howard, for example, participated in military campaigns against American Indians in the western United States and eventually became superintendent at West Point after Congress terminated the Freedmen's Bureau.) Consequently, the bureau's administrators had less incentive to distance the agency from competing policies or raise it to a dominant position in the welfare field.[23] Finally, the bureau's involvement in freedpeople's civil, political, and social rights was highly contentious, because citizenship itself was a valuable form of political capital that could facilitate access to other kinds of capital, including patronage, land, control over labor power, education, public deference, and so forth.

Although the Freedmen's Bureau encouraged struggles over the status and rights of its clients, freedpeople ultimately failed to escape the stigma of pauperism. This is evident in two ways. First, as public criticism of the Freedmen's Bureau and denigration of its clients persisted, educated middle-class whites increasingly came to regard it as a failed, misguided, and mistaken policy. In their view, it did not reward civic virtue so much as foster civic vice. Indeed, this would become the prevailing view of the Freedmen's Bureau until revisionist historians began to challenge it in the mid-twentieth century. Second, the institutional structure and practices of the bureau also reflected freedpeople's failure to avoid the taint of pauperism. As noted in chapter 1, a successful classification struggle results not only in the internalization of new classificatory schemes in the minds of social agents, but also in their objectification in institutions. To distinguish themselves from paupers, freedpeople needed to distinguish the bureau's welfare functions from traditional poor relief. As we have seen, they were unable to do so. Rather than incorporating valued policy features that would differentiate its efforts from traditional poor relief, the Freedmen's Bureau incorporated some of poor relief's worst policy features. The bureau thus organized social assistance in ways that reflected (and reinforced) public perceptions of freedpeople as a degraded pauper class. The bureau's temporary existence and the constant retrenchment during its brief and short-lived career similarly evinced freedpeople's failure to legitimize government assistance. In the end, many Americans welcomed the bureau's termination, because they believed it fostered dependence or they considered its clients unworthy of federal aid. Although freedpeople acquired American citizenship and constitutional guarantees of basic civil and political rights—at least on paper—they were never able to reconcile federal assistance with full citizenship. To use Marshall's ([1949] 1964, 80) words, the federal government provided assistance to freedpeople "only if the claimants ceased to be citizens in any true sense of the word."[24]

## CHAPTER THREE

# An Honorable Alternative to Poor Relief

## Civil War Veterans' Pensions, 1862–1890

W hy did the clients of the Freedmen's Bureau fail to avoid the stigma of pauperism? One way to answer this question is to compare their struggle with a more successful but otherwise similar struggle. Fortunately, a suitable case for comparison exists and has already been well researched by historical sociologists. While freedpeople failed to reconcile government assistance with full citizenship, a comparable and overlapping group of Americans did: The Union's Civil War veterans benefited from a generous, honorable, and permanent program of federal assistance in the form of military service pensions (Orloff 1988, 1993b; Skocpol 1992, 1995a; Williams 2003). In contrast to the Freedmen's Bureau, the Pension Bureau incorporated social rights into the status of citizenship, consistently treating veterans as independent, rights-bearing individuals who earned and deserved public aid (Skocpol 1992, 149–51, 260).[1]

### The Comparability of the Freedmen's Bureau and the Civil War Pension System

The classification of Civil War veterans as independent and deserving citizens was neither automatic nor inevitable. Like the civic classification of freedpeople, it was a result of struggle, and these struggles were comparable in several respects. First, as policy innovations, both the Freedmen's

Bureau and the Pension Bureau created new groups of clients whose status and rights were initially uncertain and up for grabs. Struggles over the classification of those clients turned upon whether new forms of federal assistance rendered them paupers and thus stripped them of civil and political rights. (To be sure, freedpeople had to acquire civil and political rights that white Civil War pensioners merely had to preserve, but in both cases, these rights were placed in jeopardy.) By shaping the "cultural characterizations" and "popular images" of their clients (Schneider and Ingram 1993, 334)—a process of social construction that was contested in both cases—the Freedmen's Bureau and the Pension Bureau shaped their civic statuses. Moreover, both policies were created at roughly the same time: Congress created the Civil War pension system in 1862, three years before it created the Freedmen's Bureau. This contemporaneous timing makes it easier to control for contextual variables that could account for the success or failure of the ensuing classification struggles.

Second, the Freedmen's Bureau and the Civil War pension system shared several policy features. Both programs were what Skocpol (1992) terms paternalist rather than maternalist social policies. Both had a semi-discretionary benefit structure that allowed public aid to be used for patronage purposes (Skocpol 1992, 120–24). And both had a noncontributory financing structure: Although Freedmen's Bureau officials tried to make freedpeople contribute to their own support, Congress financed the Freedmen's Bureau primarily from general tax revenues. Likewise, the Civil War pension system also relied upon general sources of revenue (mainly tariffs) to fund benefits. These similarities were important insofar as policy structure both reflects past classification struggles and shapes subsequent struggles. As Lieberman (1998, 16) notes, "the structure of benefits and financing . . . influences the relationship of beneficiaries to other elements of the political system, particularly their status in the public mind as 'deserving' or 'undeserving,' 'honorable' or 'dishonorable.'" However, since the Freedmen's Bureau and the Civil War pension system shared these particular policy features, they cannot account for variation in how freedpeople and veterans were classed.

Third, similar political forces created and sustained the Freedmen's Bureau and Civil War pension system: the destruction and dislocation of the Civil War, which created a large pool of potential beneficiaries; the revival of tight party competition, which encouraged the use of patronage to win close, competitive elections; and the failure of Congress to impose centralized bureaucratic controls and effective bureaucratic supervision

over federal aid, which enabled politicians to use it for patronage purposes (Skocpol 1992, 103–4, 117–20; Skocpol 1995a, 55, 57–61). Although Skocpol (1992, 117) argues that tight party competition was not
revived until the mid-1870s (after the termination of the Freedmen's Bureau), evidence suggests that the Republican Party faced considerable
competition, even during Reconstruction: "In 1865–1868, the Democratic Party controlled from 44 per cent to 50 per cent of the voters in
the North, so that if the white people of the South had been included,
undoubtedly the Democratic Party would have been in the majority. By
the exclusion of the South, the Democratic Party had been beaten in
1866, and in 1867 had carried only Maryland and Kentucky, Connecticut,
New York, Pennsylvania, New Jersey and California; nevertheless, on the
whole, the Democratic vote increased, as compared with the Republican"
(Du Bois [1935] 1962, 373). Under these circumstances, the Republican-
controlled Congress perpetuated the Freedmen's Bureau to help ensure
Grant's election as president in 1868. As noted in the previous chapter,
this use of the bureau for patronage purposes provoked angry condem-
nation from Northern Democrats and Southern whites, but it contributed
crucially to Grant's slim victory. Republicans, facing continued competition after 1877, similarly used the Civil War pension system for political advantage in closely contested elections. Furthermore, both of these
policies benefited large constituencies, fueling the growth of influential
pressure groups that allied themselves with the Republican Party to defend and expand federal aid. Just as the Freedmen's Bureau encouraged
the expansion of the Union League, the Civil War pension system fostered the growth of the Grand Army of the Republic (GAR), an association of Union veterans formed in 1866 to defend "the late soldiery of the
United States, morally, socially, and politically" (Fitzgerald 1989, 38, 71,
103; Dearing 1952; McConnell 1992; Skocpol 1992).[2]

Fourth, as shown in this chapter, Americans used remarkably similar language to contest the legitimacy of the Freedmen's Bureau and the
Civil War pension system. In both cases, policy supporters sought to distinguish federal assistance from traditional poor relief, justifying the former on civic republican grounds as a reward for the wartime services of
virtuous and loyal citizens. Policy critics also invoked similar arguments.
Like the Freedmen's Bureau, the Civil War pension system was said to
render its clients dependent on the government, stimulate a massive and
costly expansion of federal power and bureaucracy, privilege particular
groups, and foster corruption and patronage. In both cases, public debate

over the legitimacy of the policies was linked to public attitudes toward their respective clients.

## The Struggle over the Civic Classification of Civil War Pensioners

In 1862, the Civil War pension system circumscribed the class of deserving recipients narrowly, reflecting what McConnell (1992, 140) calls the "standard view" of pension eligibility. According to this view, military pensions were reserved for soldiers disabled in war.

> Other veterans, even poor or unemployed ones, had to take care of themselves. . . . Mere service as a Union veteran did not entitle a man to any special consideration, even if he happened to be sick, jobless, or destitute. Upon being mustered out, he had become a civilian, and, like other civilians, he had to take his chances in the marketplace or accept the minimal public relief provided in the almshouse. . . . With the exception of a limited group of seriously wounded or ill veterans, . . . ex-soldiers had no more claim to the public treasury than did any other group. (McConnell 1992, 140, 153)

Accordingly, the 1862 law limited benefits to soldiers actually injured in combat or to the dependents of those disabled or killed; it "allowed no pension simply for indigence and none for injuries not proved to be of service origin" (Orloff and Skocpol 1984, 728; McConnell 1992, 143; Orloff 1993b, 134–35; Skocpol 1995a, 45).

Despite these tight restrictions on military pensions, reform-minded Northern intellectuals and journalists began to question the civic virtue and worthiness of Union veterans soon after the Civil War ended. As in subsequent years, they focused on veterans' demands for patronage. Since restrictive eligibility requirements limited the number of pensioners and the amount of expenditures in those years, patronage took other forms. As noted in chapter 2, many veterans experienced unemployment after the war's end, and some blamed politicians for not appointing more veterans to political offices (Dearing 1952, 54–55). As early as 1866, these complaints prompted Charles Eliot Norton, a prominent writer and editor of the influential *North American Review,* to warn that Union veterans "would arrogate to themselves a special distinction for their services. . . . 'Nothing can be more corrupting in politics than the existence of a class of men willing to sell themselves for office and with notoriety sufficient to make them available candidates'" (Dearing 1952, 103). The newly formed GAR came under attack as well. In 1867 and 1868, Horace Greeley's influential *New York Tribune* condemned the veterans' organization as "office-beggars and politicians." "We believe the soldiers should receive abundant reward," the *Tribune* declared, " . . . but we dislike this making [of] a privileged class" (quoted in Dearing 1952, 124).

Although complaints about fraudulent pension claims began to emerge as early as the 1870s, Congress nevertheless passed the 1879 Arrears Act, the first of two major changes in the Civil War pension system (Orloff and Skocpol 1984; Orloff 1988, 1993b; McConnell 1992; Skocpol 1992, 1995a). The new law aimed to establish a common starting point for all pensions, thereby eliminating inequities in the pension system. To this end, it "allowed soldiers who 'discovered' Civil War-related disabilities to sign up and receive in one lump sum all of the pension payments they would have been eligible to receive since the 1860s" (Orloff and Skocpol 1984, 728; Orloff 1988, 46; Orloff 1993b, 134–35; Skocpol 1992, 110; Skocpol 1995a, 49). While the Arrears Act liberalized pension benefits considerably, it "did not alter the basis of pension payments" or "add any new classes of pensioners to the rolls. . . . Pensions continued to be based, as they always had been before the Civil War, on war-related disability (or, in the case of widows' pensions, war-related death)" (McConnell 1992, 149). Nevertheless, the Arrears Act intensified struggles over the worthiness of veterans by raising the stakes. The legislation increased federal pension expenditures and encouraged politicians to use pensions for patronage purposes, sharpening opposition to the pension system among Northern reformers (McConnell 1992, 147; Orloff and Skocpol 1984, 728; Skocpol 1995a, 37, 61). At the same time, the Arrears Act encouraged pension attorneys and veterans to ally themselves with the Republican Party and mobilize "to wrest further concessions from Congress" (Skocpol 1992, 130; Dearing 1952, 249, 268). As a result, the GAR expanded rapidly and "became much more active on the pension issue" (McConnell 1992, 148; Dearing 1952, 268–69, 274).

In the 1880s, middle-class reformers, joined by growing segments of the press and the Democratic Party, tied Union veterans to patronage and corruption, questioning their civic virtue and worthiness for public aid. As in earlier years, reformers continued to attack the practice of appointing veterans to political office. Indeed, the issue gained "renewed prominence" in the 1880s as veterans clashed with a growing movement for civil service reform taken up by Democrat President Grover Cleveland (Dearing 1952, 284; Skocpol 1992, 124–30; Skocpol 1995a, 66–67).[3] More importantly, Democrats "parted company [with Republicans] on the issue of pension generosity after the early 1880s" and began to attack the pension system on a variety of grounds. "From the time of Grover Cleveland's [first] presidency [1885–1889] onward, the national Democratic party and Democratic presidents stressed controls on pension expenditures, and the need to attack fraud in the system" (Skocpol 1992, 125, 150; Skocpol 1995a, 65; Dearing 1952, 330–31).[4] In addition, under Cleveland's leadership, Democrats condemned the high tariffs that funded the pension system as excess taxation and called for their reduction. "Protective tariffs, the Democrats argued, constituted hidden taxes on consumers and on most southern and western producers" (Skocpol 1995a, 66–67; cf. Skocpol 1992, 124–30). The press, who echoed this charge, deplored the growing cost of pension expenditures and opposed further pension legislation. The *New York Herald,* for example, "condemned 'a manifest intention on the part of some congressmen and politicians to go on indefinitely in the work of currying favor with the survivors of the Civil War at the expense of the taxpayers,' while the *Chicago Tribune* declared, 'It begins to look like wholesale confiscation'" (quoted in Dearing 1952, 286).

Like the attacks on the Freedmen's Bureau, these assaults on the Civil War pension system may be seen as a form of "moral entrepreneurship" (Becker 1963) intended to sway public opinion against it, which inevitably shaped public attitudes toward the Pension Bureau's clients. "For fifteen years," Edwin Godkin, the founder and editor of *The Nation,* wrote in 1885, "these [GAR] men, who professed to have fought for pure love of the Union, have devoted all the energies of a great organization to the extracting of money from the public treasury, without the smallest regard to truth, honor or decency." Four years later, Godkin declared that "'veteran' is becoming in their eyes a synonym for 'bummer' or 'dead beat,' and [non-veterans] began to listen to the clamor for pensions very much as they listen to the arguments by which the street casual enforces his demand for a quarter on a cold night'" (quoted in McConnell 1992, 159). In 1889, Harvard president and mugwump Charles Eliot raised similar questions about the civic virtue and worthiness of Civil War pensioners: "I hold it to be a hideous wrong inflicted upon the republic that the pension system instituted for the benefit of the soldiers and sailors of the United States had been prostituted and degraded. . . . *One cannot tell whether a pensioner of the United States is a disabled soldier or sailor or a perjured pauper who has foisted himself upon the public treasury"* (quoted in Orloff 1993b, 232n4, emphasis added). Civil War veterans, once regarded as independent and deserving citizens whose wartime services entitled them to public aid, were now indistinguishable from paupers to tough-minded critics like Godkin and Eliot.

In contrast, Republicans, pension attorneys, and veterans vigorously defended the pension system in what amounted to a prolonged national public relations campaign. In response to critics like Godkin and Eliot, they extolled pensions as an expression of reciprocity and public gratitude, stressing the Union's moral obligation to assist and protect those who had assisted and protected it in its darkest hour. "The failure of the Government to protect itself against [pension] frauds," President Rutherford Hayes wrote at the end of his term in 1881, "is no reason for evading just obligations" (quoted in Dearing 1952, 249). At the same time, to underscore the necessity of a generous pension system, Republicans emphasized the negative aspects of traditional poor relief, rejecting it as a degrading and dishonorable alternative unfit for veterans (Bremner 1980, 150). "As the 1888 Republican platform put it, 'The legislation of Congress should conform to the pledges made by a loyal people and be so enlarged and extended as to provide against the possibility that any man who honorably wore the Federal uniform shall be the inmate of an almshouse, or dependent upon private charity. In the presence of an overflowing treasury, it would be a public scandal to do less for those whose valorous service preserved the government'" (Skocpol 1992, 125). Thus, "the Civil War pension system, like subsequent provision for 'deserving' Americans, was . . . defined in opposition to charity or public programs for paupers at state and local levels. . . . The point was to keep these deserving men and those connected to them from the degrading fates of private charity or the public poorhouse" (Skocpol 1992, 149–50).

As these remarks suggest, struggles over the classification of Civil War veterans had important policy implications. At a time when influential thinkers like William Graham Sumner were declaring "paupers unfit for the franchise, because they might vote for public charity" (R. Smith 1997, 352), reformers like Godkin and Eliot denounced veterans in an analogous manner for extracting ever greater pension expenditures from Congress, and they urged the federal government to apply to Civil War pensioners the same kind of discipline and retrenchment that local governments typically imposed upon paupers. In contrast, veterans sought policy improvements that would set them apart from paupers and confirm their standing as honorable and deserving citizens. At the state level, the GAR successfully lobbied for the creation of new forms of public provision that were specifically earmarked for veterans and explicitly distinguished from traditional poor relief (Bremner 1980, 150; McConnell 1992, 141–43; Skocpol 1992, 139–43, 150; Skocpol 1995b, 260–61). New forms of public provision were also created for veterans at the federal level, including the National Home for Disabled Volunteer Soldiers, which "state agents self-consciously labored to differentiate . . . from the asylums and poorhouses created to assist non-veterans" (Kelly 1997, 6). In addition, veterans' groups demanded free land in the West, veteran preference in government hiring, and, above all, further liberalization of Civil War pensions (McConnell 1992, 156–57). Between 1884 and 1890, the GAR advocated a variety of dependent and service pension bills, all of which jettisoned "the old idea that pensions were compensation for injuries suffered *in war*" (McConnell 1992, 149–50; original emphasis). The new plans, like policy innovations at the state level, guaranteed benefits to veterans "simply because they were veterans" (McConnell 1992, 149–50).[5] These proposals thus aimed to broaden the class of deserving pension recipients far beyond earlier legislation. In that respect, they reflected the GAR's efforts in the 1880s to "reach out into public life" and redefine "the proper relationship between Union veteran and civilian" (McConnell 1992, 126). "Far from assuming an easy metamorphosis of veteran into civilian," the GAR's pension plans "treated ex-soldiers as a special class, to whom ordinary charity arrangements did not apply" (McConnell 1992, 153–54). In keeping with this vision and division of the social world, the GAR vigorously opposed legislative changes that would have blurred the line between pensions and traditional poor relief. In 1887, for example, GAR lobbyists objected to a "pauper provision" (a clause requiring pension claimants to prove that they could not support themselves) in a dependent pension bill that was subsequently vetoed by President Cleveland (McConnell 1992, 150).

As in struggles over the Freedmen's Bureau, debates over the merits of the new pension plans rested on a gendered conception of citizenship. Service pension advocates argued that "the Union veteran's service in saving the nation was in the nature of a contract: in return for it he was owed public support, regardless of his physical or financial condition" (McConnell 1992, 157). Pensions were thus compensation "for services already rendered" (157), and "any kind of charity based only on disability or dependence made veterans 'paupers before the country whose very existence we have preserved'" (161–62). Other veterans preferred dependent pensions over service pensions, because the former "would give money only to those in need," thereby avoiding sapping "the self-reliance of veterans" (161–62). Reformers invoked the same civic ideals to oppose both types of plans. Mugwumps like William Sloane rejected service pension proposals because "only unmanly individuals went to war for money or depended on pensions when they were perfectly capable of working" (161–62). Likewise, President Cleveland vetoed the Dependent Pension Bill of 1887 on the grounds that "it confused wounded veterans with those who were 'willing to be objects of simple charity and to gain a place upon the pension-roll through alleged dependence'" (161–62). As McConnell further points out, "the striking thing about the whole pension debate from the mid-1880s into the twentieth century is the way all parties asserted that they stood for independence and manliness, no matter what policy they were advocating. . . . Every party to the debate attempted to paint the others as advocating some kind of plan to turn veterans into helpless dependents, while picturing its own scheme as a bulwark against the decline of self-reliance" (161–62).

Ultimately, the advocates of pension liberalization prevailed. In 1890, as the GAR reached its peak membership of nearly 428,000 members and the zenith of its power, it helped to push the Dependent Pension Act through Congress (Dearing 1952, 402, 445; McConnell 1992, 206). The second major change in the Civil War pension system, this new law "severed altogether the link to combat-related injuries" (Orloff and Skocpol 1984, 728), extending eligibility to every honorably discharged veteran who had served at least ninety days in the Union military and "suffered from any disability that incapacitated him for manual labor, no matter what his financial situation and no matter how the disability had been incurred" (McConnell 1992, 152–53). Thanks to the Pension Bureau's generous interpretation of the statute and subsequent amendments, "old age alone became a sufficient disability" (Orloff and Skocpol 1984, 728). The Dependent Pension Act thus "created what was for all practical purposes a service pension system" (McConnell 1992, 152–53) that not only expanded the pension rolls and increased pension expenditures, but also confirmed and institutionalized the division between pensioners and paupers (see also Orloff 1988, 46–47; Orloff 1993b, 135; Skocpol 1992, 110–11. 128–29; Skocpol 1995a, 49, 69). "An old soldier can receive a pension as a recognition of honorable service with a feeling of pride," Green B.

Raum, commissioner of the Pension Bureau, declared in 1891, "while he would turn his back with shame upon an offer of charity" (quoted in Skocpol 1992, 150; Skocpol 1995b, 261).

Like the 1879 Arrears Act, the 1890 Dependent Pension Act generated a negative reaction from all the usual suspects: Southern whites (who opposed expansion of the pension system from the outset), Northern reformers, mugwumps, Democrats, and a broad segment of the press. This counter-mobilization also invoked familiar themes and arguments. Critics of the pension system condemned fraud and patronage, voiced alarm over growing pension expenditures, deplored high tariffs, reiterated the old "standard view" of eligibility, denounced the GAR as a "grand army of beggars" and mercenary "political engine" and urged reconciliation with the South and an end to sectionalism (Dearing 1952, 428, 434–38; McConnell 1992, 158–59; Skocpol 1992, 272–77; Skocpol 1995a, 70). As previous studies have shown, this negative reaction, especially strong among the educated middle class, prevented Civil War pensions from serving as a positive precedent for the enactment of new social spending programs (Orloff and Skocpol 1984; Orloff 1988, 1993b; Skocpol 1992, 1995a).

Despite this reaction, however, Union veterans were remarkably successful in their efforts to avoid the stigma of pauperism. Veterans' success in the struggle over their civic classification is evident in two ways. First, "the cry against pensions never became general. . . . The pension reformers . . . were in the minority, and the politicians were wise enough to know it" (McConnell 1992, 162, 164–65). Popular support for the pension system was reflected in electoral outcomes as well as in the difficulties pension investigators experienced when they questioned civilians about alleged frauds and the reluctance of juries to convict in pension fraud cases (McConnell 1992, 162, 164–65). This support stemmed, at least in part, from the GAR's symbolic work: "If civilians after 1880 were willing to fund an unprecedented level of public spending for military pensions, it may have been because they were constantly deluged with reminders of the glorious sacrifices of Union soldiers" (McConnell 1992, 167). Throughout the 1880s and 1890s, the GAR organized and participated in ritualistic "tributes to the warriors" that sustained "the image of veteran as savior" and made it "a commonplace of a postwar popular culture" (McConnell 1992, 167). Second, the success of Union veterans in avoiding the stigma of pauperism is also evident in the changing institutional structure of the Civil War pension system. As indicated above, the Civil War pension system not only provided an alternative to traditional poor relief but also incorporated valued policy features by 1890 that distinguished pensioners sharply from paupers. Veterans' successful campaign to distinguish themselves from paupers is also evidenced by the continued expansion of the pension system. Even after the 1896 presidential election, when elections became less competitive, reformers failed to dismantle or retrench Civil War pensions. Despite would-be reformers' strident denunciations of fraud and corruption, "pension laws continued to be liberalized, and pension expenditures, already high by historic standards, continued to rise until the eve of World War I" (McConnell 1992, 162–63; Orloff 1993b, 276; Skocpol 1995b, 260). Thus, the GAR's vision and division of the social world was not only institutionalized in the pension system, but it also endured over time. As McConnell (1992, 164–65) points out, this long-term success was more than "an exercise in power politics. . . . [S]uch complete success, continuing even as veteran numbers dwindled in the early twentieth century, could not have occurred without the acquiescence, and even the support, of a great many civilians." In all of these respects—the widespread perception of their worthiness and the steady improvement, upgrading, and durability of the policies upon which they depended—the success of Civil War veterans stands in sharp contrast to the failure of freedpeople.

## Why Did Outcomes Differ?

Why did similar struggles lead to such different outcomes? Previous scholarship suggests several possible reasons why freedpeople failed to avoid the stigma of pauperism. First, their failure may simply be the result of American exceptionalism and the social forces said to produce it, including America's liberal political culture and its distinctive political institutions (Lipset and Marks 2000). In line with this theory, some scholars have pointed to the ideological constraints of classical liberalism—most notably, its commitment to property rights and aversion to economic radicalism—to explain why government assistance to freedpeople was so limited (Hartz 1955; Du Bois [1935] 1962). Others have emphasized Americans' commitment to states' rights as a potent source of opposition to freedpeople's political claims (R. Smith 1997, 295–98). Another, albeit weaker, version of the exceptionalist argument emphasizes the idea that social citizenship was not impossible in the United States, just slow to develop. From this perspective, the Freedmen's Bureau was simply premature; it anticipated the twentieth-century welfare state but emerged before the social changes that made it possible (Abbott 1967, 133–34).

Second, business-centered theories of the welfare state would attribute freedpeople's failure to the power and influence of America's capitalist class (Du Bois [1935] 1962). From this perspective, Northern capitalists were careful to subordinate the legitimation and patronage functions of America's postbellum social spending regime to its capital-accumulation and labor-disciplining functions. The ritual degradation of relief recipients, this argument suggests, is an invariant feature of social welfare programs, because it "serves to celebrate the virtue of all work and deters actual or potential workers from seeking aid" (Piven and Cloward [1971] 1993, 165).[6]

Third, institutionalist perspectives on the American welfare state would point to the public reaction against the patronage and corruption of the Freedmen's Bureau. Just as a similar reaction against the use of Civil War pensions for patronage purposes discouraged the enactment of new social spending programs, so too public hostility to the bureau's patronage functions may explain why federal assistance to freedpeople was curtailed and eventually terminated.

However, the problem with all of these explanations is that they do not adequately explain *variation* in outcomes. Why did exceptional social and political conditions in the United States thwart freed slaves but not veterans? Why were attempts at ritual degradation effective against freedpeople but not Civil War pensioners? Why did the public backlash against patronage and corruption doom clients of the Freedmen's Bureau but not clients of the Pension Bureau to pauperism? While these explanations all contain some truth, they do not fully explain why similar struggles over the classification of freedpeople and veterans led to such different outcomes.[7]

### Policy structures

I suggest that the difference in outcomes was in part a product of institutional differences between the Freedmen's Bureau and the Civil War pension system that shaped struggles over the classification of their clients. Although the Freedmen's Bureau and Civil War pension system shared some policy features, they differed in other crucial ways. Moreover, these differences were already present in the 1860s, before struggles over the classification of Civil War pensioners led to changes in the pension system.

As noted earlier, the Civil War pension system, like other forms of public provision for Union veterans, was sharply and explicitly distinguished from traditional poor relief. Even in its original form, the pension system included a variety of policy features that set pensioners apart from paupers. First, the pension system was administered at the federal rather than the local level, which resulted in more-liberal treatment of clients. Second, benefits were not means tested. On the contrary, the pension system provided resource protection to its clients, meaning that pension recipients were not required to use all of their existing resources before receiving support.[8] Third, benefits were awarded in cash rather than in kind, which allowed clients greater autonomy; these benefits were also relatively generous, which allowed clients to enjoy some modicum of economic independence. Finally, the pension system avoided the tendencies toward retrenchment that were characteristic of traditional poor relief in part because of the program's quasi-entitlement status, which protected it from congressional funding threats (Skocpol 1992; Orloff 1988, 1993b; Jensen 2003).[9] These features, all part of the original 1862 Civil War pension policy, constrained efforts to stigmatize pensioners as paupers. In contrast, as the previous chapter has shown, the Freedmen's Bureau never fully divorced its welfare functions from local and conventional forms of poor relief. Rather, it incorporated many of the same policy features that made traditional poor relief stigmatizing. In addition, although the Freedmen's Bureau and Civil War pension system were both financed from general tax revenues, the Freedmen's Bureau depended on regular appropriations, which made it more vulnerable to funding threats. That vulnerability facilitated retrenchment, which made it that much more difficult to differentiate the bureau from traditional poor relief. Finally, the federal government had less control over bureau activities than the military pension program, which led to more-illiberal handling of clients. As a result of these institutional features, the bureau's welfare activities resembled traditional poor relief to a much greater extent than did the Civil War pension program. If Americans were inclined to see freedpeople as paupers, it was in part because the Freedmen's Bureau treated its clients more like paupers than citizens.

The policy structures of the Civil War pension system and the Freedmen's Bureau differed in another important respect as well. The pension system was a distributive policy, while the Freedmen's Bureau combined distributive, regulatory, and potentially even redistributive functions (Lowi 1972; Skocpol 1992, 81–87). As Skocpol (1992, 82) points out, distributive policies "tend to be positive-sum in that 'the indulged and the deprived, the loser and the recipient need never come into direct confrontation.'" In this case, high tariffs benefited Northern industrialists while generating the revenues that funded Civil War pensions (Skocpol 1992, 82–83). Although high tariffs arguably harmed consumers, the causal chain that linked tariffs to pensions was indirect and not highly visible. Consequently, the Civil War pension system generated considerable support and little opposition, making it easier for Union veterans and their allies to improve the system in ways that confirmed their status as worthy, independent, rights-bearing citizens. In contrast, regulatory and redistributive policies "are likely to be zero-sum in their consequences, imposing losses on the disfavored groups whose actions are regulated or whose advantages are redistributed" (Skocpol 1992, 82). In this case, the Freedmen's Bureau deprived many Southern whites of both symbolic and material advantages, including property, control over black labor, and even the "wages of whiteness," and it did so in a direct, coercive, and highly visible fashion.[10] In addition, the bureau's regulatory and redistributive features probably made it more threatening than the Civil War pension program to Northern capitalists. Of course, with the exception of Northern investors in Southern agriculture, Northern capitalists were not directly disfavored by the bureau's activities. However, it is likely that they considered themselves *potentially* disfavored by the regulatory and redistributive precedents that the bureau set.[11] As a result of these zero-sum consequences, the Freedmen's Bureau generated considerable opposition, and political pressure from disfavored but influential groups encouraged the bureau to treat freedpeople in an illiberal manner as dependent paupers in need of supervision and discipline.[12]

## Racial politics

Differences in the policy structures of the Freedmen's Bureau and the Civil War pension system help to explain why freedpeople were classed as paupers while veterans obtained recognition as rights-bearing citizens. However, a second major factor also contributed to these divergent outcomes. In contrast to Union veterans, freedpeople's classification struggle generated a broad and vigorous racial backlash. To be sure, this backlash was not altogether independent of policy structure. As noted in chapter 1, specific policy features can make it easier to set off a racial backlash against the policy's clients or render the policy more vulnerable to racial attacks. Perhaps the most obvious feature in this case was the confinement of Freedmen's Bureau benefits mainly to African Americans. Although Congress did include white war refugees in the bureau's relief efforts, these refugees had all returned to their homes by early 1866. Moreover, in contrast to the Civil War pensions that had proved so lucrative for pension attorneys, the Freedmen's Bureau provided few indirect benefits to more powerful groups who would thus have also had a stake in the classification of the Bureau's clients. (One important exception, of course, was the Republican Party, which benefited from black votes.) Other features of the Freedmen's Bureau invited a racial backlash as well. The bureau advanced (albeit haltingly and unreliably) black citizenship rights, expanded political, as well as other forms, of capital available to black workers (or at least threatened to do so), and, as noted above, administered benefits in a less-centralized fashion than did the Civil War pension system.

Yet it would be a mistake to see the racial backlash against the Freedmen's Bureau and its clients as a product of policy structure alone. The backlash also depended on the activity of the bureau's supporters and opponents, including the symbolic work that was required to mobilize individuals along racial lines. As I detail in the next section of this chapter, those efforts were shaped by the historical legacies of past struggles over the meaning and boundaries of American citizenship, of which the bureau's institutional structure was only one manifestation.

Much of the racial backlash was concentrated in the South, of course, where it took a variety of forms, including the countermobilization of whites by the Democratic Party, racial discrimination by local civil authorities, and the use of economic pressure, intimidation, and violence against freedpeople and their white Republican allies. Perhaps the most brutal expression of this backlash was the formation of terrorist groups, such as the Ku Klux Klan, which reached the peak of its activity in the late 1860s. Klan terrorism "destroyed the Union League as an effective political organization" and rendered freedpeople more dependent on planters for protection, shifting the balance of power on the plantations and paving the way for the eventual overthrow of Republican rule in the South (Howard 1907, 381–82; Fitzgerald 1989, 213, 226).

A similar albeit less brutal racial backlash emerged in the North as well, where it manifested initially in President Johnson's attempts to veto and later sabotage the Freedmen's Bureau. Although Johnson failed to kill the bureau, the backlash was subsequently sustained by the emergence of a self-described "liberal reform" movement in the late 1860s that sought

to restrict popular political participation and rein in the activist, reform-
ing state created by the Republican Party. This movement reflected an
incipient shift from what Schudson (1998) calls a party-based model of
citizenship, prevalent in the nineteenth century, to a newer model based
on the ideal of the "informed citizen," which would eventually crystallize
during the Progressive era. Drawn in part from the ranks of former Radical Republicans, liberal reformers were spurred by middle-class anxieties
about rising immigration, labor's campaign for an eight-hour day, and the
corruption and demagoguery of patronage politics (Sproat 1968; Ahern
1979; Montgomery [1967] 1981, 379, 385–86, 388; McGerr 1986, 9, 46,
50, 52, 65; Foner 1988, 488–511; Keyssar 2000, 119–27). Reform-minded
elites were "especially appalled by the ways in which public relief for
able-bodied unemployed men could become enmeshed with grassroots
party politics" (Skocpol 1992, 96). In Godkin's characteristic words, such
entanglement led "foreigners . . . ignorant, credulous, newly emancipated, brutalized by oppression . . . to look on the suffrage simply as a
means of getting jobs out of the public, and taxation as another name for
the forced contributions of the rich to a fund for the poor man's relief'"
(quoted in Skocpol 1992, 96). These concerns led reformers to champion
"measures designed to take public welfare provision out of 'politics'—or,
more precisely, to take it out of the grip of the patronage-oriented political parties that controlled much of the polity in the post–Civil War decades" (Skocpol 1992, 95; see also Lui 1995).

These same concerns "induced many Northern intellectuals to cast
a more kindly eye than they had hitherto toward the white foes of the
Republican regimes in the South" (Montgomery [1967] 1981, 385). Perceiving parallels between their own problems and those of Southern elites,
"reformers and Mugwumps of the North identified corruption with the
Radical wing of the Republican party, lost interest in the Negro allies of
the Radicals, and looked upon them as a means of perpetuating corrupt
government all over the nation as well as in the South" (Woodward 1957,
239–40). To be sure, concerns about corruption and patronage fueled
opposition to the Civil War pension program as well. However, attacks
on the Freedmen's Bureau differed in that Southern whites and Northern liberal reformers linked their assault on patronage politics to race.
As Du Bois ([1935] 1962) points out, "the South . . . named the Negro as
the main cause of Southern corruption," (583) linking "the Negro vote
and graft . . . in the public mind" (624). In the North, liberal reformers
were "completely taken in by the legend of 'Black Reconstruction'" and

"ready to believe the worst that Southern whites had to say about the Ne-gro in politics" (Sproat 1968, 34). They concluded that the black voter in the South, like the immigrant voter in Northern cities, "had been given a fair chance to prove his worth as a responsible citizen and that the exper-iment had proved a failure" (Woodward 1957, 239–40; cf. Sproat 1968, 29–42; Keyssar 2000, 119–20). The result, Boston reformer Charles Fran-cis Adams warned in 1869, was an impending "government of ignorance and vice" by "a European, and especially Celtic, proletariat on the At-lantic coast; an African proletariat on the shores of the Gulf, and a Chi-nese proletariat on the shores of the Pacific" (quoted in McGerr 1986, 46; Montgomery 1993, 146).

Racialized fears about political corruption and democratic excess had important policy implications, all of which made it harder for clients of the Freedmen's Bureau to preserve their status and rights as citizens. First, the liberal reform movement encouraged rapprochement with Southern landowners and reinforced reservations about black political participa-tion. In *The Nation,* Godkin mixed hostility toward Tammany Hall with "sympathy toward the taxpayers' conventions staged by 'conservatives' in the Southern states, and even toward the Ku Klux Klan. Having lost his proselytizing zeal for unlimited democracy, Godkin had come to re-gard Southern men of property and culture as allies of their Northern counterparts in a common struggle against corrupt mass politics" (Mont-gomery [1967] 1981, 385). To Godkin and like-minded reformers, "the Negro as a freedman had been a disappointment, and home rule under the old white leadership was the only way to restore honest government" (Stampp 1965, 191). Second, while liberal reformers condemned the ter-rorism of the Ku Klux Klan, they advocated what was in effect a policy of appeasement. When Congress passed a series of Enforcement Acts in 1870 and 1871 authorizing the president to use military force to suppress the Klan, liberal reformers argued that military intervention would only reinforce Southern support for the "Lost Cause" and therefore "provide no final solution. Local and federal corruption must disappear. . . . Only an end to corruption and the full participation of all Southern men in the political process [i.e., amnesty for former rebels] would reduce violence" (Ahern 1979, 58). Third, the liberal reform movement fostered a polit-ical realignment that helped to end Reconstruction. By bringing disen-chanted Radical Republicans like Godkin together with "some of their former antagonists among conservative Republicans and Northern Dem-ocrats," the liberal reform movement disorganized the old Republican coalition that had formulated Reconstruction policy (N. Cohen 2002, 31; cf. Ahern 1979, 65; Montgomery [1967] 1981, 384–86).[13] In brief, faced with a violent racial backlash in the South, blamed for political corruption by the North, and increasingly deprived of elite allies in a Republican coalition that was internally divided by new cleavages, freedpeople found it difficult to obtain recognition as honorable, rights-bearing citizens who earned and deserved public aid.

Civil War pensioners avoided this racial backlash, because veterans were overwhelmingly white. Although black soldiers played a significant role in the war, they made up only about 9 to 10 percent of Union military forces (Vinovskis 1989, 40; Skocpol 1992, 138). Furthermore, because black veterans were likely underrepresented on the pension rolls, they probably constituted an even smaller percentage of pensioners. Although black Union veterans and their survivors "formally enjoyed equal access to Civil War veterans' pensions," three-quarters of them were former slaves whose special circumstances made it more difficult for them to establish pension claims. These circumstances included illiteracy, name changes, lack of funds or written records, problems establishing proof of marriage or proving birth dates, and demographic factors that made black veterans less likely than white veterans to survive the quarter-century after the end of the Civil War (Williams 2003, 62–65).[14] In addition, the GAR marginalized black members and relegated them to second-class status, reinforcing the public image of veterans as white (Dearing 1952, 412–20; McConnell 1992, 71, 208–9, 213–19).[15]

To sum up, freedpeople's demands to be classed as rights-bearing citizens who had earned and deserved public aid, the policy implications of those demands, and the mobilization of freedpeople in support of their demands generated a strong racial backlash. This backlash, in conjunction with the consequences of policy structure, explains their failure to avoid the stigma of pauperism or to even preserve the limited forms of public aid available to them through the Freedmen's Bureau. To be sure, the racial backlash against freedpeople was linked to a more general campaign against corrupt patronage politics and related ills (political manipulation of the dependent poor, rising taxes, class legislation, and so forth), which was itself rooted in the emergence of a new model of citizenship based on the "informed citizen" (Schudson 1998). However, by itself, this reaction against patronage was insufficient to defeat Civil War pensioners in the struggle over their civic classification. Indeed, for the most part the liberal reformers' "campaign for 'good government'"

had only a circumscribed impact and limited influence (Sproat 1968, 271).
Only when it was racialized and linked to racist beliefs about blacks' incapacity for self-government did the campaign against patronage become
a potent political force. This contrast suggests that the reaction against
corrupt patronage politics generated greater antagonism to America's
nineteenth-century social spending regime when it was associated with
racial conflict. Just as the color of welfare mediated the effects of antistatist values during the War on Poverty (Quadagno 1994), so, too, did it mediate the effects of anti-patronage sentiment in the nineteenth century.[16]

## The Historical Legacies of Past Classification Struggles

*How previous classification struggles shaped freedpeople's struggle*

Previous classification struggles influence the outcome of subsequent
struggles, rendering some outcomes more likely than others. The struggle over the citizenship status and rights of Freedmen's Bureau clients in
the nineteenth century was no exception. Freedpeople's efforts to avoid
the stigma of pauperism were shaped by the antebellum struggle of white
workingmen to expand the boundaries of citizenship and by the enslavement and civic exclusion of African Americans prior to the Civil War.
These earlier patterns of civic inclusion and exclusion hindered freedpeople from reconciling citizenship with government assistance, fostered
illiberal and disciplinary policies for them, and encouraged the racial
backlash that frustrated and confounded their aspirations.

First, consider how white workingmen's antebellum struggle for political rights constrained freedpeople. As noted in chapter 1, the Anglo
American tradition initially restricted full citizenship to property owners on the grounds that property prevented their personal dependence
or subordination. Political elites deemed propertyless wage earners unfit for full citizenship because, in the words of the English jurist William
Blackstone, they were dependent, had "no will of their own," and would
therefore cast their votes "under some undue influence" (Keyssar 2000,
10). When propertyless white workingmen demanded and obtained political rights during the first half of the nineteenth century, they expanded
the boundaries of citizenship to encompass wage laborers as well as property owners. However, by severing the link between property ownership
and citizenship, they foreclosed an alternative and more radical strategy
for expanding the boundaries of citizenship: distributing property more

widely among a greater number of people. As shown in chapter 2, this was precisely what freedpeople demanded in the aftermath of the Civil War. When they asked for recognition as full and equal citizens, they did so with the understanding that citizenship implied land ownership as its material basis. Their claims were ineffective in part because white workingmen had previously broadened the meaning of economic independence to include wage labor, undercutting redistributive claims to land or other forms of property that might otherwise be deemed an integral and necessary part of citizenship. The potentially radical logic of civic republicanism was therefore lost. As freedpeople soon discovered, citizenship became easier to acquire once it was separated from property, but it was also diminished in substance and value without the material basis that property provided. In contrast to freedpeople, Civil War pensioners were unconstrained by this historical legacy. Although they, too, struggled to be classed as citizens rather than paupers, their classificatory claims entailed no redistribution of property. Consequently, their claims did not rest upon the discredited antebellum conception of citizenship that linked civic inclusion to property ownership. Nor did their classificatory claims entail any regulation of labor relations. Their claims were therefore more compatible with the emerging Lochnerian conception of citizenship that equated citizenship rights with freedom of contract. In short, freedpeople and Civil War pensioners both sought to preserve their status as citizens, but they linked this status to a different set of material and symbolic profits. Because antebellum classification struggles altered the relationships among citizenship, labor, and property, Civil War pensioners' demands for civic inclusion were more consistent with the prevailing post-bellum conception of citizenship than freedpeople's demands.

It was not only the civic inclusion of propertyless white workingmen that constrained freedpeople, but also the antebellum exclusion of slaves and paupers. As I have suggested, parallel processes of ritual degradation constituted these groups and set them apart as pariah classes, which made it easier to map the category of pauper onto former slaves after the Civil War. Stripped of their civil and political rights, paupers experienced a civil death not unlike the social death of slaves (O. Patterson 1982). In addition, both groups served as negative reference points for white wage earners. The fate of paupers "loomed large in the lives of those who lived close to indigence, warning them always of a life even worse than hard work and severe poverty" (Piven and Cloward 1977, 42–43). Likewise, slaves gave white workingmen "a wretched touchstone against which to measure their fears of unfreedom and a friendly reminder that they were by comparison not so badly off" (Roediger [1991] 1999, 49). Further strengthening the association between pauperism and slavery was the emergence of a transatlantic, "liberal capitalist, antipaternalist" discourse in the nineteenth century. In both Britain and the United States, pauperism and slavery were said to demoralize and crush "the incentive of laboring populations . . . by guaranteeing and fixing their recompense and otherwise upsetting that 'natural' correspondence between performance and reward. Increasingly during this period, these two institutions were represented as artificial drags on the formation of a wage-labor market that honored individual initiative, healthy competition, and 'freedom of contract'" (Glickstein 2002, 60). These parallels led some Americans to equate slavery and pauperism explicitly. For example, Edmund Ruffin, a leading secessionist from Virginia, charged Northern abolitionists with hypocrisy for failing to see how closely Northern relief practices resembled slavery. "Free labor must eventually degrade into the 'pauper slavery' of the poorhouse," he sneered, "where 'the pauper, whether laborer or otherwise, receiving support from the parish, [was] neither more nor less than a slave to the administrators of the law and dispensers of the public charity.' Such a person, [Ruffin] contended, ceased 'to be a free agent in any respect'" (Schmidt 1998, 82–83).

Given these cultural analogies between slaves and paupers, it is not surprising that critics of the Freedmen's Bureau would see its relief work and regulation of labor relations as a restoration of slavery in modified form. "In slavery every planter [took?] care of his own," explained Alabama resident James Gillette to a bureau official in 1868, but emancipation relieved the former master of his responsibilities and conferred them upon "the General Government" (Office of the Commissioner, Letters from the Executive Mansion, Box 19). While Gillette saw this situation as a temporary necessity, critics construed the bureau's relief efforts as a throwback to the paternalism of slavery, incompatible with "a social order in which labor relations were mediated by the impersonal market, and blacks aggressively pressed claims to autonomy and equality" (Foner 1988, 130; cf. Pierce 1904, 35, 43, 68; Belz 1976, 74; Berlin et al. 1990, 15–16). Freedpeople's former status as slaves thus made them more vulnerable than Civil War pensioners to stigmatizing charges of pauperism.[17]

Furthermore, the enslavement and civic exclusion of African Americans in the antebellum period undermined postbellum attempts to form biracial political coalitions. To preserve their status as rights-bearing citizens and avoid being classed as paupers, freedpeople needed white allies. From a class perspective, an alliance with poor white yeomen farmers against planters made the most sense. However, Democrats' appeals to white supremacy divided this potential class-based coalition along racial lines (Du Bois [1935] 1962). These appeals resonated with white yeomen farmers and white laborers, because their collective identity had been formed in opposition to the ritually degraded slave labor of blacks. Even after black workers were liberated from slavery, they retained the stigma of their former status, making it difficult for whites to identify with them. Moreover, slavery shaped whites' and blacks' access to economic and cultural capital and thus their positions in social space. There was considerable social distance between the positions occupied by white yeomen farmers and landless black plantation workers, making their political coalition unstable. The social world, as Bourdieu (1991, 233) points out, can be divided and constructed in different ways, but "one cannot group together just anyone with anyone else while ignoring the fundamental differences, particularly economic and cultural differences, between them." These differences were in large part a legacy of slavery.

Finally, slavery bequeathed a set of cultural assumptions about African Americans that continued to influence the strategies of whites long after slavery was abolished. These cultural assumptions shaped how whites defined their economic and political interests, leading many to embrace illiberal policies and join the racial backlash against freedpeople. For example, attacks on the bureau's relief efforts reflected a longstanding assumption that blacks would not work without compulsion as well as the subsequent inference that relief would reinforce this tendency. This same assumption shaped reactions to the bureau's labor policies. Southern planters opposed protective labor regulations, because they had a material interest in the exploitation of cheap black labor, but their material interests were also mediated by their belief that blacks were naturally indolent, unsuited to free labor, and worked only under duress (R. Smith 1997, 303; Foner 1988, chap. 4). Black workers were "not controlled by the same motives as white men," one planter explained, "and unless you have power to compel them, they'll only work when they can't beg or steal enough to keep from starving" (quoted in Litwack 1979, 365). Precisely because planters understood labor in racialized terms and not as the identical abstract labor of classical economics, they preferred coercive labor arrangements to other alternatives.

Another set of cultural assumptions about blacks stemmed from slavery's paternalistic features. Although slave owners ruthlessly exploited black workers, they also treated slaves as permanent children. The Freedmen's Bureau reflected and reproduced this paternalism by treating blacks as dependent wards in need of supervision and discipline. Letters in support of the bureau similarly emphasized freedpeople's ignorance and inability to take care of themselves, indicating that paternalistic assumptions were widespread even among their allies (Office of the Commissioner, Letters from the Executive Mansion, Box 19). These same paternalistic assumptions led many whites to conclude that elites were manipulating freedpeople for their own ends. Like propertyless workers in the eighteenth century, freedpeople were, in the words of William Blackstone, "esteemed to have no will of their own" and to be "under some undue influence" (quoted in Keyssar 2000, 10). While poor white yeomen farmers worried that planters would control the black vote, Redeemer Democrats and Northern reformers feared that blacks were under the sway of corrupt Republican politicians. In both instances, the assumption that blacks were childlike and therefore easily manipulated encouraged many whites to see them as a threat. In short, though material interests undoubtedly influenced the outcome of freedpeople's classification struggle, those interests were shaped by enduring cultural assumptions about blacks. Those assumptions were, in turn, a legacy of the enslavement of black laborers and their ritual degradation as a pariah class in the antebellum period. Just as degrading relief practices nurtured and reinforced "market ideology" (Piven and Cloward [1971] 1993, 149), so too did the degradation of slave labor nurture and reinforce racism.

## How freedpeople's classification struggle shaped subsequent struggles

Just as antebellum struggles influenced postbellum struggles over the citizenship status and rights of freedpeople, so, too, did struggles during Reconstruction shape those that came afterwards. Freedpeople's failure to obtain recognition as rights-bearing citizens who earned and deserved public aid and their inability to institutionalize that status had three important consequences. First, this failure enhanced the power of the Southern planter class. As we have seen, freedpeople linked their demands for full citizenship to land reform or, failing that, less coercive labor arrangements. They regarded these goals as a necessary and integral part of the citizenship they claimed, and they welcomed government assistance to achieve them. Had they even partly attained these goals, they would have been able to exercise their civil and political rights more effectively, alter the distribution of resources and social opportunities in the South, and weaken the power of the planter class. Consequently, black laborers would have been better positioned to defend and expand their citizenship rights during the Populist insurgency of the 1890s and the labor upsurge of the 1930s.[18] However, instead of land reform, freedpeople acquired only a grudging and temporary form of public assistance largely modeled on traditional poor relief and a temporary regime of labor regulations that was at least as disciplinary as it was protective. This outcome left subsequent generations of black laborers with little or no basis for economic independence or advancement. As a result, they were far more vulnerable to exploitation and domination (Ahern 1979, 65; R. Smith 1997, 299).

Second, freedpeople's failed classification struggle did not merely reflect racial divisions inherited from slavery; it also reinforced them. As Foner (1988, 604) puts it, "if racism contributed to the undoing of Reconstruction, by the same token Reconstruction's demise and the emergence of blacks as a disenfranchised class of dependent laborers greatly facilitated racism's further spread." The Freedmen's Bureau played a role in this process insofar as degrading relief practices stigmatized freedpeople and strengthened racist beliefs and assumptions about blacks. Moreover, the creation of a dual welfare system that provided honorable, relatively generous benefits to (primarily white) veterans but stingy, often degrading benefits to freedpeople racialized the division between citizens and paupers, setting a precedent for the two-tier welfare state (alluded to in chapter 1) that emerged in the twentieth century. If slaves were deemed to be analogous to paupers before the Civil War, ex-slaves and their descendants would often be identified with paupers after the war. Even after the Freedmen's Bureau was dismantled, influential journalists like James Pike continued to decry the "domination" of Southern states by "pauper blacks, fresh from a state of slavery" (quoted in Sproat 1968, 35).[19] At the same time, the Reconstruction era's dual welfare system objectified racial divisions, exacerbating unequal access to and distribution of resources and social opportunities. As a result, it widened the social distance separating white and black claimants, making the possibility of biracial coalitions even less likely in the future. These effects were further compounded by the destruction of the Union League. Although the league created "extraordinary sites of interracial cooperation," its demise demoralized supporters and encouraged them to conclude that interracial cooperation and radical reform were doomed to failure. "Once destroyed," the league's experiment in interracial cooperation "would take many more decades to replicate anywhere in the United States" (Hahn 2003, 187).

Third, postwar conflicts over the status and rights of freedpeople triggered a political learning process at the national level that, despite the erroneous conclusions that reformers drew, had a profound impact on subsequent policymaking. The strong negative reaction to the Freedmen's Bureau among educated middle-class whites, stemming from the fused politics of patronage and race, not only discouraged new social spending for blacks, but also reinforced hostility to black political participation, even in formerly sympathetic circles. In fact, these were two sides of the same reaction, since the use of social spending for patronage purposes was a key means of mobilizing black (and white) voters after the Civil War. By the end of the nineteenth century, the power of the planter class, deepening racial divisions, and the perceived threat that black enfranchisement ostensibly posed to good government paved the way in the South for the disfranchisement of black voters, Jim Crow, and the supremacy of a Democratic Party dominated by white landowners and merchants. Freedpeople's failed classification struggle contributed in this way to the under-democratization of the South, which constrained subsequent welfare-state development. Instead of civil and political rights leading to social rights, as Marshall ([1949] 1964) argued, restrictions on political participation in the South would hinder the development of social citizenship for the nation as a whole.[20]

## Summary and Conclusion

To explain why the clients of the Freedmen's Bureau failed to escape the stigma of pauperism, I have compared their classification struggle to the more successful struggle of Civil War pension recipients. First, significant analogies between the cases were identified in order to establish their comparability: The Freedmen's Bureau and the Civil War pension system were roughly contemporaneous policy innovations that created new groups of clients; both policies were created and sustained by similar political forces (most notably, patronage politics); the policies shared important institutional features that shaped the struggles over the status and rights of their clients; these struggles entailed important policy changes and involved material as well as symbolic stakes; and the participants in these struggles used similar language and invoked the same civic ideals. Second, the development of Civil War pensions and the struggle over the classification of pension recipients from the creation of the pension system in 1862 to its last major expansion in 1890 were traced. Third, I sought to explain why, despite the similarities noted above, the clients of the Freedmen's Bureau were classed as dependent paupers while Civil War pensioners were recognized as rights-bearing citizen-soldiers. Three generally accepted explanations for the treatment of Freedmen's Bureau clients—American exceptionalism, capitalist hegemony, and the under-bureaucratization of the nation's civil administration—were found to be inadequate or insufficient. Instead, I argued that the outcomes of the classification struggles depended crucially on the institutional structures of the policies and on racial politics. Although the Freedmen's Bureau and the Civil War pension program shared several policy features, they were not identical. Among other things, the Freedmen's Bureau differed from the Civil War pension system insofar as the former was institutionally linked to traditional poor relief and more similar in form. Freedpeople were also burdened by a racial backlash that Civil War pensioners avoided. This backlash required symbolic work to render racial divisions more significant than competing sources of social division, thereby mobilizing agents along racial lines. Of course, the classification of Freedmen's Bureau clients as paupers was not caused by racism alone; hostility to the Freedmen's Bureau and opposition to the claims of its clients reflected a general reaction against corrupt patronage politics and perceived democratic excess. However, the effectiveness of this reaction was mediated by racial politics. Finally, rather than taking policy structures and racial divisions as givens, I ended with a brief discussion of how these causal factors were themselves shaped by past classification struggles, and how struggles during Reconstruction shaped those that came afterwards.

# PART II

# Claiming Rights as Citizen-Workers
*Struggles during the New Deal*

## CHAPTER FOUR

# "They are just 'reliefers' and have no rights"

## The Works Progress Administration, 1935–1942

In the case of economic disasters, indeed, something like a declassification [*déclasse-ment*] occurs which suddenly casts certain individuals into a lower state than their previous one. . . . Time is required for the public conscience to reclassify men and things [*pour qu'hommes et choses soient à nouveau classés*]. . . . The limits are unknown between the possible and the impossible, what is just and what is unjust, legitimate claims and hopes and those which are immoderate. Consequently, there is no restraint upon aspirations. . . . All classes contend among themselves because no established classification [*classement*] any longer exists.—Emile Durkheim, *Suicide: A Study in Sociology*

The politics of the unemployed both in the nineteenth and twentieth centuries illustrates that not the least part of the class struggle was the struggle to create a class. —Richard Flanagan, *"Parish-Fed Bastards": A History of the Politics of the Unemployed in Britain, 1884–1939*

Like the Civil War and Reconstruction, the Great Depression and the New Deal unsettled established patterns of civic inclusion and dramatically altered the scope and content of national citizenship. The Depression declassed millions of workers, transforming them from independent citizens "into relief recipients who could be legally labeled as paupers" (Keyssar 2000, 238). The resulting disjuncture between their habitual expectations and new social conditions, combined with the fiscal breakdown of local relief programs under the strain of mass unemployment, generated a severe crisis of the welfare field. Furthermore, during the New Deal, as in Reconstruction, "extraordinary" politics superseded "normal" politics, fundamentally transforming the meaning of

the Constitution and ushering in a new "constitutional regime" (Ackerman 1991). In the course of reconstructing the welfare field, New Dealers
challenged the older, laissez-faire conception of citizenship that equated
freedom and independence with liberty of contract. In Marshallian terms,
they sought to create an activist, regulatory welfare state that would "in-
vade" the market from the outside, establishing new social rights that
would be integrated into rather than detached from the status of citizenship. At the same time, labor unions struggled to create "a sort of secondary industrial citizenship" through collective bargaining, challenging
liberty of contract from within the market. Both of these developments
implied "the subordination of market price to social justice, the replacement of the free bargain by the declaration of rights" (Marshall [1949]
1964, 93–94, 111). However, the New Deal was fiercely contested, un-
evenly implemented, and never fully completed—a "halfway revolution"
in the words of William Leuchtenburg (1963, 347) that resulted in a pattern of divided citizenship (Mettler 1998). Thus, while the New Deal expanded opportunities for welfare state claimants to resist the actual or
threatened loss of their citizenship status and rights, it did not guarantee
their success.

   This chapter focuses on one key element of the New Deal welfare
state: the WPA, an enormous public employment program that Congress created in 1935 to manage the mass unemployment generated by
the Depression and terminated in 1942. Just as the Freedmen's Bureau
provided a prime case for investigating the classification struggles of the
Reconstruction era, so the WPA serves a similar purpose here; it provides
an accessible microcosm of the broader struggles over the meaning and
boundaries of citizenship in the New Deal era. The WPA is well suited
for this purpose, because it was central to the Second New Deal in terms
of size, spending, and importance.[1] At its peak in 1938, the program put
more than three million unemployed relief recipients to work (U.S. Federal Works Agency 1946, 28). By 1939 it had become "Roosevelt's top
priority in social policy" (Amenta 1998, 83), the federal government's
"most comprehensive" and "ambitious" program, and "the cornerstone
of domestic relief" (Porter 1980, 61, 70). Accounting for 46 percent of social spending in the United States and 1.7 percent of the nation's gross national product that year, the WPA absorbed "both the greatest amount of
public spending and public attention" (Amenta 1998, 81, 144).

   Furthermore, like the Freedmen's Bureau, the WPA did not merely reflect or reveal classification struggles, but it also inadvertently contributed

to them. Although modeled on earlier experiments with public works and work relief (Salmond 1967; Schwartz 1984; Sautter 1991), the WPA created a new group of clients whose standing relative to those assisted by other policies was not immediately clear. Would WPA employment be modeled on or sharply distinguished from traditional poor relief? Would it provide relief as an alternative to citizenship rights or as an integral part of them? Punitive nineteenth-century forms of work relief served as a model for WPA workers and sympathetic New Dealers to avoid, while other policies set standards against which they could measure injustices. Particularly important in this respect were New Deal labor policies like the 1935 National Labor Relations Act, which guaranteed workers the right to organize and bargain collectively, and the 1938 Fair Labor Standards Act (FLSA), which set a federal minimum wage and maximum workday length. Furthermore, in the context of an emerging two-tiered welfare state that divided citizens along gender and racial lines (Quadagno 1994; Lieberman 1998; Mettler 1998), the WPA was a hybrid program that straddled these divisions. As a result, it positioned its clients in ambiguous and contradictory ways, which also encouraged conflict over their status and rights (Goldberg 2005).

While the struggle over the classification of WPA workers involved a variety of individuals and groups with divergent views and goals, this chapter focuses on the activities and claims of the Workers Alliance of America as one manifestation of that struggle. The Workers Alliance was a nationwide social movement organization that, from 1935 to 1941, sought to organize and represent WPA workers. The movement had its roots in earlier efforts to organize the unemployed by the Socialist Party, A. J. Muste's Conference on Progressive Labor Action, and the American Communist Party (Rosenzweig 1975, 1979, 1983). In 1935, the Socialist-led groups merged with the Musteite Unemployed Leagues to form the Workers Alliance. A year later, the Communist-led Unemployed Councils were also included, although non-Communist leaders retained a majority on the Alliance's national executive board (Piven and Cloward 1977, 75–76; Seymour 1937, 41–44; Karsh and Garman 1961, 93). "What had been three major organizations and a number of minor ones became a single entity able to bring increased pressure on behalf of the jobless" (Folsom 1991, 417).

The consolidation of the unemployed movement coincided with the movement's growing ties to the new federal works program. Despite the warnings of Workers Alliance leaders that it must avoid "becoming merely a trade union for WPA workers," Klehr (1984, 297–98) suggests, "it soon was exactly that. By 1939 some 75 percent of Workers' Alliance members were WPA employees."[2] However, this formulation elides a key component of their struggle. Since the status of WPA workers as employees was contested, the Workers Alliance had to struggle to bring into existence the very thing that trade unions presuppose and represent. Consequently, the Workers Alliance demanded not only higher wages for WPA workers but also recognition of a new identity. Just as the Union League and the GAR sought recognition of their members as virtuous citizen-soldiers, the Workers Alliance resisted the pauperization of WPA workers and insisted that they be recognized and treated with dignity as rights-bearing citizen-workers. As in previous classification struggles, the material and symbolic stakes of this conflict were inextricable: "To possess the name is to feel the right to claim the things normally associated with those words, i.e., the practices . . . and the corresponding material and symbolic profits (wage claims, etc.)" (Bourdieu and Boltanski 1981, 141–42).

## Between Public Relief and Public Employment: The Contradictory Position of WPA Workers

Previous scholarship generally treats the WPA as part of the national tier of New Deal social and labor policies that mainly benefited long-term, full-time, male wage earners (see, for example, Rose 1994, 100–4). The close connection between the federal works program and the social insurance programs created in 1935 suggests that the WPA was indeed primarily oriented to the needs of unemployed male breadwinners (Gill 1939, 201–2, 257–58; Perkins 1946, 188–90; Altmeyer 1966, 12–13; Amenta 1998, 89). Moreover, because WPA officials considered men to be the economic heads of their families and sought to avoid "public criticisms for employing 'too many women,'" unemployed men were "the first to be put on the [WPA] rolls. . . . [T]he husband's position had to be protected even if this involved putting 'some brake upon women's eagerness to be the family breadwinner, wage recipient, and controller of the family pocketbook'" (Rose 1994, 101). While women were not officially denied WPA employment, they found it harder to get work, because they were more often classified as unemployable, and because WPA employment was restricted to one family member (usually the husband or father). Consequently, the proportion of women working for the WPA (between 12 and 18 percent up until the end of June 1940) was less than the proportion of women in the country's entire labor force (25 percent, according to the 1940 census) (U.S. Federal Works Agency 1946, 44). All of these considerations support the claim that the WPA was part of the masculine tier of the U.S. welfare state (cf. Amenta et al. 1996, 17–19; Amenta 1998, 155–56).

However, closer inspection reveals that the WPA positioned relief workers in more contradictory ways, not only in a discursive manner, but also as a consequence of how policymakers and administrators organized work relief. First, because female WPA workers were ghettoized in largely feminine projects, such as sewing and white-collar clerical work (U.S. Federal Works Agency 1946, 44), the gender divisions characteristic of the welfare state as a whole were reproduced *within* the WPA itself. In this respect, the WPA was not so much a masculine as an "androgyne" program (cf. Fraser 1989, 150–51). Second, the proportion of women working for the WPA steadily increased after 1940 (reaching 40.8 percent by the end of 1942) as men left the WPA rolls for private employment more rapidly than women, in effect feminizing the program (U.S. Federal Works Agency 1946, 44). Third and most importantly, the WPA was characterized from its inception by a "Janus-like nature" (D. Howard, 1943, 251) because "neither Congress nor administrative officials" ever clarified "the perennial question of . . . how far the WPA should be regarded as a relief program as opposed to a work program" (D. Howard 1943, 246; see also D. Howard 1943, 421–22; Lescohier 1939; Bremer 1975). This can best be demonstrated by comparing the social position of WPA workers first to that of the dependent poor relegated to the feminine tier of state-administered public assistance and second to that of the long-term, full-time wage earners served by the masculine tier of social insurance.[3]

### The WPA and public relief

Policymakers created the federal works program to help the new class of "employable" unemployed generated by the Depression, rather than those whom national WPA Administrator Harry Hopkins called "unemployables" and "chronic dependents." They intended the works program to keep those who were newly poor from the degrading fates of private charity or local poor relief and to preserve their morale and skills (D. Howard 1943, 197; Bremer 1975, 639–40; Schwartz 1984, 34–35, 70; Axinn and Levin 1997, 184, 186). Nels Anderson (1935), a sociologist who became the director of the WPA's Section on Labor Relations, argued that "public work" would thus prevent the unemployed from becoming a "caste" (his word) of reliefers. California governor Culbert Olson, who promised a New Deal for his state, justified his preference for a works program on similar grounds: "We wish to rehabilitate the unemployed as workers and citizens," he explained in 1939. "We could not submit to reducing these people to the status of indigents in the counties" (quoted in *Work,* March 11, 1939, 11). These policy aims led New Dealers to emphasize the difference between their brand of work relief and earlier forms like the workhouse, which they regarded as punitive and stigmatizing (Gill 1939, 160–61; Hopkins 1936, 100–1, 114–15; D. Howard 1943, 277).

However, while the federal works program elevated relief workers above the traditionally despised pauper class, policymakers never entirely sundered it from local and conventional forms of public relief. Despite the insistence of the advisory council to President Roosevelt's Committee on Economic Security that "the Government employment program should be divorced completely from relief" (D. Howard 1943, 354), the WPA employed almost exclusively workers who were certified as needy and referred by local relief agencies (D. Howard 1943, 247; see also Brown 1999, 73–74). Indeed, policymakers restricted WPA employment to relief recipients on the grounds "that if workers are to be brought to the realization that WPA employment is a form of relief rather than 'just another job,' it is necessary to require them to accept relief as an antecedent to a job" (D. Howard 1943, 409). Most Americans perceived this link to public relief as socially polluting. As New York City WPA administrator Hugh Johnson pointed out, WPA employment failed to prevent "the humiliation of home relief," since "to go on work relief, the rules require that a man first go on home relief. To get there, he must submit to the equivalent of a pauper's oath" (quoted in D. Howard 1943, 412–13).[4] Thus, while the relief policies of Roosevelt's Second New Deal distanced WPA workers from paupers and the dependent poor, they did not entirely eliminate their relief status or the ritual degradation historically associated with it.

### The WPA and employment

Because the policy innovations of the Second New Deal did not completely separate WPA workers from paupers and the dependent poor, the WPA did not completely resemble long-term, full-time paid employment. To be sure, federal officials, WPA administrators, and the official pamphlets they distributed to WPA workers all described the program as

employment, and some of its institutional features confirmed this perception.[5] This was evident, for example, from the type of benefits the WPA
provided. The WPA paid a cash wage rather than provide in-kind assistance, and the wage was based on place and skill rather than a family's estimated need. Moreover, in a concession to organized labor, Congress determined the number of hours that WPA workers were required to work
by dividing the sum of their cash benefits by the wage rate prevailing for
that type of work.[6] However, there were limits to how closely the WPA
resembled regular paid employment. Although the wage rates of WPA
workers might have been equal to those in private industry, the sum of
their monthly "security wage" was deliberately fixed below that of wages
in private industry so as to encourage the unemployed to take private-
sector jobs when such positions became available (D. Howard 1943, 255;
Rose 1994, 98). Even though the WPA was primarily oriented to the
needs of unemployed male breadwinners, this wage differential, rooted
in the traditional poor relief principle of less eligibility, set WPA workers apart from—and placed them in an inferior position to—those in private industry (D. Howard 1943, 255–256). Indeed, as the demands of the
Workers Alliance for equal pay for equal work suggested, the WPA "security wage" had more in common with the "supplemental" wages historically paid to female dependents than the "family" or "living" wage
that male workers historically demanded (Kessler-Harris 1990). Low
wages and precarious job security thus demasculinized WPA work insofar as they hindered WPA workers from serving as reliable family breadwinners (cf. Barrett and Roediger 1997, 21).[7]

   WPA workers' conditions of employment also revealed their hybrid
status. Rather than contract work out to private employers, the WPA itself
hired, paid, and supervised workers (D. Howard 1943, 150–51). Under
these conditions, WPA workers were more likely to regard themselves as
directly employed by the federal government. The relatively long-term
duration of their employment reinforced this perception (D. Howard
1943, 519), which discouraged the unemployed from seeing the WPA as
a stopgap between jobs. In addition, the WPA guaranteed that workers
could organize, and it prohibited discrimination against workers active
in unions or other labor organizations (D. Howard 1943, 218), further
encouraging relief workers to see themselves as employees rather than
paupers. Yet significant distinctions remained. Because Congress determined WPA wages and hours, they were "beyond the pale of bargaining"
(D. Howard 1943, 219). Furthermore, federal policy prohibited WPA

workers from striking against the federal government. Although WPA workers engaged in strikes anyway, President Roosevelt and WPA officials refused publicly to describe de facto strikes as such, instead using euphemisms such as "defection from WPA employment" (D. Howard 1943, 222n1; see also 222–27; Ziskind 1940, 133–84). "What is most noteworthy about this general consensus [that WPA workers had no right to strike]," observed one contemporary, "is that many who share it do so not because the struck jobs were 'government' jobs but because they were relief, not real, jobs" (D. Howard 1943, 222).

Finally, the contradictory character of the WPA is evident when one examines whether relief workers were entitled to the existing rights and protections granted to public employees and workers in private industry. The federal government provided workers' compensation benefits to injured WPA workers through the United States Employees' Compensation Commission (D. Howard 1943, 265). However, eligibility for unemployment compensation benefits under the 1935 Social Security Act was less clear (D. Howard 1943, 435–39). "Was a worker employed by the WPA to be regarded as employed or unemployed? In some instances, the question was decided in one way, in others, differently. In Michigan it was decided both ways. At one time it was decided that WPA work was employment and not relief. . . . According to another interpretation, however, WPA workers could be regarded as 'totally unemployed' and therefore eligible not only to file claim for but also actually to receive [unemployment compensation] benefits" (D. Howard 1943, 436). These inconsistencies reveal policymakers' failure to resolve the status of WPA workers.

### Reasons for the WPA's internal contradictions

Why did the federal government organize work relief in such an incoherent way? Many of the same factors that account for the internal contradictions of the Freedmen's Bureau explain those of the WPA as well. First, like the architects of the Freedmen's Bureau, New Deal policymakers pursued multiple policy goals—relief, reform, and recovery—that were not always fully compatible (Lescohier 1939; Bremer 1975; Katz 1986, 228–34). Reform-minded New Dealers, such as WPA administrator Harry Hopkins and deputy WPA administrator Aubrey Williams, who saw "the right to work" as "the defining premise of New Deal social policy," promoted the welfare state's legitimation function (Brown 1999, 72). In contrast, policymakers like treasury secretary Henry Morgenthau and President Roosevelt himself, who remained preoccupied with balanced budgets and business confidence, placed more emphasis on the welfare state's accumulation function (Bremer 1975; Brown 1999).[8] In addition, the WPA was occasionally used for patronage purposes. Although the WPA was entangled in patronage politics to a far lesser extent than the Freedmen's Bureau, concerns about patronage were serious enough to prompt an investigation by the 1938 Senate Campaign Expenditures Committee. Finally, insofar as the works program was meant to "rehabilitate the unemployed as workers and citizens" (*Work*, March 11, 1939, 11), it also had a transformative (or at least conserving) function. Rehabilitation was especially emphasized for those workers who had the greatest difficulty finding private employment and, thus, were the last to leave the WPA rolls. "The WPA," noted Secretary of Labor Perkins (1946, 190), "had to teach some people the simplest forms of personal reliability, integrity, and cleanliness so that they would be fit to go into a workroom." In short, the WPA was pulled in divergent directions, because policymakers and administrators tried to fulfill multiple functions simultaneously.

The WPA's inconsistent treatment of its clients also reflected institutional differences between the federal and state governments (Katz 1986, 228–34; Mettler 1998). Since the WPA was a federal agency, one might expect it to have administered its policies in a "centralized, unitary manner through standardized, routinized procedures," and to govern its clients as rights-bearing "members of a liberal regime" (Mettler 1998, xi). To some extent, this was true. WPA administrators were bound by an elaborate system of internal bureaucratic regulations that was intended to minimize their discretionary power and (notwithstanding the findings of the Senate Campaign Expenditures Committee) prevent them from mixing politics with relief (see, for example, U.S. Work Projects Administration 1940, 1941, 1942). These aspects of the program were most salient to African American workers, who were generally unaccustomed to such treatment. "The gover'ment," reckoned one black WPA worker in North Carolina, "is the best boss I ever had" (D. Howard 1943, 295). However, like the Freedmen's Bureau, the WPA shared aspects of state-level as well as nationally administered social policies. Although the WPA "emanated out of Washington," it "functioned through a network of nearly 400 state and district offices, which marked what one observer called the 'relinquishment of federal control over the execution of projects'" (Schwartz 1984, 254; cf. Durant 1939). Other features weakened federal control as well, including "the necessity of getting [local] sponsors to initiate and contribute to the cost of projects" (D. Howard 1943, 291), the program's reliance on local relief agencies to certify the unemployed, and the scaling of WPA wage rates in accordance with regional wage differences (768–70). These limitations introduced discretion and variability into the WPA, resulting in less liberal treatment of the program's clients.

## From Contradiction to Contestation: The Struggle over the Classification of WPA Workers

The innovative nature of the WPA and the contradictory organization of work relief encouraged a struggle over the classification of WPA workers not unlike those studied by Bourdieu and Boltanski (1981). In those struggles, French workers modified their job titles "in order to remain aloof from certain groups and get closer to other groups." This semantic difference, they noted, was a "transformed expression of social distance" (149). The Workers Alliance contested the classification of WPA workers in a similarly twofold way. The Workers Alliance defined the collective identity of WPA workers in opposition to that of persons who had clearly lost their standing as rights-bearing citizen-workers, most notably forced laborers and paupers. While seeking to distance WPA workers from these pariah groups, the Workers Alliance simultaneously struggled to equate WPA workers with wage-earning employees.

### Defining WPA workers in opposition to forced labor

Americans have historically defined free labor in opposition to dependent, punitive, and stigmatizing forms of labor, particularly slave labor (Roediger [1991] 1999; Glickstein 2002). By 1935, of course, the United States had long since abolished slavery. However, in the context of an ominous international setting where Fascist movements were rapidly growing in strength, similarly racialized forced-labor programs in Nazi Germany provided real and vivid reminders that not all labor was honorable. Like slavery in the nineteenth century, forced labor in the twentieth century gave workers "both a wretched touchstone against which to measure their fears of unfreedom and a friendly reminder that they were by comparison not so badly off" (Roediger [1991] 1999, 49). These fears led the Workers Alliance initially to oppose the creation of the federal works program and then to attack the WPA's "slave," "coolie," "scab," and "starvation" wage rates

(*Workers Alliance,* August 15, 1935, 1–2; September 1, 1935, 2; October 2, 1935, 2; see also Salmond 1967, 114–16; Ziskind 1940). Hence, the movement did not simply demand public relief or work for the unemployed; it also struggled to define the social relationship created by work relief programs. Implicit in denunciations of forced work were claims that WPA workers were free, independent, rights-bearing citizens (or at least entitled to that status) and that the state should treat them accordingly. Moreover, as the language of these claims indicates, this was a racialized status. Even as the Workers Alliance struggled to unite the unemployed across ethnic and racial lines, it appealed to an "American standard of living" that had historically rested on "white men's wages" (R. Smith 1993, 559–60; Barrett and Roediger 1997, 6, 22–23; Roediger [1991] 1999).

Once the WPA was firmly established, the Workers Alliance dropped its initial opposition to the policy and instead mobilized to support, improve, and expand it. By the late 1930s, however, retrenchment and conservative reforms of the WPA revived old fears and led to renewed ambivalence about the works program. Workers Alliance leaders now defined the WPA in opposition to forced labor, but they pointed to forced labor programs in other countries as a vivid reminder of what the WPA could become if the unemployed were not vigilant. "Perhaps in Germany labor battalions fit the social and political scheme of things," Workers Alliance president David Lasser wrote in 1939. "But we have no use for them here. And to tell free Americans that they must work at any wages fixed for them, or starve; to tell them that they will go to jail if they strike; to tell them that they are just 'reliefers' and have no rights, is an impossible situation" (*Work,* July 15, 1939, 6). Invoking a discourse of industrial democracy that was resurgent during the New Deal and inscribed in the 1935 National Labor Relations Act (Plotke 1996, 98–99), the Workers Alliance insisted that citizenship rights, including the right to organize, had to be extended to WPA workers to prevent the program from becoming "a system of forced labor in which the workers have no rights," a "situation abhorrent to democracy" (Franklin D. Roosevelt, Papers as President, Official File, File 2366).[9]

## Defining WPA workers in opposition to paupers

The Workers Alliance defined the status of WPA workers not only in opposition to forced labor but also in opposition to those receiving "direct relief," or, on "the dole." The partial separation of the works program from direct relief and the strong desire of relief workers to avoid the taint of pauperism facilitated these efforts. Public opinion data and anecdotal evidence strongly suggest that the unemployed preferred work relief to direct relief, not only because work relief provided greater economic security, but also because it provided more social respect (Hopkins 1936, 109–10; *Work,* October 22, 1938, 12; June 3, 1939, 6; Bakke 1940a, especially 298–99; Bakke 1940b, 257, 278, 280–81, 284, 395–96, 410–11; D. Howard 1943, 411, 811–19). According to Nels Anderson (1935), this preference was a key motivation behind the political mobilization of the unemployed: "[T]he unemployed . . . say in effect: 'We claim the rights of citizens. We want work instead of relief; and we have a right to work. . . .' " (365). "Living on relief is a frowned-upon way of living. . . . That is why they band together and demand work" (367).

Resistance from the Workers Alliance to the pauperization of WPA workers tapped into and reflected this desire to avoid the stigma of direct relief. *The Professional Worker,* the newspaper of the Berkeley-based Union of Professional Workers, an affiliate of the Workers Alliance, noted with concern in 1937 that "non-relief workers . . . will be eliminated [from WPA rolls]. . . . Relief status in this program [WPA] was to have been incidental, but the inadequacy of the Congressional appropriation coupled with the need for retrenchment are making pauperdom the standard by which to determine eligibility for WPA work" (March 1, 1937). Another issue of *The Professional Worker* condemned increased investigations by social workers as "the first step in requiring pauperdom as a requisite for work relief" (March 22, 1937).

By 1939, Workers Alliance leaders were calling for the complete separation of the WPA from traditional forms of public relief and the elimination of degrading policy features associated with the latter, including resource exhaustion (destitution) as a condition of eligibility. "It is not fair nor good Americanism," Lasser testified to the Senate Appropriations Subcommittee in 1939, "to make it necessary for [the] unemployed to exhaust their last resources before they are entitled to employment on this [WPA] program. . . . This makes the program more of a relief program, it provides less morale and self-respect for those who work on it" (*Work,* July 1, 1939, 2). Indeed, Lasser continued, "we believe that the W.P.A. program suffers from its characterization as a relief program, and because the W.P.A. workers are called 'relief workers.' We believe it should not be necessary for decent self-respecting Americans to reach the relief level before they can secure useful work and earn wages on a works program." Without the relief test, Lasser emphasized, the WPA "would not stigmatize the workers as 'relief clients'" (U.S. Congress. House 1939–40, 34). While conceding that need should continue to be an important consideration in certifying the unemployed for WPA jobs, the Workers Alliance insisted that it be determined "without forcing the unemployed to go through the relief rolls" (*Work,* May 7, 1938, 1).

Conservative proposals to further decentralize the federal works program (described below) also raised fears about the pauperization of WPA workers. As late as 1945, Lasser warned that reintroducing the works program in a decentralized form would render it indistinguishable from traditional poor relief; workers would become "charity recipients as clearly marked as though they were at the county almshouse" (Lasser 1945, 215).[10] To resist decentralization was to resist pauperization, but it was also to claim a largely masculine and white standard of citizenship most completely realized in social insurance (Mettler 1998). To their credit, Lasser and other leaders of the Workers Alliance struggled to pull up all relief recipients to this national standard even as they resisted efforts to push down WPA workers to the lower standard of public assistance.

Although the Workers Alliance defined WPA workers in opposition to direct relief recipients, this opposition should not be overstated. Even when the majority of Workers Alliance members were WPA workers, the movement never defined itself exclusively as a movement of the "productive" or "employable" unemployed. On the contrary, the Workers Alliance also recruited and worked to organize direct relief recipients and consistently fought to upgrade and expand direct relief for unemployables. "Whether you are a W.P.A. worker, a direct relief client, or an unemployed worker who can't get either a W.P.A. job [or] relief, your place is with us," the Workers Alliance proclaimed in a 1937 pamphlet (Workers Alliance of America 1937, 5–6). Insisting that "the Federal government makes its contribution only in part when it provides a work program," the Work and Security Program adopted by the alliance's 1938 national convention called for restoration of federal responsibility for general assistance (that is, in addition to categorical assistance to the aged, the blind, and dependent children). Moreover, the Work and Security Program insisted that neither work nor a means test should be a condition for receiving public assistance or unemployment insurance (*Work,* November 5, 1938, 2). However, the Workers Alliance saw direct relief as a necessary evil at best: "The unemployed want work, not relief" (Workers Alliance of America 1937, 19). "Our purpose in organizing these victims of unemployment," Lasser declared in 1939, "is to help secure work—and, failing that, enough income to provide security for themselves and their families" (Lasser 1939, 3).

Why didn't the Workers Alliance define WPA workers more exclusively in opposition to other categories of relief recipients? As noted above, the social organization of the WPA made sharp distinctions difficult, and the contradictory position of WPA workers led not only to a desire for social distance from paupers, but also to a sense of grievances shared in common. Moreover, the organizational structure of the Workers Alliance itself discouraged a sharper and more exclusive division between WPA workers and other categories of relief recipients. Until the Communist-led Unemployed Councils merged with the Workers Alliance in 1936, the American Communist Party built organizations "around the 'project level,' inclusive of all [WPA] workers on a given [work] project or job location" (Seymour 1937, 40–41). Since recipients of direct relief were not employed on WPA work projects, Communist organizers relegated them to separate organizations. In contrast, the Workers Alliance "advocated inclusion of WPA workers in existing 'neighborhood locals'" (40–41). These neighborhood locals incorporated WPA workers on the basis of where they lived rather than worked, thereby bringing WPA workers "together with direct relief members" (40–41). Rather than isolating WPA workers, this form of organization encouraged fraternization, solidarity, and a shared identity among the various categories of relief recipients. Indeed, following the merger of the Communist Unemployment Councils with the Workers Alliance in 1936, "Socialist leaders defend[ed] 'neighborhood' as against 'project locals'" on precisely these grounds. The project local, they argued, "separates WPA workers from direct relief members and therefore weakens a bond that should be close, not only because both groups are unemployed, but because WPA jobs have not been secure and transfer back to relief is frequent" (Seymour 1937, 45; see also *Workers Alliance*, March 1, 1936, 3).[11]

### WPA workers as government employees

RECOGNITION FROM THE STATE. As the Workers Alliance sought to distance WPA workers from forced laborers and (to a lesser extent) paupers, it simultaneously struggled to equate them with wage-earning employees and to elicit recognition of such claims from political authorities. In a letter to Roosevelt outlining the demands of the Workers Alliance on the eve of the 1936 presidential election, Lasser wrote: "While programs such as WPA exist, the WPA workers want . . . the opportunity to do a useful day's work and receive decent pay. They want to be taken out of the twilight zone in which they are not on relief and yet have an essentially relief status. We WPA workers want to work and be treated as workers."[12] The Workers Alliance continued to press for such recognition after Roosevelt's landslide reelection. In reference to the first meeting between Lasser and Roosevelt in March 1937, a Workers Alliance pamphlet declared: "This conference between President Roosevelt and the spokesman of the Workers Alliance meant that . . . the administration now recognizes that the W.P.A. workers are its employees and are therefore entitled to a hearing, just as workers in private industry are entitled to meet with their employers" (Workers Alliance of America 1937, 13).

The Workers Alliance also acquired elite support in the classification struggle from WPA administrators, who made similar claims about the status of WPA project workers. These claims were shaped by the ideological commitments and perhaps the professional backgrounds that WPA administrators brought to their jobs, but they also sprang from the threat that an increasingly conservative and hostile policy environment posed to the continuation of the program.[13] Early on, conservative opponents of the WPA sought to decentralize administration of the program or replace it altogether with less costly direct relief (D. Howard 1943, chap. 30, chap. 31). Republican congressmen began to push these competing policies as early as 1936 with the support of organizations like the U.S. Chamber of Commerce and the National Economy League (D. Howard 1943, 740n2; 746–47, 760–61). As congressional conservatives gained strength in the late 1930s, WPA officials found themselves embroiled in a political struggle between those who favored continued federal control over the program (limited though it was) and those who opposed federal control (D. Howard 1943, 746). Concerned about the survival of their program, WPA officials mounted a nationwide public relations campaign on its behalf. Between 1938 and 1940, top-level WPA officials, including Corrington Gill, Francis C. Harrington, Harry Hopkins, Howard Hunter, and Aubrey Williams, defended federal control and administration of the WPA on a variety of grounds in testimony before Congress, radio addresses to the public, newspaper articles, and WPA press releases (Gill 1940; D. Howard 1943, 735, 740, 743–44, 747–48, 759, 761–62, 766, 768). For example, in an address delivered to the United States Conference of Mayors in 1939 and subsequently printed in the *Congressional Record,* WPA Commissioner Harrington urged his audience to continue "our

work program along its present lines." The real aim of competing policies, he warned, was "the prospective abandonment and destruction of
the work program within the various States" since decentralization would
allow state governments to "stop providing work and merely distribute
Federal funds as a dole to the able-bodied unemployed." Harrington concluded that the WPA in its existing form, "though doubtless capable of
improvement, seems to me worth preserving and defending" (U.S. Congress 1939, 2259). Echoing these sentiments, President Roosevelt himself
made a public "plea for the continuance of federal operation of the WPA
program" in April 1939 (D. Howard 1943, 759).

As part of their public relations campaign, WPA administrators tried
to distinguish the program sharply from competing policy proposals.
WPA officials argued that their program allowed the unemployed to earn
their benefits, thereby preserving their dignity and self-respect. "The
least we can do for our unemployed," explained Harrington, "is to make
it possible for them to support their families by their own toil" (*Work,*
October 12, 1939, 4). Similarly, in a press release dated June 21, 1939,
Harrington announced:

> It is a fundamental fallacy to discuss a work program in terms of 'relief.' I can
> see no reason why any of us should attempt to ignore the fact that work is
> work. I have no sympathy for the notion that work becomes something other
> than work when it is provided by public agencies to the needy unemployed.
> In a relief program, needy persons receive, for good reasons, a portion of the
> wealth produced by other members of the community, but without giving any
> immediate return for it. In the work program, needy persons perform useful
> services for the community, and are paid for those services. There is a good
> short English word for this arrangement—the word work, and I propose to use
> it. The WPA is a work program. (Harry L. Hopkins, Container 35)

At the same time, WPA officials identified competing policies with the
degradation of traditional poor relief. In 1938, for example, Aubrey Williams testified to Congress that local control of unemployment relief was
undesirable because "many local relief systems are . . . cruelly inhumane."

> Their methods . . . involve nailing people's names upon the doors of the town
> hall, publicizing them as the town's paupers, reducing this whole thing to a
> level where you force people to accept the status of pauperism, denying them

votes in many places, forfeiting their citizenship. These are ordinary unemployed people, honest citizens willing and able to work for a living. They ought not to be subjected to these things.

I believe with all my heart . . . that if you were to throw responsibility back to the States, it would not be many months until you would have this on the level of soup kitchens and paupers' oaths. You would have forfeiture of citizenship and of self-respect that no Congress could stand. (D. Howard 1943, 766)

In a press release dated May 15, 1939, WPA administrator Howard Hunter defended the WPA on similar grounds while linking his defense explicitly to the threat of policy competition: "People who propose to abandon the WPA for a system of grants-in-aid to States do not really want the unemployed to work at real wages on useful public projects. What they want is an idle labor pool, given a charity pittance. They do not like a program of work which enables these temporarily unemployed people to maintain their self-respect, bargaining power and rights of citizenship" (quoted in D. Howard 1943, 761–62). Hunter went on to suggest that earlier federal attempts to administer relief through grants to states had failed in part because "there was no recognition given to the fact that these newly unemployed people that had grown in numbers from a handful to millions, were a new kind of poor people. They were not the same old paupers who had normally been handled under the archaic poor-laws in most of our states. They were able-bodied unemployed citizens—the same kind of people as you and I" (quoted in D. Howard 1943, 768).

Thus, by the late 1930s, WPA officials and the Workers Alliance were making converging claims about the classification of WPA workers. Partly to ward off competing policy proposals from the right that would have resulted in a radical decentralization or termination of the WPA, WPA officials insisted that the program's clients were citizen-workers rather than paupers. Of course, WPA officials did not speak for the federal government as a whole. Because of divisions among New Dealers and the insistence of conservatives inside and outside of Congress that WPA workers be treated as "reliefers," official recognition of WPA workers as government employees remained partial, inconsistent, and uneven. Nevertheless, even the limited recognition provided by WPA officials undermined conservative efforts to stigmatize WPA workers as recipients of public charity. As Bourdieu (1991, 223) points out, this kind of official recognition is crucial in classification struggles, for the effectiveness of "the act of social magic which consists in trying to bring into existence the thing named . . . is directly proportional to the authority of the person doing the asserting."

RECOGNITION FROM LABOR UNIONS.   While pressuring government officials to recognize WPA workers as employees, the Workers Alliance tried at the same time to forge organizational ties to the American Federation of Labor (AFL) and the Congress of Industrial Organizations (CIO). These ties were intended not only to obtain material advantages but also to confirm the movement's claims that WPA workers were employees rather than paupers. Workers Alliance leaders sent representatives to AFL conventions, called upon AFL leaders to endorse the Workers Alliance and its program, and urged solidarity between the employed and the unemployed (*Workers Alliance*, October 2, 1935, 2; Karsh and Garman 1961, 94–95). In addition, delegates to the Alliance's 1937 national convention authorized the movement's national executive board to associate more closely with the CIO without changing "the principles of our organization" or "its attitude to those members of organized labor who find themselves in unions still affiliated to the A.F. of L." (Seymour 1937, 50–51; cf. *Work*, September 24, 1938, 6–7). By July 1937, negotiations for affiliation on fraternal or organizational lines with the CIO were in progress. According to Alliance officials, the movement sought "closer association with the C.I.O. organizationally so that we may become an integral part of that great movement."[14]

Despite these efforts, the Workers Alliance obtained only limited recognition and support from labor unions in its struggle over the classification of WPA workers. AFL leaders were willing to cooperate with and support the Workers Alliance to maintain union wage standards on WPA projects, but (like the government) the AFL was internally divided over the classification of relief workers. Although some lower-ranking AFL officials were willing to organize relief workers, national AFL policy prohibited the issuance of union charters to relief workers' organizations (Edelman 1961, 173; Lorence 1996, 85, 105–6, 113, 131). Cooperation between the Workers Alliance and the CIO was more extensive. By the late 1930s, the Workers Alliance and CIO locals (sometimes joined by AFL locals) had set up unemployment committees in cities throughout the nation to plan and carry out joint actions on issues of common concern (Karsh and Garman 1961, 95; *Work*, April 23, 1938, 1, 3, 9, 10; May 21, 1938, 2; July 2, 1938, 3; July 30, 1938, 9; September 24, 1938, 6–7;

December 3, 1938, 10). In addition, the Workers Alliance, the AFL, and the CIO jointly supported many of the strikes and protests against WPA retrenchment in 1939. Nevertheless, the Workers Alliance failed to establish "a united relationship on a national scale" with the CIO (*Work,* September 24, 1938, 6–7).

The attempts of the Workers Alliance to forge alliances with existing labor unions were complicated by fears of job displacement. These fears were especially strong among public employees and the employees of contractors performing public work: "The fact that W.P.A. workers were often mixed with the [local project] sponsors' regular employees sharpened the need for a careful check on their activities. Another difficulty that arose was the hostility of the permanent civil servants toward relief coworkers. It was feared that W.P.A.-paid persons might not only displace the regular governmental employees but also would lower existing wage standards" (Millett 1938, 118). These concerns about the WPA may have reflected workers' experiences with locally administered forms of work relief (Gill 1940, 388). Brown (1940, 378–80) notes "a rapid development of work relief under local auspices" between 1938 and 1939 "in at least one-third and probably one-half of the states." She estimates that in the fall of 1939, local governments employed between eighty thousand and one hundred thousand relief workers. These local relief workers often "displaced regular city or county employees" and were paid extremely low wages on the old budgetary deficiency basis.

Furthermore, recognition of WPA workers as employees often led to organizational rivalry and competition with existing labor unions, making it a mixed blessing for the Workers Alliance. As Karsh and Garman (1961, 94–95) point out, "many AFL leaders viewed the jobless movement as potentially dual to the established organizations of labor." Even after the AFL endorsed the Workers Alliance in June 1936, AFL president William Green continued to warn that "the Alliance should not function as a competitor." Although the Workers Alliance denied that it was "a substitute or rival to the trade union movement," fears about competition were not confined to the AFL leadership. Workers Alliance leaders harbored similar concerns about the AFL, especially as cooperation with trade unions increased (see also *Workers Alliance,* "Second January Issue" [1936], 2; March 1, 1936, 3). Turf conflicts also emerged between the Workers Alliance and the CIO. Although the two groups tried to manage these conflicts by hammering out ad hoc agreements at the local level, the Workers Alliance was not entirely satisfied with these compromises and remained wary of the CIO's ambitions (*Work,* April 23, 1938, 3, 10; May 21, 1938, 12; June 18, 1938, 3; September 24, 1938, 6–7; Karsh and Garman 1961, 95). According to a 1938 report from its national executive board, the Workers Alliance failed to establish "a united relationship on a national scale" with the CIO, because the CIO set conditions the Workers Alliance found unacceptable. CIO leaders reportedly informed their counterparts in the Workers Alliance that "a basis of unity might be worked out if the Alliance were demolished and local groups chartered as local industrial unions of the CIO" (*Work,* September 24, 1938, 6–7). In short, by recognizing WPA workers as employees, labor unions helped to create the very group they sought to organize while simultaneously triggering a struggle with the Workers Alliance over what Bourdieu (1991) calls the delegation of symbolic power, in other words, a conflict over who would have the power to speak for and represent the group. This conflict hindered the Workers Alliance and labor unions from working together to impose their shared vision and division of the social world on others.

RECOGNITION FROM WPA WORKERS.    Besides seeking recognition from the government and labor unions, the Workers Alliance also encouraged WPA workers to see themselves as employees and make claims on that basis. Movement leaders adopted appropriate organizational forms and modes of protest early on, embracing the "labor union model" even though other organizational forms were available (Lorence 1996, 81–82).[15] In addition, despite considerable disincentives against WPA strikes, a high proportion of the protest events organized by the Workers Alliance took the form of walk-out or sit-down strikes (Ziskind 1940, 175–78, 181; D. Howard 1943, 223, 225–27). Although strikes were arguably less effective against the WPA than private industry (since the WPA was a nonprofit enterprise, its profitability could not be threatened by work stoppages), these modes of protest fulfilled an important dramaturgical function. Like the labor union model of organization, strikes served as framing devices to establish and confirm the collective identity of WPA workers as employees, define their relationship to the state as one of contractual exchange for wages, and contravene efforts to define them as recipients of public charity. These practices also shaped the political alliances that organized WPA workers were likely to form, orienting them primarily to the labor movement rather than other groups such as women's or consumers' organizations.[16]

By 1939, the Workers Alliance had hundreds of thousands of members and reportedly "exercise[d] an influence over about one and a half million" (U.S. Congress. House 1939–40, 93–95; "Seeks WPA Legislation," *New York Times,* September 25, 1939). While it is difficult to determine how many WPA workers (or even Workers Alliance members) shared the views of the movement's leaders and spokesmen, there is evidence that many came to regard themselves as government employees by the late 1930s, increasingly looking upon the WPA "as work not significantly different from that in the private sector, except for the important assumption that public employment was a temporary phenomenon" (Lorence 1996, 81). Hopkins (1936, 114) noted that WPA workers considered themselves to be "working for the Government" and not "on relief any more." This view is also confirmed by newspaper accounts. According to a 1939 editorial in the *Philadelphia Record,* WPA workers "don't regard a W.P.A. job as charity. They don't want charity. They want work, consider their job IS work" (reprinted in *Work,* January 28, 1939, 7). Finally, public opinion data also provide evidence that many WPA workers came to see themselves as government employees. In July 1939, a Gallup poll asked the American public whether they approved of dropping WPA workers who went on strike for more than five days from the WPA rolls. Gallup (1999, 169) reported that 74 percent of respondents approved, and 26 percent disapproved. Gallup also broke down its findings by income (upper, middle, and lower), which revealed that approval was positively correlated with income. Among those with lower income, approval dropped to 62 percent. Among WPA workers only, the approval rate dropped still further to 49 percent. "In explaining reasons for their attitude," *The New York Times* reported in an article about the poll, "voters who approve the firing of WPA strikers say, chiefly, that WPA is a 'form of charity' and the workers should be 'glad of what they get.' On the other hand, voters who disapprove the dismissals argue that 'all workers should have the right to strike' and that the WPA 'doesn't give them enough money anyway.'"[17] These data suggest that by 1939 WPA workers were significantly less likely than others to approve punitive action against their strikes because they were more likely to consider themselves employees.[18]

## Citizenship as a Stake and Resource in the Classification Struggle

The citizenship status and rights of WPA workers were very much at stake in the struggle over their classification. At the time of the Great

Depression, "the constitutions of fourteen states [still] denied the franchise to paupers" (Piven and Cloward 1977, 42). As millions of workers became relief recipients and new federal relief programs proliferated, uncertainty arose over how and to whom these pauper exclusion clauses applied. Nevertheless, some public officials tried to enforce the laws, and their efforts were accompanied by new proposals to curb or eliminate relief recipients' citizenship rights (Keyssar 2000, 237–244). In 1934, for example, the New York State Economic Council (NYSEC), "an association of anti-New Deal businessmen headed by prominent Republicans," drew national attention with a proposal to disfranchise "'all persons receiving public unemployment relief . . . during the period in which such relief is being received'" (239). Likewise, in 1938, "a small group of conservative, anti-New Deal women, calling itself the Women's Rebellion, . . . approach[ed] the attorneys general in states with pauper exclusion laws and demand[ed] that the laws be enforced" (241–42). That same year, the Brooklyn Chamber of Commerce proposed a new constitution for New York that would have stripped public relief recipients of their right to vote (*Work,* April 9, 1938, 1–2). In 1939, the Kansas Attorney General ruled that unemployed persons who resided in Civilian Conservation Corps (CCC) camps were ineligible to vote in his state, and the California state legislature considered prohibiting recipients of public assistance from paying dues to unemployed organizations (*Work,* January 14, 1939, 9; June 3, 1939, 3; June 17, 1939, 3). Although most Americans opposed these efforts to restrict relief recipients' political rights, a substantial minority supported the idea. A survey conducted by NYSEC showed that "35 percent of all candidates for the legislature and Congress in New York" supported its proposal to disfranchise relief recipients, and "national support was sufficiently widespread that a countermovement was launched to promote a Twenty-second Amendment to the United States Constitution to guarantee the citizenship rights of the unemployed" (Keyssar 2000, 234). According to a 1938 poll conducted by the American Institute of Public Opinion, nearly one in five Americans (19 percent of those polled) supported disfranchisement of the unemployed on WPA and relief, and a similar survey conducted in 1939 by *Fortune* revealed that 18 percent of Americans favored disfranchisement of relief recipients (*Work,* October 22, 1938, 1; Keyssar 2000, 243).

In this context, one of the principal aims of the Workers Alliance was to establish "the unemployed of America as citizens with full rights under our Constitution, the same as any other group" (*Work,* September 24,

1938, 6). In 1936, the movement's newspaper warned that "big business interests have time and again urged the disenfranchisement of relief workers, and in a number of localities attempts to deny WPA workers the right to seek office are now being made." As "the nationwide
spokesman for the unemployed and relief workers," the Workers Alliance pledged to fight "vigorously any attempt to encroach upon the democratic rights of the unemployed, whether they be native or foreign-born,
Negro or white" (*Workers Alliance,* "First July Issue" [1936], 4). Similarly, at its 1938 national convention, Lasser proudly described his movement's struggle against the "conviction in high places that unemployed
people had no rights." The Workers Alliance, he declared, had not only
improved the "economic position" of the unemployed by "winning work
and relief," but also "established our right to a voice in our legislative
counsels" (*Work,* September 10, 1938, 5). Determined to protect these
achievements, the convention adopted a Work and Security Program that
vigorously opposed any "curtailment of citizenship rights to those receiving unemployment or public assistance" (*Work,* November 5, 1938, 2).

The Workers Alliance sought not only to protect the existing rights of
WPA workers but also to expand them. Just as labor unions tried to create
"a sort of secondary industrial citizenship" for workers in private industry through collective bargaining (Marshall [1949] 1964, 93–94, 111), the
Workers Alliance struggled to create something similar for WPA workers.
But what did industrial citizenship entail? What did it mean to be "treated
as workers," in Lasser's words? Shared cultural understandings of the
rights to which workers are entitled—the material and symbolic profits
that correspond to the name "worker"—are not inherent in the name or
category itself. The Workers Alliance developed these understandings by
transposing cultural schemas from federal employment, public works programs, and employment in private industry to the circumstances of WPA
workers.[19] Moreover, these cultural schemas were themselves changing.
As other New Deal institutions, such as the National Labor Relations
Board and the FLSA, granted new rights to workers in private industry,
the Workers Alliance demanded similar rights for WPA workers.

Federal employees were perhaps the most obvious reference group
with whom the Workers Alliance could demand parity. In 1936, for example, the Workers Alliance approvingly reported that "two [law] suits
to force granting of 26-day annual vacations to all WPA employees have
been filed in the United States District Court [in New York]. . . . The suits
are being filed under a federal law allowing all government employees

26 days annual vacation and sick leave, exclusive of Sundays and holi-
days" (*Workers Alliance*, "Second July Issue" [1936], 4). In its 1938 report
to the fourth national convention of the Workers Alliance, the Alliance's
WPA Labor Relations Committee called for vacation and sick leave privileges for WPA workers on similar grounds (*Work*, November 5, 1938, 4).

The Workers Alliance also demanded parity with employees of the
Public Works Administration (PWA). Unlike the WPA, which directly
hired, paid, and supervised workers, the PWA was essentially a financing
agency that channeled federal money to private contractors who hired
and supervised most of the program's employees (Meriam 1946, 358).
Congress did not require PWA employees to go through the relief rolls
like WPA workers, and it required employers to pay PWA employees the
prevailing wage from the program's inception (Edelman 1961, 173–74).
As early as 1935, Lasser criticized the federal works program for paying
PWA workers more than WPA workers, even though "the actual work
done might be the same in either case" (*Workers Alliance*, August 15,
1935, 1). Echoing claims that had long been made on behalf of women
workers (Kessler-Harris 1990, chap. 4), the Workers Alliance demanded
that equivalent work be remunerated with equal pay (*Work*, December 17,
1938, 2, 9). Furthermore, Lasser pointed out in 1939 that the WPA worker
suffered other humiliating indignities from which the PWA employee
was routinely spared: "He is 'examined' regularly, he takes 'tests' to see
that he is not an alien, or not plotting to overthrow the government, or
not earning 50 cents a week extra, or has not been on the program too
long" (*Work*, July 15, 1939, 6). By drawing analogies to PWA workers, the
Workers Alliance not only shaped WPA workers' understandings of what
constituted a just wage, but also what it meant to be treated as a worker
more broadly: Parity with PWA workers meant being positioned as a citizen whose rights extended into the workplace rather than as a dependent
person subject to pervasive surveillance and humiliating supervision.

The Workers Alliance also demanded parity with workers in private
industry. Early on, for example, Lasser rejected WPA wages as inadequate, because they were "unreasonably lower than those paid in comparable industries and the trades and professions from which WPA workers have been drawn."[20] Moreover, parity with workers in private industry
remained a constantly moving target as those workers won new gains
(Derber 1961; Babson 1999, 51–111). Successful labor struggles in private
industry inspired similar demands by relief workers on the WPA rolls,
particularly after the formation of the CIO in 1935 and its electrifying

victories against Goodyear in 1936 and U.S. Steel in 1937. According to a contemporary observer, "organization on work relief projects, previously a difficult task not successfully performed, would appear to have gained impetus from the C.I.O. 'organization' atmosphere" (Seymour 1937, 45).

As newly enacted New Deal labor policies encouraged and legitimized organizing efforts in private industry (Piven and Cloward 1977, 111–15; Skocpol 1980), the Workers Alliance invoked those same policies to encourage and legitimize protest among WPA workers. After Congress enacted the 1935 National Labor Relations Act, creating the National Labor Relations Board (NLRB) and making collective bargaining rights enforceable for workers in private industry, the Workers Alliance claimed the same rights for WPA workers. When Workers Alliance members demanded the removal of Pennsylvania WPA administrator E. N. Jones in 1936, for example, a spokesman for the protesters simply explained: "Mr. Jones has . . . violated the principles of collective bargaining as set forth in the Wagner labor disputes law" (quoted in *Workers Alliance,* "First January Issue" [1936], 4). When it became clear that the existing legislation would not cover WPA workers, the Workers Alliance demanded that Congress expand the law's protections (Workers Alliance of America 1937, 17; *Work,* March 19, 1938, 3; October 22, 1938, 5; November 5, 1938, 4).[21] As late as January 1940, Lasser complained to Roosevelt that "discrimination, intimidation, [and] terrorization of [WPA] workers for exercising their legal rights to organize is widespread and growing." He decried the "old tricks" being used against the Workers Alliance, including "tricks which would haul a private employer before the National Labor Relations Board" (Franklin D. Roosevelt, Papers as President, Official File, File 2366).

Like the NLRA, the applicability of the 1938 FLSA to WPA workers was also contested. As previously noted, the FLSA established a federal minimum wage and set maximum hours. Congress seemed to apply these standards to the WPA in the 1938 Emergency Relief Appropriation Act, which required the WPA to pay its workers the prevailing wage unless it was below the minimum set by the FLSA, in which case the federally mandated minimum would apply (*Work,* August 13, 1938, 1). However, upon closer inspection, the legislation was less clear. Conservatives argued that the standards established by the FLSA were largely inapplicable to WPA workers, because most were not engaged in interstate commerce and "because the occupations on WPA and those covered by the Wage-Hour Bill are 'not similar' to task" (*Work,* October 22, 1938, 3; see

FIGURE 4.1. The Workers Alliance demands industrial citizenship for WPA workers. ("Alas! Our Hands Are Tied," *Work,* August 13, 1938, 12)

also *Work,* December 3, 1938, 2). Nevertheless, both the leadership and the rank and file of the Workers Alliance used the FLSA as a benchmark for defining the rights of WPA workers and invoked its minimum-wage provisions to make claims on the government (Lasser 1938, 32; *Work,* October 22, 1938). "The Administration officials are always hammering away at the private enterprise or large corporate interests to shorten hours and pay good wages," Workers Alliance member B. W. Adams wrote in a letter to the movement's newspaper. "Why does not the Administration agencies of PWA and WPA take some of their own advice?" (*Work,* September 10, 1938, 12; see also *Work,* September 24, 1938, 6).

When the WPA announced wage increases for 500,000 workers in thirteen states in 1938—in part because of political pressure on the Roosevelt administration to resolve inconsistencies between WPA wage policies and the FLSA—the Workers Alliance hailed the increases as a victory (*Work,* May 21, 1938, 3; "WPA Raises Wages in South on Order of the President," *New York Times,* June 27, 1938; *Work,* July 2, 1938, 1; U.S. Congress. Senate 1939, Part II, 369–72). The movement welcomed the wage increases, not only because they expanded its potential resources (derived largely from dues payments), but also because of the social meanings inscribed in them. When the Workers Alliance first began agitating for higher WPA wages, Lasser noted, "the papers scoffed at our attempt to 'raise the wages of those on relief.' Reliefers, it was said, were being given charity. They should be thankful for whatever was bestowed!" Now, Lasser wrote, "we can appeal to WPA workers with pride and assurance. The justice of our cause has been vindicated" (*Work,* July 16, 1938, 5). Thus, these rights claims were linked to the categorization of WPA workers as employees—or, to be more precise, as employees that fell on the more privileged side of the gender and racial divide in the coverage of new U.S. labor standards. Congress excluded millions of workers who were deemed not to be involved in interstate commerce from the minimum wage provisions of the FLSA, and "women and nonwhite men fell disproportionately into those [excluded] categories, in agriculture, as domestics, and in retail and service work" (Mettler 1998, 188). Like struggles to resist further decentralization of the WPA, struggles to extend FLSA protections to WPA workers involved claims to a standard of citizenship that was largely white and masculine.

The Workers Alliance, WPA officials, and their conservative opponents understood that political and industrial citizenship were not only stakes in the struggle over the classification of relief recipients, but also forms of political capital that relief recipients could use to appropriate other valuable resources. According to the Workers Alliance, disfranchisement was intended to curb "the growing economic and political power of the organized unemployed" (*Work,* October 22, 1938, 1; see also *Work,* April 23, 1938, 12). Indeed, many of the disfranchisement proposals described above emerged in states like New York and California where the Workers Alliance was strongest, and the attempt in

California to prohibit relief recipients from paying dues to unemployed organizations was explicitly aimed at the Workers Alliance. Whether real or exaggerated, the "power of the organized unemployed" was a major concern of the movement's opponents. When the Workers Alliance sent two thousand delegates on a job march to Washington, DC, in July 1937, Virginia congressman Clifton Woodrum warned that "the WAA [Workers Alliance of America] would soon be a powerful political organization unless the federal government shifted relief back to the states and the municipalities. If this did not happen, said Woodrum, no congressman would be able to win reelection without acceding to WAA demands" (Folsom 1991, 421). A year later, in the kind of language once used to describe the GAR, an alarmed *New York Times* editorial (August 12, 1938) warned that the Workers Alliance was becoming "an enormous pressure group compared with which the American Legion and the farm lobbies may pale into insignificance."[22] Such fears had "deep historical roots." Americans who favored decentralization of relief or disfranchisement of relief recipients "saw the nightmare that [English jurist William] Blackstone had characterized and [American jurist James] Kent had predicted: an army of 'dependents' marching to the polls; a mass of propertyless men ready to seize the property of others (through taxes); men 'with no will of their own' who easily could be manipulated by a clever politician or demagogue." They echoed these eighteenth- and nineteenth-century fears when they denounced Roosevelt as "a masterful and manipulative politician" who used "federal tax dollars to build a national political machine" kept in power by "a permanent, government-supported army of indigents" (Keyssar 2000, 240–241).

## The Conservative Countermobilization

Like the Union League's claims on behalf of freedpeople during Reconstruction, the Alliance's claims on behalf of WPA workers provoked a strong negative reaction. Conservatives insisted on treating WPA workers as "reliefers" rather than employees, rejected their demands for industrial citizenship, and tried to limit their political mobilization. This countermobilization was most effective when conservatives linked it to broadly shared concerns about corrupt patronage politics and political subversion. As we have seen, the Workers Alliance invoked liberal-contractual considerations about work, mobilizing WPA workers as independent, rights-bearing citizens whose socially useful labor entitled them to a decent wage and public respect. By shifting the classification struggle from liberal-contractual considerations about work to civic republican considerations about corruption and disloyalty, conservatives effectively challenged the civic status and worthiness of WPA workers.

The conservative countermobilization against the WPA and the Workers Alliance coincided with the emergence of an increasingly powerful coalition of Republicans and Southern Democrats in Congress in the late 1930s (J. Patterson 1967; Porter 1980; Brinkley 1995; Brown 1999, chap. 3). After the 1938 election increased Republican strength in Congress, "conservative Democrats held the balance of power between liberals and conservative Republicans, and they used it to prevent completion of the structure of the Second New Deal" (Rauch 1944, 284).[23] In this shifting political context, three congressional committees spearheaded attacks on the WPA and the Workers Alliance with widely publicized and highly ritualized investigations.[24] The first was the 1938 Senate Campaign Expenditures Committee, popularly known as the Sheppard Committee after its chairman, Texas Democrat Morris Sheppard (U.S. Congress. Senate 1939; J. Patterson 1967, 246–247). By linking the WPA and the Workers Alliance to patronage, the Sheppard Committee made it easier to attack them as sources of civic corruption that threatened cherished republican ideals like independence and the subordination of private self-interest to the public good.[25] The second was the 1938 House Special Committee on Un-American Activities, known as the Dies Committee after its chairman, Texas Democrat Martin Dies (U.S. Congress. House 1938; Ogden 1945).[26] The third was the 1939 House Subcommittee on the Works Progress Administration, composed of members of the powerful House Appropriations Committee, and known as the Woodrum Committee after its leader, conservative Virginia Democrat Clifton Woodrum (U.S. Congress. House 1939–40; Macmahon, Millett, and Ogden 1941, 289–290).[27] The Dies and Woodrum committees questioned the loyalty, allegiance, and Americanism of WPA workers who mobilized through the Workers Alliance to expand their rights and, by extension, they questioned the loyalty of the WPA officials and New Dealers who facilitated such mobilization. Like freedpeople had been sixty years earlier, politically mobilized WPA workers were classed as anti-citizens whose civic inclusion and political participation threatened to pollute the Republic in various ways. All three committees sought to expose this pollution and rectify it through greater supervision and disciplining of relief workers.

The work of the Sheppard, Dies, and Woodrum committees, in turn, laid the groundwork for two key developments in the late 1930s that would profoundly influence the citizenship status and rights of WPA workers. On the one hand, investigations of the WPA encouraged conservative reforms of the program that strengthened its illiberal features and reinforced its resemblance to traditional poor relief. On the other hand, investigations of the Workers Alliance helped to delegitimize and disorganize the movement, alienate its elite allies among WPA officials and in the Roosevelt administration, weaken the commitment of existing members, hinder recruitment of new members, and prepare the way for government repression. Though only a fraction of WPA workers were ever members of the Workers Alliance, conservative attacks on the organization had repercussions for all WPA workers, because the Workers Alliance was their chief spokesman and advocate in the struggle over their classification. These two developments were closely linked, because structural reforms of the WPA were intended among other things to cripple the Workers Alliance, and because reform of the WPA and repression of the Workers Alliance were both grounded in the same anti-Communist vision and division of the social world. While the conservative assault on the WPA and the Workers Alliance did not deprive WPA workers of citizenship, it did curtail their citizenship rights, restrict their capacity to mobilize, and hinder their efforts to convert their political capital into greater social spending for the unemployed.

## The campaign against patronage

As with the Freedmen's Bureau, allegations that the WPA provided patronage in return for votes aroused hostility to the policy and encouraged demands to curb the political activity of its clients. Although allegations of patronage were exaggerated, such concerns were not unfounded. "Patronage had been dealt some blows by the civil service reforms of the 1910s," but it "remained a concern of elites into the 1930s. . . . The United States entered the Depression with federal, state, and local administrations only partially delivered from the patronage system" (Orloff 1993b, 270, 273). Moreover, "at a time when polls found nearly 90 percent of Americans in favor of civil service and with the League of Women voters engaged (from 1934 to 1936) in a massive publicity campaign on its behalf, Roosevelt was restoring patronage politics. . . . He increased the number of patronage positions not so much to control the Democratic Party as to achieve ideological control of the government" (Schudson 1998, 229–30). Not surprisingly, in this context, the WPA was occasionally used for patronage purposes. Thus, critics of the program did not invent these abuses, but they did serve as moral entrepreneurs who created or enforced rules against patronage and publicly brought infractions to the attention of others. Due to their efforts, debate over the WPA, like debates about other social spending programs, "took place against the backdrop of a continuing struggle . . . between those who favored civil service reform and patronage politicians" (Orloff 1993b, 274; see also Keyssar 2000, 241).[28]

Concerns about patronage came to a head when the 1938 Sheppard Committee investigated "charges of undue political activity in connection with the administration and conduct of the Works Progress Administration" (U.S. Congress. Senate 1939, Part I, 39). The investigation was triggered by three developments. First, beginning in early 1938, the President intervened in several Democratic primaries (including some in the South) to oppose anti–New Deal candidates. Although Roosevelt's attempt to purge the party of its conservatives was largely unsuccessful, it "heightened fears that [Harry] Hopkins was using the WPA to build a national political machine" (Leuchtenburg 1963, 269). Indeed, "several New Deal liberals either seeking renomination or attempting to unseat conservative incumbents [in the 1938 midterm election] were accused of manipulating the WPA to enhance their prospects at the polls" (Porter 1980, 110). For example, G. Tom Hawkins, a candidate in the 1938 Kentucky primary, complained that WPA rolls were padded before the primary, in effect purchasing voters "as slaves with public funds or taxpayers' money" (quoted in U.S. Congress. Senate 1939, Part II, 73–74). (This language not only underscored WPA workers' alleged political dependency on party bosses, but, like denunciations of "slave wages," reflected the historically racialized development of American citizenship.) Although the Sheppard Committee's investigation failed to sustain most of these charges, it did find some evidence of "unjustifiable political activity" in several states where "funds appropriated by the Congress for the relief of those in need and distress" were "diverted from these high purposes to political ends" (U.S. Congress. Senate 1939, Part I, 39). In its final report, the committee recommended new legislation to prohibit elected officials from "promising work, employment, money, or other benefits in connection with public relief" ( U.S. Congress. Senate 1939, Part I, 39–41; see also "WPA Chief Sounds Appeal for Votes," *New York Times,* June 28, 1938; *Work,* July 16, 1938, 2; U.S. Congress. Senate 1939, Part I, 32; Part II, 191–93, 363–69).

Second, the National Civic Federation accused "'high relief officials' in Washington" of "fostering the growth of Communist-led unions of WPA workers," including the Workers Alliance, "in the hope that their agitation would influence Congress to increase Federal relief appropriations."[29] On the eve of the 1938 election, public remarks by WPA officials added credibility to these charges. Hopkins told the press that at least 90 percent of WPA workers would "vote for Roosevelt without being told" to do so (U.S. Congress. Senate 1939, Part II, 372), and Aubrey Williams urged WPA workers to organize and use their votes to "keep our friends in power" (quoted in "WPA Chief Sounds Appeal for Votes," *New York Times,* June 28, 1938; *Work,* July 16, 1938, 2; U.S. Congress. Senate 1939, Part II, 363–69) The Sheppard Committee construed these remarks as "a form of coercion contrary to public policy and the spirit of our Government" (U.S. Congress. Senate 1939, Part I, 32), and its final report recommended new legislation that would forbid relief officials from using "their official authority or influence to coerce the political action of any person or body" (U.S. Congress. Senate 1939, Part I, 39–41; see also U.S. Congress. House 1939–40, 78, 114).

Third, the Workers Alliance, having already elected some of its leaders to local offices, boasted that it could deliver half a million votes in the 1938 election and announced that it would raise a $50,000 campaign fund from WPA workers to elect congressmen who would increase relief expenditures. In response, the Sheppard Committee warned the Workers Alliance that it was illegal to collect campaign contributions from federal employees under the 1883 Pendleton Civil Service Act, and it threatened to refer the matter to the United States Department of Justice if the Workers Alliance proceeded with its plan.[30] In addition, the committee's final report recommended new legislation that would ban political contributions by relief recipients or administrators (*Work,* July 16, 1938, 2–3; U.S. Congress. Senate 1939, Part I, 32, 39–41; Part II, 363–69, 372–77; Keyssar 2000, 241).[31]

The Workers Alliance denounced the Sheppard Committee's investigation as part of the larger assault (described above) on the political rights of WPA workers, relief recipients, and the unemployed. In newspaper articles, public speeches, and letters to Senator Sheppard, Workers Alliance leaders accused the committee of deliberately trying to "gag three million WPA workers" and "deprive them" of their "citizenship rights" (*Work,* September 10, 1938, 1–2).[32] The committee's attacks, they added, "encouraged the reactionary organizations who have always resented our right to vote openly and insistently demand that we be *utterly* disfranchised" (Lasser 1938, 14–15; original emphasis).[33] Hence, the Workers Alliance insisted, the Sheppard Committee served the interests of the powerful and privileged. According to an editorial in the movement's newspaper *Work,* "these tory interests . . . harbor a deep and abiding fear of the awakening political power of the 16,000,000 jobless. These reactionaries . . . look with fear and trembling upon the fact that the unemployed are organizing, and voting according to their own social and economic interests" (*Work,* July 16, 1938, 12; cf. Lasser's comments in U.S. Congress. Senate 1939, Part II, 365). Finally, the Workers Alliance pointed out that the 1883 Pendleton Act was only applicable if WPA workers were classed as federal employees, which legislators did selectively and inconsistently (U.S. Congress. Senate 1939, Part II, 375; "Alliance Ignores Fund-Raising Ban," *New York Times,* August 28, 1938). "Certainly the W.P.A. worker is not regarded as being an employee of the United States for any other purposes," Lasser objected, "and is not entitled and does not receive the various rights and privileges accorded to the employees of the Federal Government" (U.S. Congress. Senate 1939, Part II, 375). Following up on this point, Willis Morgan, the president of the Workers Alliance of Greater New York, demanded consistent treatment in a telegram to Sheppard:

> You forbid us to collect money from WPA workers on the ground that they are Federal employes [sic] and therefore fall under the provision of the Criminal Code dealing with campaign expenditures. If WPA workers are Federal employes, we call upon you to see to it that the Works Progress Administration immediately grant us all the rights and privileges of non-civil service employes. We expect to be immediately granted vacations, sick leave, seniority rights and so forth otherwise you are indulging in blatant hypocrisy and trying to deprive us of those political rights granted to us by Congress in the 1938 Relief Act. If we are Federal employes we want all their rights besides their responsibilities. If we are not we do not fall under your interpretation of the law. ("Alliance Ignores Fund-Raising Ban," *New York Times,* August 28, 1938)

As the Workers Alliance feared, the Sheppard Committee's investigation discouraged the political mobilization of WPA workers. The committee's selective recognition of WPA workers as government employees constrained the Alliance's capacity to mobilize economic capital and convert it into political capital, limiting its access to the political system. In

FIGURE 4.2. The Sheppard Committee as an attack on democracy by the powerful and privileged. ("A New 'Interpretation,'" *Work,* September 10, 1938, 12)

addition, by tainting the Workers Alliance with the stigma of corrupt patronage politics, the committee placed the movement's elite allies on the defensive. Backing away from his previous support for the political mobilization of WPA workers, Hopkins vowed to "deal swiftly and summarily with any proven charge of political coercion" (quoted in U.S. Congress. Senate 1939, Part II, 53), and he condemned the Workers Alliance plan to raise campaign funds on the grounds that WPA workers should be free of political pressures and that their wages were too meager for campaign contributions. President Roosevelt backed Hopkins, urging WPA workers to spurn appeals of the Workers Alliance for contributions, while George Kondolf, director of the WPA's Federal Theater Project in New York City, threatened to dismiss any employee who solicited political contributions for the Workers Alliance (*Work*, September 10, 1938, 1–2; Hopkins, Container 80, "Analysis of Cases Investigated by the Special Committee to Investigate Senatorial Campaign Expenditures Which Affect the Works Progress Administration," December 29, 1938).[34] Faced with the threat of criminal prosecution and deserted by its allies in the Roosevelt administration, the Workers Alliance eventually backed down and abandoned its plan to solicit contributions from WPA workers, though it vowed to continue its electoral campaign with other funds ("Workers Alliance Drops $50,000 Fund Plan to Elect Friends of Relief to Congress," *New York Times*, September 8, 1938; *Work*, September 10, 1938, 1; U.S. Congress. Senate 1939, Part II, 377).

## The campaign against Communism

CONGRESSIONAL INVESTIGATIONS, 1938–1940.   Like the Sheppard Committee, the Dies and Woodrum committees also tied social provision to civic virtue, but instead of linking the Workers Alliance to corrupt patronage politics, they branded it a treasonous and disloyal front for the Communist Party.[35] As Dies put it, "Moscow dictates to the Communist Party, and if the Workers Alliance is a part of this Communist organization, there you have a direct tie-up with Moscow" (U.S. Congress. House 1938, 822). Furthermore, both committees sought to uncover political ties between the Workers Alliance and the WPA in order to extend the stigma of Communist subversion to the latter as well. Woodrum, openly acknowledging that his committee was "interested in . . . what contact there is between the Workers Alliance and the W.P.A. and what influence, if any, it has had in its affairs" (U.S. Congress. House 1939–40, 24–25), asked committee investigators to estimate "the total amount of money per month that is being drawn from the Federal Treasury by these Communists" (1128). Dies similarly concluded that "public funds are indirectly being used to forward the movement of communism in the United States; that is the ultimate effect, that the taxpayers' money is being appropriated for the W.P.A., and Communists are entering this organization and dominating it, and using it to further their purposes" (U.S. Congress. House 1938, 433–35). In fact, Dies alleged that "thousands of

Communists and Communist sympathizers worked in the federal government," and his 1940 book *The Trojan Horse in America* claimed that the WPA was the Communist Party's "greatest financial boon" (Sexton 1991, 145–46). "The whole purpose" of these congressional investigations, Lasser ruefully concluded, was "to discredit the Workers Alliance and thereby render it less effective in leading the struggle to preserve and defend the WPA. It is really a compliment to our organization that these Congressional tories feel they must first destroy us before proceeding with the main purpose of their campaign—the destruction of WPA and eventually of the New Deal itself" (*Work,* May 20, 1939, 2).

The Dies and Woodrum committees did not create anti-Communist sentiment in the United States, nor did they conjure up or manufacture a Communist menace out of whole cloth. While allegations of Communist subversion were exaggerated, supported with flimsy or circumstantial evidence, and reliant on biased testimony, they did have some basis in reality, which made them credible. Communists were indeed active in the Workers Alliance, they tried to use the Alliance and the WPA to further their political aims, and the Communist Party did oppose the American system of government. Nevertheless, without the moral entrepreneurship of the Dies and Woodrum committees, an anti-Communist reaction might never have materialized. As Becker (1963, 132) points out, "rules do not flow automatically from values," and "the existence of a rule does not automatically guarantee that it will be enforced" (121). The degree to which others respond to a deviant act—including those political in nature—depends largely on the activities of the moral entrepreneurs who create rules, publicly bring infractions to the attention of others, and enforce rules. In these ways, moral entrepreneurs can mobilize new or alternative criteria of legitimacy, as conservatives did when they shifted public debate about the WPA and the Workers Alliance from dependency to disloyalty. Of course, like all moral entrepreneurs, congressional conservatives were not merely disinterested guardians of society's values; they were motivated by particular interests that prompted them to take the initiative as much as a fervent belief in the righteousness of their cause. And since congressional conservatives could not accomplish their aims without help, they did what moral entrepreneurs usually do—they "enlist[ed] the support of other interested organizations and develop[ed], through the use of the press and other communications media, a favorable public attitude" (139) toward the rules they sought to create and enforce. Since political taboos against communism were hardly new, there was ample historical precedent for this kind of symbolic work, most notably the Red Scare of 1919 to 1920.

Moral entrepreneurship is especially evident in regard to the Dies Committee. Although it received little attention at first, publicity began to grow in July 1938. By the time formal hearings opened in Washington in August 1938, committee chairman Martin Dies had "become front-page news," and "from that time on his name was destined to become a familiar one to millions of newspaper readers throughout the United States" (Ogden 1945, 48). By December 1938, public opinion polls "showed that three out of five voters were familiar with the work of the [Dies] Committee and that three out of four of those who knew of it believed that it should be continued. . . . Of all the voters polled, 74 per cent were in favor of continuing the investigation" (101–2). By March 1939, two out of every three voters reported having heard of the Dies Committee (114), and a subsequent poll conducted in December 1939 revealed that public support for the committee remained strong (173). Following the release of the Dies Committee's second report in January 1940, a poll revealed that "70 per cent of the people interviewed thought it more important to investigate Communism than Nazism, a definite change from the attitude expressed in the Poll a year before" (179).

According to Sexton (1991, 145), "Dies's assault on the labor-left" not only "overshadowed in scope and influence even the McCarthy hearings in the post–World War II years," but also helped to change "the country's political balance." In October 1938, Dies boasted that his committee had "destroyed the legislative influence of the Workers' Alliance" in Congress (Ogden 1945, 152). The Dies Committee probably influenced the outcome of the 1938 election as well, which proved to be detrimental to the WPA and disastrous for the Workers Alliance. The changing balance of power in Congress ensured, in turn, that the committee's work would continue. After receiving the Dies Committee's first report, Congress voted overwhelmingly in February 1939 to continue the committee and appropriated $100,000 for that purpose (113). Congress again voted overwhelmingly to continue the Dies Committee after the release of its second report in January 1940 (177–88). Even President Roosevelt was prompted to praise the committee in May 1940 as "one of his sources of information on fifth columnists" (208).

Although the Workers Alliance struggled to resist the stigma of treason and disloyalty, its efforts were largely ineffective. To begin with, greater financial resources and widespread and favorable press coverage allowed congressional conservatives to mold public opinion more effectively than the Workers Alliance. "At all times newspaper coverage . . . favored the [Dies] Committee and by means of it favorable public opinion had been built up" (Ogden 1945, 101–2). "We may justly claim," the Dies Committee announced in its January 1941 report to Congress, "to have been the decisive force in shaping the present attitudes of the American people towards the activities of the 'fifth columns' which aim at our destruction. Our work has been a type of public education whose importance cannot be exaggerated" (230). In contrast, the Workers Alliance had much greater difficulty disseminating its vision and division of the social world. In April 1938, for example, the circulation of its official newspaper *Work* reached only seven thousand (*Work,* April 23, 1938, 4). Moreover, conservative warnings of Communist subversion fell on fertile ground, because they were compatible with the preexisting political inclinations of diverse groups, including some factions within the Workers Alliance itself. Anti-Communism signified different things to different people: principled opposition to Stalin's murderous dictatorship, patriotic nationalism, hostility to organized labor and the political left, even (as the next chapter reveals) racial segregation and white supremacy. Anti-Communism was effective at realigning social forces into a new political formation, in part because diverse groups could rally around the same symbol while attributing different meanings to it (cf. Klatch 1987).

DISORGANIZING THE WORKERS ALLIANCE, 1938–1940. The symbolic work of the Dies and Woodrum committees helped to delegitimize and disorganize the Workers Alliance. As previously shown, the Workers Alliance represented WPA workers as employees and mobilized them on that basis. However, by reviving and strengthening the opposition between Americanism and Communism, the committees furnished a competing and cross-cutting source of social division that could be used to demobilize the movement. This symbolic reordering of the social world challenged how the Workers Alliance represented and constituted WPA workers, not with the stigma of pauperism, but with the stigma of un-Americanism. Rather than defining WPA workers as paupers in opposition to the citizen-worker, congressional conservatives now sought to construct WPA workers—at least those who mobilized under the aegis of the Workers Alliance to make contentious claims on the government—as internal enemies in opposition to the citizen-soldier. This alternative mode of ritual degradation increasingly resonated with the American public as social turmoil at home (the sit-down strike wave of 1936–1937) and abroad (the outbreak of war in Europe in 1939 and the fall of the French Republic in 1940) intensified concerns about national security.[36]

At the same time, anti-Communism threatened to destabilize another important identity upon which the unity of the Workers Alliance and the mobilization of WPA workers was based: the Popular Front against Fascism, which had temporarily brought Communists together with their erstwhile enemies for a limited set of aims. The Popular Front made possible the merger of the Communist Unemployment Councils with the Workers Alliance in 1936, and anti-Fascism continued to provide a basis for solidarity (tenuous though it was) between Communists and non-Communists in the Workers Alliance until the late 1930s. For the Communist Party's leadership and inner circle, of course, the Popular Front was a tactical move orchestrated by the Comintern, not a principled rejection of the party's earlier opposition to liberal democracy. Nevertheless, the Popular Front was partly successful in disarticulating old political formations and, by brokering new alliances, reworking their elements into new formations. As Howe and Coser (1957) point out, "the Popular Front strategy, particularly through its appeal to the emotions of anti-fascist fraternity, was extremely successful in this country. It was the first approach the CP had found that enabled it to gain a measure of acceptance, respectability, and power within ordinary American life" (325, see also 362–63, 385). Although the American Communist Party never gained a mass membership, more Americans came to see the party as a legitimate political partner during the Popular Front phase than in any other period in American history (cf. Karsh and Garman 1961, 103–4; Klehr 1984). Ultimately, however, the Popular Front proved to be fragile and short-lived, and by the late 1930s, conservatives were once again successfully opposing what the Popular Front had tried to align: Americanism and Communism.

Conservative efforts to disrupt the Popular Front's vision and division of the social world, though modestly successful before 1939, were greatly facilitated by a nonaggression pact between Nazi Germany and the Soviet Union in August 1939. The pact helped conservatives to equate Communism and Fascism as two sides of the same coin, equally threatening to Americanism. "The Nazi-Soviet Pact," wrote Workers Alliance organizer Eli Jaffe, "gave new impetus to the anti-communist feeling latent in many Americans, notably the policy-makers in Washington. . . . It became increasingly clear to me that [the] Nazi-Soviet Pact was providing a green light to anti-communist witch hunters" (Jaffe 1993, 91). At the same time, the pact—and the American Communist Party's resulting about-face when it came to support for the New Deal and vigilance against the threat of fascism—disillusioned and alienated many former allies, sympathizers, and "fellow travelers" (Howe and Coser 1957, 391–92; Klehr 1984, 400–9).

Within the Workers Alliance, these developments led to intensified conflicts over the movement's collective identity. At stake in these struggles was the internal delegation of symbolic power: not only how the movement would define itself, but also who within the movement would have the power to do so. Of course, the conflicts within the Workers Alliance between Communists and non-Communists did not emerge *de novo*. Rather, conservative efforts to reorder the social world exacerbated existing tensions and provided additional incentives for non-Communists to break with their Communist colleagues. Beginning in 1938, these tensions erupted into a series of splits, purges, and defections that quickly spread from New York to Alabama, Georgia, Idaho, Illinois, Ohio, Maryland, New Jersey, and Wisconsin. Although the Workers Alliance took steps to contain internal conflicts and prevent the hemorrhaging of members and leaders, matters worsened the following year as the Nazi-Soviet non-aggression pact widened rifts within the organization. Prior to the pact, the Workers Alliance had been strongly anti-Fascist, prompting the movement to endorse the principle of collective security at its 1938 national convention. By 1940, however, the Workers Alliance had taken a strongly antiwar position and insisted on maintaining strict American neutrality in the face of Nazi aggression in Europe. These antiwar and isolationist sentiments alienated members like Lasser who felt that the Workers Alliance should condemn the Soviet Union, side with the Allies, and support American rearmament "as steps toward fighting Fascism" (Folsom 1991, 427–28). The Alliance's new antiwar line also seemed to confirm conservative charges that Communists controlled the Workers Alliance and were subservient to the Soviet Union. Many non-Communist members who opposed the Alliance's antiwar and isolationist stance expressed their dissent through exit rather than voice. While these defections may partly have been an attempt to evade delegitimation and political repression, they also indicated that the collective identity of some Workers Alliance members no longer lined up with the movement.[37]

ANTI-COMMUNIST LEGISLATION AND WPA RETRENCHMENT, 1939–1940.
Unlike the Workers Alliance, congressional conservatives were members
of what Fraser (1992) calls a "strong public," which could make binding
and authoritative decisions as well as deliberate, and they used their growing influence within Congress to inscribe new principles of social division
and new criteria of legitimacy into law. Congressional conservatives began to institutionalize their vision and division of the social world in 1939,
when Congress passed legislation that explicitly excluded Communists
from participation in the federal works program ("City WPA to Purge
1,000 Nazis, Reds," *New York Times,* June 23,1940; Macmahon, Millett,
and Ogden 1941, 336; D. Howard 1943, 119, 138–39, 303–24; Meriam
1946, 369–70; Sexton 1991, 148; Rose 1994, 112–14, 137–38nn56–57).
These anti-Communist provisions were intended, among other things, to
limit the political activity of WPA workers and restrict the use of relief
expenditures for such activities.[38] As one member of the Woodrum Committee, quoted in *The New York Times* on condition of anonymity, explained:

> Unless there is assurance given us that the Workers Alliance will no longer be
> welcomed at the WPA as the representative of the workers, then I shall pro-
> pose an amendment to the law forbidding payment of relief funds to those who
> are members of the alliance. I take the position that since the testimony of the
> alliance officials shows clearly that it leans toward communism, which has as
> its aim the overthrow of our form of government, then the funds of this gov-
> ernment should not continue to go into the hands of those who are themselves
> Communists, or who by their membership in this organization give force to its
> aims. Of course, the proposal to deny relief money to members of this orga-
> nization is a drastic one. I do not feel that the workers ought not to organize.
> But I am convinced that, if in organizing they place themselves under the ban-
> ner of an organization whose executive committee is honeycombed with Com-
> munists, they cannot in good conscience protest against the action of members
> of Congress in upholding their oaths to support the Constitution and to wage
> a relentless fight against enemies, both within and without this country. Many
> of us have known for a long time that the alliance was furthering—whether
> consciously or otherwise—the aims of the Communist party by preying upon
> those in want, organizing them and gradually spreading the Communist cloak
> over a large segment of those who must ask the government for subsistence. I,
> for one, do not propose to let money appropriated for relief go into the coffers

of an organization such as the alliance. ("Drive to Bar Reds from WPA Activity Forms at Capitol," April 20, 1939)

Congress supplemented its anti-Communist reforms of the WPA with broader and more far-reaching legislation to repress the political influence of the Communist Party more generally. These measures included the 1939 Hatch Act, an anti-patronage measure arising from the work of the Sheppard Committee that also prohibited federal employment of Communists, and the 1940 Smith Act, which made it a crime to advocate the overthrow of the U.S. government (Macmahon, Millett, and Ogden 1941, 287; Leuchtenburg 1963, 270; Porter 1980, 109; Sexton 1991, 148–49; Jaffe 1993; Brinkley 1995, 141; Schudson 1998, 229–30). By means of these reforms, congressional conservatives not only purged Communists from the works program, but also severely hindered the organizing efforts of the Workers Alliance (*Work,* November 9, 1939, 4; February 15, 1940, 1; June 20, 1940, 1; "City WPA to Purge 1,000 Nazis, Reds," *New York Times,* June 23, 1940; "3 on WPA Who Denied Being Reds Indicted for False Swearing in Loyalty Affidavits," July 19, 1941). Despite the Alliance's denials that it advocated the overthrow of the government, Lasser complained in 1940, "WPA workers on the projects are told . . . that *they cannot belong to the Workers Alliance and work on the WPA program*" (Roosevelt, Papers as President, Official File, File 2366, emphasis in the original). For unemployed workers who depended on WPA employment to survive, such threats were a powerful disincentive against participating in radical political activity.

Fears of Communist subversion were related to suspicion of foreign-born workers, who were historically viewed as social carriers of un-American radicalism. As a result, the anti-Communist campaign of the 1930s defined Americanism in ways that conflated allegiance with nationality. The investigations of the Woodrum and Dies committees, in particular, helped link these meanings. Committee hearings examined whether the membership of the Workers Alliance included foreigners "who owe their allegiance to the Russian Government" (U.S. Congress. House 1939–40, 124–25; it accepted foreigners without regard to their political views); whether its leaders traveled to the Soviet Union or other countries (133–34; they did); whether it was "part of an international organization" or sought to establish a "world-wide organization of the unemployed" (67; 103–4; Lasser denied the allegations); and whether it received "any [financial] contributions from any foreign source" (67; its

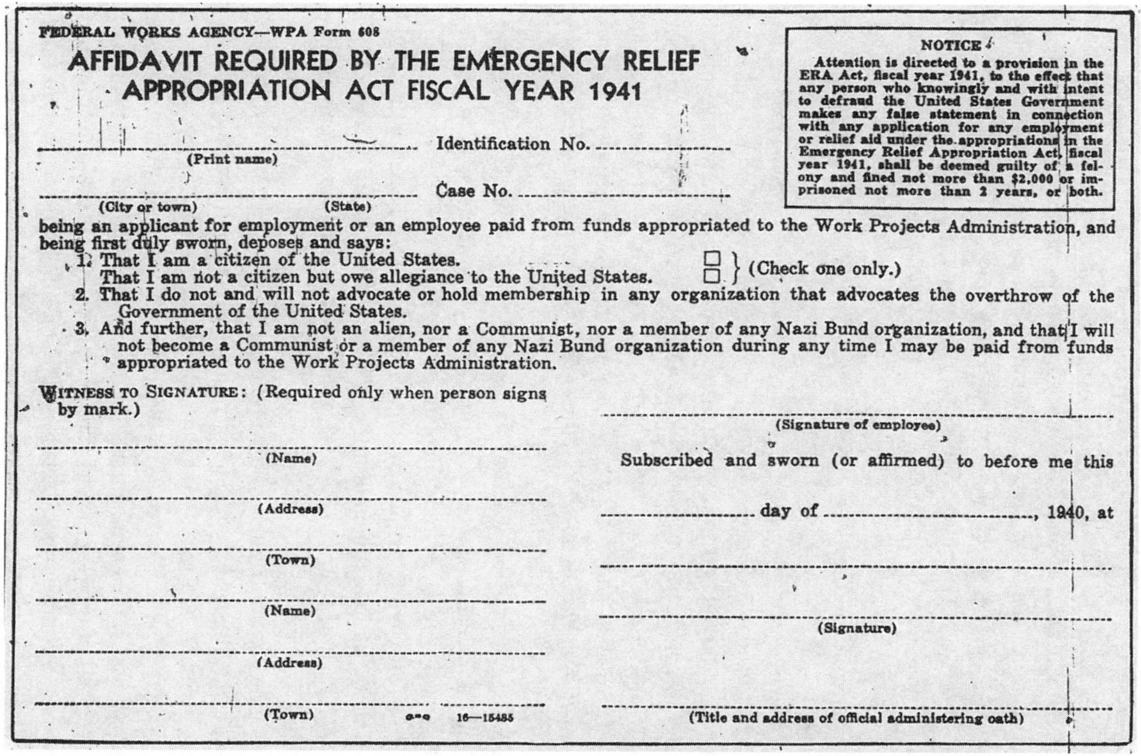

FEDERAL WORKS AGENCY—WPA Form 608

## AFFIDAVIT REQUIRED BY THE EMERGENCY RELIEF APPROPRIATION ACT FISCAL YEAR 1941

Identification No. _____

................................. ........................
(Print name)

................................. ........................
(City or town)        (State)

Case No. _____

being an applicant for employment or an employee paid from funds appropriated to the Work Projects Administration, and being first duly sworn, deposes and says:

1. That I am a citizen of the United States.
2. That I am not a citizen but owe allegiance to the United States. ☐ } (Check one only.)
   That I do not and will not advocate or hold membership in any organization that advocates the overthrow of the Government of the United States. ☐
3. And further, that I am not an alien, nor a Communist, nor a member of any Nazi Bund organization, and that I will not become a Communist or a member of any Nazi Bund organization during any time I may be paid from funds appropriated to the Work Projects Administration.

WITNESS TO SIGNATURE: (Required only when person signs by mark.)

................................. ........................
(Name)

................................. ........................
(Address)

................................. ........................
(Town)

................................. ........................
(Name)

................................. ........................
(Address)

................................. ........................
(Town)

16—15485

................................. ........................
(Signature of employee)

Subscribed and sworn (or affirmed) to before me this

................. day of ................., 1940, at

................................. ........................

................................. ........................
(Signature)

................................. ........................
(Title and address of official administering oath)

FIGURE 4.3.  Affidavit to purge Communists from WPA rolls. (*New York Times*, June 23, 1940, 13)

leaders insisted that it did not). Suspicion of foreigners also appeared in congressional investigations of the WPA. The Woodrum Committee, for example, called witnesses who complained that the WPA kept aliens on work projects while firing veterans (268, 650–56). In fact, Congress had already begun to restrict the eligibility of aliens for federal unemployment relief before the Dies and Woodrum committees started their investigations. The investigations simply legitimized existing restrictions as anti-Communist measures while encouraging new ones. Moreover, the 1936, 1937, 1938, and 1939 Emergency Relief Appropriation Acts not only limited aid to aliens, but increasingly gave preference to veterans (Millet 1938, 65; D. Howard 1943, 523; Meriam 1946, 381–82; Rose 1994, 112–14, 137–38nn56–57). While the unemployed had struggled since the inception of the WPA to define themselves as worthy citizen-workers—"to work and be treated as workers," in Lasser's words—it was the icon of the citizen-soldier that Congress increasingly held up as deserving. This icon could only be defined in opposition to a foreign and subversive threat against which the nation had to be defended. Hence, the preference given to veterans went hand in hand with the exclusion of aliens (because they were foreigners) and Communists (because they were perceived as dangerous proponents of an alien philosophy and tools of a hostile foreign power).[39]

By stigmatizing the Workers Alliance, delegitimizing the WPA, and calling into question the civic worthiness of WPA workers, anti-Communist measures fostered retrenchment of the federal works program. In the late 1930s, congressional conservatives succeeded in restricting eligibility and curtailing funding for the WPA (Porter 1980; Rose 1994, 111–14). A key strategy was to limit WPA employment and make it more precarious. The Emergency Relief Appropriation Act of 1939 instituted a new eighteen-month rule, which required those on the WPA rolls who had been employed for eighteen months or more to relinquish their WPA standing and remain off the rolls for sixty days, after which time they could be reconsidered for WPA employment if recertified as eligible.[40] Although the eighteen-month rule was devastating for WPA workers, "efforts of the [Roosevelt] administration and others to mitigate the rigor of the eighteen-month clause did not deter Congress in 1940 from re-enacting essentially the same provision" (D. Howard 1943, 522–23; see also *Work*, February 15, 1940, 1; September 28, 1939, 1). As the next chapter shows, these measures were not simply a response to falling unemployment in the late 1930s; retrenchment of the WPA was also motivated by political concerns. While conservatives justified the eighteen-month rule as a way of spreading around WPA employment to as many people as possible (thus implicitly acknowledging the inadequacy of relief expenditures), they also intended the rule to defund the Workers Alliance, discredit the Alliance's claims to guarantee WPA employment to its members, hinder its organizing tasks, and dissuade WPA workers from participating in unsanctioned political activity that might potentially jeopardize their chances of recertification (*Work,* June 17, 1939, 2; July 1, 1939, 7; July 29, 1939, 7; Kelley 1990, 157; Amenta 1998, 141, 222).[41]

DISSOLUTION OF THE WORKERS ALLIANCE AND TERMINATION OF THE WPA, 1940–1942.   The internal purges and defections that weakened the Workers Alliance in the late 1930s continued into the early 1940s, reaching the organization's highest ranks. Herbert Benjamin, the most prominent Communist in the Workers Alliance, resigned as national secretary-treasurer in January 1940, reportedly to remove "the most obvious target of the red-baiters." While dramatic, this gesture ultimately failed to protect the Workers Alliance, and "attacks by reactionaries" remained "intense" (Folsom 1991, 428–29). In June 1940, David Lasser resigned as president of the Workers Alliance, taking most of the non-Communist members of the national executive board with him and vowing to form "a new national unemployment movement which will be 100 per cent American and free of isms" (Roosevelt, President's Personal File, File 7649). Writing to Roosevelt, Lasser predicted that the unemployed, freed from Communist influence, would readily respond to the president's calls "to preserve our freedom and democracy. . . . As loyal, patriotic Americans, we are ready to do our part in defense of our homes, our shores and our institutions against attack or aggression" (Roosevelt, Papers as President, Official File, File 2366). Lasser's new movement (aptly named the American Security Union to underscore its double commitment to economic and national security) was short lived and ineffectual, and the Workers Alliance, crippled by external repression and internal schisms, was dissolved by its new leaders in 1941 ("Workers Alliance Disbanded in U.S.," *New York Times,* November 20, 1941). While the organizations that represented and mobilized WPA workers declined, the conservative bloc in Congress maintained and then increased its strength. Democrats made no substantial gains in 1940 (despite Roosevelt's reelection) and lost seats in 1942. With congressional attacks on public employment programs mounting, President Roosevelt agreed to the termination of the

WPA in December 1942. The program ceased operations in 1943, eliminating the clients whose classification had been so contested for the past
seven years.

## Summary and Conclusion

Struggles over the fate of the WPA and the status and rights of its clients
reveal striking parallels to earlier struggles over the Freedmen's Bureau.
In both cases, these struggles were part of an ongoing and more general
conflict over the meaning and boundaries of citizenship in the United
States; the struggles reflected enduring civic ideals and related anxieties
about patronage, disloyalty, and dependency (a status that was itself an
object of contention in each case); and the claims of welfare-state clients
revealed the contested intersection of citizenship rights with class, gender, race, and national allegiance. Furthermore, like struggles over the
Freedmen's Bureau, struggles over the WPA were partly the product of
large-scale, historically specific social forces that unsettled the structure
of citizenship and dislocated millions of Americans, rendering their status and rights uncertain. Yet the WPA, like the Freedmen's Bureau, did
not merely reflect the broader citizenship struggles of which it was a part;
it also contributed to those struggles through its policy feedback effects.
First, the WPA created a new group of welfare-state clients out of a disparate mass of unemployed and declassed workers. Because of the program's innovative nature, their status and rights relative to other clients in
the welfare field were initially undefined. In particular, it remained to be
determined whether WPA workers would be treated like recipients of traditional poor relief or sharply distinguished from them. Second, because
of conflicting policy goals and institutional features, the WPA treated its
clients in a contradictory manner, placing them in an intermediate position within the welfare field. As shown by comparison of the WPA to
public relief and public employment, the program sometimes treated its
clients in a liberal manner as autonomous, rights-bearing citizen-workers,
while at other times treating them in a nonliberal manner as dependent
persons subject to humiliating supervision and discipline. These contradictory practices provided a plausible basis for competing classificatory
claims. Third, policy competition also provided an impetus for struggles
over the classification of WPA workers. As shown above, proposals to decentralize the WPA or replace it with direct relief threatened the survival

of the program, prompting WPA administrators to downplay its relief aspects and emphasize its preservation of WPA workers' dignity and rights as citizens. While these efforts bolstered the claims made by the Workers Alliance, they also encouraged the program's opponents to challenge WPA workers' fitness for full citizenship. Fourth, claims to citizenship, including industrial citizenship, were contested, because citizenship itself was a valuable form of political capital that WPA workers could use to obtain access to other forms of capital.

The Alliance's struggle to obtain recognition of WPA workers as worthy, rights-bearing citizen-workers failed, at least in part, insofar as WPA workers' fitness for full citizenship remained contested. First, this is evident from public opinion. To be sure, most Americans opposed disenfranchising WPA workers (in that respect, their citizenship rights remained secure) and supported continuation of the WPA, even during the late 1930s. However, probably due to criticism of the WPA, the percentage of Americans who favored continuation of the program fell (from 79 percent in 1937 to 73 percent in 1939), and it was significantly less than the proportion of Americans (about 90 percent) who preferred work relief to direct relief (Schiltz 1970, 114–17). Moreover, while New Deal labor legislation was expanding the rights of workers in private industry, public opinion data suggest that most Americans opposed any extension of industrial citizenship to WPA workers. As noted earlier, a 1939 poll showed broad public support for the dismissal of striking WPA workers. Similarly, in a nationwide poll conducted in January 1940, 79 percent of those polled said that WPA workers should not be allowed to form unions, and 85 percent said that WPA workers should not have the right to strike ("Unions in the WPA Opposed by Voters," *New York Times,* January 10, 1940; *Work,* January 18, 1940, 3). In short, public opinion seems to have supported continuation of a works program, but one shorn of the valued policy features that the Workers Alliance demanded. Relative to workers in private industry—or at least those on the more privileged side of the gender and racial divide in the coverage of new U.S. labor standards—relief workers remained second-class citizens.

Second, the demise of the Workers Alliance itself in 1941 is evidence of failure. The classification struggles in which the Workers Alliance was engaged shaped its collective identity in ways that hindered its capacity to mobilize resources, thereby contributing crucially to the movement's collapse (Goldberg 2003). Thus, the demise of the Workers Alliance was in part an outcome of the classification struggles in which it was involved and the failure of the movement to impose a favorable vision and division of the social world.

Third, the institutional structure of the WPA provides further evidence of the failure of relief workers to avoid the stigmas of dependency, corruption, and subversion, all of which were understood to be incompatible with full citizenship. A successful classification struggle results not only in the internalization of new classificatory schemes in the minds of social agents but also in their objectification in institutions. To distinguish WPA workers from paupers, the Workers Alliance needed to distinguish the WPA more sharply from traditional work relief. As we have seen, it was unable to do so. The rhetoric of WPA administrators notwithstanding, the program was never entirely divorced from local and conventional forms of poor relief, nor did Congress eliminate the stigmatizing policy features it shared with traditional poor relief. On the contrary, institutional reforms of the WPA in the late 1930s reinforced those features of the program that treated WPA workers as dependent persons in need of discipline and supervision, pushing an already ambiguous program in a less, rather than more, liberal direction.

## CHAPTER FIVE

# "A different class from the ordinary relief case"

## Old Age Insurance, 1935–1949

W hy did WPA workers fail to obtain recognition as honorable, rights-bearing citizens who earned and deserved public aid? This question can be answered by comparing their struggle to a roughly similar but more successful one. Fortunately, a suitable case exists: in 1935, Congress established a contributory Old Age Insurance (OAI) program, popularly known as social security, which is comparable to the WPA in many respects.[1] Like the WPA, OAI was a policy innovation that created a new group of clients in the welfare field. Since the program's "basic principles and financing remain[ed] unsettled" in its early years (Campbell 2003, 83), the availability of competing organizational models created considerable uncertainty about the status and rights of OAI recipients relative to the clients of other policies. In this respect, OAI recipients and WPA workers found themselves in similar situations. Furthermore, the timing of OAI and the WPA (both created in 1935) make them comparable cases; implementation of the policies and the ensuing struggles over the status and rights of their clients were roughly contemporary, which makes it easier to control for contextual variables that may account for the successes or failures of those struggles.

OAI and the WPA are also comparable insofar as both policies were designed to maintain income that had been lost due to old age or unemployment. These risks were not so different as they might first appear. While today, the elderly are more likely to be seen as deserving of long-term governmental support than the able-bodied unemployed, the worthiness of the elderly is in no way inherent. Similar to worthiness of unemployed persons, it was socially constructed and contested (Powell, Branco, and Williamson 1996, 58–93).

Opponents of old-age pensions invoked many of the same criticisms that were made against the WPA; they argued that pensions undermined self-reliance, encouraged idleness and dependency, required excessive taxation and a wasteful and inefficient government bureaucracy, were so-cialistic and un-American, and could be better provided through the pri-vate sector. Advocates for the elderly and the unemployed also invoked similar arguments. Reformers argued that the insecurity of both groups was caused not by personal failings, but by structural forces beyond indi-vidual control. In fact, they attributed the risks of old age and unemploy-ment to the same forces. "Pension reformers argued that the immediate cause of old-age insecurity was to be found in the 'spectre [sic] of un-employment' and the discriminatory industrial hiring and firing practices that were responsible for it." As one pension advocate put it, "American industrial concerns . . . flung older workers, like 'less effective machines, onto the scrap heap'" (Powell, Branco, and Williamson 1996, 70–71). From this perspective, the elderly were not so much worthier than the un-employed as they were a subset of them.[2] Furthermore, like WPA officials and the Workers Alliance, pension reformers invoked the negative sym-bolism of the poorhouse to rally support for new income-maintenance policies, and they defined the benefits of those policies as compensation for recipients' contributions to society rather than public charity (Pow-ell, Branco, and Williamson 1996, 61–66, 76–77). Making this parallel ex-plicit, New Dealers argued that "the right to work for the non-elderly" was "a corollary to an earned right to a pension" (Brown 1999, 72). Since OAI and the WPA both tied income support to work, past or present, the structure of the policies facilitated these claims. From 1935 into the 1940s, policy advocates used this link between income support and work to le-gitimize OAI and the WPA, to distinguish them from traditional poor relief and public assistance, and to ward off competing policies.[3] Finally, supporters presented both policies as self-sustaining. In the case of OAI, payroll taxes funded the program, which eliminated the need for financ-ing from general tax revenues (J. Zelizer 1998, chap. 2). In the case of the WPA, policymakers designed "self-liquidating" public works projects "to recover project costs over time, much as a loan was repaid" (Brown 1999, 51; see also 52–53, 57–58). Like the link between benefits and work, this,

FIGURE 5.1. Old-age pensions as an honorable alternative to pauperism. (Cartoon by John Miller Baer, *American Labor Legislation Review,* June 1930)

too, was meant to distinguish the policies from conventional poor relief and their recipients from paupers.

Even if OAI and the WPA were comparable in the 1930s, it is generally assumed that the fates of the policies diverged as a result of America's entry into the Second World War. According to this view, wartime mobilization (and later, postwar prosperity) eliminated mass unemployment, making WPA jobs unnecessary. These conditions are presumed to explain the demise of the Workers Alliance, the movement's failure to rid the WPA of its relief aspects, and the eventual termination of the program. In contrast, though the war halted the expansion of OAI and caused it to stagnate through the 1940s (Sparrow 1996), old age remained a permanent risk presumably necessitating, or at least making possible, the continuation and eventual expansion of OAI.

Despite some truth to this argument, it does not adequately explain why struggles to preserve and upgrade the WPA were less successful than those concerning OAI. First, retrenchment of the WPA and repression of the Workers Alliance began in the late 1930s, when unemployment was still high (in fact, it rose sharply during the recession of 1937–1938) and before America's entry into the war. Thus, the war did not so much halt the expansion of the works program as reinforce political trends that had emerged beforehand. Second, there was no tight connection between the unemployment rate and political efforts to retrench the WPA. To be sure, falling unemployment provided conservatives with an expedient justification for retrenchment, but so too did rising unemployment from 1937 to 1938, which conservatives blamed on the "anti-business" policies of the Roosevelt administration (Rauch 1944, 295). Although conservative efforts to restrict relief spending enjoyed more success after 1938, the efforts began earlier.[4] Third, as shown in the previous chapter, retrenchment and disciplinary reforms of the WPA were motivated by political concerns as well as changing economic conditions. Fourth, economic recovery did not necessitate the termination of the WPA. Because many New Dealers believed that unemployment would again become a serious problem after the war ended, they planned to make the works program a permanent feature of the postwar welfare state (Harvey 1989, 18–19, 106–7; Amenta 1998, 199, 237–40).[5] Furthermore, the WPA could have been reoriented to solve new problems other than mass unemployment. Some congressmen "clearly envisaged an increase in projects undertaken by the WPA to further the national defense," and some leaders of the unemployed movement sought cooperation with national defense agencies to promote the training of the unemployed (D. Howard 1943, 132–33; see also *Work,* November 23, 1939, 1; Rauch 1944, 314–15, 326; Roosevelt, President's Personal File, File 6794). In fact, by 1942 the WPA was already "becoming more of a work agency to carry on defense and war projects than a work relief agency. Projects were then selected more on the basis of their value for the major task of the nation than on the basis of their suitability for furnishing employment to unemployed on relief rolls" (Meriam 1946, 403). These considerations suggest that economic recovery alone does not account for why WPA workers were less successful than OAI recipients in their classification struggles. While changing economic conditions undoubtedly affected the fate of WPA workers, the impact of those conditions was politically mediated.

The divergent fates of OAI recipients and WPA workers therefore remain in need of explanation. Despite the similarities between the cases, efforts to legitimize OAI and class its clients as rights-bearing citizen-workers were more successful. As shown in the previous chapter, the civic worthiness of WPA workers remained contested throughout the program's existence. Critics of the policy portrayed "the WPA worker . . . as entirely lazy and unwilling to work for private industry" (Rauch 1944, 249), and allegations of patronage and Communist subversion in the late 1930s reinforced the perception of WPA workers as dependent wards of the state who required discipline and supervision. In contrast, OAI recipients came to be widely regarded as self-supporting individuals who earned their benefits (Schiltz 1970; Cates 1983; Berkowitz 1991, chap. 3; Tynes 1996; Mettler 1998). Why did attempts to class OAI recipients as independent, rights-bearing citizen-workers succeed while similar efforts on behalf of WPA workers failed? Why did tying income support to work legitimize social citizenship for OAI recipients but not for WPA workers? To explain these divergent outcomes, this chapter compares the two policies and the political struggles that emerged over the classification of their respective clients.

## The Struggle over the Civic Classification of OAI Recipients

*Policy competition and the classification of OAI recipients*

The mechanism of policy competition contributed crucially to the classification of OAI recipients as independent, rights-bearing citizen-workers. The 1935 Social Security Act created the potential for such competition, because instead of establishing a unified system of social security as Harry Hopkins recommended (Perkins 1946, 284), it provided social security through two separate vehicles: social insurance and public assistance. Social insurance would eventually emerge as the primary vehicle for providing social security, and the struggle to achieve this primacy would have favorable consequences for the status and rights of OAI recipients, but this outcome was neither immediate nor inevitable. "Within six months of the Social Security Act's passage," the leadership of the Social Security Board (SSB) was privately "speaking of a growing race between conservative social insurance and [public] assistance as to which one would be embraced by the nation as the primary income-support model" (Cates 1983, 28). Although President Roosevelt, legislative leaders in Congress, and SSB officials favored social insurance, its fate remained uncertain.

According to Arthur Altmeyer (1966, 169–70, 187), the longtime chairman of the Social Security Board, the primacy of social insurance over public assistance was not fully secured until the 1950 amendments to the Social Security Act (cf. Derthick 1979, 273–74; Berkowitz 1995, 65–66, 69–70; J. Zelizer 1998, chap. 2).[6]

Why did the primacy of social insurance remain in doubt for so long? To begin with, OAI faced an unstable policy environment in the years immediately following enactment of the Social Security Act. "Despite a great deal of support for Social Security in the 1930s, the [OAI] program was very controversial, especially in the Congress, in the early years (unlike the relative complacency and acceptance of the 1950s and 1960s). . . . The passage of the Social Security Act in 1935 did not necessarily imply its long-term success; on the contrary, the early years were shaky ones for the program" (Tynes 1996, 55, 64). Republican presidential candidate Alf Landon called for its repeal in the 1936 election while congressional opponents delayed appropriations, attacked the program's financing system, and denounced OAI as a "step toward sovietizing our distinctive American institutions" (Tynes 1996, 58). Outside of Congress, the National Association of Manufacturers, the U.S. Chamber of Commerce, and the American Liberty League also attacked OAI. Some business firms refused to pay the new payroll tax as the Business Advisory Council and the National Association of Manufacturers mounted "a concerted 'employers' campaign' . . . against Social Security" (Tynes 1996, 67–68), including a legal challenge to the constitutionality of the Social Security Act (Cates 1983; Lieberman 1998, 90; Tynes 1996, 65). At the same time, many congressmen and a variety of groups outside of Congress favored competing policies that continued to threaten the primacy of social insurance throughout the 1940s: public assistance (especially Old Age Assistance [OAA]) or flat pensions (paid out of general revenues to all elderly persons, without regard to need). As Derthick (1979, 135) points out, "the public assistance alternative (which would have confined federal support to the needy, linked it to a means test, and left administration to state and local governments) was always more acceptable to the conservatives than a federally administered program that gave benefits independently of need." Flat-pension proposals came from a wide variety of sources, including the old age pension movement, the CIO, the Brookings Institution, Congress, Keynesian economists in the U.S. Department of the Treasury, the head of the Federal Security Agency (which supervised the SSB from 1939 to 1952), and even dissident actuaries within the

Social Security Administration itself (Altmeyer 1966, 11, 16, 108, 122–26, 128–30, 175, 181–83; Derthick 1979, 135–36, 159–60, 194–95, 217–22, 273–74; Cates 1983; Berkowitz 1991, chap. 3; Berkowitz 1995, 29–30, 54–55, 57, 62, 65–66; Sparrow 1996, 34, 44, 58; Mettler 1998, 93–97; J. Zelizer 1998, 67–68, 73–78; Hacker 2002, 86, 97–98, 136).[7]

As these remarks indicate, the status and rights of OAI recipients were shaped not only by struggles among elites but also by social movements from below. Perhaps the most notable was the Townsend movement, which pressured the federal government to provide a $200-per-month flat pension to every citizen sixty years of age or older (Holtzman 1963; Amenta and Zylan 1991; Amenta, Carruthers, and Zylan 1992; Amenta, Halfmann, and Young 1999; Mitchell 2000, chap. 4; Amenta, Carren, and Olasky 2005; Amenta 2006). Other pro-pension groups included Ham and Eggs in California and the National Annuity League in Colorado (Powell, Branco, and Williamson 1996, chap. 3–4; Mitchell 2000). These pro-pension groups were in some ways analogous to the Workers Alliance; they too sought to mobilize a mass constituency on behalf of new income-maintenance programs that would be distinguished from traditional poor relief and provide generous benefits as an earned right. Indeed, when the Workers Alliance began to push its own "$60 at 60" flat-pension plan in 1939 to win the backing of Townsend Plan supporters, the *New York Times* noted the potential for a "fusion of the political strength of two of the nation's most powerful pressure groups, the unemployed and the aged."[8]

However, because the Townsend movement favored a flat pension, its relation to OAI was quite different from that of the Workers Alliance to the WPA. As shown in the previous chapter, the Workers Alliance mobilized to support and expand the works program and push for improvements within it. These improvements, though never fully achieved, would have established and confirmed the status of WPA workers as full, rights-bearing citizens. In contrast, the Townsend movement viewed the Social Security Act as an undesirable competitor and obstacle to its own plan; it attacked OAI for paying inadequate benefits, "condemned [OAA] as constituting charity" (Holtzman 1963, 117), and criticized the legislation as a whole for "providing 'pauper's' benefits" (Amenta 2006, 94). To be sure, in the late 1930s and 1940s the Townsend movement began to operate more like the Workers Alliance; it softened its initial opposition to the Social Security Act and (with other pro-pension groups) began to seek improvements to existing pension programs at the state level (Holtzman

1963, 191–98). These improvements generally took the form of higher benefits rather than expanded coverage (Amenta, Carruthers, and Zylan 1992; Amenta, Halfmann, and Young 1999; Amenta, Carren, and Olasky 2005; Amenta 2006, chap. 7–8). In addition, the Townsend movement helped rid California's OAA program of degrading features like its lien provision, which "treated [recipients] as paupers" in the eyes of many elderly residents (Amenta, Halfmann, and Young 1999, 12–13, 19; see also Amenta 2006, 193–94). SSB leaders worried that "in some states Townsendites might even rally sufficient support to convert an OAA system into a flat pension system" (Cates 1983, 105; see also Holtzman 1963, 101–5, 191–98; Altmeyer 1966, 60–61, 169–70; Schiltz 1970, 40–44; Derthick 1979, 194–95, 218–19; Amenta 2006, chap. 7–9). In California and a few other states, they came close to succeeding (Amenta 2006, 131–32).[9] Yet this change in strategy did little to benefit OAI recipients, for it was it was invariably OAA—OAI's chief competitor—that pro-pension groups promoted. Thus, the Townsend movement never championed the status and rights of OAI recipients in the same way the Workers Alliance championed the status and rights of WPA workers.

Finally, in addition to being threatened by political opposition, endangered by competing policies, and deprived of "its strongest natural support" (Witte 1962, 96)—that of the old age pension movement—OAI was hobbled by major drawbacks relative to public assistance. First, eligibility for OAI benefits was restrictive. Statutory exclusion of agricultural workers, domestic workers, and other occupational groups left large gaps in OAI coverage, and OAI did not include allowances for dependents until 1939.[10] As a result of these restrictions, more Americans received OAA than OAI benefits until 1950, a disparity that alarmed SSB leaders. Second, OAI benefits remained low until 1950, which made it necessary for some people to supplement them with public assistance.[11] Third, under the original legislation, payroll tax collection for OAI benefits would begin in 1937, but the first OAI benefits would not be paid until 1942. (Even then, Republicans suggested that benefits might not be paid because the government was using payroll taxes to finance current expenditures.) In contrast, public assistance payments began within a year of Congress passing the Social Security Act (Altmeyer 1966, 169–70; Derthick 1979, 273–74; Cates 1983, 106; Sparrow 1996, 53; Mettler 1998, 95–96; J. Zelizer 1998, 67–68; Hacker 2002, 97, 108, 112, 129; Amenta 2006, 164, 169). To sum up, in the midst of an unstable policy environment, "the SSB was confronted with the task of selling a conservative program that would take seven years for the first benefits to get off the ground, of relying on a prime policy competitor, assistance, to deal with need until insurance matured, and yet making sure that the stopgap assistance competitor did not usurp insurance's place" (Cates 1983, 28–29).

To contain the threat that competing policies posed to OAI, the SSB initiated a national public relations campaign on its behalf, extolling the virtues and advantages of social insurance in speeches, radio presentations, short films, pamphlets, and newspaper articles (Derthick 1979, 198–204; Lieberman 1998, 78–79; Metter 1998, 95; J. Zelizer 1998, 59). Fearing that resemblance between OAI and competing policies would encourage policy opponents who wanted to replace social insurance or force a policy compromise, SSB officials used insurance imagery to distinguish OAI sharply from public assistance and other competitors (Derthick 1979, 224–227; Cates 1983; Berkowitz 1991, chap. 3; Tynes 1996, 95). On the one hand, social security officials represented public assistance as a degrading, demoralizing, humiliating, charitable gratuity; stressed its negative aspects, including investigations by caseworkers and resource exhaustion (destitution) as a condition of eligibility; and identified it with traditional poor relief. On the other hand, the SSB drew an analogy between private insurance and social insurance to represent the latter as an earned right that embodied American values of initiative, self-support, self-respect, and self-confidence. The "analogy between private insurance and social security" was "the principal means of legitimating this social welfare program . . . especially during the first twenty years while the [SSB] was pursuing political institutionalization" (Cates 1983, 10). Moreover, this analogy was also deployed by social insurance advocates in Congress, who had already begun to class OAI recipients in opposition to paupers. During congressional debate in 1935 on the bill that would become the Social Security Act, House Ways and Means chairman Robert Doughton (a Southern Democrat from a rural North Carolina district) insisted that because "the worker's right to benefits is conditioned upon his previous employment," social insurance would not "break down the sacred American tradition of self-reliance and initiative. . . . It must be recognized that the aged person in need of public assistance is in a different class from the ordinary relief case" (quoted in Tynes 1996, 52). While critics repeatedly challenged the insurance imagery as misleading—economist Milton Friedman would later describe Old Age Insurance as "a triumph of imaginative packaging and Madison Avenue advertising"—it nevertheless proved effective. "In the mythic construction begun in 1935 and elaborated thereafter on the basis of the payroll tax," social insurance appeared as "a vast enterprise of self-help in which government participation was almost incidental" (Derthick 1979, 165, 231–232).[12]

## Institutionalizing the status of OAI recipients as deserving citizens

The SSB's strategy to legitimize and promote social insurance, though ultimately triumphant, was initially constrained by the limitations of the Social Security Act itself: "The language of the 1935 Social Security Act did not characterize the program as 'insurance'—social or otherwise—nor were there any references to contributions or premiums. The Act spoke simply of taxes and benefits" (Cates 1983, 31). In fact, those who drafted the legislation intentionally avoided insurance terminology in order to minimize the likelihood that the Supreme Court would strike the law down as unconstitutional. Mindful of this uncertainty, the SSB avoided insurance terminology in official publications (although not in its public relations campaign) until 1937, when the Supreme Court upheld the Social Security Act. "Immediately after the constitutionality of the program was established . . . the analogy to private insurance was heavily emphasized in documents published by the SSB" (Tynes 1996, 95). Two years later, the 1939 amendments to the Social Security Act reinforced the analogy by incorporating insurance terminology into the legislation for the first time. Ironically, however, even as the 1939 amendments increased benefits and popularized the insurance metaphor, they weakened "the link between contributions and benefits by granting benefits in case of death to the dependents and survivors of covered workers, and changing the starting date for benefit payments from 1942 to 1940" (Tynes 1996, 65). In addition, the 1939 amendments abandoned "two of the main fiscal mechanisms" that distinguished Old Age Insurance from public assistance, namely, "the principle of accumulating large reserves" and the program's avoidance of general-revenue financing (J. Zelizer 1998, 56, 61–66). These changes, compounded by payroll tax freezes throughout the 1940s and the 1944 Vandenberg-Murray amendment, significantly diminished "the insurance design of the program" (Campbell 2003, 83) and "blurred the thin line that separated old-age insurance from public welfare" (J. Zelizer 1998, 56). Furthermore, authorization to use general revenue jeopardized another distinctive policy feature of social insurance: "distribution of government benefits regardless of need." After all, if benefits were no longer entirely "earned" through "contributions" (payroll taxes), the chief objection to means-testing would be substantially weakened (J. Zelizer 1998, 66). Although the 1950 amendments to the Social Security Act would later bar the use of general-revenue financing for Old Age Insurance, strengthen the program's payroll tax system, and firmly establish the distinctiveness and primacy of social insurance, these achievements were not automatic, and discrepancies between the institutional reality of Old Age Insurance and the insurance imagery used to legitimize the program persisted throughout the 1940s.[13]

If the institutional reality of social insurance did not completely conform to the SSB's rhetoric, there was greater consistency when it came to public assistance. In fact, the SSB made sure of it. From 1935 until the mid-1940s, the SSB worked to monopolize valued policy features for social insurance while excluding those same features from public assistance. In this way, it prevented a "loss of distinction between the two systems" and confirmed the expectations it created through its public relations campaign (Cates 1983, 104–135; cf. Derthick 1979, 159–160). First, social insurance provided automatic benefits, meaning that social insurance programs delivered income support "without individual case investigation that exposes virtually all aspects of an applicant's life to inquiry" (Cates 1983, 107). In contrast, public assistance programs were means-tested. The SSB maintained and sharpened this distinction by resisting reform proposals at the state level (typically pushed by the old-age pension movement) to establish alternative methods of determining eligibility for public assistance, including group eligibility and declaration methods.[14] Second, the SSB represented social insurance payments as rights and public assistance payments as gratuities. SSB officials resisted state plans that would have blurred this distinction by providing a guaranteed minimum income or clearly establishing a right to cash support under public assistance. Third, social insurance provided resource protection, meaning that recipients were not required to use all of their existing resources before receiving support. In contrast, public assistance programs generally came to require resource exhaustion (destitution) as a condition of eligibility. Here again, "resource exhaustion was not an inevitable element of public assistance, but something that the SSB imposed on states, many of which [under pressure from pro-pension groups] were eager to protect applicants from resource exhaustion." In short, "the SSB intentionally created a self-fulfilling prophecy regarding public assistance's negative features, for the SSB needed a weakened, restrictive assistance system to make conservative social insurance look good by contrast and

to contain a powerful policy competitor" (Cates 1983, 107–108; cf. Altmeyer 1966, 60–61, 119; Mettler 1998, 94–95).

To sum up, the classification of OAI recipients as independent, rights-
bearing citizen-workers was in part a by-product of policy competition,
which pushed SSB officials to extol OAI and sharply distinguish it from
public assistance. The board's efforts were not merely discursive; the SSB
institutionalized the distinction between OAI recipients and paupers by
reserving valued policy features for OAI and excluding those features
from public assistance. These efforts were, in turn, made easier by the organizational features of the SSB itself. Most importantly, Congress gave
the SSB the institutional authority to administer not only OAI but also
its chief competitor, OAA. From 1935 to 1963 and again after 1971, the
SSB (renamed the Social Security Administration in 1946) administered
both public assistance and social insurance systems (Derthick 1979, 159–
160; Cates 1983, 104). Under this arrangement, the SSB exercised broad
discretion over the institutional design of public assistance policies. "Under the 1935 Act, the SSB was given the authority to approve state plans
for public assistance systems; this approval was a prerequisite for federal matching funds. . . . Once a plan was in place, the SSB made quarterly reviews of state operations; the continued flow of federal funds was
contingent on these reviews" (Cates 1983, 108). The SSB's relatively autonomous administrative control over both OAI and public assistance enabled it to shape the policies in accordance with the classificatory scheme
it sought to impose. By institutionalizing its preferred vision and division
of the social world, the SSB sought to ensure a close correspondence between the expectations generated by its public relations campaign and
the lived reality of social insurance and public assistance.[15]

While the Social Security Board played a key role in promoting the
primacy of social insurance and distinguishing its recipients from paupers, the success of the board's efforts depended in turn upon the support (or at least the consent) of other governmental actors and interest
groups. Often, these allies were motivated less by a commitment to social
insurance than a fear of more radical alternatives. Persistent agitation on
behalf of the Townsend Plan, promotion of state-level "baby Townsend
plans," and the efforts of pro-pension groups to liberalize OAA strengthened congressional support for the creation of OAI in 1935 and improvements to the program in 1939 and 1950 (Perkins 1946, 294; Witte 1962,
103n65; Holtzman 1963, chap. 4; Altmeyer 1966, 10, 32; Amenta, Halfmann, and Young 1999, 10; Amenta 2006, 62, 80, 173–175, 186–187, 195,

215–217). In effect, by pushing more radical alternatives to OAI, the old-age pension movement inadvertently brought together a broader constituency for the program's liberalization. (Ironically, without ever mobilizing OAI recipients or pressuring the government on their behalf, the old-age pension movement may thus have accomplished more for them than the Workers Alliance did for WPA workers.) In addition to the SSB and President Roosevelt, this pro-OAI coalition eventually came to include Southern Democrats, fiscal conservatives and organized business (who reversed their previous opposition to the program), and state-level welfare administrators worried about the rising costs of OAA.[16] With the backing of this coalition, the SSB was able to promote the expansion and improvement of OAI much more effectively, which (especially after 1950) had favorable consequences for the status and rights of OAI recipients.

### Forestalling political opposition to the SSB's classification of OAI recipients

Among the various groups whose tacit consent and cooperation the SSB needed in order to promote Old Age Insurance, Southern Democrats were undoubtedly one of the most important. Southern support for the expansion and improvement of OAI depended, in turn, upon how the program affected Southern race relations. The SSB's classification of OAI recipients as full, rights-bearing citizens and its efforts to institutionalize that status were successful in part because the policy benefited relatively few black workers in the 1930s and 1940s. To understand why this was an important and even indispensable condition for the success of the SSB's efforts, it is necessary to examine Southern interests and the means with which Southern congressmen were able to protect them.

In the 1930s, the Southern economy was labor-intensive, largely agrarian, and heavily dependent on a black workforce. As a result, Southern politicians opposed social spending programs that "might reduce the supply of low-wage labor" or "provide sufficient benefits for African Americans to disrupt the Southern agrarian economy" (Manza 2000a, 309; see also Quadagno 1988b, 1994; Alston and Ferrie 1999; Brown 1999). At stake was not just the cost of labor, but the paternalistic method of labor control upon which the Southern economy depended: "The political economy of the South . . . was based on the utter economic dependence of mostly black agricultural labor. Any welfare policy that gave

Southern farm workers sources of income independent of the planter elite and the political institutions that it dominated had the potential to undermine the rigid racial and class structures of the South" (Lieberman 1998, 27; cf. Tynes 1996, 23; Alston and Ferrie 1999, chap. 1). For similar reasons, Southern planters and their political representatives in Congress opposed "nationalization of . . . potentially intrusive labor market regulations" (Manza 2000a, 309–310; cf. Katznelson, Geiger, and Kryder 1993; Alston and Ferrie 1999; Brown 1999).

These material interests did not necessarily lead Southern congressmen to oppose social spending programs or federal labor standards during the New Deal, but they did demand that new policies accommodate their interests by sacrificing either federal control or inclusiveness (Lieberman 1998, 30, 37–38; Manza 2000a, 308). Southerners were willing to support social policies such as Aid to Dependent Children (ADC) and OAA that sacrificed federal control, allowing states to set low benefit levels and restrict eligibility when expedient. In fact, "Southern politicians aggressively embraced programs that combined federal resources with local control" (Manza 2000a, 309–10; cf. Katznelson, Geiger, and Kryder 1993; Lieberman 1998, 37; Brown 1999). Alternatively, Southerners were willing to support federally administered social and labor policies that excluded most African American workers and limited coverage as far as possible to white, urban, industrial workers. Thus, the FLSA covered neither agricultural nor domestic workers, occupational categories that accounted for two-thirds of black employment (Mettler 1998, 186; Valocchi 1994, 354; Palmer 1995).

OAI excluded agricultural and domestic workers for similar reasons (Quadagno 1988a, 1988b; Tynes 1996, 55–56; Hamilton and Hamilton 1997, 27–42, 83–89; Lieberman 1998, 39–48; Alston and Ferrie 1999, chap. 3).[17] Indeed, these occupational exclusions prompted Charles Houston, a board member of the National Association for the Advancement of Colored People (NAACP), to describe the Social Security Act as "a sieve with holes just big enough for the majority of Negroes to fall through" (Hamilton and Hamilton 1997, 30). Those holes ensured that the SSB's strategy to legitimize OAI did not threaten the economic and political subordination of African-American workers within the Southern agrarian economy. The SSB's attempt to raise the status of OAI recipients relative to public assistance recipients therefore raised few concerns and provoked little interference from Southern Democrats in Congress (Amenta 1998, 226–27).[18]

The consent of Southern Democrats was important, because institutional arrangements in the 1930s and 1940s created a powerful "Southern veto" in Congress. Between 1890 and 1910, the threat of Southern Populism led the Redeemer governments of the former Confederate states to disfranchise African Americans and poor whites by means of literacy tests, property qualifications, and poll taxes. As a result, Southern states became essentially one-party regimes dominated by the Democratic Party, which served the interests of a shrunken electorate composed mainly of white landowners and merchants in counties where plantation agriculture prevailed. Since these institutional arrangements at the state level precluded serious electoral competition, they ensured that Southern Democrats would repeatedly be reelected to Congress and accumulate greater seniority than congressmen from outside the South. Seniority, in turn, allowed Southern Democrats to dominate crucial committees that determined if and when legislation came up for a vote. Hence, institutional arrangements at the state level and within Congress itself amplified the power of Southern Democrats (Key 1949; Quadagno 1988a, 1988b; Katznelson, Geiger, and Kryder 1993; Lieberman 1998, 36; Alston and Ferrie 1999, chap. 2).

## Why Did Outcomes Differ?

*Policy structure and race in the classification of WPA workers*

The struggle to class OAI recipients as rights-bearing citizen-workers was more successful than the campaign on behalf of WPA workers, in part because SSB officials were subject to fewer institutional constraints than WPA officials. As previously noted, the SSB had greater administrative control over competing policies than the WPA, which allowed it to shape those policies in accordance with its preferred vision and division of the social world. As a result of these institutional arrangements, the SSB could distinguish OAI from public assistance more effectively than WPA officials could differentiate the WPA from public assistance. In contrast to OAI, the WPA was never entirely divorced from local and conventional forms of poor relief. On the contrary, it employed almost exclusively workers who were certified as needy and referred by local relief agencies.[19] As shown in the previous chapter, this did not prevent WPA administrators from contrasting their program to locally administered relief. However, policy competition placed them in the contradictory position of denigrating the very relief programs to which the WPA remained tied. Furthermore, WPA officials were subject to financial constraints that the SSB was spared. Although OAI and the WPA were both supposed to be financially self sustaining, their financing structures differed in important respects. Unlike OAI, the WPA was not an entitlement program. Consequently, the WPA depended on regular annual appropriations, which made it more vulnerable to funding threats in Congress. That vulnerability facilitated retrenchment, which constrained the efforts of WPA administrators to differentiate their program from conventional poor relief and thus distinguish their clients from paupers. The WPA's dependence on regular appropriations from Congress does not explain the timing of the program's retrenchment and termination, but it does indicate the extent to which the WPA's institutional structure and policy features were out of the hands of the program's administrators. In short, WPA officials had less autonomy than their counterparts on the SSB, operated under less favorable conditions, and faced greater limitations. While the SSB had the institutional means to shape and sharply differentiate public assistance and social insurance policies, sharper separation of the WPA from conventional poor relief required congressional action.

However, the institutional constraints to which WPA officials were subjected only partly explain the failed classification struggle on behalf of WPA workers; in fact, it only pushes the question back a step. If WPA officials lacked the authority to upgrade the WPA and separate it from local and conventional forms of relief, why didn't Congress grant them the necessary authority or do the task itself? The answer to this question points to a more fundamental reason for the failure to legitimize and improve the WPA. Attempts to class WPA workers as independent, rights-bearing citizen-workers were more threatening to powerful Southern interests in Congress than similar efforts on behalf of OAI recipients. To understand why, it is necessary to examine both the institutional structure of the WPA and the changes that would have been required to class WPA workers as independent, rights-bearing citizen-workers.

In its existing form, four lines of defense mitigated the WPA's disruptive potential and ensured that it would not pose a serious threat to the Southern agrarian economy. First, regional differences in WPA wage rates minimized the danger that the WPA would reduce the dependence of black workers on Southern planters or diminish the supply of low-wage labor. To be sure, WPA wages were more generous than general relief, especially in the South, and "southern Negroes working on government projects frequently earned more than they would have received in private employment" (D. Howard 1943, 188; cf. Wolters 1970, 206–7). However, WPA wages varied widely among states and were set especially low in the South (D. Howard 1943, 182–83, 201, 206–7, 395, 770). African Americans, who were concentrated in the South and were therefore already disadvantaged by regional wage disparities, were further disadvantaged by the WPA policy of setting wages according to skill (Hamilton and Hamilton 1997, 24–25). As NAACP officials pointed out, because black workers in the South were "uniformly classed as unskilled," they were typically subjected to the WPA's lowest wage rates (Wolters 1970, 206–7; cf. Amenta 1998, 158).

Second, WPA officials set up elaborate administrative safeguards against the danger of labor shortages, including "discontinuance of projects in areas likely to need labor, wholesale dismissal of workers thought to be needed by private enterprise, and selected dismissal of WPA employes [sic] having previous experience necessary to performance of specific kinds of work likely to be available" (D. Howard 1943, 487–88, 490). In the South, this meant releasing black workers at harvest time, which "forced them to take low-paying, seasonal jobs in the fields" (Wolters 1970, 207–8; see also Rose 1994, 100–4; Valocchi 1994, 353; Hamilton and Hamilton 1997, 25; Brown 1999, 85–87). Indeed, from 1935 to 1936 and again after 1938, Congress required WPA workers to accept private employment even if it paid wages *below* the WPA security wage, "providing these jobs paid rates prevailing in the community for the type of work offered" (D. Howard 1943, 486–87, 490–92).[20]

Third, some states established special restrictions on WPA employment of sharecroppers, tenants, and farm laborers that further minimized any threat the WPA posed to the Southern agrarian economy. "In Louisiana, for example, it [had] been prescribed that: 'Sharecroppers living on plantations in the plantation quarters should not be considered for referral [to the WPA] without consultation with the plantation management to determine if there is employment available for them on the plantation and whether the usual source of credit, namely, the landlord, is available to them" (D. Howard 1943, 506). These state-level restrictions were strengthened by agreements between the WPA and the Farm Security Administration. At best, these agreements restricted WPA employment of farm laborers to "the periods of inactivity in farm operations." At worst, they ended the WPA employment of farm laborers altogether, even between seasons (D. Howard 1943, 506–509). These restrictions were evidently effective. In 1939, deputy WPA administrator Howard Hunter noted that only 8 percent of WPA workers were agricultural laborers (U.S. Congress 1939, 2488).

Fourth, selective exclusion of African Americans from the WPA rolls also minimized the WPA's threat to the Southern agrarian economy. Of course, Congress and WPA policy prohibited racial discrimination in WPA employment, and WPA administrators at the federal level were generally committed to racial fairness. Federal control over the WPA therefore reduced discrimination, and African Americans expressed appreciation for these efforts (U.S. Department of Labor 1940, 638; D. Howard 1943, 285–87; Wolters 1970, x–xi, 204; Hamilton and Hamilton 1997, 24–26; Amenta 1998, 157–59). However, local authorities were generally less committed to racial fairness and were able to circumvent the federal prohibition against racial discrimination in a variety of ways (Durant 1939; D. Howard 1943, 291–96, 386, 390, 452–53, 768–69; Rose 1994, 100–4; Valocchi 1994, 353; Foley 1997, 175, 178–80; Goldfield 1997, 205; Brown 1999, 83).

> In at least two ways current policies of the WPA permit discrimination by state and local agencies against minority groups (or individuals) in such a way as to leave the WPA powerless to aid even those who may improperly be denied benefits under its own program. First of these policies is that which authorizes state and local relief agencies to refer or certify workers for employment. The second is that requiring sponsors to initiate and contribute to the cost of projects. . . . Most amazing in this respect is not the degree of control over its own program the WPA has delegated to others, but the fact that . . . no effective provision is made for . . . avoiding at these vital points discrimination that might prevent disadvantaged groups or individuals from benefiting under the very program which federal officials aver is more humane and less discriminatory because it is administered by the federal government. (D. Howard 1943, 768–69)

Of course, the WPA supervised local certifying agencies, and it could punish recalcitrant agencies by withdrawing its approval and assuming responsibility for certification itself. The WPA also began to supervise certification work more closely in 1939 (D. Howard 1943, 360, 362–63). However, even with tightened supervision, state and local agencies in the South continued to act as gatekeepers, referring only those applicants they deemed suitable for WPA jobs.

To be sure, African Americans were overrepresented on the WPA rolls overall, which reflected greater need among blacks (Brown 1999, 77–79, 84). While the proportion of nonwhite persons in the labor force was about 11 percent in 1940, African Americans constituted 15.2 percent of WPA workers in 1937 and approximately 14 percent of WPA workers in 1939 (U.S. Department of Labor 1940, 636; D. Howard 1943, 288–89; U.S. Federal Works Agency 1946, 45; Amenta 1998, 158). However, these national percentages obscure significant geographical variation that is consistent with a pattern of selective exclusion:

> Northern Negroes were generally overrepresented on WPA rolls. . . . *In the southern and border states, on the other hand, black workers did not fare so well,* though conditions varied from state to state and even from county to county within the same state. On comparison of southern counties having one or more cities with a population of at least ten thousand with counties having no such city revealed that *it was particularly in the rural areas that Negroes had difficulty getting WPA jobs.* In large southern cities, on the other hand, Negroes were well represented on the WPA rolls. (Wolters 1970, 205–206, emphasis added)

In short, African Americans were sometimes overrepresented on WPA rolls, but not in the rural South, where the WPA would pose the greatest threat to the Southern agrarian economy.[21]

Although the WPA in its existing form did not seriously challenge the Southern racial order, the struggle over the classification of WPA workers did. This struggle, like the struggle over the classification of OAI recipients, was not merely discursive. When the Workers Alliance (later joined by the CIO) demanded recognition of WPA workers as independent, rights-bearing citizen-workers, it sought to objectify this classificatory scheme by incorporating valued policy features into the WPA. Thus, the struggle over the classification of WPA workers, like the struggle over OAI recipients, had institutional implications and involved material as well as symbolic stakes. The struggle threatened Southern interests in at least three ways: by potentially strengthening federal control, extending federal labor standards, and mobilizing black workers.

STRENGTHENING FEDERAL CONTROL.   First, the struggle over the status and rights of WPA workers threatened the capacity of local authorities to selectively exclude black farm laborers from WPA employment. Insofar as local and state relief agencies certified the unemployed for WPA employment, the WPA allowed local authorities to exercise considerable control over who got onto WPA rolls. However, successful classification of WPA workers as independent, rights-bearing citizen-workers would have entailed the separation of the WPA from relief. As shown in the previous chapter, this was a key demand of the Workers Alliance. Separation of the WPA from relief would, in turn, have eliminated the role of local relief agencies in certifying the unemployed for WPA employment, thereby undermining the influence of local authorities and increasing federal control over certification.

EXTENDING FEDERAL LABOR STANDARDS.    Second, the classification of WPA workers as independent, rights-bearing citizen-workers would have entailed the extension of new federal labor standards to WPA workers. As noted in the previous chapter, the 1935 National Labor Relations Act did not cover WPA workers, and application of the 1938 FLSA to WPA workers was contested. Nevertheless, extension of this legislation to WPA workers was another key demand of the Workers Alliance, and struggles over WPA wage rates in the South were closely tied to controversy over the FLSA (D. Howard 1943, 162). Conservatives complained that the federal government maintained regional differences in WPA wage rates, which were set lowest in the South, but penalized private industry by "refusing them the same right" in the FLSA. In response, Workers Alliance president David Lasser declared that his movement was "absolutely in favor of eliminating the differential in wages on WPA and in private industry, between the North and the South. But this does not and can not mean pulling the Northern wages down to the Southern level. The only policy we will support is to raise the Southern wages up to the Northern level" (*Work,* May 21, 1938, 3). Admittedly, the FLSA provided "extremely low minimum wage rates: twenty-five cents an hour in 1938 increasing to a maximum of forty cents an hour by 1945" (Mettler 1998, 195). However, as Workers Alliance leaders pointed out, since WPA wages in the South were as low as fifteen cents an hour, extension of the newly established national minimum wage would make possible "a substantial increase in the [wages of the] lowest paid WPA workers" (*Work,* September 24, 1938, 6). Many of these low-paid WPA workers would be African American, especially if Congress reduced the role of local authorities in certifying the jobless for WPA employment. Since the FLSA (like OAI) excluded agricultural and domestic workers, extending the FLSA to WPA workers would potentially extend its coverage to many black workers who would otherwise be left out. Barred at the front door by the law's occupational exclusions, African Americans might thus enter through the back door via the WPA.

Although application of the FLSA to WPA workers remained contested, the Workers Alliance received open support from some WPA officials on wage issues. WPA wages in Southern states increased markedly after 1935, and after the program's 1938 wage increases (noted in chapter 4) some WPA administrators "expected further increases in the southern wage rates even to wiping out all sectional differences as soon as public opinion would 'stand for it'" (D. Howard 1943, 162n3) In line with this goal, Nels Anderson, director of the WPA's labor relations section, "boasted that the $21 paid unskilled workers for 140 hours of work in rural areas of the South was 'about double the wage for the same amount of labor on a farm.' Far from apologizing for this, Mr. Anderson defended it as 'good public policy in areas of extremely low living standards'" (166).[22] Moreover, in 1939 Congress "required that differences in wage rates paid for similar work in various sections of the country should not be greater than could be justified by differences in the cost of living" (159). By reformulating national WPA wage policies, the 1939 Emergency Relief Act sharply raised WPA wages in the South (while lowering wage standards in some regions outside the South). In particular, monthly "wages for unskilled in the rural South jump[ed] from $26 to $35" (*American Federationist,* September 1939, 916). If the efforts of the Workers Alliance to extend federal labor standards to WPA workers alarmed Southern congressmen, these trends toward higher and more uniform WPA wages rates probably reinforced their concerns.[23]

MOBILIZING BLACK WORKERS.    Third and finally, it was not only the demands of the Workers Alliance and the backing of WPA officials in Washington that alarmed Southern Democrats; it was also the efforts of the Workers Alliance to mobilize Southern black workers in support of those demands. These efforts were most clearly evident in the Alliance's 1936 Southern organizing drive and its 1938 campaign to "raise the wages of 2,600,000 WPA laborers in low-wage categories," which was also primarily concentrated in the South (*Workers Alliance,* "Second March Issue" [1936], 1; *Work,* July 16, 1938, 1; August 13, 1938, 1; August 26, 1939, 3). Black WPA workers, who were often among the lowest paid, stood to benefit the most from the wage increases demanded (and sometimes won) by the Workers Alliance. A sit-down strike of WPA workers led by the Workers Alliance in Birmingham, Alabama, for example, succeeded in raising the minimum WPA wage there from $36 to $40.80 per month; opposing the raise was none other than Public Safety Commissioner Eugene "Bull" Connor (*Work,* September 24, 1938, 3).[24] The Workers Alliance also fought WPA discrimination against blacks, and its leaders demanded in 1938 that eligibility for old-age and unemployment insurance be extended to a broader range of occupations, including agricultural, migrant, and domestic workers, among whom blacks were disproportionately represented (*Work,* November 5, 1938, 2; October 26, 1939, 1, 4).

In addition to fighting for social rights, the Workers Alliance struggled to expand the political rights of Southern blacks, particularly through the abolition of the poll tax, which the movement regarded as a tool for disfranchising the poor and unemployed (*Work,* May 7, 1938, 7; July 16, 1938, 7; September 24, 1938, 1; October 22, 1938, 6; April 8, 1939, 7; September 14, 1939, 6; September 28, 1939, 7). When congressman Lee Geyer, a California Democrat and ally of the Workers Alliance, introduced a bill in 1939 to make payment of a poll tax illegal as a prerequisite for voting, the Workers Alliance testified in support of the bill and advised its Southern locals "to mobilize an active campaign for its passage" (*Work,* October 12, 1939, 2; April 25, 1940, 1; Porter 1980, 133). The Workers Alliance also worked to register black voters. In Greenville, South Carolina, for example, the Workers Alliance helped the Negro Youth Council and the NAACP register African Americans for municipal elections in 1939, despite threats and violent assaults from the local police and Ku Klux Klan (*Work,* July 29, 1939, 9; Bunche 1973, 422–24; Sullivan 1996, 144–45). Although the president of the Greenville Workers Alliance local was arrested three times before election day, the Alliance "gave the strongest backing to the [voter registration] movement," and almost everyone who registered for the first time was a relief worker or unemployed (Bunche 1973, 422, 424; Sullivan 1996, 145). These efforts to organize the black unemployed in the face of intense and often brutal repression earned the Workers Alliance the loyalty of thousands of African Americans, many of whom were drawn into the movement and worked actively to expand and strengthen it. On the basis of reports by delegates to the 1938 national convention of the Workers Alliance, movement leaders estimated in 1939 that 10 percent of the Alliance's members were African American (U.S. Congress. House 1939–40, 104). Younger blacks in particular turned to the Alliance, whose aid they were happy to use in the struggle for equal rights (Kelley 1990, 202).

FIGURE 5.2. Blacks and whites listening to organizer at Workers Alliance meeting in Muskogee County, Oklahoma, July 1939. (Library of Congress)

The Alliance's role in the political mobilization of Southern blacks is also evident from its growing ties to black civil rights organizations in the late 1930s. Delegates to the Alliance's 1938 national convention recommended greater cooperation with the National Urban League (NUL), the National Negro Congress (NNC), and the NAACP, called for the Workers Alliance to exchange representatives with black organizations and work with their "jobs and unemployed committees," and urged the Alliance to support the "Southern Conference on Human Rights [sic]" (*Work,* December 3, 1938, 5).[25] In keeping with these proposals, the Workers Alliance participated in the 1938 meeting in Birmingham, Alabama, that gave birth to the Southern Conference for Human Welfare, a voluntary organization devoted to propagating the New Deal in the South. The conference received widespread news coverage and drew two thousand delegates, "a who's who in Southern liberalism" and "Southern liberal organizations," including 120 African Americans and several prominent New Dealers (Krueger 1967, 22–23). In addition, Lee Morgan, the black secretary-treasurer of the Ohio Workers Alliance, served as an officer of the NAACP and the NNC; John P. Davis, chairman of the NNC, addressed the Alliance's 1938 national convention; and the Alliance returned the gesture by sending one of the largest delegations to the Third National Negro Congress in April 1940 (*Work,* May 21, 1938, 5; September 24, 1938, 1; November 5, 1938, 5; April 25, 1940, 1).[26] The Workers Alliance also forged stronger ties to blacks at the local level. For example, Hazel Dawson, the national Workers Alliance representative in North Carolina, reported that the movement "set the pace for inter-racial work" in her state and "started forming a united front of Negro fraternal and church organizations to cooperate with the Workers Alliance on the problems of the Negro people" (*Work,* October 8, 1938, 9).

*Political opposition to the classification of*
*WPA workers as deserving citizens*

The efforts of WPA officials and the Workers Alliance to class WPA workers as rights-bearing citizens, the policy changes needed to institutionalize that status, and the Alliance's efforts to mobilize blacks in support of those policy changes generated a strong racial backlash against the Workers Alliance and the WPA, a backlash that partly expressed itself in the guise of anti-Communism.[27] As shown in chapter 4, Communists were indeed active in the Workers Alliance, and it is this Communist influence that largely accounts for the Alliance's efforts on behalf of Southern blacks. In the 1930s, the American Communist Party was an aggressive advocate of racial equality (Howe and Coser 1957, 204-216; Goldfield 1997, chap. 6; Babson 1999, 64; Stepan-Norris and Zeitlin 2003, chap. 8-9). Southern racial conservatives were aware of this connection between Communism and black political mobilization, which helps to explain why prominent Southern Democrats, such as Martin Dies, chairman of the 1938 House Un-American Activities Committee, and Clifton Woodrum, chairman of the 1939 House Subcommittee on the Works Progress Administration, played leading roles in the anti-Communist crusade against the Workers Alliance and the WPA in the late 1930s. As shown in the previous chapter, these Southern Democrats worked with Republicans to delegitimize the Workers Alliance as a front for the Communist Party, discredit the WPA as a source of funding for Communist subversion, cut WPA expenditures, and eventually dismantle the program. Analysis of congressional roll call votes confirms this view. Although Southern Democrats were generally favorable to the WPA on budgetary votes during the program's early years, their support for spending declined over time, and by 1939 most of them were voting against WPA spending (either against increases or for reductions). In addition, most Southern Democrats joined Republicans to maintain a prohibition on deficiency appropriations in 1938, oppose payment of prevailing wages in 1939, and support time limits on WPA work between 1939 and 1941. Of the thirty staunchest opponents of the WPA in the U.S. Senate, nearly half were from the South (Amenta and Halfmann 2000; Amenta 2001, 267-75).[28]

The racial concerns that fueled anti-Communist attacks on the Workers Alliance and the WPA were evident in the work of both the Woodrum and Dies committees. Appealing to ascriptive forms of Americanism and deep-rooted fears of African Americans as an internal domestic enemy, witnesses testified to the Woodrum Committee in 1939 that Communists sought to establish "an independent black republic" in the United States "under the domination of the Communist commissars" (U.S. Congress. House 1939-40, 1096).[29] In this context, the Alliance's vigorous multiracial organizing efforts in the South appeared to confirm charges of Communist domination. Similar anxiety about the mobilization of black workers is evident in the work of the Dies Committee. In September 1942—four years after Dies boasted that his committee had "destroyed the legislative influence of the Workers' Alliance" in Congress, one year after the Workers Alliance dissolved, and the same year that Congress abolished the WPA—Dies made explicit the relationship between his anti-Communist convictions and his opposition to racial equality. On the floor of Congress, Dies "deplore[d] the fact that throughout the South today subversive elements are attempting to convince the Negro that he should be placed on social equality with the white people; that now is the time for him to assert his rights" (quoted in Gellermann 1944, 245–46; Ogden 1945, 107, 152). The following year, Dies defended the poll tax against its liberal critics, decrying "the effort of Northerners to exploit the poverty of the South 'for political purposes.'" Southerners, Dies added, could "'solve our own problems'" (Gellermann 1944, 261–62). Finally, in February 1943, again on the floor of Congress, Dies denounced "'a well-organized attempt to build up in this country a united front of radicals—a united front of Communists, crackpots, Socialists, men of different shades of totalitarian beliefs,' and an effort by this group to bring the Negro population under its influence. 'Constantly,' said Dies, 'the Negroes are told that now is the time for them to achieve that degree of social equality to which they are entitled'" (249). For Southern Democrats like Dies, the struggle to class WPA workers as rights-bearing citizens, institutionalize that status, and extend it to black workers was clearly the work of this radical front.

The involvement of Southern Democrats was a crucial element in the racial backlash against the Workers Alliance. As we have seen, Southern Democrats wielded disproportionate power in Congress, and the discourse of anti-Communism helped to discredit, disorganize, and legitimize repression of the movement. However, the backlash against the Workers Alliance was not confined to Southern congressmen alone. Their efforts to repress the Workers Alliance at the national level dovetailed with strong, often violent, and frequently racialized resistance to the movement at the local level. Workers Alliance members and organizers were harassed, prohibited from meeting, forced out of town, tear gassed, jailed, beaten, and shot ("Socialists Urged to Support Labor," *New York Times,* December 22, 1935; *Workers Alliance,* "Second January Issue" [1936], 2; *Work,* May 7, 1938, 2; June 4, 1938, 3, 9, 10; June 18, 1938, 4; July 15, 1939, 3; Bunche 1973, 501). Perhaps the most notorious case of intimidation occurred in Tampa, Florida, where a Workers Alliance organizer was tarred, feathered, and beaten to death by Ku Klux Klansmen (*Workers Alliance,* "First January Issue" [1936], 1). Also notorious was the conviction of Angelo Herndon, a black Communist organizer and later a vice president of the Workers Alliance, who was convicted of attempting to overthrow the government of the state of Georgia under an 1866 insurrection code and sentenced to twenty years on a chain gang (*Workers Alliance,* "First July Issue" [1936], 1; Herndon 1937; Moore 1971).[30] These incidents reflected the anxieties that Southern Democrats like Dies expressed on the floor of the Congress. By the early 1940s, "militant and organized demands" for the "abolition of segregation" coincided with "the war crisis" to generate an "atmosphere of suspicion and fear" in the South. "The flying rumors of plot and counterplot, of bands armed with icepick and switch-blade knife, of Eleanor Clubs, conspiratorial societies, and subversive Northern agitators" led at least one contemporary observer to conclude that "'the South and the Negro . . . faced their greatest crisis since the days of the re-construction'" (Woodward 1957, 105–7). In this context, the efforts of the Workers Alliance to secure full civil, political, and industrial citizenship for WPA workers, black as well as white, made the movement a prime target for political reaction.

A racial backlash also emerged within the ranks of the Workers Alliance itself, contributing to the movement's internal conflicts over its own collective identity. Although the Workers Alliance officially condemned racial discrimination and prohibited it within the movement, its leaders sometimes had to make concessions to the "'backward prejudices'" of local authorities and "new Alliance members" in order to build the movement (Workers Alliance of America 1937, 21–22; *Workers Alliance,* "Second January Issue" [1936], 1; *Work,* December 3, 1938, 3; June 17, 1939, 3; Naison 1983, 264–65). In Atlanta, Georgia, for example, the Workers Alliance was forced to hold separate meetings for blacks and whites and to organize blacks into separate locals as a result of Jim Crow legislation. Workers Alliance leaders also had to rid the Atlanta local of "disturbing Ku Klux Klan elements," whom movement leaders expelled by December 1938 (*Work,* July 30, 1938, 2; September 24, 1938, 11; December 17, 1938, 4). In Alabama, "racial equality and Communism were seen as two sides of the same coin," leading many whites to leave the Workers Alliance in that state "on the pretext that its racial practices alone proved it was a Communist front" (Kelley 1990, 156). In this context, condemnations of the WPA as a "slave-labor scheme" paying "coolie" wages may have reflected anxieties among white WPA workers about the erosion of the status and rights they associated with whiteness. These anxieties may, in turn, have reinforced a desire for social distance from non-whites that expressed itself as racial exclusion. To be sure, instances of racial discrimination within the movement were more the exception than the rule; most Workers Alliance members refused to make political claims on the basis of race and generally forswore the wages of whiteness. However, when racial divisions were aligned with the division between Americanism and communism, political purges could take a racialized form.

Finally, efforts to class WPA workers as full, rights-bearing citizens may have been undermined by a broad racial backlash against the WPA itself. The proportion of African Americans on the WPA rolls increased from 14 percent in 1939 to 20 percent in 1940 at a time when non-whites made up only 11 percent of the country's total labor force. Despite continued exclusion in the rural South, the proportion of blacks on WPA rolls grew nationwide because African Americans faced greater difficulty finding private employment and left the rolls less rapidly than whites (U.S. Federal Works Agency 1946, 45).[31] Brown (1999, 77–79, 89) argues that "the increasing proportion of blacks on both WPA and general relief rolls" in the late 1930s, combined with "widespread racist stereotypes" of black workers as "'lazy, irresponsible, [and] indolent,'" "undoubtedly contributed to the erosion of public support after 1938 for expanding WPA and relief expenditures, despite continuing high levels of unemployment." If so, Southern hostility to the Workers Alliance and its demands merged with a larger racial backlash against the WPA among the American public. In sum, as the Workers Alliance and the WPA became vehicles for challenging racialized patterns of social closure, they became targets of racial hostility from elites and mass publics alike.

## The Historical Legacies of Past Classification Struggles

*How previous classification struggles shaped struggles*
*during the New Deal*

While the material interests and power resources of Southern planters played a crucial role in the classification of OAI recipients and WPA workers, these determinants should not be reified merely as given features of the Southern political economy. They are better understood as the product of past political struggles during Reconstruction and the Populist insurgency of the 1890s (Du Bois [1935] 1962; Woodward 1957; Goodwyn 1976; Foner 1988). What Marx says about the production of textiles thus applies equally well to the Southern political economy: Human beings not only "produce cloth, linen, [and] silks," but, "according to their abilities, also produce the *social relations* amid which they prepare cloth and linen" (Tucker 1978, 140, original emphasis). Moreover, the political struggles that produced these relations were not simply conflicts between existing classes; they involved efforts to build biracial, cross-sectional or class-based political coalitions and competing efforts to disorganize those coalitions along racial and sectional lines. Such classification struggles are a key dimension, though often a concealed one, of class struggle (Bourdieu and Boltanski 1981, 151). As I have argued in previous chapters, these classification struggles frequently result in social closure as agents monopolize the material and symbolic profits of privileged names, titles, or categories while excluding others. The resources and interests of Southern elites, insofar as they derived from monopolization of land and political power, can be understood in precisely these terms. In short, while material interests and power resources partly determined the outcome of the classification struggles over OAI recipients and WPA workers, these determinants must themselves be seen, at least in part, as the outcome of previous classification struggles.

Like the material interests and power resources of Southern planters, the broader racial backlash against the Workers Alliance and the WPA at the local level, within the movement itself, and among the general public was also rooted in previous classification struggles during and after Reconstruction. Those struggles not only helped planters to accrue enormous material and symbolic advantages but also reinforced a racialized vision and division of the social world. Internalized by social agents, racial divisions shaped their identities, structured their preferences, and mediated their strategic choices, constraining subsequent efforts to regroup them along non- or biracial lines. Objectified in economic, political, and educational institutions, racial divisions generated unequal access to economic, political, and cultural capital, widening the distance in social space between agents categorized as white or black and thereby making biracial coalitions unstable. Insofar as racial divisions were both internalized and objectified, a social world fractured along racial lines came to appear self-evident and taken for granted to agents whose very categories of thought were produced by it. Past classification struggles did not prevent agents from re-envisioning the social world or dividing it differently, but they did make it harder for such efforts to succeed.

*How classification struggles during the New Deal*
*shaped subsequent struggles*

The classificatory schemes objectified in the New Deal welfare state did not merely reflect but also reinforced racial divisions (Quadagno 1994, 19–24; Goldfield 1997; Hamilton and Hamilton 1997; Brown 1999). Thus, during the New Deal, as during Reconstruction, citizenship operated as an instrument of social closure and stratification. As we have seen, the failed struggle over the classification of WPA workers shaped the program's structure, enabling conservatives to reinforce its illiberal and disciplinary policy features. In addition, the stigmatization of the Workers Alliance and the WPA facilitated the retrenchment and eventual termination of the program. These policy outcomes, coupled with the exclusion of most black workers from social insurance, relegated many blacks to local poor relief or the newly established public assistance programs created by the Social Security Act (Hamilton and Hamilton 1997, chap. 2; Brown 1999, 16–17, 76–90).[32] The parallels with Reconstruction are striking. By the 1930s, a living wage had replaced property ownership as the primary signifier of freedom, independence, and citizenship (Glickman 1997); yet black workers were unable to secure either through state intervention. Just as Reconstruction furnished freedpeople with relief instead of land, the New Deal gave black workers public assistance instead of a right to work or industrial citizenship. At the same time, the SSB stigmatized public assistance recipients, identified them with paupers, and shaped the policy structure of public assistance accordingly. Consequently, these programs treated their clientele—a clientele that over time became disproportionately black—in a nonliberal manner as dependent persons requiring supervision and discipline. This outcome was well understood by black civil rights activists at the time, who strongly supported the New Deal's work and work-relief programs and firmly "believed that some kind of permanent public works program was needed" (Hamilton and Hamilton 1997, 26). Without the federal works program or access to social insurance, they predicted, "a large proportion of the Negro population would become permanently dependent on public assistance. They feared that this would place the Negro population in a tenuous position in a society with a strong work ethic; it would limit Negroes' ability to advance, to be viewed as responsible, contributing members of society" (26–27; see also 30).

The classification struggles of the New Deal era thus combined to denigrate public assistance in both the literal and figurative sense of the term, objectifying racial divisions in the welfare state and reinforcing the association of blacks with idleness, dependence, and pauperism. As in the case of the Freedmen's Bureau, ritually degrading relief practices strengthened racist assumptions that blacks were lazy and irresponsible and set a precedent for punitive and disciplinary policies in the future. In addition, a racially bifurcated welfare state reinforced unequal access to economic and cultural capital, further widening the social distance separating white and black clients. These consequences, compounded by labor-market discrimination and later by structural changes in the economy, constrained the upward mobility of black workers. The result was a divided working class, "characterized at one extreme by the inner-city poor subsisting on low-wage jobs and meager welfare benefits," and at the other extreme by a "working 'middle class'" that secured high wages and "private pension and healthcare plans" through strong unions (Babson 1999, 151–52; cf. Orloff 2002, 101–102). Solidarity between these class fractions, already weakened by their diverging positions in social space, was further undermined by segregation in physical space and by renewed struggles in the 1960s to appropriate "the occupational and political benefits attached to public employment," including money, influence on the policies of municipal agencies, and the jobs themselves (Piven and Cloward 1974, 226–27, 237).

## Summary and Conclusion

To explain why WPA workers failed to obtain recognition as honorable, rights-bearing citizens who earned and deserved public aid, this chapter compared their classification struggle to the more successful struggle over the status and rights of OAI recipients. First, analogous features of the cases were identified in order to establish their comparability: OAI and the WPA were roughly contemporaneous policy innovations that created new groups of clients whose status and rights relative to other clients in the welfare field were initially uncertain. In both cases, the policies tied income support to work and were said to be financially self-sustaining; supporters used these institutional features to legitimize the policies, distinguish them from public relief, and ward off competing policies; and these struggles had important implications (material and symbolic) for the status and rights of the policies' clients. Second, the struggle over the classification of OAI recipients was traced from the program's creation in 1935 through the 1940s, and significant parallels with the concurrent struggle over the classification of WPA workers were noted. Third, an explanation was sought of why, despite these similarities, struggles over the classification of WPA workers and OAI recipients resulted in different outcomes. It was argued that policy structure and racial politics, both shaped by previous classification struggles, contributed crucially to these outcomes. Finally, rather than taking policy structures and racial divisions as givens, a brief account of how these causal factors were themselves shaped by past classification struggles, and how struggles during the New Deal shaped those that came afterwards was provided.

Elite efforts to class OAI recipients as rights-bearing citizen-workers succeeded, even without the mobilization of those recipients, because Old Age Insurance was racially biased. Although efforts to position OAI recipients as deserving citizens required the incorporation of valued policy features into OAI and a high degree of federal administrative control over the program, these efforts posed no serious threat to the Southern agrarian economy, because OAI excluded agricultural and domestic workers, who were disproportionately black. Neither administrative elites nor mass movements seriously challenged the racially biased character of OAI. In part, this may be because there was no Communist-influenced movement of OAI recipients (in contrast to that of the Workers Alliance). As a result, the SSB and OAI sidestepped the anti-Communist campaign against the Workers Alliance and the WPA. Although Congress did eventually expand OAI coverage to include agricultural and domestic workers, it was not until the 1950s, after the mechanization of Southern agriculture and black migration to the North began to weaken Southern opposition (Piven and Cloward 1977; Quadagno 1988a; Tynes 1996, 106–7; Mettler 1998, 217–18; Alston and Ferrie 1999, chap. 6).

Like the classification of OAI recipients, the classification of WPA workers had important implications for the policy's structure. The Workers Alliance sought not only to elicit recognition of WPA workers as independent, rights-bearing citizen-workers but also to institutionalize that status. Achievement of this goal required structural reforms of the WPA, including its separation from local poor relief, greater federal control over the program, and the extension of new federal labor laws to WPA workers, all of which the Workers Alliance promoted. WPA officials, who had a shared interest in such reforms, often supported them, and the Workers Alliance also mobilized black workers in the South to advance its demands. While the WPA in its existing form did not pose a serious threat to the Southern agrarian economy, the activities and demands of the Workers Alliance did, which triggered the "Southern veto" in Congress. This reaction was compounded by a broader racialized backlash at the local level, within the Workers Alliance itself, and perhaps in public attitudes toward the WPA. Efforts to class WPA workers as independent, rights-bearing citizen-workers failed in part because they pushed a program that was racially biased in the rural South in the direction of greater inclusion, federal control, and standardization in the 1930s and 1940s.

Of course, hostility to the Workers Alliance and the WPA was not confined to the South, nor was racism its only source (Harvey 1989, chap. 6). Amenta (1998, 219–30) argues that a variety of institutional features made the WPA's demise more likely, including its provision of public work, which generated business opposition; the high cost of the program, which generated opposition from fiscal conservatives as well as business; and executive control over the WPA, which antagonized Congress. Presumably, these same features generated opposition to the Workers Alliance and its demands as well. Nevertheless, the veto power that Southern Democrats wielded in Congress made their stance crucial. As Amenta (1998, 142) points out, "organized business and the Republicans could not have been effective as they were without the aid and leadership of southern Democrats." While Southern Democrats (like other groups) surely had nonracial reasons to oppose the Workers Alliance and the WPA, those reasons do not negate their interest in preserving the Southern racial order. Indeed, without attending to the racial politics of work relief, it would be difficult to explain why Southern Democrats shifted their stance toward the WPA (from acquiescence to hostility) or the timing of the anti-Communist campaign against the Workers Alliance and the WPA in the late 1930s. Policy features that were relatively constant throughout the program's existence simply cannot account for such variation. Furthermore, it is possible that racial politics was not merely an additional source of opposition to the Workers Alliance and the WPA, but also one that augmented the effects of others. By linking fears about government competition with private business, excessive relief spending, and the growth of executive power to racial conflict, Southern Democrats probably magnified the opposition those fears generated.

These findings have more general implications for U.S. welfare state development. According to one influential view, Americans are generally hostile to social welfare programs because of their historical commitment to classical liberal values: antistatism, laissez-faire, individualism, and so forth. In line with this view, scholars and policymakers alike have frequently assumed that work-based benefits will receive more support in the United States than other kinds of programs, because they more fully embody liberal American values of self-reliance. This view remains, at best, an overly simple explanation of how liberal values inhibit or facilitate the development of the American welfare state. Contrary to conventional wisdom, conditioning social rights upon work does not invariably legitimize them, nor does it ensure that clients' other rights—civil, political, or industrial—will be respected. Just as antistatist antagonism to the welfare state was stronger when the welfare state was linked to racial conflict and black political mobilization (Quadagno 1994), so the work ethic generated less support for work-based social welfare policies when those policies were linked to the pursuit of civil, political, and social rights for African Americans. The color of work mediated the effects of liberal values during the New Deal, much as the color of welfare would mediate their effects during the War on Poverty.

# PART III

# From Citizen-Mothers to Citizen-Workers

*Struggles after the New Deal*

## CHAPTER SIX

# "Work with no rights and no pay equals slavery"

## Workfare in New York City, 1993–2001

In 1996, President Bill Clinton fulfilled a campaign pledge to "end welfare as we know it" (Clinton 1993) by signing into law the Personal Responsibility and Work Opportunity Act (PRWOA). Among other things, this legislation encouraged a rapid and dramatic expansion of workfare in the United States. Workfare programs require public assistance recipients "to 'work off' their grants by contributing labor to non-profit organizations or to government agencies . . . on the supposition that work experiences would prepare recipients to seek real jobs" (Piven and Cloward [1971] 1993, 382). In New York, Los Angeles, and other large cities, these reforms fostered the largest publicly subsidized work programs since the Great Depression.[1] Sixty years after the creation of the WPA, the nation had once again embarked on a large-scale, long-term experiment with work relief for the "employable" poor, a category now broadened to encompass single mothers.

This chapter investigates struggles over the civic classification of workfare workers in the 1990s through an examination of New York City's Work Experience Program (WEP) during the mayoral administration of Rudolph Giuliani (1993–2001).[2] Just as the Freedmen's Bureau and the Works Progress Administration served as microcosms for the study of earlier struggles over the meaning and boundaries of citizenship, so the WEP serves a similar purpose here.[3] The program is well suited for this task because of the size and importance of New York City's welfare system. Even after the rapid decline in New York's welfare rolls in the 1990s, the city still represented the largest urban federal welfare caseload in the United States, responsible for one out of every thirteen cases nationwide in 2001. Though it was not the only element of "New York City's work-based welfare system," the WEP was its "centerpiece" (Nightingale et al. 2002, iii, 3). By December 1999, 14 percent of the adult federal welfare recipients in New York City participated in WEP, "compared with a national monthly average of just 4 percent [in similar workfare programs throughout the country] in fiscal year 2000. With 21,933 work experience participants, New York City accounted for more than one-third of the nation's 61,643 work experience participants, and it far exceeded the average monthly number of participants in other states with a relatively high reliance on work experience programs, including New Jersey (6,016), Ohio (14,127), and Wisconsin (3,227)" (Besharov and Germanis 2004, 47, 56). As the largest and most ambitious experiment with workfare in the nation, New York's WEP served as a model for other cities and states (Fuentes 1996; "Don't Unionize Workfare," *New York Times,* February 21, 1997).

While the struggle over the classification of New York's workfare workers involved a variety of individuals and groups with divergent aims and views, this chapter focuses on the activities and claims of the Association of Community Organizations for Reform Now (ACORN), a national community-organizing group. ACORN was not the only organization trying to mobilize welfare recipients as workers, but it was arguably the most effective. The group was created in the 1970s as an effort to expand the constituency of the National Welfare Rights Organization beyond welfare recipients (Delgado 1986). In 1996, building on decades of experience organizing unemployed and underemployed workers, ACORN began to organize workfare workers in New York, New Jersey, Milwaukee, and Los Angeles (Reese 2002). Since the status of workfare workers as employees was contested, ACORN organizers struggled to obtain not only better working conditions for workfare workers but also recognition of a new identity. Like the Union League during Reconstruction and the Workers Alliance during the New Deal, ACORN opposed the pauperization of its members and demanded that they be recognized as honorable, independent, rights-bearing citizens.

As these remarks suggest, this chapter aims to draw analogies from earlier struggles over the classification of Freedmen's Bureau clients and WPA workers to more recent struggles over New York's workfare workers. Such a comparison poses an obvious problem: strictly speaking, a local policy like New York's WEP is not comparable to a federal policy like the Freedmen's Bureau or the WPA. However, to categorize the cases in this way would be misleading. All three of these policies are better understood as collaborative arrangements among the federal, state, and local governments, though the influence and role of the federal government within these collaborative arrangements varied from case to case. Although the Freedmen's Bureau and the WPA were ostensibly administered at the federal level, federal control was limited in both programs, allowing for significant local discretion and variability. Likewise, although the WEP was primarily administered at the local level, neither the policy's dramatic expansion under Mayor Giuliani nor the ensuing struggles over the classification of its clients can be understood apart from related policy developments at the state and federal levels. In short, all three of these cases cut across levels of government. Accordingly, while this chapter concentrates on classification struggles in New York City, it pays careful attention to the interplay of events at the local, state, and federal levels.

## The Prehistory of Classification Struggles over Workfare

The majority of New York's workfare workers in the 1990s qualified for federal welfare benefits because they were poor, single mothers. Their classification struggle must therefore be seen as part of a broader historical struggle over the social rights and obligations of female citizens that can be traced back to the Progressive era. In those years, maternalist reformers struggled to create state-administered pensions for needy single mothers who had to raise children without the wages of a male breadwinner. Like the Freedmen's Bureau and the WPA, the creation of mothers' pensions spurred classification struggles as maternalist reformers sought to distinguish these pensions sharply from traditional poor relief. Reworking civic ideals of republican motherhood, they represented pensions as compensation for mothers' services to the nation rather than public charity (Skocpol 1992, chap. 8; Kornbluh 1996). "We cannot afford to let a mother, one who has divided her body by creating other lives for the good of the state, one who has contributed to citizenship, be classed as a pauper, a dependent," declared the president of the Tennessee Congress of Mothers in 1911. Mothers' pensions were "given for service rendered," another advocate proclaimed, "just as the soldier service is recognized [by veterans' pensions]. Charity has nothing to do with it. The mothers are not to be classed with paupers for no court would grant the pension to mothers who come under that category" (quoted in Skocpol 1992, 450, 452). Thus, maternalist reformers rooted women's claims to pensions in their status as citizen-mothers, not citizen-soldiers (like clients of the Freedmen's Bureau) or citizen-workers (like WPA workers). Yet in all three of these cases, claims to social provision rested on some form of reciprocity; benefits were reserved for those who had proven their civic virtue through some socially useful public service.

In 1935, when Congress created the WPA for the able-bodied unemployed, it also created the ADC program for poor single mothers. ADC was modeled on the mothers' pensions created during the Progressive era and marked the federal government's partial assumption of responsibility for them. Later renamed Aid to Families with Dependent Children (AFDC) and popularly known as "welfare," the program served as the primary source of public assistance for poor single mothers in the United States for sixty years. However, during that period, classificatory changes, the program's shifting clientele, and the rising employment of women undermined the maternalist vision of the social world, calling into question the perceived worthiness of AFDC clients and paving the way for a radical overhaul of the program in the 1990s. First, New Deal policymakers divided welfare state clients into "employables" and "unemployables," reorienting public discourse about social provision from a broad conception of public service, originally construed by maternalists to include social reproduction, to a narrower focus on production and paid employment. Within this classificatory scheme, the categorization of single mothers as unemployables emphasized their status as dependents, obscuring maternalists' emphasis on the public service through which citizen-mothers earned their pensions. Second, the 1939 amendments to the Social Security Act shifted "many 'worthy' widows of working husbands out of ADC and into the social insurance system. . . . Left eligible for ADC were abandoned or unmarried mothers, women whose husbands were in jail, or widows whose husbands had worked either in noncovered occupations or not at all" (Lieberman 1998, 150). In addition, "during the 1940s and 1950s, the racial composition of the ADC caseload shifted dramatically, with black families making up considerably more of the caseload" (Lieberman 1998, 129). This trend continued as the welfare rolls expanded rapidly in the 1960s and early 1970s (Mettler

1998, 169–72). These changes encouraged the perception that AFDC clients were unworthy of social provision and transformed the program into a target for the expression of racial antagonism toward African Americans. Third, the rising participation of women in the paid workforce altered expectations about women's employment and encouraged a gradual reclassification of single mothers as employables. As early as the 1940s, the implementation of ADC "reflected the prevailing ambiguity as to whether women," especially women of color, "should be exempted from the requirement to work" (Piven and Cloward [1971] 1993, 123). Although ADC rules initially prohibited recipients from working, the program was adjusted to keep women in the labor pool when men did not provide a sufficient supply of low-wage labor (Piven and Cloward [1971] 1993; Abramovitz 1996). Furthermore, from the 1960s onward, various welfare-to-work reforms signaled that single mothers were increasingly expected to support themselves and their children through paid employment.[4] "Against the backdrop of poorly developed welfare state provision for non-poor working-age people, politicians could paint welfare as a 'privilege' and construe welfare reform as simply extending the compulsion of the market to welfare recipients" (Orloff 2002, 110). As a result of these changes, the classificatory principles and corresponding expectations institutionalized in AFDC lagged behind those embraced by political elites and the broader public. Although successive reforms helped to close the gap, the lag encouraged demands for a more sweeping transformation of the program.

## Policy Innovation at the Federal Level

Federal welfare reform culminated with the 1996 PRWOA, which terminated AFDC and replaced it with Temporary Assistance to Needy Families (TANF; National Governors' Association et al. 1997; Mink 1998; Schram 2000; Katz 2001, chap. 12). Several features of the legislation deserve mention. First, unlike AFDC, which reimbursed states for a percentage of their welfare expenditures, TANF provided states with lump sums of federal money known as block grants. Since the amount of the grant was fixed, this method of funding discouraged states from increasing their welfare expenditures or raising benefit levels (Committee on Social Welfare Law 2001, 324). The transformation of AFDC into a program issuing block grants also expanded the discretionary power of state and local officials, thereby increasing local variability in the administration of welfare. In this respect, the 1996 welfare reform strengthened a longstanding trend. Even before the legislation, AFDC was characterized by considerable administrative discretion and variability, a tendency reinforced by the use of federal waivers in the 1980s and 1990s (Mettler 1998, 225–28; Teles 1998, chap. 7). As noted in previous chapters, this kind of decentralized administration has generally resulted in less generous and more punitive redistributive policies (Mettler 1998). Second, TANF eliminated the federal statutory entitlement to public assistance for those who met prescribed standards of eligibility (Committee on Social Welfare Law 2001, 324). In so doing, the reform eliminated the federal mandate on states to serve all qualified applicants, permitted states to cut off aid to children as a penalty for parental misconduct, and jeopardized federal due process protections that the Supreme Court had applied to the administration of public assistance programs since the 1960s (Abramovitz 1996, 43; Mettler 1998, 225–28; Jeffrey 2002).[5] Third, the PRWOA restricted immigrants' access to TANF and other public benefits (Zimmermann and Tumlin 1999; Fix and Passel 2002). Although Congress partly restored access to some of these benefits in subsequent years, many restrictions remained in place. Welfare reform thus promoted both internal and external social closure, limiting the rights of citizens on public assistance while simultaneously fostering the exclusion of noncitizens. These immigrant provisions recall similar reforms in the past, including charity reformers' attempts to curb relief for the new immigrant working class in the late nineteenth century and restrictions on the eligibility of aliens for federal unemployment relief in the 1930s. Fourth, unlike AFDC, TANF imposed a five-year cumulative lifetime limit on federal public assistance payments. As a result of this restriction, hundreds of thousands of poor families throughout the United States started to exhaust their TANF benefits in 2001. These families were eliminated from the welfare rolls unless states continued to assist them with state funds (Committee on Social Welfare Law 2001, 324).[6] Fifth, TANF required most adult public assistance recipients to work within two years of receiving aid. Building upon precedents set by earlier welfare reforms, these work requirements completed the transformation of welfare from a maternalist to an employment-based policy.

The 1996 welfare reform did not constitute a comprehensive and radical reconstruction of American citizenship on par with Reconstruction or the New Deal, but it did reflect a significant and ongoing transformation of social rights in the United States. Just as the reconstruction of the welfare field during the New Deal challenged the older, Lochnerian vision of citizenship based on liberty of contract, so more recent reforms have eroded the limited forms of social and industrial citizenship bequeathed by the New Deal.[7] Whether the PRWOA ultimately points to the transformation of the New Deal welfare state into something new—a "Schumpeterian workfare state" (Jessop 1993, 1994), a Third Way "social investment state" (Giddens 1998; Myles and Quadagno 2000), a postindustrial welfare state (Piven 1991; Esping-Andersen 1999), or a "capital investment welfare state" (Quadagno 1999)—remains to be seen.[8] What is certain is that efforts to recast the welfare state, whatever form they may ultimately take, have already begun to foster a new round of classification struggles over the citizenship status and rights of welfare state claimants. While the transformation of AFDC into a program of work relief laid to rest maternalist claims to social provision, it also provided a new basis for welfare recipients to make claims: as citizen-workers rather than citizen-mothers.

## Policy Innovation at the Local Level

Although workfare experiments in New York City can be traced back to the 1970s, local welfare reforms implemented by Mayor Rudolph Giuliani significantly expanded and transformed the city's workfare program. Assisted by the federal government's 1996 PRWOA and New York State's 1997 Welfare Reform Act, Giuliani created "an ever-increasing number of administrative obstacles" to receiving welfare benefits, assigned growing numbers of welfare recipients to the Work Experience Program, and imposed strict sanctions on those who failed to comply (Committee on Social Welfare Law 2001, 327). Four features of the WEP under Giuliani are worth noting.[9]

First, the WEP embodied Giuliani's emphasis on "work first." The Giuliani administration extended workfare requirements to more and more welfare recipients while reducing (until mid-1999) the training and education options available to them, making New York's welfare system one of the nation's strictest in terms of work participation requirements (Fuentes 1996; Green 1997, 27; "Evidence is Scant That Workfare Leads to Full-Time Jobs," *New York Times,* April 12, 1998; Committee on Social Welfare Law 2001, 343; Nightingale et al. 2002, iii–v). The administration began by pushing recipients of general assistance (known as Home

Relief in New York; it was later renamed Safety Net Assistance, or, SNA)
into the WEP in 1995.[10] Workfare was then expanded in 1996 to include
AFDC (and later, TANF) recipients, some of whom were forced to leave
college in order to fulfill the program's work requirements. Although the
city was legally obliged to help working welfare mothers find child care,
child care shortages led caseworkers to pressure some parents to leave
their children in substandard care and forced the city to excuse from
work requirements thousands of others who were unable to obtain child
care ("Mothers Poised for Workfare Face Acute Lack of Day Care," *New
York Times,* April 14, 1998; Committee on Social Welfare Law 2001, 331–
332, 341–343).[11] The Giuliani administration expanded workfare again in
the late 1990s to include public assistance recipients with special needs,
including recipients who were disabled, pregnant, new mothers, and substance abusers—many of whom were previously work exempt. These initiatives helped to raise the proportion of adult SNA and TANF recipients
"subject to mandatory work requirements . . . from about half of all recipients in 1996 to about 80 percent in 1999" (Nightingale et al. 2002, 43).[12]
The mayor also tried to extend workfare requirements to residents of the
city's publicly funded homeless shelters in 1999, but the plan was delayed
by legal challenges and ultimately ruled illegal by the New York State Supreme Court.[13]

Second, as a result of this growing extension of work requirements,
the WEP expanded rapidly and dramatically under Giuliani. According
to Weikart (2003, 224), "Mayor [David] Dinkins [Giuliani's predecessor
from 1989 to 1993] had about 8,000 WEP slots." Under Giuliani, WEP
caseloads grew from 23,000 Home Relief recipients in September 1995 to
35,000 participants (including both Home Relief and AFDC recipients)
in 1996, and peaked at nearly 40,000 participants in May 1997. "Over the
next three years [from 1997 to 2000], the total number of WEP participants gradually declined to about 33,000. . . . Then, from May 2000 to September 2001, the WEP caseload fell by nearly 50 percent, to about 17,000"
(Besharov and Germanis 2004, 59; cf. Nightingale et al. 2002, B2–B3).
This decline was the result of variety of factors, including the city's shrink-
ing welfare rolls and a rising proportion of welfare recipients with conditions that prevented them from working.

Third, although a small proportion of WEP workers (about 2,500) la-
bored for nonprofit organizations, most worked directly for the City of
New York, mainly in its HRA (the city's welfare department) or its Parks,
Sanitation, or General Services (later renamed Citywide Administrative

Services) departments (Green 1997, 27; Tait 1998; Besharov and Germanis 2004, 62).[14] To ensure that WEP workers did not "get too comfortable in work assignments," HRA guidelines limited assignments from six months to a year (Nightingale et al. 2002, 41). WEP workers "worked off" their cash and food stamp benefits at these assignments, generally performing one of three types of activities: "clerical, custodial/maintenance, and human services (such as work at day care and senior citizen centers)" (Nightingale et al. 2002, 39). The number of hours worked were "based on the minimum wage rather than the prevailing wage for the activity performed" (Committee on Social Welfare Law 2001, 327). Home Relief (and later, SNA) recipients initially worked twenty-five to thirty-five hours every two weeks in six- or seven-hour shifts and were not provided with training or educational programs. AFDC (and later, TANF) recipients worked five days a week from 9 A.M. to 1 P.M. For every six months they worked in WEP, the city permitted them to spend one month in job-search classes. Most did not find jobs in the private sector and were reassigned to WEP (Green 1997, 26–28).[15] By the end of Giuliani's second term, his administration shifted from this "basic" model to a "three-plus-two" model, in which most welfare recipients (SNA as well as TANF) spent three days a week in WEP and two days a week engaged in other activities, such as job search, training, substance abuse treatment, or education (Nightingale et al. 2002, 34–38).

Fourth, the location and nature of WEP work assignments influenced the collective identity and claims of public assistance recipients in distinctive ways. As shown below, the assignment of WEP workers to city agencies encouraged them see the city as their employer. In contrast, past welfare-to-work reforms typically focused on finding private-sector employment for welfare recipients, thereby keeping the recipient's employer institutionally distinct from the welfare agency providing the benefits. Under these conditions, clients were less likely to transpose employment-related norms and expectations to their welfare administrators.

Furthermore, WEP reduced the social isolation of public assistance recipients. To be sure, rather than being completely atomized, welfare recipients were typically embedded in kin-based networks of cooperation and reciprocity that linked households (Stack 1974). However, these networks tended to confine solidarity and cooperation to family and close friends. Workfare, in contrast, facilitated interaction and social ties across such networks by placing clients from different kin-based networks in a shared work site. Although the durability of new ties was limited by labor turnover, this arrangement fostered a collective identity centered on work rather than kin or community. What Schwartz (1984, 196–97) says about the federal works program in the 1930s was therefore also true of New York's WEP in the 1990s; a "new sense of collective identity on the [work] projects" was made possible by the formation of new social ties through which meanings could be communicated and reinforced.

Finally, the WEP not only reduced the isolation of WEP workers from each other but also precluded their isolation from unionized municipal employees. This arrangement shaped the aspirations and expectations of WEP workers in important ways. As indicated in chapter 4, an individual's understanding of the rights to which he or she is entitled as a worker is dependent in part on which sets of workers serve as reference groups. Consequently, welfare recipients are likely to perceive less deprivation relative to non-unionized, low-wage, or part-time workers in the secondary sector than they will relative to unionized, high-wage, full-time civil servants.[16] The assignment of WEP workers to city agencies not only encouraged them to regard the city as their employer but also fostered face-to-face interaction and permitted fraternization with primary-sector unionized workers, alongside whom their deprivation became glaringly apparent. While WEP workers were paid the equivalent of $5,000 to $12,000 per year with no fringe benefits, "a unionized city worker made from two to eight times that amount—about $20,000 a year plus benefits for clerical and service workers, or $40,000 for trades people like painters and carpenters" (Tait 2005, 164). These disparities became salient once WEP workers looked upon themselves as municipal employees engaged in the same work as their unionized counterparts: As Tocqueville ([1835] 1972, 373) noted, "men are much more forcibly struck by those inequalities which exist within the same class than by those which may be noted between different classes." The location and nature of WEP work assignments thus mediated the effects of work requirements, raising the aspirations and expectations of WEP workers in ways that previous welfare-to-work reforms did not necessarily do.


## Between Public Welfare and Public Employment:
## The Contradictory Position of New York's Workfare Workers

Like the WPA in the 1930s, New York's WEP was a hybrid policy. On the one hand, the program's inclusion of welfare mothers, decentralized administration, and illiberal features were characteristic of the welfare state's feminine tier of public assistance. As shown in chapter 5, the proponents of social insurance intentionally equated this tier with traditional poor relief in the 1930s and 1940s. Accordingly, the WEP treated its clients in many respects as dependent paupers in need of discipline and supervision. The policy remained tightly linked to the older forms of public assistance it was supposed to supplant, WEP workers lost commonly accepted citizenship rights, and they were subjected to ritual degradation, as relief recipients in the past had been. These features of the program ensured that WEP workers remained close to other public assistance recipients in the welfare field. On the other hand, the program also resembled public employment in certain respects, which encouraged WEP workers to claim the independent status and rights of the city's regular employees. Since most WEP workers labored for and were directly paid and supervised by the City of New York, the dependent labor of WEP workers was difficult to distinguish from the independent labor of regular city employees. In addition, long-term changes in welfare policy and in the composition of New York's public-sector workforce ensured that WEP workers and regular municipal employees were not sharply differentiated along gender or racial lines, which further reduced the social distance between workfare workers and municipal employees. WEP workers therefore occupied an intermediate position in the welfare field, straddling the divisions between relief and work, dependency and independence, pauperism and full citizenship.

## WEP and public welfare

THE RELATION OF WEP TO WELFARE.   When Giuliani began his expansion of New York's WEP in the mid-1990s, he promoted it to the public as a radical and much needed break with past policies. Welfare, he argued, had sapped New York City of the entrepreneurial spirit that once made it great, a "spirit that embraces individual initiative, responsibility, and drive" (Giuliani 1997a). Past welfare policies thus perpetuated a "cycle of dependency" (Giuliani 1996b) that prevented each recipient from "utilizing his or her potential" (Giuliani 1996a) or developing "the self-worth that comes from having a job" (Giuliani 1996c). In contrast, the mayor claimed, the WEP allowed "welfare recipients to contribute to their city and their society by performing work that needs to be done" (1996b). Appealing to the "ethos of reciprocity" that fueled hostility to welfare among the city's white, ethnic, middle-class voters (Rieder 1985, 101–5), Giuliani extolled workfare for restoring "the social contract" between welfare recipients and "the rest of society" (quoted in "Evidence is Scant That Workfare Leads to Full-Time Jobs," *New York Times,* April 12, 1998). In this way, the program was said to foster dignity, hope, opportunity, self-sufficiency, and independence. Rhetoric like this linked the policy to longstanding civic republican themes in American political culture while distinguishing WEP favorably from the discredited welfare policies of the past. Yet this emphasis on the reciprocal and innovative character of the city's workfare program also fostered uncertainty about the standing of its clients. After all, reciprocity worked both ways; if workfare workers fulfilled the social contract and contributed to their city, did they remain recipients of public charity or were they now municipal employees who earned their benefits and were entitled to the same rights and protections as other city workers?

Whenever workfare workers made claims on the city as public employees, however, the Giuliani administration reversed its emphasis on the work aspects of WEP and instead emphasized its relief aspects. Again and again, city and state officials vehemently insisted that workfare was not a public employment program. City welfare administrators maintained that workfare workers were not and should not be considered public employees, they carefully referred to them as WEP participants rather than WEP workers, and they emphasized the transitional or temporary nature of workfare. Moreover, the workfare program's institutional ties to welfare reinforced its relief aspects. Despite the mayor's depiction of workfare as a bold alternative to older and more permissive policies, WEP was never clearly separated from public assistance. Just as WPA workers were certified as needy and referred by local relief agencies, New York's workfare workers were drawn from the ranks of Home Relief (and later, SNA) and AFDC (and later, TANF) recipients. The Giuliani administration's contradictory cues suggested that work, like military service, could provide a route to full and equal citizenship, but only when it was remunerated in the form of wages rather than welfare benefits.

CURTAILMENT OF CITIZENSHIP RIGHTS.   Federal courts have been unreceptive to arguments that workfare violated constitutional rights, such as the Thirteenth Amendment's prohibition of involuntary servitude or the Fourteenth Amendment's guarantee of equal protection (Mahmoudov 1998, 372–86; Reese 2000, 902–7). Yet WEP clearly limited the citizenship rights of workfare workers, even if these infringements did not rise to the standard of unconstitutional conditions (Mink 1998). First, WEP workers experienced a curtailment of their civil rights. Assisted by the federal government's termination of the statutory entitlement to welfare, the Giuliani administration "employed aggressive strategies to circumvent [the] due process rights" that courts applied to the administration of public assistance programs (Jeffrey 2002, 142; cf. Green 1995). Furthermore, the Giuliani administration maintained that workfare workers were not employees and therefore were not entitled to the protection of federal civil rights laws against sexual harassment and sex discrimination in the workplace. When the U.S. Equal Employment Opportunity Commission tried to investigate workfare workers' complaints of sexual harassment, the city refused to cooperate on the grounds that the commission lacked the necessary authority, because workfare workers were not employees. The commission subsequently found the city to be in violation of the 1964 Civil Rights Act, which led to a federal lawsuit in 2001 ("City Must Shield Workfare Force on Harassment," *New York Times,* October 1, 1999; "Federal Suit Accuses City of Not Acting on Harassment Complaints in Workfare Jobs," July 15, 2001; Committee on Social Welfare Law 2001, 340–41; Kean 2004).

Second, while there were no efforts to disfranchise WEP workers, ACORN sued New York State in 1996 for "neglecting to register welfare recipients at public assistance offices" in violation of the 1993 National Voter Registration Act, and it organized protests to pressure the state's Department of Social Services to comply with the law. According to ACORN, state officials registered "98,000 people . . . at public assistance offices in the first nine months of 1995, compared with the potential registration of nearly half a million." In effect, argued Brooklyn ACORN chairman Vernon Druses, New York State made it "more difficult for women, low-income and minority citizens to vote" by "neglecting people applying for assistance" ("State is Sued on Voter Signup," *New York Daily News,* March 24, 1996; see also ACORN 1997h).

Third, WEP workers lacked the industrial citizenship that American workers struggled to create in the 1930s and partly achieved through New Deal labor legislation. As described later in this chapter, local, state, and federal authorities denied workfare workers the most essential component of industrial citizenship: the right to organize and bargain collectively. In addition, WEP workers were "required to fulfill the obligations of employees without receiving the same legal protections and rights, social standing, or degree of control over their lives that employees enjoy" (Diller 1998, 29). Echoing the grievances expressed by WPA workers sixty years earlier, WEP workers complained that they occupied "a new basement tier in the labor force" that lacked fringe benefits (sick leave, vacations, pensions) and "regulations on hours, wages and safety that other workers take for granted" ("Discontented Workfare Laborers Murmur Union,'" *New York Times,* September 27, 1996; Fuentes 1996, 14).

RITUAL DEGRADATION.    Continuities between welfare and workfare are also evident from the ritual degradation of workfare workers. As Piven and Cloward ([1971] 1993, 1977) have shown, degradation is a longstanding feature of traditional poor relief; it is ritualistic insofar as it communicates something about work and welfare to both relief recipients and those who remain in the labor market. This dramaturgical function can be better understood by comparison to the ceremonial profanations and mortification processes through which the self is desecrated and destroyed (Goffman 1961, 1967). As Goffman (1961) points out, these processes are especially prominent in total institutions, which systematically attack the inmate's former view of herself, prevent "role carry-over" from her past, and force her to embrace "the life of the establishment" (120). Although New York's WEP was not a total institution (and thus not as effective), it operated in a similar, albeit less extreme, fashion. Like those recruited into total institutions, the workfare worker entered the program "with a conception of [herself] made possible by certain stable social arrangements in [her] home world," but was "immediately stripped of the support provided by these arrangements." As a result, she experienced "radical shifts in [her] *moral career,* a career composed of the progressive changes that occur in the beliefs that [she] has concerning [herself] and significant others" (Goffman 1961, 14; original emphasis). Degradation of the workfare worker dramatically failed to corroborate her prior self-conception while inducing her to internalize a new conception of self that was more consistent with the practices of welfare officials. Just as mortification of the self induces a "passage from civilian to patient status" in total institutions (Goffman 1961, 135), similar processes induced a passage from citizen to pauper status in the WEP.

Ritual degradation of workfare workers began with the interview process preceding work assignments. Just as WPA workers were fingerprinted in the 1930s, public assistance applicants in New York were subjected to finger imaging in the 1990s, which, in effect, criminalized them

(Green 1997). Moreover, chaotic and overcrowded conditions during the interview process deprived welfare applicants of even a modicum of privacy ("Workfare Screening of Homeless Starts, Then Stops," *New York Times,* August 21, 1996). Such conditions violated what Goffman (1967, 62–63) calls avoidance rules, norms that require an actor to keep at a distance (spatial and social) from others and not to violate the other's privacy and personal reserve. Lack of privacy also deprived applicants of their "front," expressive equipment employed to control the presentation and construction of self and to resist role dispossession (Goffman 1959, 22–30). In these ways, workfare interviews resembled the admission procedures found in total institutions; they ensured "a deep initial break with past roles," shaping and coding the applicant "into an object that can be fed into the administrative machinery of the establishment" and "worked on smoothly by routine operations" (Goffman 1961, 16).

WEP workers experienced further degradation at their work assignments, not only from welfare administrators, but also at times from the municipal employees who worked alongside them. This degradation took a variety of forms, including social avoidance. Just as the violation of avoidance rules may pollute or defile another person, an individual may avoid others so as not to be polluted or defiled by them (Goffman 1967, 69). Avoidance of "anomalous things" also "affirms and strengthens the definitions to which they do not conform" (Douglas 1966, 40). Insofar as WEP workers were perceived to be unworthy individuals with an anomalous status (between public assistance and public employment), avoidance of WEP workers served both of these dramaturgical functions. WEP workers were set apart by special uniforms and were sometimes prohibited from using the same bathrooms or cafeterias as regular employees (Fuentes 1996; "Discontented Workfare Laborers Murmur 'Union,'" *New York Times,* September 27, 1996; NYWRB 1997; Besharov and Germanis 2004, 68–69). Similarly, the transit workers' union insisted that WEP workers be prohibited from working together on the same squads as unionized workers ("Transit Union Agrees to Allow Workfare Plan," *New York Times,* September 19, 1996). In addition, workfare workers frequently experienced what Goffman (1961, 21) calls "mortification of the self by way of the body." This was typically accomplished by contaminative exposure, the "besmearing and defiling of the body or of other objects closely identified with the self." Contaminative exposure constitutes "a breakdown of the usual environmental arrangements for insulating oneself" (25), resulting in what Goffman describes as a loss of demeanor, the ability to control the way the self is constructed and presented. The testimony of workfare workers in lawsuits and public hearings provides vivid examples of this kind of humiliation: being ordered to pick up filthy garbage, bloody animal carcasses, urine-soaked mattresses, feces, condoms, dirty needles, rusty nails, glass, and other hazardous materials without protective clothing or gloves; being denied access to toilets and instead being forced to urinate on the street or on the sides of highways; and a lack of raincoats, warm clothing, winter coats, safety equipment, and protective gear (NYWRB 1997; CGO 1998; Mahmoudov 1998, 353–55). WEP workers also reported more serious abuses resulting in injury or even death (NYWRB 1997; CGO 1998). Consistent with this testimony, a 1997 lawsuit filed on behalf of workfare workers alleged that "the City [of New York] was routinely assigning people whom its own medical contractors found to be employable with limitations . . . to work sites at which their physical and/or mental limitations were in no way taken into account" or "reasonably accommodated," thereby exacerbating "the workers' medical problems and disabilities" (CGO 1998, 188–89; cf. Mahmoudov 1998, 353–55).

It is clear from their testimony that WEP workers perceived these abuses as presentational rituals, intentional "acts through which [an] individual makes specific attestations to recipients concerning how he regards them" (Goffman 1967, 71), and not mere oversights. "When I think of the degradement [sic] and disrespect I suffer here," WEP worker Elliott Roseboro testified to the New York City Council's Committee on Governmental Operations, "it literally brings a tear to my eye" (CGO 1998, 212). "We are being held back," complained WEP worker Parthinia Williams, "beaten down and being punished for what?" (CGW/CHE 1998, 16). Workfare worker Nick LeBraun angrily suggested that unionized municipal employees were complicit in the degradation: "As far as Sanitation [Department] workers, Parks [Department] workers, housing managers and stuff, they look down on WEP workers like, you know, we do their dirty work for them. . . . [W]e get treated like sluts" (NYWRB 1997). As LeBraun's comments suggest, male workfare workers often perceived the degradation to be demasculinizing and therefore doubly disrespectful. Again and again, workfare workers testified about a persistent lack of dignity, fairness, and respect.

Although the impact of degradation on workfare workers has been emphasized here, degradation also exercised an important influence on those outside the WEP. Legislative investigations, press releases and public announcements from welfare officials, journalistic exposés, and newspaper editorials periodically set forth these rituals of degradation for public display, lifting them out of localized contexts of face-to-face interaction and transmitting their effects to a broader public (Piven and Cloward [1971] 1993, 169). In this way, the "spectacle of the degraded pauper" (Piven and Cloward [1971] 1993, 173) served as a "punitive semiotechnique," an "art of images linked by association . . . circulating discreetly but necessarily and evidently in the minds of all" (Foucault [1975] 1977, 101, 103–4). By stigmatizing workfare and communicating that stigma to a broader public, the Giuliani administration sought to deter potential applicants from seeking public aid. At the same time, ritual degradation served as a vehicle for moral entrepreneurship. During his administration, Mayor Giuliani repeatedly denounced public assistance as morally polluting to both the city and to recipients themselves. By presenting rituals of degradation for public display, the mayor and his allies sought to enlist the vicarious participation and involvement of the public in "guarding against and exorcising the moral and personal defects that are the presumed source of poverty" (Piven and Cloward [1971] 1993, 170–71; cf. Nissen 1999).

## WEP and public employment

DEPENDENT AND INDEPENDENT LABOR.   While institutional ties between WEP and welfare, curtailment of citizenship rights, and ritual humiliation served to constitute WEP workers as a degraded pauper class and set them apart from public employees, these effects were mitigated and partly offset by other features of the policy. Chief among these mitigating features were the location and nature of the program's work assignments, which, as previously noted, led many WEP workers to regard New York City as their employer. Of course, work requirements, per se, were not sufficient to blur the social distinction between welfare recipients and municipal employees. After all, traditional poor relief often imposed work as a form of ritual degradation, most notably in the nineteenth-century workhouse system established in England and the United States (Piven and Cloward [1971] 1993). However, the workhouse's "semiotics of deterrence" depended on "a clear distinction between 'independent' and 'dependent' labour" (Driver 1993, 24). In other words, ritual degradation did not serve to "celebrate the virtue of all work," as Piven and Cloward ([1971] 1993, 165) suggest, but rather, to celebrate the virtue of free labor. Like slave or convict labor, the forced labor performed by workhouse inmates gave free laborers "a wretched touchstone against which to measure their fears of unfreedom and a friendly reminder that they were by comparison not so badly off" (Roediger [1991] 1999, 49; cf. Glickstein 2002).[17] This is not to suggest that wage labor has never been degraded or stigmatized, only that the architects of the workhouse system tried to make relief less desirable than even the worst employment. As England's nineteenth-century Poor Law Commissioners put it, the pauper's situation " 'shall not be made really or apparently so eligible as the situation of the independent labourer of the lowest class.' The entire strategy . . . thus rested on the drawing of 'a broad line of distinction between the class of independent labourers and the class of paupers' " (Driver 1993, 24, 49; cf. Glickstein 2002, 70).

New York's WEP differed from the nineteenth-century workhouse insofar as WEP workers performed labor that was virtually indistinguishable from that of municipal employees. To be sure, city officials pledged not to replace unionized municipal employees with workfare workers, and the PRWOA sought to institutionalize this distinction by prohibiting the direct replacement of employees by public assistance recipients ("New York Girding For Surge in Workfare Jobs," *New York Times,* August 13, 1996; National Governors' Association et al. 1997). However, the legislation allowed vacancies to be filled by workfare workers, and the Giuliani administration took advantage of this loophole to employ large numbers of workfare workers in city agencies (Besharov and Germanis 2004, 75–76). Consequently, the WEP created "a pool of contingent workers, doing the same work as city employees and often working shoulder to shoulder with them, but for a fraction of their pay. . . . [P]ublic sector unions have mostly watched with fear and loathing as WEP workers have begun to fill slots once occupied by their civil-service colleagues" (Fuentes 1996, 14–15). Indeed, a 1998 survey of 482 New York City welfare recipients found that 88 percent of respondents claimed to do the same work as regular municipal employees (Stettner 1999, 79–80). Perhaps the best examples of this job displacement occurred in the city's Sanitation and Parks departments. The Sanitation Department's regular workforce fell from 8,296 in 1990 to 6,328 in 1998, when it was supplemented with five thousand workfare workers. Job displacement was even more dramatic in the Parks Department. In 1990, the nonadministrative workforce of the Parks Department numbered 2,786. By April 1998, that number had dropped to 1,156, and WEP workers assigned to the Parks Department outnumbered nonadministrative employees by more than five to one ("Many Participants in Workfare Take the Place of City Workers," *New*

*York Times,* April 13, 1998; see also Tait 1998, 141; City of New York Independent Budget Office 2000). Similar trends were evident in New York
State's Metropolitan Transportation Authority (MTA). In return for a
pledge not to lay off any union workers through 1999, a 1996 contract between the city's transit workers' union and the MTA allowed the MTA to
cut up to five hundred cleaning jobs (from a total of 2,800) through attrition and use thousands of workfare workers to clean subways and buses.[18]
The agreement was the first in New York to explicitly state that workfare workers would perform duties formerly done by union workers, and
it specified that workfare workers working for the MTA would be given
credit for their experience in the civil service point system that regulated
the advancement of municipal workers.[19] Although the activities of WEP
workers did not coincide completely with those of city employees, they
overlapped sufficiently to subvert the distinction between dependent and
independent labor (Committee on Social Welfare Law 2001, 343–44). As
one union official put it to the press, "workfare people are doing the jobs
that our members used to do" ("Union Head is Assailed on Workfare
Concessions," *New York Times,* October 1, 1996).

GENDER AND RACIAL CLEAVAGES.    It was not only the assignment of
WEP workers to city agencies that encouraged WEP workers to see
themselves as public employees; it was also a series of long-term shifts in
welfare policy and the changing composition of New York City's public-
sector workforce. These trends blurred gender and racial divisions between WEP workers and regular city employees in the 1990s, which further reduced the social distance between them. Even before the 1996
welfare reform, welfare had become increasingly masculinized while paid
employment (especially public-sector employment) became increasingly
feminized. On the one hand, the extension of AFDC benefits to families
with unemployed fathers and the introduction of work incentives to push
female recipients into paid employment eroded the feminine subtext of
welfare. New York's WEP reinforced this trend by bringing AFDC recipients (mostly single women) together with Home Relief recipients (more
than half of whom were unemployed men) and subjecting them to similar
requirements.[20] On the other hand, paid employment became less masculine as more women entered the workforce. By the late 1990s, women
made up 60 percent of new workers each year, accounted for more than
48 percent of the labor force, and represented 60 percent of new unionists
and 38 percent of union membership nationally (Needleman 1998, 151).

This feminization of paid labor was especially evident in public-sector employment in New York City. Although men continued to hold "a monopoly of the top positions" in New York City's public-sector and service unions in the 1980s and 1990s, "women made up a majority of the members of many substantial groups" in the New York labor movement (Freeman 2000, 317–18). These trends toward the masculinization of welfare and the feminization of public employment helped to bridge gender differences between WEP workers and regular municipal employees.

For many years, welfare recipients were distinguished as much by race as by gender. As conflicts over civil rights heightened racial antagonism in the 1960s and 1970s, the growing proportion of African Americans among AFDC recipients (especially in the cities) fostered increasingly racialized attacks upon welfare. "The animosity surrounding public assistance shifted from immigrants to blacks, and the justification for cutting aid changed from preserving the 'purity of the racial stock' to evoking racial stereotypes of black women as promiscuous, matriarchal, and welfare dependent" (Abramovitz 1996, 72). Critics assailed AFDC for "discouraging work and family formation and for rewarding laziness" in language strikingly reminiscent of earlier attacks on the Freedmen's Bureau, communicating "subtly veiled messages about family structures and employment patterns among African Americans" (Quadagno 1994, 117). In this context, many white workers came to perceive welfare as a "black problem" (Piven and Cloward 1974, 141). At the same time, racial minorities began to challenge predominantly white civil servants in New York and other urban areas for control over "the occupational and political benefits attached to public employment," including money, influence on the policies of municipal agencies, and the jobs themselves. Whites had "the bulk of these benefits," Piven and Cloward (1974, 226–27, 237) wrote in 1969, and blacks wanted "a greater share of them."[21]

By the 1990s, however, the racial divisions that once distinguished welfare recipients from city workers in New York had blurred considerably. To be sure, the 1996 welfare reform reinforced welfare's black subtext. Following enactment of the PRWOA, whites left the welfare system faster than minorities, leaving an overwhelmingly African-American and Latina caseload in urban areas (Orloff 2002, 98, 105; "Hispanic Mothers Lagging as Others Leave Welfare," *New York Times,* September 15, 1998). In addition, workfare encouraged public employees once again to see public assistance recipients as "a problematic and dangerous underclass" threatening their jobs (Tait 1998, 145–46). Yet the struggle over the classification of workfare workers in the 1990s was not simply a continuation of the racially polarized struggles between white civil servants and racial minorities in the late 1960s. As a result of those earlier struggles, nonwhites *did* acquire a greater share of the material and symbolic profits that accrued from public employment. By 1997, minority employees made up more than half the civil service in New York (Mollenkopf 1997, 102), and this shift was reflected in the city's municipal labor unions. District Council 37 of the American Federation of State, County, and Municipal Employees (AFSCME), New York's largest union of municipal workers, "provided a model of racial harmony, or at least peaceful coexistence. With a membership highly heterogeneous in racial and ethnic background, type of work, skill level, and income, the union's survival depended on sensitivity to internal diversity and the creation of broad solidarity" (Freeman 2000, 312). The union's 120,000 members were drawn largely from minority groups, and it was strongly backed by the black and Hispanic caucus of the New York City Council ("With No Clear Leader or Strategy, Unions Prepare to Face Giuliani," *New York Times,* February 21, 1994). In addition, Stanley Hill, the union's president from 1986 to 1998, was not only the head of "a major, racially integrated institution" (Freeman 2000, 313), but also one of the city's most prominent African-American leaders. In fact, "during the 1980s and 1990s, throughout D.C. 37, African-Americans, and to a lesser extent Hispanics, moved into positions of power" (313). With the election of Dennis Rivera to National Health and Human Service Employees Union 1199 in 1989, "the leadership of two of the city's largest and most influential unions" was brought squarely "in line with the increasingly black and Hispanic workforce in government and service jobs." Furthermore, "by the mid-1990s, D.C. 37, 1199, TWU [Transit Workers Union] Local 100, and Teamsters Local 237 all had African-American or Hispanic heads" (317). Just as the increasingly feminine subtext of the city's public-sector workforce made it difficult to distinguish city employees from workfare workers along gender lines, the increasingly nonwhite subtext of that workforce made it difficult for municipal unions to distinguish their membership along racial lines.[22]

In summary, two key developments reduced the social distance between WEP workers and municipal employees in the 1990s. First, WEP workers were generally assigned to municipal agencies, where they worked alongside municipal employees doing virtually identical work. Insofar as this arrangement blurred the line between dependent and independent labor, it made the WEP similar in form to public employment and provided a basis for WEP workers to make claims as public employees. Second, long-term shifts in welfare policy and in the composition of New York City's public-sector workforce diminished gender and racial divisions between workfare workers and city employees. These trends helped to limit or mitigate other features of the program that set WEP workers apart as a degraded pauper class.

## Reasons for the Contradictions of the WEP

Why did the WEP resemble public assistance in some respects and public employment in others? What accounts for the hybrid nature of the policy and its inconsistent treatment of workfare workers? Many of the same factors that accounted for the contradictory features of the Freedmen's Bureau and the WPA explain those of the WEP, as well.

### Clashing policy goals

As in previous cases, policymakers designed the WEP to achieve multiple goals. In this case, the policy was intended to discourage actual or potential workers from seeking public assistance, to provide a cheap supply of labor for the city, and to transform an urban underclass that was viewed as dependent and potentially dangerous into a conscientious, industrious, and disciplined labor force imbued with the spirit of capitalism. All of these goals reflected the emergence of a new urban regime in New York that began in the 1980s that sought to stimulate private economic development through reduced public spending, curtailment of the public payroll, tax breaks for private capital, and (under Giuliani) privatization of government services and more effective crime control (Mollenkopf 1991, 1992, 1997; Dreier, Mollenkopf, and Swanstrom 2001; Weikart 2003). However, this did not mean that the WEP conformed to a coherent functionalist logic. On the contrary, its multiple goals generated conflicting imperatives and, from the perspective of policymakers, unintended and potentially dysfunctional consequences. The program encouraged illiberal treatment of WEP workers as dependent persons in need of discipline and supervision while simultaneously generating demands to treat the program's clients more liberally, as independent, rights-bearing citizen-workers.

The WEP strengthened the accumulation and labor-disciplining functions of the welfare state (O'Connor 1973; Piven and Cloward [1971] 1993) insofar as the program's punitive and stigmatizing features deterred claims to public assistance, reduced the welfare rolls, and pushed welfare recipients into private-sector employment. The WEP's deterrent effects (in tandem with the expansion of the EITC and a booming economy in the late 1990s) contributed to a steady decline in the number of persons receiving public assistance in New York City, from 1.14 million in fiscal year 1994 to 497,100 in fiscal year 2001 (City of New York 1994–2001; see also Besharov and Germanis 2004, 127–42). Reduction of the city's welfare rolls, in turn, helped curb redistributive spending. Although New York City's spending actually rose slightly (2.2 percent) in Giuliani's second term, he reduced spending for redistributive functions from 31.5 percent of the city's budget in fiscal year 1994 to 25.9 percent in fiscal year 2001 (Weikart 2003, 220–21, 228). According to Piven and Cloward ([1971] 1993, 381–99), reduction of welfare rolls also increases competition for jobs, thereby driving down private-sector wages, particularly in low-wage industries that rely on "a predominantly female and minority service proletariat" (Piven and Cloward [1971] 1993, 397; cf. Tilly 1996; Adler 2002; Levitan 2003). Among eight low-wage industries in New York City, half of which relied on a predominantly female workforce, total payroll employment increased by 9.3 percent, while average annual wages declined by 0.5 percent between 1994 and 1999 (O'Neill et al. 2001, 22–24). Although a variety of factors (including immigration) may have contributed to these trends, they are consistent with Piven and Cloward's thesis ([1971] 1993) and with Mayor Giuliani's own publicly avowed goal of providing, in his words, "the climate that will make it possible for the private sector to earn profits and provide jobs" (quoted in Weikart 2003, 217).

As the previous discussion of job displacement suggests, the Giuliani administration also used workfare workers as a cheap labor force for the city. In contrast to the Freedmen's Bureau and the WPA, this was not patronage (since workfare jobs were punitive and undesirable) but rather a way of containing public-sector labor costs. While Giuliani reduced the city's workforce by nearly twenty-three thousand people in his first three years in office, the city increasingly relied upon WEP workers, few of whom (about one thousand between 1995 and 1998) were hired full-time by city agencies.[23] However, the WEP was not entirely successful at reducing the public payroll; Giuliani ultimately increased the total number of full-time New York City government employees by nearly 6 percent, from 235,752 in fiscal year 1994 to 249,824 in fiscal year 2001 (Weikart 2003, 222). Moreover, the use of workfare workers as a cheap labor source clashed with the goal of reducing welfare rolls. "Because WEP workers perform useful tasks" for city agencies, "especially tasks that may be critical but burdensome or undesirable to regular staff . . . , there is a potential conflict between the interests of the host agency to keep participants engaged in productive WEP assignments versus transitioning participants into permanent wage-paying employment" (Nightingale et al. 2002, 41). The city's Independent Budget Office, a publicly financed nonpartisan fiscal monitor, also recognized this problem. "In the four years from 1995 to 1999 the WEP program grew rapidly, creating a pool of low-cost labor available to city agencies, in some cases enabling the restoration of services lost to previous budget cuts. The continuing decline in this labor supply poses a challenge for agencies such as parks and sanitation, which have come to depend upon these workers" (City of New York Independent Budget Office 2002, 1–2; cf. City of New York Independent Budget Office 2000, 1; City of New York Independent Budget Office 2001, 2). Furthermore, the city's use of workfare workers as a cheap labor source clashed with the policy's labor-disciplining functions. The employment and exploitation of WEP workers by the city encouraged protests and efforts to organize them, the city's growing reliance on the labor of workfare workers gave them potential leverage that welfare recipients did not previously have, and the partial replacement of municipal employees with WEP workers created potentially disruptive conflicts with the city's municipal unions.

City officials tried to legitimize the WEP by emphasizing the policy's capacity to transform its clients. As noted above, this strategy drew upon and reworked elements of the republican tradition in American political culture, particularly its emphasis on the need to cultivate civic virtue. In contrast to the WPA, which was intended to prevent the able-bodied unemployed from joining the ranks of "chronic dependents" (as Harry Hopkins put it), workfare was typically understood in reverse fashion as a form of rehabilitation for those who were already (presumed to be) chronic dependents. In this respect, the WEP was closer to the Freedmen's Bureau. Just as the bureau sought to remake its clients into self-disciplined workers fit for citizenship in a free-labor society, the WEP aimed to instill a "lost" work ethic in clients who were also overwhelmingly people of color (Giuliani 1995, 1996a, 1996b, 1996c, 1997a, 1997b, 1998; "Evidence is Scant That Workfare Leads to Full-Time Jobs," *New York Times,* April 12, 1998; cf. Schram 2000). The program punished workfare workers for their putative civic vices (dependency, indolence, pauperism, and promiscuity, for example), thereby stigmatizing them as unworthy, yet at the same time it was supposed to move them to a state of civic virtue (responsibility, self-reliance, and self-control). Accordingly, the Giuliani administration presented WEP as a rite of passage and consecration that would regenerate its underclass clientele and enable them to obtain employment and social respect. As Mayor Giuliani put it in 1998, "those who passed through our welfare to work programs prove to be excellent, motivated, dedicated workers" (quoted in CGO 1998, 177).[24] Promises from city officials that work should and would be rewarded, especially when combined with the employment of workfare workers by the city and the availability of municipal employees as a reference group, inevitably raised the expectations of workfare workers and encouraged them to make new claims upon the city. This is evident from the 1998 survey of New York City welfare recipients that found that more than one-third of the city's workfare workers expected to obtain permanent city jobs if they did well in the WEP. For many of the respondents, this would have represented significant upward mobility (Stettner 1999, 79–80, 89). The policy's rehabilitative function thus generated expectations and demands that directly clashed with the goal of reducing the city's labor costs.

*Federalism*

Treatment of WEP workers was also shaped by collaboration and conflict among local, state, and federal governments. As previously noted, social welfare and labor policies administered at the local or state level have historically tended to treat their clients in a less liberal fashion than federally administered policies (Mettler 1998). This disparity is partly the result of political-economic factors. Because cities and states have less taxing power than the national government and are more vulnerable to outflows of capital, they face greater competition to "attract and retain businesses" and therefore tend to have less generous and more punitive redistributive policies (Mettler 1998, 14–15). In this case, New York City's spending was limited by a host of factors after its 1975 fiscal crisis, including declining federal and state aid, oversight of the city's financial management by the State Financial Control Board, the city's inability to "raise taxes other than the property tax (which has a ceiling imposed by the state) without permission from the state legislature," declining tax revenues during a severe recession that stretched into the first two years of Giuliani's first term, and demographic changes (including immigration) that reduced the proportion of the city's African-American voters, who tended to be more supportive of redistributive policies (Weikart 2003, 211).[25] According to a study of mayoral spending policies in New York from 1978 to 2001, these constraints limited mayoral control over "how much to spend," though they allowed mayors significant control over "what to spend it on" (219). As noted above, Giuliani shifted the city's fiscal resources from redistributive functions to public safety and education (220–21, 228).

The political-institutional aspects of federalism also influenced the treatment of WEP workers. As already indicated, state and federal welfare reforms facilitated and reinforced many of the WEP's illiberal features. The administrative decentralization of welfare was especially consequential. In their study of New York City politics and policy since 1960, Brecher et al. (1993, 44–45) found that "whatever benefits the urban poor gain are derived primarily from the interventions of higher governments rather than their own local power. . . . Stated differently, the poor did less well when local politics became more important." However, administrative decentralization did not completely eliminate "the interventions of higher governments," some of which (court rulings, minimum wage laws, and the like) reduced administrative discretion and mitigated the policy's most egregious infringements upon clients' rights. In fact, state involvement was more liberalizing in the case of the WEP than in previous cases (the Freedmen's Bureau or the WPA) because of evolving constraints on states' police powers. States were "relatively unrestrained in their application of the police power . . . until the late 1950s and 1960s, when they were restrained by various reforms and court decisions at the national level." As a result, "the oppressive qualities of state governance for marginalized groups lessened. National government and social forces pushed states to reform, transforming various of the political-institutional features that had characterized state governance for so long" (Mettler 1998, 13–14, 223–25). These changes help to explain why New York's state courts stepped in to protect WEP workers from some of the program's worst abuses, at times even going further than the federal government.[26]

## From Contradiction to Contestation:
## The Struggle over the Classification of Workfare Workers

As in past struggles, the contradictory policy features of the WEP provided plausible bases for competing classificatory claims. Mobilized by community-organizing groups and labor unions, workfare workers sought to contest their classification as dependent paupers in need of discipline and supervision and reclaim their standing as independent citizen-workers. The ensuing conflict about how to class workfare workers was, in turn, linked to important material and symbolic stakes, including the rights to which they were entitled and the policy features that would be incorporated into or excluded from the program. To obtain recognition as citizen-workers, workfare workers invoked a variety of political traditions, civic ideals, and historical precedents from past struggles. Like Freedmen's Bureau clients, they reworked liberalism's emphasis on productive labor to demand fair compensation for their toil and to counter criticisms that they were freeloaders or exploiters of taxpayers' generosity. They also drew upon the Reconstruction amendments, invoking liberal guarantees of freedom of contract, due process, and equal protection to denounce workfare as a new form of involuntary servitude. Like WPA workers, workfare workers drew analogies between themselves and public employees in order to demand similar rights and protections, and they invoked the ideals of industrial citizenship embedded in New Deal labor legislation to articulate grievances and define injustices. Finally, workfare workers drew upon the legacy of the civil rights movement of the 1960s, including the rights-based model of citizenship that emerged in its wake (Schudson 1998). However, the struggle over the classification of workfare workers was not merely a conflict between workers and the state; it also involved internal disputes within the labor movement and conflicts among the various levels and branches of government. As in past struggles, labor and the state rarely acted in a unitary fashion.

## Mobilization of workfare workers

As New York's WEP expanded in the mid-1990s, community-organizing groups began to mobilize the city's workfare workers in opposition to it. This was not an easy task. The program's institutional structure discouraged participation in protests or other forms of political action. The benefits were meager at best, leaving clients with little cash with which to pay dues or engage in organized political activities, and administrative sanctions could deprive them of benefits entirely. Nevertheless, by the summer of 1996, workfare workers had formed an organization called WEP Workers Together with the support of three nonprofit welfare advocacy organizations: Community Voices Heard, the Fifth Avenue Committee, and the Urban Justice Center (Fuentes 1996; "New York Girding for Surge in Workfare Jobs," *New York Times,* August 13, 1996; "Discontented Workfare Laborers Murmur 'Union,'" September 27, 1996). In addition, two other organizations began to mobilize workfare workers: Workfairness (an affiliate of the Trotskyist Workers World Party) and, beginning in November 1996, ACORN. From September 1996 to February 1997, these groups helped WEP workers organize more than thirty demonstrations throughout the city (Vila 1997; Tait 2005, 168). Among these protests were "recognition actions," which ACORN began to stage in December 1996 and during which WEP workers confronted their site supervisors and demanded training opportunities, child care, and immediate improvements in their working conditions, including coats, warm clothing, gloves, protective gear, rest breaks, and access to bathroom facilities (ACORN 1997c, 1997f, 1997g, 1997h; "Divided They Fall?" *Village Voice,* January 28, 1997). ACORN also organized pickets, sit-ins, work slowdowns, and public demonstrations to demand better working conditions, health and safety protections, and later, a grievance procedure for WEP workers (Tait 1998, 142; 2005, 167–68).

While intended to obtain material improvements, these protests served an important dramaturgical function, as well. The organizers of those on workfare adopted modes of discourse, organization, and collective action that would disidentify WEP workers as paupers and affirm their collective identity as citizen-workers. In September 1996, for example, roughly forty workfare workers marched in the city's Labor Day parade alongside municipal employees ("Discontented Workfare Laborers Murmur 'Union,'" *New York Times,* September 27, 1996). Work slowdowns and the adoption of a labor-union model of organization communicated similar claims about WEP workers' collective identity. Workfare organizers sought to obtain recognition of these claims from political authorities, labor unions, and WEP workers themselves.[27]

Recruitment of WEP workers rose steadily from 1996 through 1997. Only about one hundred workfare workers had joined WEP Workers Together in August 1996, but that number doubled within a month ("New York Girding for Surge in Workfare Jobs," *New York Times,* August 13, 1996; "Discontented Workfare Laborers Murmur 'Union,'" September 27, 1996). By the end of January 1997, WEP Workers Together claimed to have expanded its contact list from an initial one or two hundred to five hundred, and Workfairness claimed to have collected 1,200 cards signed by WEP workers authorizing the group to represent them in any future talks with the city (ACORN 1997a; "Divided They Fall?" *Village Voice,* January 28, 1997). By June 1997, Workfairness reported three thousand members, and District Council 37 (now engaged in a unionization effort of its own) had signed up one hundred workfare workers (*Workers World,* June 26, 1997). ACORN quickly emerged at the forefront of recruitment efforts and surpassed the achievements of all the other groups. Between December 1996 and February 1997, ACORN signed two thousand workfare workers to its unionizing campaign ("Divided They Fall?" *Village Voice,* January 28, 1997). By April 1997, between 6,000 and 6,500 workfare workers had signed cards authorizing ACORN's WEP Workers Organizing Committee to represent them. When ACORN announced plans to raise that number to ten or twelve thousand by May 1997, the press called it "the area's most ambitious unionization drive in years" ("Welfare's Labor Pains," *Newsweek,* March 31, 1997; ACORN 1997f, 1997h).

Although WEP Workers Together eventually disbanded in 1997, Workfairness and ACORN continued to organize protests directed at a broad range of targets, from WEP workers' immediate supervisors to the mayor, the state legislature, and the federal government. Rallies of workfare workers and supporters were organized in December 1996 and at city hall in January 1997 ("Divided They Fall?" *Village Voice,* January 28, 1997). In addition, ACORN staged a rally of workfare workers and supporters in Washington, DC, in March 1997 to pressure the Clinton administration to apply the FLSA to workfare workers. Protesters chanted "day's work, day's pay" and held signs reading "Work with No Rights and No Pay Equals Slavery." Of the five hundred protesters who marched, more than two hundred were New York City workfare workers ("Welfare's Labor Pains," *Newsweek,* March 31, 1997; ACORN 1997f, 1997h). Two months later, Community Voices Heard organized another demonstration of workfare workers in Albany outside the New York State Assembly chamber ("Welfare Recipients Rally to Press for Jobs, Benefits," *Albany Times Union,* July 16, 1997).

ACORN's WEP Workers' Organizing Committee also sought to obtain recognition as a collective bargaining agency for workfare workers ("Union Seeks to Enlist 35,000 in New York City's Workfare Program," *New York Times,* June 29, 1997). In July 1997, 250 WEP workers marched to City Hall with thirteen thousand authorization cards to demand that the mayor recognize a union of workfare workers. As organizers pointed out, the signatures that ACORN collected represented more than one-third

of the city's WEP workers, exceeding the 30 percent required under federal labor law to call a union election for private-sector workers ("Petitions Seek Vote on Union for Workfare," *New York Times*, July 3, 1997;
Tait 1998, 142–43; 2005, 168). Although Mayor Giuliani refused to budge,
ACORN moved forward with a unionization vote in October 1997. For
four days, volunteers from unions, community organizations, and religious groups collected ballots at 150 WEP worksites around the city. The
election was supervised by a committee of labor, religious, academic,
and political leaders, and was headed by a former union official. More
than 45 percent of the city's WEP workers participated in the election,
exceeding the 38 percent voter turnout for the city's 1993 mayoral election. Of the more than seventeen thousand workfare workers who voted,
207 voted against unionization, and 16,989 voted to designate ACORN's
WEP Workers Organizing Committee as their representative in any future talks with the city.[28] Though it was not binding, the election served
an important dramaturgical function; it contested the dominant vision
and division of the social world and revived the possibility that people
and things could be classed differently. By affirming the status of WEP
participants as employees, the election aimed to bring into existence the
very thing that labor unions presuppose and represent. Subsequent protests reaffirmed those claims. In December 1997, more than four hundred WEP workers and supporters from local labor unions marched in
lower Manhattan to demand that the Giuliani administration recognize
workfare workers' right to unionize. Ed Ott, an official from the New
York City Central Labor Council, told the crowd that they were workers with "a right to a day's pay for a day's work" and "a right to be organized." Nick Unger, a union organizer for UNITE (Union of Needle-
trades, Industrial, and Textile Employees), promised workfare workers
that they would "not be alone" because "we will stand with you in your
fight for representation" ("Marchers Call on Giuliani to Support Workfare Union," *New York Times*, December 11, 1997).

WEP workers with previous union experience may have been more
likely to embrace ACORN's organizing campaign. Of course, many WEP
workers lacked such experience. The 1998 survey of New York City welfare recipients found that the respondents "earned an average of $772
per month [in past jobs], *less* than the federal poverty line for a family
of three ($1066 per month)" (Stettner 1999, 89, original emphasis). It is
unlikely that such low-paying jobs were unionized. However, based on
a random sample of 115 ACORN union authorization cards that I ex-

amined in April 1998, it may be estimated that about 17 percent of the WEP workers who signed the cards reported they had prior union experience. This experience could not be independently confirmed, nor is it clear to what exactly "prior union experience" refers. Nevertheless, given New York City's union density of 14.6 percent in the private sector and 23.3 percent overall in 2000 (Labor Research Association 2001), the data suggest a relatively high level of prior union experience among WEP workers who joined ACORN's campaign. If this is the case, habits acquired through previous experience with unions may have disposed them to embrace a labor-union model of organization. Conversely, among WEP workers who declined to join the unionization campaign, the proportion with prior union experience was probably lower. Unfortunately, the data necessary for comparison are not available.

Despite its achievements, ACORN's unionization campaign had reached an impasse by 1998. The organization had obtained the signatures of seventeen thousand workfare workers and had successfully used protests and lawsuits to improve WEP participants' working conditions. However, "courts and labor relations boards around the country . . . repeatedly ruled" that workfare workers could not "bargain collectively with a government" ("He Fights, Patiently, for Workfare Laborers," *New York Times,* January 16, 1998). Like mayors in other big cities, Giuliani refused to recognize workfare workers as employees or negotiate with ACORN. Nevertheless, ACORN began a major expansion of its workfare organizing efforts in New Jersey and Long Island in January 1998. As part of that effort, ACORN and the Communications Workers of America (a public employees' union) began trying to enroll ten thousand workfare workers in a new organization, People Organizing Workfare Workers ("Group Tries to Organize Workfare Recipients," *New York Times,* January 6, 1998). Jon Kest, ACORN's chief workfare organizer, acknowledged to the press that the organization was not a union, because workfare workers were not recognized as state employees, but he added that ACORN ultimately sought to achieve union status for them. "I'd liken it . . . to the farmworkers' struggles in the early '60s and mid-'70s," Kest told the *New York Times.* "It was 15 years before they were classified as employees in the state of California. So we don't necessarily view it as imperative to win everything today. We know that's not going to happen. But the whole debate in the city is going to shift in the next few years." Alarmed by this suggestion, Deputy Mayor Randy Levine warned that ACORN was "doing a very dangerous thing, raising the expectations and hopes of people" ("He Fights, Patiently, for Workfare Laborers," *New York Times,* January 16, 1998; see also Tait 2005, 147, 177–78).

*Gender and race in the mobilization of WEP workers*

Women were active in the groups struggling to organize workfare workers in the 1990s. Based on a random sample of 115 ACORN union authorization cards examined in April 1998, it can be estimated that roughly 60 to 70 percent of the WEP workers recruited by ACORN were female. This finding is also consistent with what I witnessed as a participant observer in ACORN activities from 1997 to 1998. This suggests that the participation of women in organized collective action was at least proportionate to and perhaps slightly higher than the percentage of women among adult public assistance recipients in New York. Moreover, women (often black or Latina and sometimes former workfare workers) held important leadership positions as ACORN organizers or staff members. Yet WEP workers rarely made claims as "welfare mothers" or framed workfare as a women's issue. In contrast to earlier struggles, which based women's claims to economic welfare and security on their relationships to husbands and children, female workfare participants were more likely to make claims as workers (cf. Reese and Newcombe 2003). This shift can be explained as a product of previously discussed trends. The rising participation of women in the paid workforce, the feminization of New York City's public-sector workforce in particular, the growing orientation of AFDC (and later, TANF) to employment rather than mothering, and the mass induction of welfare mothers into the city's workfare program after 1995 all discouraged female welfare recipients from defining their struggle in maternalist terms. As in the 1930s, a "work-related consciousness rather than . . . domestic concerns" was more typical of women whose daily existence straddled family and paid work and who did not view their work status as temporary (Kessler-Harris 1990, 64). Even WEP workers' demands for better child care typically rested on what Stoltzfus (2003) calls a "productive citizenship" rationale. WEP workers generally acknowledged single mothers' obligation to earn wages in support of their families, and they called for improved child care to help them meet this obligation. Thus, what Stoltzfus (1999, 3) says about the working mothers who fought to maintain publicly subsidized child care after the Second World War applies equally well to WEP workers in the 1990s. "Access to affordable and quality child care allowed them to engage in what they understood as productive citizenship, and, conversely, as productive citizens, they had the right to claim child care as a social wage." These developments encouraged workfare organizers and workers to emphasize workers' rights, orienting them primarily to the labor movement rather than feminist or women's groups.

Based on my participant observation of ACORN activities from 1997 to 1998, I have estimated that the overwhelming majority of organized WEP workers were African-American or Hispanic. At times, WEP workers downplayed racial differences as irrelevant. As one worker testified in 1997, "Whether it be color or creed, we will stick together and we will have this [workfare workers'] union" (NYWRB 1997). However, like public assistance itself, WEP workers' claims had an obvious and unmistakable racial subtext. In 1998, for example, WEP worker and ACORN member José Nicolau invoked Rosa Parks and the 1955 Montgomery bus boycott in his testimony to the New York City Council's Committee on Governmental Operations (CGO). "They didn't get off that seat in the bus to let somebody else sit who had more money and was better," Nicolau told the committee. "We are going to sit on this seat until we get . . . the dignity and respect we want" (CGO 1998, 215–16). This allusion to the civil rights movement implicitly cast workfare as a form of racial injustice.

The frequent equation of workfare with slavery communicated a similar message. One workfare worker testified in 1997 that workfare "violates not only the minimum wage laws, but also violates the Emancipation Proclamation. . . . [It is] nothing short of slavery" (NYWRB 1997). Other workfare workers referred to workfare as "slave labor," "legalized slavery," or "workfare slavery" (NYWRB 1997; CGO 1998). Advocates for WEP workers often used similar language. In 1997, a coalition of seventy churches, synagogues, and nonprofit groups publicly refused to employ workfare workers on the grounds that the WEP was unjust ("Nonprofit and Religious Groups Vow to Fight Workfare Program," *New York Times,* July 24, 1997; "2 Well-Known Churches Say No to Workfare Jobs," August 4, 1997). Seeking to mobilize public opinion against the WEP, religious leaders described WEP workers' hardships in terms of Christian suffering and redemption, portrayed their struggle in language drawn from the Bible and the abolitionist movement, and repeatedly compared workfare to slavery ("Nonprofit and Religious Groups Vow to Fight Workfare Program," *New York Times,* July 24, 1997; CGO 1998, 155–65; Tait 2005, 175). Like the allusions to slavery made by WEP workers

themselves, these references emphasized the exploitation of welfare recipients (inverting conservative charges that welfare recipients exploited
taxpayers) and implicitly criticized workfare in racial terms. Such language reflected the complicated, intertwined, and conflicted history of republicanism and class formation in the United States: WEP workers and
their supporters used the language of slavery to simultaneously invoke
collective memories of past racial injustices and appeal to an "American
standard of living" that rested historically on "white men's wages." Like
nineteenth-century white workingmen, WEP workers concurrently made
and denied comparisons between themselves and slaves. As WEP worker
Glenn Turner put it, "they treat us like we're slaves," but "we are not
slaves; slaves been banned a long time ago" (NYWRB 1997). These kinds
of criticisms were generally not directed against the city's racially integrated municipal unions, but rather at Mayor Giuliani, who was unpopular with African Americans. Given the close connection between the
city's workfare program and the mayor, the language of slavery resonated
strongly with many black WEP workers.

## Municipal unions and workfare workers

The relationship between municipal labor unions and workfare workers involved both conflict and cooperation.[29] On the one hand, several
factors hindered an alliance between them. First, public spending preferences divided WEP workers from municipal labor unions. To be sure,
"the dependent poor and civil servants" both "prefer[red] increased expenditure" (Brecher et al. 1993, 33). Indeed, public-sector unions could
hardly stigmatize welfare recipients as threats to taxpayers' pocketbooks
since they themselves were vulnerable to the same charge, especially after New York City's fiscal crisis in 1975. As Freeman (2000, 291) points
out, many New Yorkers blamed the crisis on "overly-paid [city] workers"
as well as "overly-liberal government policies." However, "the dependent
poor and civil servants" typically "compete for spending increments." In
this case, a more generous workfare program could have resulted in less
money for the public payroll. Second, even if WEP workers and municipal unions had agreed on "labor's share of expenditure," they would have
probably disagreed about how to divide it. The poor "favor increased employment over higher compensation," while civil servants generally prefer to cut jobs rather than salaries and fringe benefits (Brecher et al. 1993,
33, 39–40). Third, job displacement revived longstanding cultural anxiet-

ies about the debasement, pollution, and demoralization of independent, respectable, and free labor by servile, degraded, unfree, or cheap labor (Glickstein 2002). On the other hand, the threat of job displacement and unionizing efforts by organizational competitors encouraged municipal unions to take up the cause of WEP workers. While competition from cheap and degraded labor may lead labor unions to try to exclude competitors from employment, it may also spur them to organize the competitors, especially if the union is incapable of excluding them. In New York, District Council 37 pursued both strategies in regard to workfare workers, first extracting non-displacement pledges from Mayor Giuliani and then seeking to organize WEP workers when the mayor failed to satisfy the union. In addition, when ACORN began its own well-publicized organizing campaign in 1996, organizational rivalry and competition for members induced District Council 37 to make similar efforts. As these remarks suggest, the economic and organizational interests of municipal unions strongly influenced their relationship with workfare workers; yet labor's interests could be defined in various ways according to alternative inferential logics, leading to uncertainty, internal disagreements, and diverse lines of political action.

Mutual wariness between the city's municipal unions and the mayor in the early years of the Giuliani administration eventually gave way to political accommodation. In response to Giuliani's efforts to curb public spending and the public payroll, District Council 37 president Stanley Hill criticized Giuliani's first budget as "a plan of pain for people of color and city workers" ("With No Clear Leader or Strategy, Unions Prepare to Face Giuliani," New York Times, February 21, 1994). According to Barrett (2000, 294), "the mayor was so nervous about labor's opposition" after the 1993 mayoral election that he "backed off" his plans to expand the city's workfare program. "Instead of workfare and other radical alterations of city policy, the 1994 Rudy was passive on public assistance policy, silently acquiescing to new record highs in the city's caseload." However, by 1995, antagonistic rhetoric between Hill and Giuliani had "given way to a remarkable period of labor peace in New York City" (Barrett 2000, 294). Giuliani avoided layoffs of unionized city employees, provided sizable incentives for those who left the payroll voluntarily, and courted the city's municipal unions in preparation for the 1997 mayoral election. In return, District Council 37 contributed money to Giuliani's re-election campaign and publicly endorsed the mayor's budget ("Defending Abrasiveness, Giuliani Cites Successes," New York Times, July 25,

1995; Mollenkopf 1997, 112). Giuliani also talked Hill into accepting the mayor's workfare program. "The Mayor promised that there would be no [public employee] layoffs (in at least some areas of DC 37 membership) [due to budget cuts] if the union agreed to an expanded WEP program. Thus, in major aspects, WEP seems to have been expanded in exchange for a no-layoff pledge" (Besharov and Germanis 2004, 75; cf. Kirtzman 2000, 171–74). This strategy weakened the unions' "traditional bond" with advocates for the poor, who criticized labor for shifting the cost of budget cuts to those who could least bear them ("Defending Abrasiveness, Giuliani Cites Successes," *New York Times,* July 25, 1995). Finally, in February 1996, District Council 37 approved a five-year contract with the city—described as the "linchpin" of Giuliani's "budgetary and labor policy" and later revealed to be passed by means of voting fraud—which promised three years of job security for most union members in exchange for a two-year wage freeze. The agreement set a pattern for contracts with other public-sector unions and helped the mayor end the city's budget deficit without upsetting labor relations.[30] With the 1996 contract approved, the mayor's accommodation with the city's municipal unions appeared complete.

Yet the labor peace was repeatedly strained as new developments pushed Hill to take a harder line on workfare. First, Hill was alarmed by the 1996 contract between the Transport Workers' Union and New York State's MTA, which allowed the MTA to use WEP workers while eliminating union jobs through attrition. Second, Hill came under increasing pressure from three powerful locals in District Council 37 that represented municipal hospital workers, park employees, and social workers, all of whom voiced growing complaints that WEP workers were doing union work. Finally, Hill found himself outflanked by more militant unionists inside and outside of District Council 37 who urged the city to train WEP workers and hire them for permanent unionized jobs; pushed for state legislation that would provide workfare workers with the same wages, benefits, and protections as others doing the same work; and lobbied Congress to tighten federal rules against job displacement and improve wages and benefits for workfare workers. In response to these developments, Hill announced that he would not allow the creation of a "separate, second-class workforce" as large or larger than the membership of his union, called for a moratorium on the expansion of workfare, demanded that the city hire union workers to fill vacancies in municipal hospitals, and insisted that the city provide permanent unionized jobs for at least some of the WEP workers assigned to the Parks Department. To back up these demands, Hill and other labor officials threatened to endorse Giuliani's opponent in the 1997 mayoral election, hold demonstrations at City Hall, and organize WEP workers.[31]

WEP workers also obtained recognition and publicity from the New York Workers' Rights Board (NYWRB), a private watchdog organization funded by unions and charity organizations (NYWRB 1996; New York Jobs with Justice 1996; "Union Forum is New Tool to Air Woes of Workers," New York Times, November 22, 1996). At the board's first public hearing on workfare in November 1996, a panel made up of academics, clergy, and union leaders heard testimony from WEP workers and others. The board's findings did not carry legal authority, but instead served as a vehicle for moral entrepreneurship. Attended by more than 250 people and reported in the press, the hearing aimed to develop a critical public attitude toward the city's workfare program. As executive director Dominic Chan put it, "Embarrassment is our primary tool. We want to embarrass the powers that be whenever we see intolerable exploitation. We want to tell them this is unacceptable" (quoted in "Union Forum is New Tool to Air Woes of Workers," New York Times, November 22, 1996). Although the hearing devoted considerable attention to the displacement of municipal employees by WEP workers, it also provided a public forum for WEP workers to voice their grievances. "Not one City agency or any other group has sought to view WEP participants as workers," the board concluded, but it was nevertheless clear that "WEP participants are workers." In its follow-up report, the board decried the "exploitation and abuse of these low paid workers throughout the WEP program" and their "hazardous working conditions, the lack of on-the-job training, unaddressed child care needs and poverty wages." The board insisted that "anyone who works is entitled to a living wage and [to] be treated with dignity and respect" (New York Jobs with Justice 1996, 4–5).

Solidarity with WEP workers became more prominent the following year. In February 1997, Hill publicly announced his support for the efforts of community activists to organize WEP workers, and he added that District Council 37 would join those efforts. At the same time, the national executive council of the AFL-CIO announced that it would to seek to organize more than one million workfare workers in New York and other states to improve their working conditions and pressure states and cities to give them permanent jobs ("Labor Leaders Seek to Unionize Welfare Recipients Who Must Go to Work," New York Times, February 19,

1997). "Are workfare participants really 'workers'? Our answer is: yes," declared the AFL-CIO Executive Council (1997). "Everyone who works should enjoy the same rights and have the opportunity to join a union. We should not create a sub-class of workers." Similarly, AFSCME (District Council 37's parent union) demanded "recognition of the rights of workfare workers to organize and to be treated as full-fledged employees" (AFSCME 1997b). In March 1997, the NYWRB held a second hearing on workfare to mobilize public support for these claims. Although the hearing was held in Albany, many of the workfare workers who testified were New York City residents and members of WEP Workers Together, Workfairness, or ACORN. A month later, the New York City Central Labor Council offered workfare workers free "associate memberships" ("Workfare Rights," Newsday, April 20, 1997). Finally, in June 1997, the New York Times reported that District Council 37 had begun "a major campaign" with strong backing from the AFL-CIO "to unionize the city's 35,000 workfare participants in what is widely considered by far the largest effort nationwide to organize such workers. . . . Because New York City's workfare program is the nation's largest, unions around the country are looking at District Council 37's campaign as a potential model" ("Union Seeks to Enlist 35,000 in New York City's Workfare Program," June 29, 1997). As "the opening salvo" in the AFL-CIO's national workfare organizing drive, District Council 37's efforts were considered "likely to expand the frontiers of union organizing and perhaps change traditional definitions of who is a worker." Union leaders clearly understood this. Jim Schmitz, AFSCME's deputy organizing director, described the campaign as "a fundamental battle to define a worker as a worker and give them the same labor law protections as other workers" (quoted in "Wages of Workfare," New York Times, July 7, 1997).

District Council 37's organizing drive was immediately complicated by competition and rivalry with ACORN. ACORN had collected about thirteen thousand signatures from WEP workers in June 1997, while District Council 37 eventually collected about ten thousand union authorization cards. Many WEP workers signed authorization cards for both organizations ("Union Seeks to Enlist 35,000 in New York City's Workfare Program," New York Times, June 29, 1997; Tait 1998, 143; 2005, 169). Although ACORN and District Council 37 discussed collaborating to organize workfare workers, several factors prevented them from reaching an agreement. First, union leaders were often territorial. "Other groups involved in activities with workfare workers are not unions," AFSCME

(1997b) declared. "They do not qualify as labor organizations and we should not seek to join with them." Some union leaders were also dismissive of ACORN's efforts. For example, James Butler, president of the local that represented municipal hospital workers, predicted that District Council 37 would recruit more WEP workers than ACORN because of its "history as a powerful union" ("Union Seeks to Enlist 35,000 in New York City's Workfare Program," *New York Times*, June 29, 1997). According to ACORN organizer Milagros "Milly" Silva, District Council 37 "wanted us to stop organizing [workfare workers] and let them do it, but we don't want to bow out totally. We want to be sure WEP rights are protected. It was a question of trust and turf. They felt we were attacking their members since some of them were supervisors of WEP workers. If we were to win collective bargaining rights, they said they should represent WEP workers" (quoted in Tait 1998, 144). Disagreements over strategy also hindered District Council 37's cooperation with ACORN. While the union focused on lobbying the state legislature to grant collective bargaining rights to WEP workers, ACORN emphasized the importance of immediately organizing WEP work sites (Tait 1998, 143). Indeed, according to union officials, Giuliani preferred to have District Council 37 represent WEP workers rather than ACORN, because the latter "had never been bashful about attacking the Mayor or organizing street protests" ("Union Seeks to Enlist 35,000 in New York City's Workfare Program," *New York Times*, June 29, 1997). In summary, the willingness of labor unions to recognize WEP workers as employees had mixed consequences for the struggle over their classification. As in the case of the WPA, recognition from unions helped to define relief workers as employees whom labor unions could then represent while triggering a struggle over who would have the power to speak for and represent them. This conflict hindered ACORN and District Council 37 from working together to impose their shared vision and division of the social world on recalcitrant public officials.

Although ACORN and the city's municipal labor unions were willing to mobilize WEP workers as employees, the state failed to guarantee this classification as the "official" and "legitimate point of view . . . that everyone has to recognize" (Bourdieu 1989, 21–22). Mayor Giuliani initially announced that he was "willing to begin talks" with District Council 37 about its efforts to organize the city's workfare workers if union leaders lobbied the federal government "to cover the increased costs" ("Mayor Says Cash Needed for Workfare Union Plan," *New York Times*,

June 30, 1997). However, the Giuliani administration subsequently refused to recognize a union of workfare workers on the basis of four rulings issued by the city's Office of Collective Bargaining between 1972 and
1981, which held that welfare recipients in past work programs were not
workers. Helping to construct the very reality he appeared merely to describe, New York City Labor Commissioner James Hanley explained that
"it would be illegal for us to bargain with people who are not our employees" (quoted in "Petitions Seek Vote on Union for Workfare," *New
York Times,* July 3, 1997). While District Council 37 and AFSCME pressured the New York State legislature to give workfare workers the right
to unionize and bargain collectively (similar to legislation proposed at the
federal level by the AFL-CIO), the Giuliani administration lobbied vigorously against such legislation on the grounds that workfare was a "transition program" and not a permanent or "regular job" ("Union Seeks to
Enlist 35,000 in New York City's Workfare Program," *New York Times,*
June 29, 1997; "Nonprofit and Religious Groups Vow to Fight Workfare
Program," July 24, 1997). New York Governor George Pataki concurred,
suggesting that workfare merely "models a real-life job" (quoted in testimony, NYWRB 1997). These claims infuriated WEP workers. Even when
they demanded "real jobs" or better access to education and training as
alternatives to workfare, they still resisted efforts to distinguish their labor from that of regular city workers. As welfare recipient Mary Conklin
told the NYWRB, "the work that I and other WEP workers perform is
genuine." "Workfare is real work," Conklin added, "it's not job training"
(NYWRB 1997). Nevertheless, the mayor and the governor prevailed.
In August 1997, the state legislature refused to pass the bill that District
Council 37 and AFSCME had proposed ("Compromise With Unions on
Workfare," *New York Times,* August 8, 1997). "We will not have unionization of workfare workers, [and] we will not have employee status of
workfare recipients," Pataki flatly declared (quoted in "Unions Irked by
Workfare," *Albany Times Union,* July 30, 1997). Consequently, District
Council 37 backed away from its organizing campaign and negotiated another compromise with the city: Giuliani promised that he would provide
adequate health and safety protections for WEP workers and avoid displacement of unionized municipal employees. In return, District Council 37 endorsed Giuliani in the 1997 mayoral election on the grounds that
he had not laid off any union members ("Compromise With Unions on
Workfare," *New York Times,* August 8, 1997; "In Agreement on Workfare, Little Change Is Provided," August 9, 1997; "Giuliani Endorsed by

Municipal Workers Union," September 12, 1997; Kirtzman 2000, 213–14). As Kirtzman points out, "the probability of Giuliani's reelection and the knowledge that he rewarded his friends and punished his enemies" (214) provided strong incentives for the union to compromise.

Following Giuliani's reelection in late 1997, the steady expansion of the city's workfare program generated new conflicts between the mayor and municipal labor unions. In April 1998, District Council 37 filed a lawsuit with the New York Supreme Court alleging that the city was preparing to lay off 900 unionized workers at city-run hospitals and replace them with workfare workers in violation of state law. "You just can't have workfare workers with nowhere to go," Hill told the press. "That to me is slavery. If you're not prepared to give these people meaningful jobs, you're not really helping." The mayor then pulled all WEP workers out of the city's public hospitals and reassigned them to other city agencies in order to rebut the union's allegations of job displacement and remove the basis for the lawsuit. The move failed to satisfy ACORN. "The losers will be those who will be laid off and those WEP workers who just keep getting shifted around," Kest complained to the press, "which is why they need a union." Several days later, Giuliani agreed to delay the layoffs for a month, promised that he would try to place laid-off hospital employees in other city jobs, and agreed to provide severance or early retirement for workers who were unable to find other employment. Hill, admitting candidly that District Council 37's "main goal" was to "avoid layoffs," agreed to suspend its lawsuit in return. As ACORN predicted, the agreement between the city and the union did nothing for the roughly 900 workfare workers whom Giuliani had dismissed from city hospitals.[32]

The fragile labor peace restored by Hill and Giuliani was again broken when a change in the leadership of District Council 37 led it to adopt a more militant and confrontational stance toward the city's workfare program. During the fall and winter of 1998–1999, Robert Morgenthau, district attorney for Manhattan, began to investigate corruption in the city's municipal labor unions, including allegations of embezzlement, kickbacks, and fraudulent ratification of District Council 37's unpopular 1996 contract with the city. Morgenthau's investigation placed District Council 37 on the defensive and bolstered challenges to Hill's leadership from dissidents within the union. AFSCME responded to the growing crisis by taking direct control of the union on November 29, 1998. As part of the takeover, AFSCME forced Hill to take unpaid leave and named Lee Saunders as the district council's trustee. Although the city's municipal labor unions agreed that they would not seek to reopen the contracts that were fraudulently ratified in 1996 (due to fears that the move might backfire), Saunders reportedly warned Giuliani that he would take a harder stance than Hill on workfare and other issues.[33] Saunders followed through with these threats the following year, starting "a small-scale war against Mr. Giuliani's workfare program" ("Vowing to Go from Scandal to Strength, City Union Looks for a Fight," *New York Times,* July 12, 1999). In 1999, District Council 37 sued the Giuliani administration in the New York State Supreme Court for substituting workfare workers for full-time city employees in four city agencies (the Parks Department, the Sanitation Department, the HRA, and the Administration for Children's Services) in violation of state law. In comments to the press about the lawsuits, Saunders blamed the WEP for creating "a second-class workforce of exploited WEP workers while attempting to eliminate union workers" ("Union Again Files Lawsuit Seeking End to Workfare," *New York Times,* April 15, 1999; see also "Union to Sue Giuliani Administration Over Use of Welfare Recipients in Jobs," *New York Times,* February 4, 1999). Union leaders also organized a rally at city hall on May 12, 1999, to protest the city's workfare program and other policies ("Unions to Protest Cuts, Vouchers and Workfare," *New York Times,* April 30, 1999). By July 1999, city officials were reportedly "displeased with the many demonstrations that Mr. Saunders helped organize to protest workfare and the Mayor's privatization plans." "Workfare is very unfair to the participants," Saunders retorted. "They're essentially performing functions performed by permanent employees who used to receive wages and benefits while the workfare workers receive none. A number of them say it is a kind of servitude" ("Vowing to Go from Scandal to Strength, City Union Looks for a Fight," *New York Times,* July 12, 1999).

## The Material and Symbolic Stakes of the Classification Struggle

As shown in previous chapters, a successful classification struggle not only internalizes new classificatory schemes in the minds of social agents, but also objectifies them in institutions. Agents institutionalize their preferred classificatory schemes by incorporating or excluding valued policy features that reflect and reinforce the status of policy clients. Consequently, classification struggles involve important material as well as symbolic stakes. In this case, the stakes included compensation and benefits comparable to those of regular municipal employees, the application of state and federal labor laws to workfare workers, and institutional changes or alternatives to the city's workfare program, ranging from a grievance procedure to the creation of a more generous form of work relief.

## Analogies to unionized municipal employees

Workers have historically been drawn to public-sector jobs for the security they provided. As Freeman (2000) points out, "government workers rarely got laid off, and they received pensions before they became common in the private sector. The civil-service system provided an element of protection against arbitrary, unfair, or discriminatory treatment, since hiring and promotions depended, theoretically, on objective measures, like examinations" (201). Moreover, in New York City, an upsurge of municipal unionism from the mid-1960s to the early 1970s "provided city workers and their families with a range of social benefits and protections that, even in the age of the Great Society, remained rare elsewhere" (214). As municipal employees became a salient reference group for New York's workfare workers in the 1990s, their historical achievements shaped workfare workers' understandings of the rights to which they were entitled. Again and again, in public testimony to the NYWRB and the New York City Council, in statements to the press, and in their political programs, WEP workers demanded parity with regular city employees (Urban Justice Center 1996; NYWRB 1997; "Petitions Seek Vote on Union for Workfare," *New York Times,* July 3, 1997; "Wages of Workfare," July 7, 1997; CGO 1998).

For starters, parity meant comparable wages and fringe benefits. The complaints made by Nick LeBraun, a WEP worker and member of WEP Workers Together, were typical. "I am working hard and I at least deserve . . . a real paycheck," LeBraun told the NYWRB. "Regular Parks workers receive sick days, they get vacation days, and they get lots of other benefits. WEP workers don't. Is this fair? I put in a hard day's work. I think I deserve what a Parks [Department] employee gets, don't I? . . . I am not getting paid for the very real work that I do" (NYWRB 1997). Making similar claims, WEP worker and ACORN member Elliott Roseboro asked the New York City Council: "What is it about me that allows this Mayor and political figures across this country to say that my work is different or of less value than the same work done by someone else?" (CGO 1998, 210–12). As in the case of the WPA, the substandard remuneration that WEP workers received had more in common with the "supplemental" wages historically paid to female dependents than the "family" or "living" wage that male workers historically demanded, and WEP workers' demands that equivalent work be remunerated with equal pay echoed claims made on behalf of women workers (Kessler-Harris 1990, chap. 4). In this respect, WEP workers appealed to a standard of living that was gendered as well as racialized.

Analogies to regular municipal employees did not merely shape WEP workers' understandings of what constituted a just wage; they also defined more broadly what it meant to be treated as a worker. Above all, parity meant being treated as a rights-bearing individual. WEP workers claimed a right to the same civil rights, health benefits, and safety protections as regular municipal employees, a right to "monitor implementation of welfare work programs," and an effective grievance procedure to safeguard their rights (Urban Justice Center 1996). Equal rights also included the right to organize. Although the National Labor Relations Act specifically exempted public employees, and New York state law prohibited strikes by state and local government workers, reforms in the 1950s and 1960s established and strengthened a genuine pattern of collective bargaining for New York's municipal employees that workfare workers sought to emulate (Freeman 2000, 202, 206). "You're a union man yourself," one WEP worker told the NYWRB in 1997. "You know how hard your people fought to get a union. That's what we are doing now. We need people like you to come out and say, 'Yes, these people need a union.' Union to union, this is what we need" (NYWRB 1997).

*State and federal labor laws*

The rights inscribed in previously enacted labor laws were an important stake in the struggle over the civic classification of workfare workers. The application of these laws, always partial and inconsistent, was an outcome of the struggle itself and therefore reflected "the previous state of the relations of power in the field of struggle" (Bourdieu 1991, 222). At the same time, the partial and inconsistent application of labor laws provided a basis for new claims and thus a stimulus to further struggle. If workfare workers were covered by some employment and labor laws, union officials asked, why not others (AFSCME 1997a)? Even when workfare workers failed to obtain legal protection, labor laws continued to shape their aspirations and claims, providing them with a language for articulating grievances and a benchmark for defining injustices. As the discussion below reveals, the state played a complicated but crucial role in these struggles as a collective actor (though hardly a unified one), an arena in which to contest the status of workfare workers, and a tribunal to adjudicate competing classificatory claims. In all of these respects, the struggle over the classification of workfare workers was strikingly reminiscent of conflicts over the status and rights of WPA workers more than half a century earlier.

STATE LABOR LAWS. As AFSCME (1997b) pointed out, the 1996 PRWOA was "largely silent on . . . whether workfare workers are considered 'employees' for purposes of coverage under state labor laws and other safety and health legislation." Under New York State law, workfare workers were not recognized as employees for most purposes. However, in 1997, the New York State legislature gave the New York State Department of Labor jurisdiction over the workplace conditions of workfare workers ("Judge Orders Health and Safety Items for 5,000 in Workfare," *New York Times,* August 19, 1997). In addition, WEP workers working in city agencies were eligible to receive workers' compensation through the Public Employee Safety and Health Bureau of the New York State Department of Labor (AFSCME 1997a). State courts went even further to recognize workfare workers as employees, though the most sweeping rulings were later overturned. Most notably, state Supreme Court Justice Jane Solomon ruled in *Brukhman v. Giuliani* that New York State law required WEP workers to be paid the prevailing wage paid to other public employees ("White House Calls for Minimum Wage in Workfare Plan," *New York Times,* May 16, 1997; Wise 1997). The decision was based upon New York's state constitution, which extended prevailing wage protection to employees of contractors and subcontractors performing public work. Solomon concluded that these provisions applied to workfare workers and consequently ordered the Giuliani administration to calculate the number of hours workfare workers were required to work on the basis of what it paid unionized city employees for similar tasks ("Court Backs Giuliani's Way of Assigning Workfare Hours," *New York Times,* September 19, 1998; *New York Law Journal,* September 21, 1998, 26; Mahmoudov 1998, 368–69). When Solomon's interpretation was rejected by the New York State Court of Appeals in 2000, a spokesman for the New York State AFL-CIO denounced the court for making "welfare workers second-class citizens" and excluding them "from the State Constitution by saying they're not employees."[34]

FEDERAL LABOR LAWS.    The PRWOA was equally ambiguous about the application of federal labor laws to workfare workers. "The new federal law is silent on many of the workplace protections workfare workers had been entitled to under the old law," the AFL-CIO Executive Council (1997) concluded, "including minimum wage, health and safety coverage, the right to join a union, and protection against discrimination." As a result, coverage of federal labor laws was also uncertain and contested. Consider, for example, the 1935 National Labor Relations Act. Since the PRWOA neglected to address whether workfare workers could join unions, some commentators concluded that it left the matter in the hands of the NLRB and the courts (Briskin and Thomas 1998, 576–86). According to the *New York Times,* however, workfare workers were "not entitled [under federal law] to bargain as a group with an employer," nor did they "come under the jurisdiction of the National Labor Relations Board, which administers union elections" ("Discontented Workfare Laborers Murmur 'Union,'" September 27, 1996; see also "Compromise with Unions on Workfare," *New York Times,* August 8, 1997). The minimum wage provisions of the 1938 FLSA also generated controversy (Briskin and Thomas 1998; Luers 1998; Mahmoudov 1998, 358–68; Reese 2000; Ellis 2003). Congress expanded the FLSA in the 1960s and 1970s to cover most categories of employees (Mettler 1998, 223), but the U.S. Court of Appeals for the Tenth Circuit ruled in *Johns v. Stewart* (1995) that workfare workers were not covered by the FLSA because they were not employees.

In 1997, labor, civil rights, women's, and religious groups began pressuring the Clinton administration to declare that workfare workers were employees who were therefore eligible to join unions and benefit from federal labor laws ("Workfare Rights," *Newsday,* April 20, 1997; NELP 1997). While the Clinton administration considered "issuing a statement to the states declaring workfare workers to be protected by [existing] federal employment laws, including the Occupational Safety and Health Act, Title VII of the Civil Rights Act of 1964, and the Fair Labor Standards Act" (NELP 1997), the Democratic minority leaders of the Senate and House of Representatives proposed new legislation (which was subsequently defeated) that would have explicitly defined workfare workers as employees covered by minimum wage laws and by laws giving workers the right to unionize (see also "Labor Leaders Seek to Unionize Welfare Recipients Who Must Go to Work," *New York Times,* February 19, 1997; Briskin and Thomas 1998; Mahmoudov 1998, 356). These moves provoked strong opposition. The American Public Welfare Association, representing the interests of state governments, sought to persuade the president that workfare workers should not be protected under the FLSA ("Workfare Rights," *Newsday,* April 20, 1997). In New York, the Giuliani administration declared that workfare jobs were "not real jobs and it is a mistake for anyone on welfare to think they ever will be" ("Welfare's Labor Pains," *Newsweek,* March 31, 1997). Likewise, in an editorial entitled "Don't Unionize Workfare," the *New York Times* (February 21, 1997) insisted that "what they [workfare workers] are doing does not amount to a job." Despite these objections, the Clinton administration concluded in a 1997 advisory interpretation that the FLSA did indeed cover workfare workers, meaning that the number of hours workfare workers were required to work had to be calculated on the basis of the federal minimum wage ("White House Calls for Minimum Wage in Workfare Plan," *New York Times,* May 16, 1997). Although New York and several other states already calculated workfare hours in this fashion, even this limited federal recognition of workfare participants as rights-bearing citizen-workers proved controversial. The *New York Daily News* ("Welfare Union is Fool's Gold," October 25, 1997) called for a "reality check: They're WEPies, not Wobblies. They're not employees. And they never will be." Some state governors and congressmen also criticized the Clinton administration's legal interpretation, prompting the National Employment Law Project (NELP) to publish a full-page advertisement in the *New York Times* warning that the critics wanted to exempt workfare workers "from the minimum wage and other basic employment rights—civil rights, organizing rights, job safety, family and medical leave and protections against sexual harassment" ("They're Chomping at the Minimum Wage Again," June 11, 1997). As the NELP predicted, Republican congressmen inserted a provision in the 1997 federal budget legislation to overturn the Clinton administration's advisory interpretation and explicitly deprive workfare workers of FLSA coverage, but they subsequently withdrew the provision when Clinton threatened to veto the entire budget. The Clinton administration's interpretation of the FLSA therefore remained in effect, but the administration failed to enforce it, and the application of the law to workfare workers remained contentious in the absence of a Supreme Court decision to settle the matter (Briskin and Thomas 1998, 566–69; Mahmoudov 1998, 367–68; Mink 1998, 110–11).

### Reforms of and institutional alternatives to workfare

When Congress and the New York State legislature failed to give work-fare workers an explicit right to unionize and bargain collectively, advocacy groups sought to introduce more modest changes in New York City's workfare program that would nevertheless position participants as rights-bearing citizen-workers. Among the proposed changes was a grievance system that would allow WEP workers to complain about dangerous work site conditions. Along with its obvious safety benefits, the proposal aimed to reduce the discretionary power of workfare supervisors and curb abusive treatment of workers. ACORN's WEP Workers Organizing Committee pressured the New York City Council to create such a system, and a bill was eventually drafted to do so (ACORN 1997a, 1997b, 1997d, 1997e, 1997g, 1997h). In addition, city councilman Stephen DiBrienza introduced a bill in September 1999 to create a "transitional employment program." As the *New York Times* pointed out ("Council's Vote on Three Bills Could Provoke Mayoral Vetoes," February 16, 2000), the bill would have provided "a limited, but sharply different, form of employment assistance than has been championed by the mayor in his workfare program." The bill allocated $3 million to create seven thousand jobs in city agencies and three thousand jobs in nonprofit organizations over five years. Welfare recipients would compete for the jobs, and those hired would give up their benefits to become regular, full-time employees. They would work for forty hours per week, including eight hours of work-related training, earn $7.50 an hour rather than the $5.15 federal minimum wage, and pay income taxes on their wages. The bill also required those who filled the transitional jobs to find other employment within a year. While ACORN focused on the grievance procedure bill, Workfairness became a strong supporter of the transitional jobs bill and began pressuring the city council to pass it ("Council Weighs New Jobs Bill as Alternative to Workfare," *New York Times,* September 29, 1999; "Council's Vote on Three Bills Could Provoke Mayoral Vetoes," February 16, 2000; "Council Votes to Guarantee Union Access at Markets," March 1, 2000).

Since the grievance procedure and transitional employment bills represented competing and more-liberal alternatives to the mayor's workfare program in its existing form, they generated considerable debate. As might be expected, the Giuliani administration sought to contrast workfare favorably to the city council's new policy proposals by identifying flaws in the latter. Giuliani opposed the grievance procedure bill on the grounds that it conflicted with state law. The mayor, the deputy mayor, and their Republican allies on the city council also scorned the transitional jobs bill as "a product of the philosophy of dependency," condemned it as too expensive because it created jobs paying more than the minimum wage, and criticized it as too limited because it did not provide enough jobs for all of the city's welfare recipients ("Council Weighs New Jobs Bill as Alternative to Workfare," *New York Times,* September 29, 1999; "Council's Vote on Three Bills Could Provoke Mayoral Vetoes," February 16, 2000; "Council Kayos 3 Rudy Vetoes," *New York Daily News,* March 30, 2000). Interestingly, advocates for both the mayor's workfare program and the transitional employment program invoked the WPA as a positive policy precedent. Author and newspaper columnist Mickey Kaus praised the WEP in the *New York Times* ("Workfare's Misguided Critics," May 5, 1998) as a reinvention of the WPA, though similarities between the policies were disputed in subsequent letters to the editor. Likewise, during debates on the transitional jobs bill, city council members explicitly referred to the WPA as well as the 1973 Comprehensive Employment and Training Act (CETA; "Council's Vote on Three Bills Could Provoke Mayoral Vetoes," *New York Times,* February 16, 2000).[35] Perhaps it was the WPA's contradictory policy features (described in chapter 4) that allowed it to serve as a model for both illiberal forms of employment assistance like workfare and more-liberal alternatives like the transitional employment program.

The New York City Council passed the grievance procedure and transitional employment bills in February 2000, and it subsequently overrode vetoes of both bills by Mayor Giuliani in March 2000. The mayor insisted that the city council did not have the power to create new social welfare programs, mounted legal challenges to the new policies in the courts, and refused to assign public assistance recipients to the newly legislated transitional jobs. In August 2001, five welfare recipients, Community Voices Heard, and the Fifth Avenue Committee sued the city for failing to create any of the transitional jobs legislated by the city council. Ironically, the Giuliani administration had quietly implemented a transitional employment program of its own, offering thousands of temporary city jobs to TANF recipients who had reached their five-year time limit on federal cash assistance. The jobs paid $9 an hour and were financed by New York State's federal block grant. These arrangements benefited the city, because they allowed it to continue to use federal funds to support clients whose income-support costs would have otherwise shifted to the city and state.[36]

## Summary and Conclusion

Like the Freedmen's Bureau and the WPA, New York City's workfare program became a focal point for broader conflicts over the meaning of citizenship and its relationship to labor, gender, and race in the United States. As in previous cases, the struggles were shaped by large-scale social changes, including economic restructuring and the transformation of the labor force, the crisis of the welfare state, and the emergence of new political forces (most notably, the New Right) that sought to challenge and reconstruct older visions of citizenship inherited from the past. Yet workfare was not merely a site of conflicts originating elsewhere; workfare itself encouraged conflict in a variety of ways. First, related policy innovations at the federal and local levels constituted workfare workers as a new group of clients within the welfare field. To be sure, the innovative character of these reforms should not be exaggerated. Federal policy changes sometimes built upon past precedents or continued long-term trends, and New York's workfare program predated the reforms of the Giuliani administration. Nevertheless, the policy changes of the mid-1990s generated significant political and legal uncertainty concerning the status and rights of workfare workers. In this context, past welfare policies served as models for workfare workers and their allies to avoid, while contemporary labor laws, positive precedents like the WPA or CETA, and the historical achievements of unionized municipal employees set standards of treatment to which they could aspire. Second, the hybrid nature of New York's workfare program placed its clients in an intermediate position within the welfare field. Workfare remained institutionally tied to the discredited welfare policies of the past, and key policy features made it similar in form to traditional poor relief. These features included the ritual degradation of workfare workers and the curtailment of their civil rights and industrial citizenship. In other respects, however, workfare resembled public employment: the assignment of workfare workers to city agencies, where they worked alongside municipal employees doing virtually identical work; long-term shifts in welfare policy and in the composition of New York City's public-sector workforce, which reduced gender and racial differences between workfare workers and city employees; and the application, albeit partial and uneven, of state and federal labor laws to workfare workers. These contradictory policy features provided a plausible basis for competing classificatory claims. Third, the Giuliani administration sought to attract public support for the mayor's workfare program by contrasting its putative merits to the alleged flaws of past policies and alternative policy proposals. City officials emphasized the program's work aspects and downplayed its relief aspects, praised it for restoring reciprocity between welfare recipients and "the rest of society," and held out the promise that workfare would enable clients to achieve employment, economic independence, and social respect. These strategies raised the expectations of workfare workers and encouraged them to make new claims on the city. Finally, workfare workers' claims to civil rights and industrial citizenship were sharply contested, because citizenship itself was a valuable form of political capital that could facilitate access to other kinds of capital, including more generous benefits and greater influence over the administration of the program. As George Gilder and other conservative intellectuals recognized, "the Republicans were clearly treading a fine line in seeking to move toward workfare without . . . facilitating the expansion of (work-oriented) welfarism in a different form, replacing the entitlement to a welfare check with a new entitlement to a government-financed job" (Peck 2001, 106).

Gilder's fears were never realized. Like the struggles of Freedmen's Bureau clients and WPA workers, the struggle of workfare workers to obtain recognition as rights-bearing citizen-workers must largely be deemed a failure. Although workfare workers did obtain recognition from some groups, most notably labor unions, there is little evidence of broad public support for their struggle. Indeed, because workfare workers' claims would have likely entailed increased public expenditures, the city's business community and privately employed residents had a shared incentive to oppose them (Brecher et al. 1993, 30–33). Moreover, public opinion data suggests widespread support for punitive welfare reforms in the mid-1990s. In a national survey of registered voters conducted in August 1996, a total of 68 percent of respondents favored the changes that Congress had made to the welfare system in the PRWOA (Gallup 1997, 199). To be sure, support for punitive welfare reforms was probably lower in New York City, which is generally more liberal than the nation as a whole. However, Giuliani's reelection in 1997 suggests that a majority of voters in New York were at least willing to acquiesce to the mayor's welfare reforms. Exit polls indicated that crime and "improving the quality of life" were voters' highest priorities ("Latinos, Blacks Show Equal Power, Poll Sez," *New York Daily News,* November 7, 1997), but the mayor's welfare reforms were well publicized and touted during the campaign as an important achievement. Finally, the clearest indicator of failure was the structure of the city's workfare program. Despite eight years of struggle, workfare workers and their allies were unable to incorporate valued policy features into the workfare program that would have distinguished its clients from paupers and institutionalized their status as rights-bearing citizen-workers. Congress and the New York State legislature refused to grant workfare workers the right to unionize, President Clinton's application of the federal minimum wage to workfare workers remained contested, and even more modest policy changes were obstructed by legal challenges and the mayor's unwillingness to implement them. Workfare workers retained their political rights and some of their civil rights, of course, but like WPA workers in the 1930s, they remained second-class citizens, only partly covered by state and federal labor standards and dispossessed of the New Deal's promise of industrial citizenship.

## CHAPTER SEVEN

# Respectable Aid for the Working Poor

*The Earned Income Tax Credit, 1975–2001*

W hy did workfare workers fail to escape the stigma of pauperism? To answer this question, this chapter compares struggles over the classification of workfare workers to similar but more successful struggles involving the EITC, a federal, means-tested tax credit for poor wage earners. Originally created in 1975 as a small credit "available only to wage-earning families with at least one dependent child" (C. Howard 1997, 69), the EITC was subsequently liberalized and expanded four times (in 1978, 1986, 1990, and 1993), adding "several million more families and several billion more dollars to the program"(139–40). As a result of these expansions, as well as the 1996 federal welfare reform, the EITC became "the largest cash transfer program for the poor and the near-poor" in the United States (Hoffman and Seidman 2003, 4). Despite efforts in the 1990s to stigmatize EITC recipients as welfare cheats and subject them to the kind of discipline and retrenchment typically reserved for paupers, the policy continued to confirm recipients' standing as independent, rights-bearing citizen-workers who earned and deserved public aid.[1] This chapter explains in what respects workfare and the EITC were comparable policies, demonstrates that similar mechanisms encouraged analogous struggles over the classification of their clients, and then shows how differences in policy structures and racial politics account for the divergent outcomes of those struggles.

## The Comparability of Workfare and the EITC

Like the classification of workfare workers, the classification of EITC recipients was the result of a contingent process of social, cultural, and political struggle. Those struggles were comparable in several respects. First, as policy innovations, workfare and the EITC created new groups of clients whose status and rights relative to other clients in the welfare field were uncertain and contested. Although workfare and the EITC can be traced back to the 1970s, the dramatic expansion of both policies in the 1990s encouraged struggles over the classification of their clients. This contemporaneous timing also makes it easier to control for contextual variables that could account for the success or failure of those struggles.

Second, though workfare and the EITC were not identical, they shared several policy features, which were important insofar as policy structure reflected past classification struggles and shaped subsequent struggles. In particular, the programs were comparable in terms of their eligibility criteria, benefit structures, and finance structures. In terms of eligibility, both policies provided means-tested support for individuals who fell below a specified income threshold. Like the WPA and OAI, workfare and the EITC were also employment-oriented policies that conditioned income support on work, past or present. In addition, both programs directed benefits largely, but not exclusively, to parents of dependent children.[2] Similar eligibility rules for workfare and the EITC, in turn, resulted in clients who were comparable in most respects. Indeed, "welfare recipients and former welfare recipients" who "left welfare and entered the workforce" were "among those most likely to benefit" from the EITC (Johnson 2000, 413). Workfare and the EITC were also comparable in terms of their benefit structures, which provided cash transfers rather than services or in-kind assistance, and their finance structures, which relied on general tax revenues (C. Howard 1997, 14–16, 69, 158–59; Hoffman and Seidman 2003, 1–2, 11, 14–15). Finally, the EITC was comparable in terms of size and cost to the public assistance programs through which workfare workers received their benefits and even outpaced those programs in the 1990s.[3]

Of course, unlike New York City's WEP, the federal EITC was designed, implemented, and administered at the national level. This difference complicates comparison, but the task is not impossible. As shown in the previous chapter, New York's locally administered workfare program was heavily shaped by and inseparable from policy developments at the federal level. When this federal involvement is borne in mind, the program appears more commensurable with the EITC. Commensurability can also be increased by broadening the comparison beyond the federal EITC to encompass similar policies at the local and state levels. In the 1980s, states began to create their own EITCs to supplement the federal EITC. New York State introduced its version in 1994, and by December 2001, nearly a third of the states had enacted similar policies (Johnson 2000, 407–8; 2001, 6; O'Neill et al. 2001, 45; Hoffman and Seidman 2003, 31–33). Likewise, the New York City Council approved the creation of a refundable city EITC during the Giuliani administration, though the New York State legislature refused to enact enabling legislation, thereby preventing the proposal from becoming law (O'Neill et al. 2001, 68). These locally and state-administered EITCs were not only modeled on the federal policy but were also institutionally linked to it. "All but two states simply 'piggyback' on the Federal EITC by providing a state EITC equal to X percent [20 percent in New York] of the federal EITC credit. This approach avoids subjecting potential recipients to another round of filling out complex EITC schedules. Once a household has done this process for the federal income tax return, the household is automatically entitled to X percent of this amount on its state income tax return" (Hoffman and Seidman 2003, 31–33). Consequently, state EITCs shared the federal credit's eligibility rules. In addition, nearly all of them shared its basic structure, and most of them (including New York's) were refundable for those who owed no taxes, like the federal EITC (Johnson 2000, 411; 2001, 8; Hoffman and Seidman 2003, 31–33). Furthermore, New York and other states used federal funds from TANF block grants to finance refundable state EITCs, and the New York City Council sought to finance its city EITC in the same way (Johnson 2000, 414; 2001, 29–31; O'Neill et al. 2001, 67–68).[4] As a result, the federal government not only influenced benefit levels and determined eligibility for state EITCs, but it funded many of them, as well. Thus, just as New York's workfare program was linked to and shaped by broader policy developments at the state and federal levels, so the federal EITC shaped and was linked to policy developments at the state and local levels. Broadening the comparison in this fashion reveals that struggles over the classification of EITC recipients, like those involving workfare workers, spilled across levels of government. Accordingly, while this chapter concentrates on the federal level, it attends carefully to related developments at the state and local levels.

Third and finally, struggles over workfare and the EITC are comparable insofar as Americans used similar language and invoked the same civic ideals to contest the status and rights of workfare workers and EITC recipients. In both of these cases, advocates for the policies' clients used the policies' links between income support and work to distinguish clients from undeserving paupers, legitimize public aid on liberal-contractual grounds as an earned benefit, and defend favored policies or policy proposals from undesired alternatives. These claims resembled the claims made on behalf of WPA workers and OAI recipients sixty years earlier. Conversely, those who promoted more punitive policies raised similar concerns to stigmatize workfare workers and EITC recipients as paupers in need of discipline and supervision. Critics denounced the EITC as an excessively large and fraudulent program that discouraged work and redistributed income to undeserving clients who paid little or no taxes. As noted in the previous chapter, workfare supporters used the same language to attack past welfare policies, promote workfare as a more desirable alternative, and oppose reforms of workfare that would strengthen clients' rights. These themes were, of course, hardly new. Dependency, special privileges for particular groups provided at taxpayers' expense, excessive costs, fraud, and corruption were all familiar and longstanding elements in the discursive repertoire of welfare-state critics from Reconstruction through the New Deal to the 1990s.

Despite these parallels, efforts to class EITC recipients as citizen-workers were more successful. Unlike workfare workers, whose classification remained contested, elites and the general public came to regard EITC recipients as self-supporting and rights-bearing individuals who had earned their benefits, rather than as dependent wards of the state. This difference in outcomes raises the question: why did attempts to class EITC recipients as independent, rights-bearing citizen-workers succeed while similar efforts on behalf of workfare workers failed? To explain these divergent outcomes, the remainder of this chapter compares the two policies and the struggles that emerged over the civic status, worthiness, and rights of their respective clients.

## The Struggle over the Civic Classification of EITC Recipients

The federal EITC was the product of a minor amendment to the 1975 Tax Reduction Act, enacted with support from congressional moderates and conservatives but with little controversy, publicity, or input from inter-est groups (C. Howard 1997, 69, 72, 139). Policy competition contributed crucially to the creation of the program. Like the leadership of the SSB in the 1930s and 1940s, proponents of the EITC perceived the growth of public assistance as a grave danger that could only be contained by estab-lishing and promoting an alternative model of income support.

> The roots of EITC can be traced to the explosive growth in AFDC during the 1960s and subsequent attempts at welfare reform. As a result of northern im-migration, public protest, and a series of favorable court decisions, the number of AFDC recipients more than tripled between 1962 and 1967, reaching five million. . . . The AFDC rolls continued to swell, and by 1970 the total hit eight million. (C. Howard 1997, 65)

Political elites sought to stem this expansion of AFDC by experiment-ing with a variety of alternative policies. These included early precur-sors to workfare, most notably the 1967 Work Incentive Program, which proved to be largely ineffective; President Richard Nixon's proposed Family Assistance Plan, which was never enacted; and a legislative proposal from Senator Russell Long for a "work bonus," which became the EITC (C. Howard 1997, chap. 3). Long, a Southern Democrat from Louisiana, was the chairman of the powerful Senate Finance Commit-tee when the EITC was enacted and the "chief architect" of the program (C. Howard 1997, 64). Like his original proposal, which "directed benefits to the 'deserving' poor, that is, those willing to work," the EITC embod-ied Long's "vision of a program that . . . covered only working poor fami-lies with children and forced the 'undeserving' poor either to choose paid employment or resort to stigmatized and inadequate AFDC services." In other words, "Long perceived his work bonus as a substitute for conven-tional welfare programs—in particular, for AFDC" (Ventry 2001, 22–23, 25). This strategy attracted support from other Southern Democrats in Congress, who played an important role in struggles over the EITC not unlike their part in the classification of OAI recipients. Indeed, "Southern Democrats, who . . . repeatedly blocked or reduced social welfare benefits for the poor (including Aid to Dependent Children and its successor AFDC), paved the way for the EITC" (C. Howard 1997, 64). With their support and Long's guidance, the Senate Finance Committee "insisted on targeting the [1975] EITC at those most likely to land on the AFDC rolls, namely, the low-income workers with dependent children: 'The most significant objective of the provision should be to assist in encouraging people to obtain employment, reducing the unemployment rate and reducing the welfare rolls'" (C. Howard 1997, 71). In contrast, "no welfare rights organization or representative of the poor advocated anything like the EITC, and none lobbied for the tax credit once it had been proposed. They tried instead to increase benefit levels and expand eligibility for the existing AFDC program" (C. Howard 1997, 73). This competition between the EITC and AFDC seems to have had a racial subtext; Long, for example, "allegedly referred to the National Welfare Rights Organization as 'Black Brood Mares, Inc.'" (C. Howard 1997, 67).

Policy competition contributed not only to the creation of the EITC but also to its subsequent expansion. Just as the SSB reserved valued policy features for OAI in order to distinguish OAI recipients from dependent paupers (see chapter 5), federal policymakers sought to liberalize the EITC for similar reasons. In 1977, the Carter administration proposed an expansion of the program on the grounds that it "it would assist the working poor 'without labeling them as welfare recipients.' An expanded EITC, moreover, . . . provided aid 'in a form relatively less stigmatizing' than traditional public assistance programs." As Americans had done since Reconstruction, EITC advocates reworked the liberal political tradition to legitimize public aid as an earned entitlement: "To its supporters, an expanded EITC was a reward for 'playing by the rules' and choosing self-reliance over dependency." Although the Carter administration originally intended to expand the EITC as part of a larger and more comprehensive overhaul of the nation's social welfare policies, the president's proposed Program for Better Jobs and Income was ultimately defeated. However, "opponents of the bill rarely attacked the EITC's proposed liberalization. In fact, most observers praised it as a positive antipoverty reform directed at the 'deserving' poor" (Ventry 2001, 29–31). This perception facilitated the program's expansion in 1978, when Congress liberalized EITC benefits and eligibility and made the program permanent (C. Howard 1997, 144). As with subsequent improvements, the need to make the EITC look good in contrast to competing policies drove policymakers to shape it accordingly, resulting in a kind of self-fulfilling prophecy. "By the end of the 1970s, the EITC had become 'everybody's favorite program,'" allowing it to survive welfare retrenchment during the late 1970s and early 1980s (Ventry 2001, 31–32).

Although concerns about the growth of AFDC eventually subsided, tight party competition encouraged policymakers to make additional changes to the EITC that reinforced the status of recipients as independent and deserving citizen-workers. After 1980, electoral de-alignment and volatility encouraged both Democrats and Republicans to try to "forge a new majority coalition of voters." Moreover, "one of the most volatile blocs of voters consisted of the working poor," many of whom were "recent blue-collar and working-class defectors from the Democratic Party, the so-called Reagan Democrats" (C. Howard 1997, 142).

> Numerous opinion polls, focus groups, and elections persuaded leaders of both parties that the allegiance of the working poor was up for grabs. Comprising roughly 20 percent of voters, the working poor represented a substantial target of opportunity. . . . These voters tended to view Republicans as the party of the rich and Democrats as the party of special interests, especially blacks. . . . [Consequently,] Politicians hoping to improve their . . . electoral chances became more receptive to programs that benefited the working poor. (C. Howard 1997, 142)

In this context, the EITC, like the Civil War pension program, became an "object of party competition" (C. Howard 1997, 145). As in the Gilded Age, the use of social welfare policies for electoral advantage encouraged interest groups to ally themselves with political parties to defend and expand federal aid. Although public interest groups representing the poor and near poor had previously "restricted their lobbying and research activities to direct spending programs" (146), congressional Democrats mobilized these groups to support tax reform in the early 1980s. These developments further broadened support for the EITC in Washington and contributed to a significant expansion of the program under the 1986 Tax Reform Act.

In the late 1980s and early 1990s, a revival of policy competition encouraged Congress to make further improvements to the EITC that again confirmed and strengthened the status of recipients as deserving citizen-workers. After the GOP lost control of the Senate in 1986, Republicans, conservative Democrats, and the U.S. Chamber of Commerce embraced the EITC as an alternative to the minimum-wage increases pushed by liberals, organized labor, and other Democratic constituencies. The 1988 Republican Party platform explicitly endorsed this strategy, praising the EITC "as an alternative to inflationary—and job-destroying—increases in the minimum wage" (quoted in C. Howard 1997, 150–52). (Liberal antipoverty groups, in contrast, supported both the EITC and a higher minimum wage.) Republicans and conservative Democrats also embraced the EITC in the late 1980s as an alternative to family legislation introduced by liberal Democrats in Congress, most notably the Act for Better Child Care (C. Howard 1997, 152–56). Due in part to the threat of these competing policies, "the EITC enjoyed strong support across the entire political spectrum" at the end of the decade, setting the stage for a "dramatic expansion" of the program (Hoffman and Seidman 2003, 14). In 1990, Congress broadened eligibility for the EITC, adjusted it for family size for the first time, and increased the maximum possible credit (C. Howard 1997, 156; Hoffman and Seidman 2003, 15).

Further improvements were introduced at the beginning of the Clinton administration, which aspired to use the EITC in conjunction with welfare reform to reorient political debate about social policy in favor of support for the poor ("Clinton Wages a Quiet War Against Poverty," *New York Times,* March 30, 1994; "Euphemisms Mask Fervor in Latest Attack on Poverty," April 17, 1994; Katz 2001, 294–98). The *New York Times* described the gambit this way: "Once taxpayers started viewing the poor as workers, not welfare cheats, a more generous era would ensue. Harmful stereotypes would fade. New benefits would flow." Though Clinton's "new 'social bargain with the poor'" would be "sold in race-neutral terms," "members of minorities, being disproportionately poor, would disproportionately benefit" ("A War on Poverty Subtly Linked to Race," December 26, 2000). Welfare reform took a more draconian form than the administration wanted. However, the Omnibus Budget and Reconciliation Act of 1993 expanded eligibility for the EITC to "higher income levels than before," extended the credit to those without dependent children for the first time, and increased "the dollar value of the tax credit across all incomes" (C. Howard 1997, 158; cf. Hoffman and Seidman 2003, 15). These expansions in the 1990s were the most significant in the program's history. According to Hoffman and Seidman (2003, 4, 26), the EITC's most rapid growth occurred after 1990. Moreover, Myles and Pierson (1997, 461) note that the expansion of the EITC in 1993 "represented the largest funding increase in any program for low-income people in the past two decades. By 1996, spending on the EITC reached $25 billion," more than double what the federal government spent on AFDC, making the EITC "a central component of national income maintenance policy."

The large gains made by the GOP in the 1994 election allowed the party to take control of both houses of Congress for the first time in forty years. In the House of Representatives, conservative Republicans led by Speaker Newt Gingrich aggressively championed a new "Contract with America" that included a balanced-budget amendment to the Constitution and harsh retrenchment of federal welfare programs (Gillespie and Schellhas 1994). Fueled by the ideological fervor of the "Gingrich revolutionaries," alarmed by the rapid growth of the EITC, and less concerned about the threat of electoral and policy competition after the 1994 election, the Republican-controlled Congress began trying to retrench the EITC in 1995 (Newman 2003, 189). As in the past, these efforts required conservatives to engage in moral entrepreneurship, identifying deviance, bringing it to the attention of others, and enlisting public support to create and enforce rules against it. Reversing previous attempts to distinguish the EITC from the discredited and stigmatized welfare policies of the past, conservatives now sought to equate them. Accordingly, "the Republican Contract with America associated the EITC with the old, failed regime of social provision" (Ventry 2001, 49n2). Republican congressmen argued that the program had "grown too big and too fast" (34), created work disincentives, and "had begun to look less like tax policy and more like welfare policy. . . . As Bill Archer (Rep.-Tex.) complained, 'Is it fair to ask middle-income taxpayers to give additional public assistance to those who pay little or no taxes?'" (34–35). Similarly, "Senator Phil Gramm (Rep.-Tex.) bluntly stated in 1995, 'It's just welfare, it's a subsidy'" (37). Conservative pundits made similar criticisms in the press, calling the EITC "a program that pays taxpayer dollars to people who don't even earn enough to be taxpayers" (49n2).

Just as opponents of the Freedmen's Bureau, the Civil War pensions, and the WPA attacked those policies as fraudulent and corrupt, tapping into republican anxieties about civic vice, conservatives denounced the EITC on similar grounds. "In 1995, Senator Don Nickles (Rep.-Okla.) called the EITC 'the fastest growing, most fraudulent program that we have in Government today.'" Likewise, Senator William Roth, a Republican from Delaware, argued that the EITC "allowed individuals to make 'millions of dollars off [the program] by scam.'" Commentators made similar allegations in the press, condemning the EITC as "'the biggest . . . transfer swindle in the history of the nation'" (Ventry 2001, 49n2). Though exaggerated, these charges gained credibility when the Internal Revenue Service (IRS) released studies showing "unusually high error rates for the EITC. Critics of the program interpreted these findings to mean that a large proportion of EITC beneficiaries were defrauders and cheats. The

EITC, they concluded, amounted to 'a tax credit for crooks'" (35). Both houses of Congress conducted hearings between 1993 and 1997 to investigate the EITC's compliance problems, and in 1994, Senator Roth "asked the General Accounting Office to investigate the noncompliance charges and determine what the IRS was doing to reduce the error rates" (35–36). As in the 1930s, congressional hearings and investigations provided opportune vehicles for moral entrepreneurship. Conservatives used the hearings to discredit the EITC and call for stricter discipline and supervision in the administration of the program. "Legislators considered suggestions designed to reform, simplify, and even repeal the credit. No stone was left unturned in the effort to locate perpetrators of EITC fraud. . . . Critics tied the EITC to a host of national problems, including reduced economic growth, the growing tax gap (the yearly difference between federal income taxes owed and federal income taxes collected), and rising taxes for the middle class" (36). Conservatives also proposed reforms that would link the EITC to welfare. "Some critics believed the IRS so incapable of administering the EITC that the program might be better run through welfare offices. . . . Not only were welfare offices more efficient than the IRS, EITC critics argued, but caseworkers could also more easily evaluate qualifying characteristics for EITC eligibles" (36). Like the institutional ties between the WPA and public relief in the 1930s, these proposed changes would have contaminated the EITC with the stigma of pauperism.

These efforts in the 1990s to discredit the EITC and stigmatize its recipients as paupers ultimately failed. In response to conservative attacks, defenders of the program continued to "differentiate the EITC from welfare" (Ventry 2001, 38). Senator John Rockefeller, a Democrat from West Virginia, praised the program for "helping parents who are teetering on the economic edge to be able to choose work over welfare, independence over dependence, dignity over the indignities of the welfare system" (37). Likewise, Leslie Samuels, the assistant treasury secretary for tax policy, argued that the EITC "should still be considered a tax refund" rather than a "welfare subsidy," because only a small proportion of the credit "exceeded total tax liabilities" (38). Furthermore, Congress and the IRS took effective steps in the 1990s to reduce the program's high error rates, and "new studies revealed that the program's work disincentive effects were not as severe as its critics insisted" (40). These developments improved "confidence in the IRS's administrative capabilities" (40) and rendered conservatives' allegations against the EITC less plausible, weakening their case. By 2001, "the intense political debate surrounding the EITC [had] subsided" (41), and "critics stopped calling the credit a welfare program" (42). Rather than retrenching the EITC, the tax act of 2001 actually increased EITC benefits for married couples (Hoffman and Seidman 2003, chap. 1).

The development of state-administered EITCs followed a similar pattern. Like the federal government's 1996 welfare reform, the expansions of the federal EITC in 1990 and 1993 spurred policy innovations at the state level. Nearly all of the sixteen state EITCs were enacted after Congress expanded the federal EITC in 1986, and half of them were enacted after the 1993 expansion (Johnson 2000, 407–8; Johnson 2001, 6). The creation of New York State's EITC in 1994 was therefore typical in terms of timing. Furthermore, at the state level as well as the federal level, policy competition contributed crucially to the creation of EITCs and encouraged efforts to distinguish their recipients from welfare recipients. Like their federal counterparts, state-level policymakers pushed the program as an alternative to welfare. They designed state EITCs to encourage welfare recipients to "enter and remain in the workforce" and ensure that "low- and moderate-income families who have never been on welfare . . . remain off public assistance" (Johnson 2000, 413). Policy competition also encouraged state legislatures to upgrade and expand their EITCs. New York's EITC, for example, "was initially pegged at 7.5 percent of the federal credit, and was later increased to 20 percent. Legislation enacted in 2000 authorized a further increase to 30 percent of the federal credit, to be phased in between 2000 and 2003" (O'Neill et al. 2001, 45). Consequently, the value of New York's EITC grew sharply. "In 1994, some 478,144 tax filers living in New York City claimed $40.7 million in state tax credits, an average of $85 per filer. In 1998, some 634,367 filers living in the five boroughs claimed $198.9 million—an average of about $314 per filer. This represents an average increase of $229 per filer between 1994 and 1998" (45). By 1998, the combined total value of federal and state EITCs in New York amounted to nearly $1.3 billion, significantly enhancing "the income of low-income working families" (45). Perhaps most telling of all, "research conducted in the 1990s . . . found that 80 to 85 percent of those eligible for the EITC [in New York] were using it" (46). This high participation rate, well above the rate for "most social benefit programs," suggests that the EITC carried little or no stigma (46). The absence of a stigma, in turn, reflected and reinforced the popularity of the program. Like the federal EITC, state EITCs "gained support across the political spectrum. . . . The credits are supported by business groups as well as social service advocates" (Johnson 2001, 6).

In conclusion, the rapid and dramatic expansion of workfare and the EITC in the 1990s encouraged analogous struggles over the worthiness, status, and rights of their clients, but these struggles had sharply contrasting outcomes. While workfare workers were largely classed as dependent paupers, EITC recipients obtained widespread and official recognition at both the federal and state levels as independent and deserving citizen-workers. This is evident from the broad support the EITC attracted from political elites, organized pressure groups, and the public. By the 1990s, the EITC was "one of the most popular programs in Washington" (C. Howard 1997, 139), repeatedly "hailed . . . as the policy equivalent of penicillin" (64), almost universally acclaimed "among political elites," praised by "the national media and officials from both major parties," and supported by a wide range of interest groups, including "organized labor, business, antipoverty groups, and children's advocates" (159). Even at the height of Republican attacks on the EITC in 1995, a national survey found that most respondents (53 percent) opposed reducing the EITC for the working poor (Gallup 1996, 272). Subsequent surveys found even more support for the EITC. A national poll conducted in April 2001 by Peter D. Hart Research Associates found that 43 percent of voters were "very or fairly familiar with the term 'earned income tax credit'"; 66 percent of respondents described their reaction to the EITC as "very or somewhat favorable" after it was described to them; and "support for the policy extended across the political and income spectrum," though it was especially high among Democrats and "those with incomes of less than $30,000" (Draut 2002, 15). "Considering the prevailing skepticism, if not hostility, toward public assistance programs," Howard (1997, 64) concludes, "the popularity of the EITC is remarkable." Since the legitimacy of a policy is usually associated with positive public attitudes toward the policy's clients, it is reasonable to conclude that broad support for the EITC indicated a favorable classification of EITC recipients.

The EITC's increasingly liberalized policy structure provides additional evidence of a favorable classification. As repeatedly emphasized in this study, a successful classification struggle does not merely internalize new classificatory schemes in the minds of social agents, but also objectifies them in institutions. Like Civil War pensions and OAI, the federal EITC and its state-administered counterparts underwent a steady process of improvement and expansion that reflected and reinforced the classification of recipients as independent, deserving, rights-bearing citizen-workers. Indeed, the "[federal] EITC expanded faster than every other major means-tested program between 1980 and 1992, and its growth even surpassed that of inclusive [and broadly popular] programs like Social Security and Medicare" (C. Howard 1997, 139–40). Moreover, in contrast to the expansion of AFDC in the late 1960s and early 1970s, the expansion of the EITC was "surprisingly uncontroversial. Backed by Republican and Democratic presidents alike, the EITC failed to generate anything like the virulent opposition which efforts to expand other income transfer programs provoked. Although the Republican Congress did try to scale back the EITC after 1994, even this effort was essentially limited to a (failed) attempt to repeal the EITC expansion enacted in 1993. Compared with their (much more successful) assaults on other antipoverty programs, this was a very muted response" (Myles and Pierson 1997, 461).

## Why Did Outcomes Differ?

Why did struggles over the classification of workfare workers and EITC recipients result in such different outcomes? A comparative approach allows three commonly accepted explanations to be ruled out or at least qualified. First, proponents of the EITC contend that the program was successful because it conformed to the classical liberal values that are presumed to be hegemonic in the United States. Christopher Howard (1997, 140) summarizes the argument this way: "Because benefits go only to people who work for wages, the EITC reinforces the work ethic. AFDC, by contrast, allegedly undermines the work ethic by providing payments to those who do not work at all." Consequently, Americans opposed welfare but accepted an expansion of the EITC (cf. Hoffman and Seidman 2003, 1–2, 14). However, this explanation fails to explain why workfare workers, who also worked in exchange for benefits, were classed as undeserving paupers. Tying benefits to work may have been necessary to avoid the stigma of pauperism, but it could not have been sufficient (cf. C. Howard 1997, 140).

Second, according to another widely shared view, policymakers adopted punitive policies like workfare in response to the growth of AFDC. According to this view, the program's excessive size and rising costs generated opposition from taxpayers and encouraged politicians to impose stricter discipline and supervision on clients, which reinforced the stigma of welfare. This explanation is unpersuasive for several reasons. To begin with, the number of AFDC recipients was falling, not rising, before the 1996 welfare reform (U.S. Council of Economic Advisors 1997). Furthermore, this argument fails to explain why EITC recipients escaped the stigma of pauperism even though the EITC grew dramatically after 1990, eventually outpacing AFDC in terms of size and cost. Finally, retrenchment and discipline do not automatically follow program expansion but instead depend on the effectiveness of moral entrepreneurs who identify expansion as a problem, draw it to the attention of the public, and mobilize opposition to it.

Third, business-centered theories of the welfare state would explain the divergent classification of workfare workers and EITC recipients in terms of how these classification struggles affected capitalist class interests. According to Brecher et al. (1993, 30–31), "the business community's major interest in local fiscal policy is to reduce, or at least contain the growth of, public expenditure," especially redistributive expenditures, because "the dependent poor are not purchasers of advanced business services," the business community does "not want public sector compensation levels to drive up the cost of labor generally," and businesses associate increased local spending with higher taxes and lower profits. Furthermore, as in the case of the WPA, the partial and potential extension of federal labor laws to workfare workers gave New York's workfare program a quasi-regulatory aspect that the EITC lacked, which also threatened to increase labor costs. From this perspective, it might be surmised that the business community vetoed workfare workers' demands because they were incompatible with business interests.[5] In contrast, one would expect efforts to class EITC recipients as rights-bearing citizens who earned and deserved public aid to be more successful, because the expansion of the policy did not threaten business interests: "Because the [EITC] program operates as a wage subsidy, benefiting only those who work, it poses no threat to businesses or regions dependent on low-wage jobs. On the contrary, by making low-wage jobs more attractive to potential workers, the EITC was particularly helpful to industries . . . which rely heavily on low-wage labor" (Myles and Pierson 1997, 461–62).

This business-centered explanation contains some truth, but it needs to be qualified in significant ways. To begin with, business support for punitive and disciplinary workfare policies did not simply reflect capitalist class interests per se; it also reflected implicit assumptions, beliefs, and expectations about welfare recipients, namely, that (1) welfare recipients did not work because (2) they lacked the proper habits and dispositions,

but that (3) they were employable or could be made so (4) through punitive and disciplinary means. These cultural assumptions did not automatically follow from capitalist class interests. Like social movements, collective action by employers presupposes a consensus about the nature of the
problems they face, the sources of those problems, and the most effective
solutions, which in turn requires interpretive work (Snow and Benford
1988; Plotke 1992). Only in conjunction with these particular cultural assumptions did Mayor Giuliani's workfare program appear to best serve
capitalist class interests. As in Max Weber's famous "switchman" metaphor (1946, 280), employers' vision and division of the social world determined the tracks along which their material interests pushed them.

Furthermore, capitalists were hardly monolithic in terms of their class
interests. In particular, the interests of financial capital diverged in significant ways from the interests of other capitalists. "Whereas the business
community prefers reduced municipal expenditure, the municipal financiers prefer more spending since some of that spending is likely to be supported by increased borrowings" (Brecher et al. 1993, 31). Consequently,
political coalitions in New York did not always reflect a simple class division between capitalists and workers. Instead, particular fractions of
the capitalist and working classes could and sometimes did unite in pro-
spending alliances that cut across class lines. In New York City, these coalitions typically included municipal financiers, civil servants, and the dependent poor (Brecher et al. 1993, 33, 43–44).[6] Thus, like labor and the
state, capital was divided (or at least potentially divisible) in struggles
over the status and rights of workfare workers. Of course, even with a
pro-spending coalition in power, workfare workers would not have obtained everything they demanded, but they would have achieved more
success than they did under Giuliani. In short, while the nature of New
York City's governing coalition influenced the outcome of the classification struggle, the formation and dissolution of political coalitions cannot
be explained by reference to class interests alone. As in previously examined cases, symbolic work was needed to provide a concrete definition of
interests, broker alliances, form coalitions, and disorganize alternative or
competing political formations.

*Policy structure*

If the EITC's conformity to classical liberal values, the size and cost of
welfare, and capitalist class interests do not fully explain the divergent

classification of workfare workers and EITC recipients, what more is needed? I suggest that the difference in outcomes was, in part, a product of institutional differences between workfare and the EITC. Though analogous in many respects, the policies were not indistinguishable. One key difference concerns the degree of federal control over the policies. Although both workfare and the EITC involved some form of collaboration among the local, state, and federal governments, these arrangements were hardly the same. In contrast to TANF, which allowed considerable variation and discretion in the amount and administration of benefits, the federal EITC provided a floor of standard national benefits upon which cities and states could only build. This made it harder to class EITC recipients as paupers. As in previous cases, nationally centralized and uniform administration tended to result in more liberal treatment of welfare state claimants (Mettler 1998).

Another key difference is that the EITC, unlike workfare, was a tax expenditure. This policy feature, part of the EITC's original institutional design, had several important consequences. While local welfare agencies provided cash benefits to workfare workers through the welfare system, the IRS (or analogous state agencies) administered EITC benefits through the tax system. Furthermore, though workfare and the EITC both provided means-tested benefits, welfare administrators relied upon more stringent, intrusive, and stigmatizing methods than the IRS to determine an applicant's financial means. Eligibility for welfare benefits depended on "a test of assets as well as income," requiring workfare workers and their families to "'spend down' their resources" in order to qualify. In contrast, eligibility for the EITC was "determined uniquely by an income test." Workfare workers were also subjected to greater supervision than EITC recipients, including individual case investigations that exposed their lives to intrusive examination and inspection (Myles and Quadagno 2000, 157, 159, 161). These institutional features provided more liberal treatment of EITC recipients as rights-bearers and distinguished the EITC from conventional public assistance, making it more difficult to class recipients as paupers (cf. Newman 2003, 183–84).

In addition, the EITC's institutional structure reduced political opposition to the program, which also had important consequences for the classification struggle. First, the administration of EITC benefits through the tax system "protected the program from social policy veto players" and provided a "less politically contested funding mechanism" (Newman 2003, 184). As a result, the program's supporters could more easily enact liberalizing reforms that reinforced the status of EITC recipients as rights-bearing citizen-workers. Second, because the EITC distributed benefits through the tax system, it did not require "new bureaucratic delivery mechanisms" (184). In this respect, the program differed from "many of the social policies implemented during the Great Society," which "entailed extensive institutional substructure creation, typified by job training initiatives" (184). As one recent study points out, conservatives sought to eliminate many of these programs on the grounds that "their weak institutional integrity bordered on patronage" (184). Workfare programs were potentially vulnerable to the same criticism, especially if they provided extensive support services or came to resemble public employment. As shown in previous chapters, such concerns about patronage tended to stigmatize policy clients as undeserving. In contrast, the "EITC avoided these criticisms, because it relied on the tax system, which did not require any new institutional support to function" (184).[7] Third, the EITC's status as a tax policy enabled it to serve policy objectives that appealed to employers and conservatives, such as reducing taxes or providing an alternative to direct expenditures and government regulation. As a result, the EITC attracted a wider and more powerful base of support among political elites (C. Howard 1997, 141; cf. Myles and Pierson 1997, 450–52), which further reduced the likelihood that EITC recipients would be singled out and stigmatized as paupers.[8]

### Racial politics

Differences in policy structure only partly explain the divergent classification of workfare workers and EITC recipients. As in previous cases, the classification of policy clients and the policy structures themselves were shaped by racial politics. Consequently, the institutionalist explanation suggested above must be supplemented by an account of how and why agents mobilized along racial lines. To understand how racial politics contributed to the divergent classification of workfare workers and EITC recipients, it is helpful to draw upon a perspective known as urban regime theory (Stone 1993; Stoker 1995; Mossberger and Stoker 2001).[9] This approach, which was developed to explain variation in how cities address poverty, assumes that "urban governance requires cooperation among an array of public and private actors." In other words, politicians must not only assemble a "majority electoral coalition" that will provide sufficient votes and campaign contributions to win elections, but also recruit "private-sector power centers" into a supportive governing coalition in order to "carry out their programs once they are in office." Since diverse economic, political, and civic interests can be combined and organized in alternative ways (a process that requires political-ideological work), multiple regime types are possible (Dreier, Mollenkopf, and Swanstrom 2001, 147; cf. Fainstein 1990). Dreier, Mollenkopf, and Swanstrom (2001, chap. 5) distinguish three ideal-typical urban regimes, each of which is "based on a different kind of coalition" and has "a distinct philosophy about the appropriate role of government in addressing urban poverty." In New York City, the mayoral administrations of Edward Koch (1977–1989) and especially Rudolph Giuliani (1993–2001) represented what the authors call a conservative urban regime. "Urban conservatism emphasizes reducing government regulation, promoting business growth, and 'freeing' the marketplace to create 'trickle-down' benefits for the poor" (147). "In office, urban conservatives typically seek to reduce taxes and regulations on business and to alter the social services practices that they think reward bad behavior by the poor and repel middle-class residents. They prescribe the unfettered promotion of private investment" (166; see also Fainstein and Fainstein 1988; Fainstein 1990; Mollenkopf 1988b, 1991, 1992, 1997). As previously indicated, workfare workers were unlikely to obtain recognition as rights-bearing citizen-workers in the context of an urban conservative regime, particularly the version that Giuliani represented. This was the result not only of the opposition of business interests in the mayor's governing coalition but also, as we shall see, of opposition within the mayor's electoral coalition.

Racial politics contributed to the emergence and perpetuation of a conservative urban regime in New York in two ways. First, racial conflict from the mid-1960s to the mid-1970s helped to disorganize the city's once-dominant liberal coalition (Mollenkopf 1988b, 1991, 1992). In those years, "demands by racial and ethnic minorities for school desegregation, the ending of job discrimination, and improved services" (Fainstein 1990, 561) pitted community groups for blacks and Hispanics against the city bureaucracy, which was predominantly white, in a struggle for "control [over] the administration of schools, hospitals, housing projects, and poverty programs" (Fainstein and Fainstein 1988, 177; see also 178–82). "Competition between blacks and whites . . . [thus] moved from the sphere of jobs to the enjoyment of public goods, like schools and entitlements" (Rieder 1985, 101). Welfare played an important symbolic role in this process. Growing publicity for federal antipoverty programs, the rapid expansion of the welfare rolls, allegations of welfare fraud, the association of welfare with urban riots, and the increasingly militant claims of welfare recipients themselves changed the meaning of welfare for many working- and middle-class whites, particularly white ethnic groups. These voters came to perceive welfare as a program for blacks that violated cherished norms of reciprocity and deference, and they began to feel that "they were subsidizing blacks to engage in any number of socially undesirable behaviors" (Rieder 1985, 101–7; quote from C. Howard 1997, 66). The city's liberal coalition unraveled under these strains. "White voters refused to support programmes that they saw as primarily benefiting minorities"; Jews, who had been staunchly liberal, and non-Hispanic Catholics became more conservative; and "public service unions, which formerly had joined forces with their clienteles to press for the enlargement of social programmes, now regarded their vociferous clients as hostile and vice versa" (Fainstein and Fainstein 1988, 177–82; Fainstein 1990, 561; see also Windhoff-Heritier 1992, 43–45). These conflicts "divided New Yorkers over racial issues in enduring ways" (Brecher et al. 1993, 89–90). Although the election of David Dinkins as mayor in 1989 showed that a coalition of white liberals and racial minorities could be reassembled, such coalitions were now more difficult to form and less stable than in the past. As in the case of the Freedmen's Bureau and the WPA, past conflicts internalized racial divisions in social agents and objectified them in institutions, thereby impeding subsequent efforts to regroup agents along cross-racial lines. This is perhaps most evident from the growing salience of race relations in New York's mayoral elections. By the 1980s, race relations had become the "critical dividing line" in elections, while other important cleavages—between service-demanders and money-providers, between party regulars and reformers, and between white ethnic groups—faded (Brecher et al. 1993, 108–9). Of course, the racial conflicts of the 1960s and 1970s did not prevent agents from reenvisioning or dividing the social world differently, but they made it less likely that such efforts would succeed.

Second, racial politics did not merely disorganize New York's old liberal coalition (a coalition that would have been more supportive of workfare workers' demands); it also provided an effective means for conservative political entrepreneurs to reorganize some of its elements into a new coalition. In the 1980s, Koch combined "formerly opposed tendencies, namely the relatively liberal Jewish population and the more conservative white Catholic population," thereby forging a dominant electoral

coalition "centered among white, ethnic, middle-class voters" (Mollenkopf 1992, 4–5, 191; see also Fainstein and Fainstein 1988, 183, 189; Mollenkopf 1991, 333, 345–48). As this feat suggests, the new urban regime
that Koch represented was "not simply the passive consequence of an
increasingly assertive stratum of capitalists and a declining progressive
movement." The mayor, "within the setting of national ideological conservatism, actively shaped his political context," not only giving voice to
"but also influencing his middle and working class supporters," shaping
their perceived interests, and persuading them that "a more generous city
government would siphon off hard-earned dollars to welfare payments
and . . . cause jobs to leave the city" (Fainstein 1990, 563, see also 567,
569, 571). Drawing upon and reinforcing past racial divisions, Koch mobilized "middle-class white fears of black and Latino encroachment" (Mollenkopf 1992, 18), "criticized the use of public spending to curry minority
support" (Mollenkopf 1988b, 247), and used symbolic terms and issues to
signal his indifference or antipathy to minority concerns.

In the 1990s, Giuliani pursued a similar strategy, attempting to "reconstruct the Koch coalition of white Catholics and Jews along somewhat more conservative lines than Mayor Koch had pursued" (Mollenkopf 1992, 180–85; see also Mollenkopf 1991, 352; 1997, 109–10). Exit
polls suggest the strategy worked. In both the 1993 and 1997 mayoral
elections, whites voted overwhelmingly for Giuliani while the vast majority of blacks and a sizable majority of Hispanics voted against him.[10]
Furthermore, when Giuliani was elected mayor in 1993, "more than half
the margin of change since 1989 [when he narrowly lost to David Dinkins]
came from middle-class white Catholic and Jewish election districts. . . .
The increased mobilization of relatively conservative white voters was
enough to make the difference for Giuliani" (Mollenkopf 1997, 109–
10).[11] Not surprisingly, Giuliani's policies reflected his core constituency's
hostility to redistributive spending for racial minorities. After 1994, the
mayor's budget was a "color-coded stacked deck. Police, fire and sanitation took 1 percent cuts while Medicaid, public assistance, foster care, day
care and child protective services plummeted 28 percent" (Barrett 2000,
309). These budget cuts disproportionately affected the city agencies that
employed the biggest proportion of racial minorities while largely spar-
ing the agencies with predominantly white employees (Windhoff-Heritier
1992, 36). Moreover, "black New Yorkers depended more heavily upon
municipal services than any other group" (Kirtzman 2000, 181). Giuliani's
fiscal policies were therefore doubly disadvantageous to New York's

black residents. In this context, workfare workers, who were overwhelmingly black or Hispanic and who received benefits through a racially stigmatized welfare program, stood little chance of obtaining recognition as honorable, independent, rights-bearing citizen-workers.

Why didn't New York's racial minorities mobilize to challenge their exclusion from the dominant electoral and governing coalitions? Workfare workers would have probably joined and benefited from this kind of challenge. However, along with the loss of liberal white allies, at least three other major obstacles discouraged racial minorities from mounting a political insurgency during the Giuliani administration. First, as shown in the previous chapter, Giuliani was able to incorporate municipal unions into his governing coalition, thereby preventing them from forming a base for an electoral challenge against him. Second, New York's black and Latino constituencies were internally divided by cross-cutting social divisions, including ethnic, class, gender, and (due to immigration) nativity differences, which deterred the formation of a challenging coalition and provided "fertile ground for the dominant coalition to divide and conquer" (quote from Mollenkopf 1991, 348; see also Mollenkopf 1988b, 252; 1992, 18, 20). Third, demographic, social, and political obstacles generated significant disparities between the political participation of whites and nonwhites. "Although whites comprise only 43% of the population of New York, they still represent three quarters of active voters, because—on an average—they are older than other population groups, because they are American citizens, and because they register as voters more often than non-whites. . . . Hence, the white electorate still plays a dominating role in City politics and accounts for the majority of the political elite in the City" (Windhoff-Heritier 1992, 42–43; cf. Mollenkopf 1988b, 224, 242). As a result of these impediments, "the reform process that forced earlier dominant coalitions to incorporate growing but underrepresented groups . . . stalled or failed for blacks and Hispanics" in New York (Mollenkopf 1991, 336). The stalling of this reform process further reduced the chances that workfare workers would obtain recognition as rights-bearing citizen-workers in the 1990s.

Of course, even with a different urban regime in New York during the 1990s, struggles over the classification of workfare workers would still have been constrained by the broader political context at the state and national levels. As Kirtzman (2000, 174) points out, Giuliani "came to power at a time when welfare was being reexamined across America and Bill Clinton, intent upon steering the Democrats on a moderate course, was pledging to 'end welfare as we know it.'" Moreover, the election of Republican George Pataki as governor of New York and the Republican Party's newly gained control of the U.S. House of Representatives in 1994 also pushed Giuliani to the right on social policy. The mayor engaged in a balancing act, trying to win reelection in New York City by taking more liberal positions on abortion, gay rights, and immigrant rights, while adopting the Republican Party's national stance on "core economic issues, each of which had a racial underside," in order to avoid appearing "awkwardly out of step with the party and the times" (Barrett 2000, 306; see also 305–12).[12] Furthermore, since New York's workfare program involved the collaboration of the local, state, and federal governments, political reforms at the state and national levels had a direct impact on the institutional design and implementation of the policy. Any mayor, regardless of the local electoral and governing coalitions he represented, would have been bound by the mandates imposed by the U.S. Congress in the 1996 Personal Responsibility and Work Opportunity Act and by the New York State legislature in the 1997 Welfare Reform Act. Nevertheless, the emphasis placed here on New York's urban regime in the 1990s is warranted for two reasons. First, the effects of the broader political context at the state and national levels were mediated by the local urban regime. Indeed, local officials partly shaped their context, as when Giuliani asked the New York State legislature to cut $1.2 billion in welfare and Medicaid spending to save the city "a comparable amount in matching funds" (Kirtzman 2000, 173). Second, the importance of racial politics was not confined to the local level. On the contrary, from the 1960s onward, racial politics contributed to the disorganization of the old New Deal Democratic coalition and the rise of more conservative regimes at the state and national levels as well (Quadagno 1994). New York City may be distinctive or unique in certain respects, but in terms of how racial conflict reorganized the city's politics and undermined efforts to class workfare workers as rights-bearing citizens, New York provides a microcosm of the political forces that thwarted workfare workers in the rest of the nation. Indeed, New York provides the strongest support for this argument: if racial politics thwarted workfare workers in a city renowned for its racial diversity, strong labor movement, longstanding liberal tradition, and Democratic dominance, what chance would workfare workers have elsewhere in the nation?

EITC recipients avoided the kind of racial backlash that thwarted workfare workers for several reasons. To begin with, a smaller proportion of EITC recipients were people of color. While the welfare caseload in big cities like New York was overwhelmingly African-American and Latina, especially after the 1996 federal welfare reform, roughly half of all EITC recipient households in 1996 were white, only 20 percent were black, and about 20 percent were Hispanic (Orloff 2002, 98, 105; Hoffman and Seidman 2003, 36).[13] Still, a relatively high proportion of recipients were racial minorities. The *salience* of racial divisions in the classification struggle was also important. As in previous cases, symbolic work was needed to make racial divisions explicit and to persuade social agents to recognize them as significant, thereby turning potential racial groupings into real, mobilized racial groups. This occurred to a greater extent in struggles over workfare than in struggles over the EITC. In part, this was because of the structure of the policies. The institutional links that tied New York's workfare program to existing welfare policies (Home Relief and AFDC) also transmitted the racial stigma that welfare had acquired in the past. Simply put, workfare workers were unable to escape the racial stigma associated with welfare, because workfare was not separated from existing welfare policies. In contrast, because the EITC was created as an alternative to welfare and separated from it, EITC recipients avoided welfare's racial stigma. Moreover, historical timing contributed to the perception of the EITC as a race-neutral policy. Welfare acquired a racial stigma in part because it became entangled with struggles over civil rights and racial integration in the 1960s and 1970s. In contrast, the most significant expansions of the EITC did not occur until the 1990s. Consequently, unlike welfare and other antipoverty programs, the EITC was never embroiled in or linked to divisive racial conflicts. Indeed, the Clinton administration deliberately promoted the EITC in race-neutral terms in order to avoid the kind of racial backlash that undermined the War on Poverty. Finally, workfare received far more publicity than the EITC, in part because workfare workers were mobilized while EITC recipients were not.[14] For example, between 1993 and 2001, the *New York Times* published 578 articles with "workfare" in the headline or lead paragraphs, but only 48 featuring "EITC" or "Earned Income Tax Credit."[15] This pattern suggests that fewer Americans may have been familiar with the EITC, which perhaps also helped to shield EITC recipients from the racial backlash that burdened workfare workers. After all, a policy is less likely to become a target if fewer people know about it. In summary, because there were fewer racial minorities among EITC recipients, and because their racial backgrounds were less salient to the public, the

EITC was "not viewed through the race or permanent underclass lens" (Newman 2003, 189), and it lacked "the cultural (and racialized) baggage associated with programs for welfare mothers" (Myles and Quadagno 2000, 161).

## The Historical Legacies of Past Classification Struggles

I have alluded to three earlier sets of political struggles that shaped the conflicts in the 1990s over the classification of workfare workers and EITC recipients. Although these earlier political struggles involved more than the classification of welfare state claimants, classification struggles were nonetheless an important dimension of them. First, workfare had distant roots in the pension programs that maternalist reformers established for poor, single mothers during the Progressive era. Classification struggles were crucial to the creation and promotion of these mothers' pensions. Maternalists argued that pension recipients were not paupers who were dependent on public charity, but rather, they were rights-bearing citizen-mothers who were entitled to public compensation for their services to the nation. Although these political struggles were not entirely successful, they provided single mothers with a new basis for claiming social rights that allowed them to circumvent the degradation of traditional poor relief. However, when the federal government assumed partial responsibility for mothers' pensions with the creation of the ADC in 1935, a second set of struggles proved to be far more detrimental to the status and rights of pension recipients. On the one hand, the categorization of WPA workers as unworthy, the eventual dismantlement of the federal works program, and the exclusion of agricultural and domestic workers from nationally administered social and labor policies like OAI and the FLSA tended to shunt women and African Americans into public assistance programs like ADC. On the other hand, the classification of ADC clients as "unemployables" rather than citizen-mothers engaged in valuable public service, the transfer of most widows into the social insurance system after 1939, and the efforts of the SSB to promote social insurance and undermine public assistance encouraged Americans to question the worthiness of ADC clients and equate ADC (and other public assistance programs) with traditional poor relief. These trends converged. Black families made up a growing share of the ADC caseload as the program became increasingly stigmatized. Finally, a third set of political struggles in the 1960s and 1970s also left historical legacies. As the War on Poverty became enmeshed in divisive conflicts over civil rights and racial integration, many whites came to perceive welfare as a program for blacks. In addition, concerns about the expansion of AFDC, changing expectations about women's employment, and the negative reaction to the welfare rights movement fostered work requirements and other forms of discipline for welfare recipients while simultaneously triggering a process of policy competition that gave birth to the EITC. Neither the racial stigma associated with welfare, which came to burden workfare workers, nor the widely recognized distinction between welfare and the EITC, which benefited EITC recipients, can be understood without reference to these earlier historical struggles.

How will the classification struggles of the 1990s influence subsequent conflicts over the status and rights of welfare state clients in the twenty-first century? Predictions are always risky and uncertain in the social sciences, but several consequences seem likely. First, the expansions of workfare and the EITC have reinforced the link between paid employment and social rights in the United States, weakening alternative bases for claiming social rights. As a result, future welfare-state clients will be more likely to make claims as citizen-workers. Second, although workfare and the EITC both link social rights to work, workfare tends to detach social rights from the status of citizenship, while the EITC incorporates them. Consequently, in a manner similar to traditional poor relief and public assistance programs, workfare programs will set a negative precedent that future welfare-state claimants will seek to avoid, a model in which the state provides meager public aid and miserly employment assistance as an alternative to full citizenship. In contrast, the EITC, like OAI, will provide a positive model for claiming social rights without forfeiting one's civil and political rights. Third, since workfare workers are more likely than EITC recipients to be either black or Latina, the classification struggles of the 1990s will stratify welfare-state claimants along racial lines. Although policy reforms in the 1950s, 1960s, and 1970s made once exclusionary social and labor policies like OAI and the FLSA more racially inclusive (Mettler 1998, 217–18, 223–25), the struggles over workfare and the EITC will likely create new racial divisions in the American welfare state. Fourth, the classification struggles of the 1990s may encourage future demands for some kind of "post-industrial citizenship" analogous to the "industrial citizenship" described by T. H. Marshall ([1949] 1964, 93–94, 111). Just as the Workers Alliance "functioned as a training

ground for unionism," returning hundreds of thousands of WPA workers to private industry as dedicated unionists (Lorence 1996, 150), more
recent efforts by community-organizing groups and labor unions to organize workfare workers may have similar effects, predisposing them to organizing campaigns in the private sector. Although EITC recipients were
not similarly mobilized, they may prove receptive to organizing drives as
well. While the policy positions EITC recipients as rights-bearing citizen-
workers, it does not require their employers to do so. Consequently, a disjuncture may emerge between the expectations generated by the policy
and the treatment of EITC recipients by their employers. This disjuncture may, in turn, encourage EITC recipients to demand some form of
post-industrial citizenship from their employers that is more consonant
with the social citizenship they have obtained from the state.

## Summary and Conclusion

To explain why workfare workers failed to escape the stigma of pauperism, this chapter compared their classification struggle with a similar but
more successful struggle involving EITC recipients. First, the chapter
pointed out analogous features of each case in order to establish their
comparability. These features included policy reforms in the 1990s that
dramatically expanded workfare and the EITC, which encouraged subsequent struggles over the classification of their clients; institutional features shared by both policies, including the involvement of the federal
government and (for workfare and state EITCs) state governments in
their administration, which shaped the outcomes of those struggles; and
the use of similar language and civic ideals to contest the status and rights
of workfare workers and EITC recipients. Second, the chapter traced
the development of the EITC and the classification of EITC recipients at
both the federal and state levels from 1975 through the 1990s. Although
the classification of EITC recipients was uncontroversial for most the program's history, it was sharply contested in the mid-1990s, at roughly the
same time as struggles over the classification of workfare workers. Third,
the chapter sought to explain why, despite these similarities, workfare
workers were classed as dependent paupers, but EITC recipients were
recognized as rights-bearing citizen-workers. Three commonly accepted
explanations—classical liberal values, excessive spending, and capitalist
class interests—were found to be insufficient reasons. The outcomes of

the classification struggles also depended crucially on the institutional structures of the policies and racial politics. Although workfare and the EITC shared some policy structures, they were not identical. New York's workfare program differed from the EITC insofar as it was institutionally linked to existing welfare programs and incorporated more of their illiberal and stigmatizing policy features. As in the cases of the Freedmen's Bureau and the WPA, policy clients were more likely to be classed as paupers when the policy was linked to or resembled conventional poor relief. In addition, workfare workers were constrained by a racial backlash that EITC recipients largely avoided—a backlash that required symbolic work to make racial divisions socially significant and a basis for mobilization. As in previous cases, this kind of backlash also made welfare-state claimants more likely to be classed as paupers. Of course, opposition to the demands of workfare workers was not a product of racism alone; many groups opposed their demands for a variety of reasons. However, racial antagonism contributed crucially to the formation of the political coalition that thwarted workfare workers, and opposition from the business community, fiscal conservatives, and others would probably not have been as effective without such a coalition. Finally, rather than taking policy structures and racial divisions as givens, the chapter ended with a brief discussion of how these causal factors were themselves shaped by past classification struggles. In this respect, too, struggles over the classification of workfare workers and EITC recipients resembled earlier cases.

Perhaps the most striking parallel between the classification struggles of the 1990s and those in previous decades lay in the attempt to link income support to employment. As in the 1930s, scholars and policymakers believed that conditioning benefits on work would allow recipients to preserve their dignity as citizen-workers and avoid the stigma of pauperism.[16] As Hasenfeld, Rafferty, and Zald (1987, 412) put it, workfare programs would have "greater legitimacy" in a liberal welfare-state regime, because "government support is earned on the basis of labor force claims." This was a key reason the Clinton administration supported work requirements for welfare recipients in the 1990s; it hoped that such requirements would bolster public support for antipoverty programs and forestall the kind of racial backlash that undermined earlier programs. Similarly, proponents of the EITC attributed the program's success to the "earned" nature of its benefits and its consistency with the work ethic. However, like struggles over the classification of WPA workers and OAI recipients, the struggles over workfare and the EITC indicate a need to qualify this view of social citizenship. Judging from the meager benefits received by workfare workers, conditioning social rights on work did not invariably legitimize state social provision, nor did it ensure that clients' civil and other rights would be respected. As in the 1930s, work-based income support took a more punitive and disciplinary form when claims to such support were linked to racial conflict or when they challenged racialized patterns of social closure. In sum, work requirements for welfare recipients did not forestall a racial backlash in the 1990s. Rather, racial politics mediated the legitimizing effects of work and even the very recognition of welfare-state claimants as workers.

## CHAPTER EIGHT

# Conclusion

*Relief, Rights, and Race in the Development*
*of the Welfare State*

On October 26, 1936, President Franklin Delano Roosevelt made a brief address at Howard University in Washington, DC, to mark the dedication of a new chemistry building ("Roosevelt at Howard," *New York Times*, October 27, 1936; Roosevelt 1938, 537–39). This historically black university was founded in 1867, at the beginning of Radical Reconstruction, and was named for Oliver Otis Howard, the commissioner of the Freedmen's Bureau who had persuaded Congress to support the institution financially. Alluding to this history, President Roosevelt declared that the university "typified America's faith in the ability of man to respond to opportunity regardless of race or creed or color" ("Roosevelt at Howard," *New York Times*, October 27, 1936). At the height of another great transformation of American citizenship seventy years after Reconstruction, Roosevelt reaffirmed that faith. The university's new chemistry building, he pointed out, had been erected as "part of our nationwide projects to reduce unemployment by building useful public works." This was not government charity, he insisted, for the students and faculty of Howard University had "shared as of right in our public works program." Echoing the claims made by freedpeople in an earlier era, Roosevelt described economic security as essential for democracy, social solidarity, and full membership in the national community. The purpose of the federal works program, he explained, "was not only to provide work in all sections for all parts of the population, but to enable them all to share in the benefits to be obtained from these works. . . . As far as it was humanly possible, the Government has followed the policy that among American citizens there should be no forgotten men and no forgotten races. It is a wise and truly American policy" ("Roosevelt at Howard," *New York Times,* October 27, 1936).

The civic ideals that President Roosevelt articulated at Howard University represented but one set of claims in an ongoing struggle over the meaning and boundaries of American citizenship. They clashed with a longstanding and enduring tradition in the United States, a tradition that "treated the claims of the poor, not as an integral part of the rights of the citizen, but as an alternative to them—as claims which could be met only if the claimants ceased to be citizens in any true sense of the word" (Marshall [1949] 1964, 80). This tradition constrained what Radical Republicans and New Dealers were able to accomplish, ensuring that Roosevelt's promises at Howard University would remain at least partly unfulfilled. While the Civil War pension system, OAI, and the EITC remind us that the poor-law tradition is not the defining feature of the American welfare state, the Freedmen's Bureau, the WPA, and the dramatic expansion of punitive workfare programs in the 1990s demonstrate its persistence and strength. As shown in the preceding chapters, this tradition was more likely to prevail when a new policy remained tied to traditional poor relief or resembled it in form and when the policy's opponents mobilized a significant racial backlash against it. Policy structure and racial politics, in turn, reflected previous struggles over the meaning and boundaries of citizenship. Just as the citizenship struggles of the Reconstruction era structured those of the New Deal, so too would the legacies of the New Deal enable and constrain President Clinton's new "social bargain with the poor" ("A War on Poverty Subtly Linked to Race," *New York Times,* December 26, 2000) at the end of the twentieth century.

The citizenship struggles examined in this book mattered in another way as well. Although the struggles were analogous in important respects, they did not simply reiterate the past. On the contrary, earlier struggles often pushed forward the frontier on which subsequent struggles were engaged, ensuring that there was in fact something new under the sun to contest. Consider, for example, the struggles of workfare workers. Like freedpeople and WPA workers, workfare workers had to fight to acquire or retain important citizenship rights, but they were not always the same rights that were at stake. For freedpeople, civil rights meant elementary rights to justice and personal liberty. For workfare workers, these rights were never seriously jeopardized. Instead, their struggle involved new civil rights that had only emerged since the 1960s: federal due process protections in the administration of public assistance programs, for example, or protection against sexual harassment and sex discrimination in the workplace. Nor did workfare workers have to contend with serious challenges to their voting rights like freedpeople and WPA workers did. This does not mean that the development of the American welfare state should be read simply as a Whiggish history of steadily expanding citizenship rights. As I argue below, this is a one-sided view of welfare-state development, for rights were sometimes lost as well as gained. What it does mean is that the material and symbolic profits associated with citizenship—and thus the stakes of citizenship struggles—are historically specific and have changed over time.

A central goal of this book has been to reexamine welfare-state development in the United States in terms of these citizenship struggles. In the introduction, I argued that placing the history of the American welfare state in this broader context would enrich our understanding and assessment of it. The pages that follow summarize the book's substantive and empirical contributions to our knowledge of the Freedmen's Bureau, the WPA, and workfare, and then turn to its more general analytical and theoretical contributions to the sociology of citizenship and the welfare state.

## Substantive and Empirical Contributions

### The Freedmen's Bureau

Although the Freedmen's Bureau was the nation's first federal welfare and regulatory agency, "most scholars of American social policy tend to ignore the historical significance of the Bureau" (Williams 2003, 30; for notable exceptions, see Trattner 1984, 82–84; Lieberman 1994; and Williams 2003, 25–68). This failure to integrate the Freedmen's Bureau into theories of welfare state development is especially surprising after the groundbreaking studies of the Civil War pension program by Skocpol (1992), Orloff (1993b), and Jensen (2003). By dispelling the longstanding assumption that "the U.S. federal government did virtually nothing about public social provision until the Great Depression and the New Deal" (Skocpol 1992, 3–4), these studies invited further investigation of America's "precocious [nineteenth-century] social spending regime."

Taking up this invitation, chapters 2 and 3 explored the Freedmen's Bureau as an important innovation in national social welfare policy that existed alongside and in relation to the Civil War pension system. This perspective yielded new insights into the nature of the bureau, its limitations and demise, its relation to labor and class politics in the nineteenth century, and its long-term historical significance.

To begin with, I have attempted to move scholarly studies of the Freedmen's Bureau beyond the antinomy of revisionism, which viewed the bureau as a well-intentioned attempt to protect the rights of the freed slaves, and post-revisionism, which viewed the bureau as an instrument of social control. By stressing the hybrid nature of the bureau, its inconsistent policy features, and its intermediate position in the welfare field between traditional poor relief and more honorable alternatives like the Civil War pension program, I have tried to reveal revisionism and post-revisionism as two poles of a false dichotomy. Rather than comprising competing or mutually exclusive interpretations, each of these perspectives has selectively emphasized some features of the bureau over others. Scholarly disputes between revisionists and post-revisionists are thus symptomatic of the bureau's own internal contradictions.

Furthermore, by integrating the Freedmen's Bureau into the sociology of the welfare state, I have attempted to deepen and refine our understanding of the social forces that constrained the bureau's accomplishments and hastened its demise. In particular, this study sought to shed new light on the role of classical liberal values, patronage politics, and the historical legacy of the pauper exclusion laws that were enacted in the first half of the nineteenth century. First, my findings challenge the longstanding argument that the dominance of liberal values in American political culture doomed the bureau to failure. In fact, the liberal political tradition proved surprisingly flexible. Just as later American reformers would rework liberalism to justify new welfare-state measures, so too freedpeople used liberal notions of property rights to justify and legitimize their demands for land reform or protective labor regulations. Second, my findings qualify another influential theory: that the emergence of mass suffrage for white men in the United States before the bureaucratization of the nation's civil administration caused social provision to become entangled with patronage politics. This entanglement, it has been argued, fostered opposition to new social spending programs among the educated middle class, constraining the formation of cross-class alliances that were necessary to enact such programs (Skocpol 1992; Orloff 1993b).

While my comparison of the Freedmen's Bureau to the Civil War pension system confirms the importance of patronage politics in U.S. welfare-state development, it also suggests that racial politics mediated the impact of anti-patronage reform movements; the reaction against patronage politics was more effective against the Freedmen's Bureau, where it coincided with racial divisions, than against the Civil War pension system, which mainly benefited white veterans. Third, I argued that the pauper exclusion laws enacted in the first half of the nineteenth century constrained struggles to establish social rights for freed slaves in the second half of the nineteenth century. To the extent that political elites and the general public identified the Freedmen's Bureau with traditional poor relief, the historical precedent set by pauper exclusion laws made it difficult for freedpeople to reconcile their claims to social protection with claims to civil and political rights.

Linking the Freedmen's Bureau to the sociology of the welfare state also shed new light on the bureau's relationship to labor and class politics in the nineteenth century. Previous research has shown how a family or living wage replaced self-employment as the primary standard of freedom, independence, and citizenship for Northern workers after the Civil War. The Freedmen's Bureau, I argued, encouraged a similar shift in the South. Prevented by President Johnson's restoration policies from creating a class of black yeoman farmers, the bureau instead encouraged freedpeople to accept permanent wage labor and promoted the ideal of the family wage as an alternative basis for independence. (This campaign was, of course, inseparable from the bureau's efforts to reconstruct the black family and to define and regulate appropriate gender roles among freedpeople.) Yet the bureau's inability to make the family wage a reality for freedmen ensured that the bureau's clients would fall short of the new standard of freedom, independence, and citizenship that the bureau helped to establish. In this context, most freedmen continued to regard land ownership as an essential aspect of full citizenship, and they made claims to land on that basis. However, this link between citizenship and property was perilous for freedpeople insofar as their propertyless condition could conversely be used to deny their claims to full citizenship. Ultimately, the efforts of freedpeople to turn the Freedmen's Bureau to their advantage posed many of the same problems for Radical Republicans in the South as the labor reform movement's demand for an eight-hour-day did in the North. In both cases, these movements challenged Radicals' reluctance to interfere with freedom of contract and confounded their attempts to subordinate the categories of race and class (seen as particularistic and divisive) to the "general welfare" and "common interest" of the nation.

Finally, placing the Freedmen's Bureau in the context of U.S. welfare-state development has also provided insight into its long-term legacies and historical significance. Though the Freedmen's Bureau was a hybrid institution that occupied an intermediate position in the welfare field, its clients were ultimately classed as paupers. In contrast, a more successful struggle over the classification of Civil War pension recipients positioned them as honorable, rights-bearing citizens who earned and deserved public aid. The outcomes of these classification struggles, objectified in the institutional structures of the respective policies, reproduced in new form the antebellum division between citizens and paupers and reinforced the precedent it set for the creation of a bifurcated welfare state in the twentieth century. Lastly, the Freedmen's Bureau was significant not only for U.S. welfare-state development but also for the development of American citizenship more generally. More was at stake in conflicts over the Freedmen's Bureau than the fate of its clients. Insofar as these conflicts turned on crucial questions about who could acquire full citizenship, the criteria that governed access to that status, and the specific rights attached to it, they had implications for all Americans.

## The Works Progress Administration

Like the Freedmen's Bureau, the WPA has been relatively neglected in sociological studies of the U.S. welfare state. Previous research has focused instead on the more enduring legacies of the New Deal like the Social Security Act and the National Labor Relations Act. One aim of this study has been to expand that focus. The federal works program was an important and institutionally distinctive component of the New Deal welfare state alongside social insurance, public assistance, and new federal labor laws, and it was politically consequential in ways that outlasted the program itself. Scholarly neglect of this component has produced a significant gap in our knowledge of the New Deal welfare state that arguably distorts our understanding of it as a whole.

I have sought to build upon two notable exceptions to this pattern of neglect, the studies of Weir (1992) and Amenta (1998), while at the same time moving beyond the limitations of these works. Weir (1992) points to weak state capacity to explain why employment policies gained only a tenuous foothold in the United States. Amenta (1998) argues that the U.S. welfare state was not a laggard, but was in fact more generous than those in Europe by the end of the 1930s, largely as a result of public-employment programs like the WPA. He attributes the demise of this generous "work and relief state" to institutional factors, such as under-democratization in the Southern states and patronage politics in the North and Midwest. Thus, Weir and Amenta both provide institutionalist accounts of the origins and underdevelopment of U.S. social and employ-ment policies. However, while correctly characterizing the New Deal wel-fare state as providing work for "employables" and relief for "unemploy-ables," they neglect the controversial and sharply contested relationship between the works program and relief. Consequently, they do not explore the struggles that emerged over the status of WPA workers or the broader implications of those struggles. These are precisely the contributions I have tried to make to our knowledge of New Deal social policy.

In addition, I have attempted to reorient our focus from how already existing institutions constrained New Deal policymaking to how the insti-tutions created by New Dealers themselves (particularly the WPA) influ-enced the collective identity and mobilization of the unemployed. In this respect, the book follows the precedent set by Piven and Cloward ([1971] 1993). The policy feedback effects of the WPA were limited, of course, because its reach was limited. Even at the peak of its expansion in 1938, the WPA did not hire all or even most unemployed workers. Nor did the WPA in any sense generate the unemployed movement, which formed well before the program was implemented. However, by positioning WPA workers in ambiguous and contradictory ways—between employment and relief—the program inadvertently fostered new conflicts over their status, identity, and rights. The WPA was therefore not simply a disciplinary re-form that served to moderate civil disorder, as Piven and Cloward ([1971] 1993, 94–100) emphasize, but a far less coherent policy that was itself a site of struggle and contestation. The significance of these struggles be-comes clearer when they are understood as part of the intertwined his-tory of citizenship and class formation in the United States. Early democ-ratization made political rights a constitutive part of the identity of white workingmen in the United States, while pauperism and slavery served as negative reference points. Hence, efforts in the 1930s to curtail relief workers' political rights or stigmatize them as paupers were not merely struggles between already existing class actors; they were also struggles to reconstruct citizenship and class boundaries. (Furthermore, insofar as pauperism and forced labor were seen as antithetical to manly independence, whiteness, or both, these struggles intersected with gender and racial divisions as well.) The classification of the unemployed as *citizen-workers* not only provided a basis for their mobilization and their claims on the state but also influenced how they mobilized. This identity entailed particular repertoires of action, discourse, and organization (even though others were available), and it influenced the political alliances that organized WPA workers were likely to form, orienting them primarily to the labor movement rather than other groups, such as women's or consumers' organizations. As a result, hundreds of thousands of relief workers returned to private industry with experience in and dedication to unionism. In all these ways, the WPA was historically consequential, as were the classification struggles that the program encouraged.

This study has also yielded new insights about the social forces that hastened the WPA's demise. According to conventional wisdom, the program was intended as a temporary form of unemployment relief that was subsequently terminated once the nation's wartime economic recovery made it unnecessary. However, as the preceding chapters have shown, the retrenchment and termination of the WPA were not the result of changing economic conditions alone. Rather, the impact of these conditions was politically mediated. First, in line with previous research by Skocpol (1992), Orloff (1993b), and Amenta (1998), I showed that the entanglement of social welfare provision with patronage politics continued to constrain U.S. welfare-state development into the 1930s. Although this entanglement was much less extensive for the WPA than for the Freedmen's Bureau, it nonetheless encouraged opposition to the program. Second, the entanglement of the WPA with Communism via the Workers Alliance proved even more detrimental to the program. Although denunciations of the WPA as a funding source for Communist subversion were exaggerated, they raised new concerns about the program, particularly after the international political context began to shift in the late 1930s. While anti-Communism provided a basis for a new cross-party conservative bloc in Congress that impeded completion of the New Deal, the 1939 nonaggression pact between the Soviet Union and Nazi Germany helped to disorganize the political forces that had previously joined forces to preserve and defend the WPA. Finally, this study has drawn attention to the role of racial politics in the demise of the WPA. My research has shown how the struggle to class WPA workers as full, rights-bearing citizen-workers threatened to weaken the dependence of black laborers on the South's planter elite and thereby undermine the Southern agrarian economy. Consequently, the struggle provoked strong opposition from Southern racial conservatives. Furthermore, insofar as Communist organizers played a key role in the struggle and were explicitly committed to racial equality, racial politics became intertwined with the politics of anti-Communism. In sum, it was only in conjunction with the politics of patronage, Communism, and race that economic factors contributed to the retrenchment and eventual termination of the WPA.

## Workfare

Just as this study has important substantive and empirical implications for our understanding of the Freedmen's Bureau and the Works Progress Administration, so too does it encourage us to rethink the expansion of workfare in the 1990s. To begin with, I have tried to broaden the focus of sociological research beyond the narrow terms set by policy evaluation studies. A major problem with such studies is that they assess workfare programs in a technocratic manner according to the policy goals set by politicians and employers. In contrast, I have endeavored to examine the politics of workfare and the organized resistance of workfare workers in a critical, historically minded, and theoretically informed way. This kind of analysis aims not to adjust welfare recipients to the social relations of a new post-Fordist economy, but rather to assess how welfare reform has enabled or constrained the capacity of workers to reconstruct their social context. Thus, my research construes the social impact of welfare reform more expansively than most policy evaluation studies, and it uses a broader set of criteria to assess it. Even if workfare programs do integrate welfare recipients into the labor market, we must go on to ask on what (and whose) terms. It is one thing to be integrated with the rights and protections guaranteed to other workers by state and federal labor laws and quite another to be integrated as a subclass of workers who lack those rights. Moreover, struggles over workfare were not merely about whether and how to integrate welfare recipients into the labor market; they were also about citizenship. Indeed, as I have shown throughout the book, the economic and civic implications of social policy are closely related, for class formation and the development of citizenship have been historically intertwined. Accordingly, I have emphasized the impact of workfare on the citizenship status and rights of welfare recipients. While this impact was perhaps most visible in the weakening of what T. H. Marshall ([1949] 1964) called "industrial citizenship," the civil rights of welfare recipients were also eroded.

Policy evaluation studies of workfare are also limited because they are generally ahistorical and uninformed by comparisons with similar policies. In contrast, I have tried to deepen our understanding of workfare by situating it within broad comparative and historical contexts. This allowed me to link workfare to slavery, the workhouse, mothers' pensions, the New Deal, the racial and welfare politics of the 1960s, and the emergence of a more conservative urban regime in New York in the late 1970s. By adopting this kind of comparative-historical approach to workfare, I have followed in the footsteps of a handful of like-minded scholars, including Piven and Cloward ([1971] 1993), Rose (1994, 1995), and Peck (2001). At the same time, however, my findings challenge or qualify some of the conclusions these scholars have previously drawn about workfare.

According to Piven and Cloward ([1971] 1993), the workfare programs of the twentieth century are functionally analogous to the workhouse system of the nineteenth century. In both cases, they argue, work requirements were intended to ritually degrade welfare recipients, thereby deterring claims to public assistance. "With the rise of a predominantly female and minority service proletariat, the degradation of female relief recipients as a means of regulating labor became entirely consistent with the historic uses of welfare to enforce market discipline" (397). As shown in chapters 6 and 7, this was indeed an important purpose, though not the only one, of New York City's workfare program in the 1990s. However, rather than communicating "meanings which reinforced labor discipline" (381), New York's workfare program fostered protests and legal challenges from workfare workers and municipal labor unions. Workfare posed a new and different threat to labor discipline that was precisely opposite of that associated with generous welfare benefits—not that workers would go on relief, but that that those on relief would demand the same rights and protections enjoyed by workers. Hence, two important implications of this book are that workfare (like the WPA) was more contradictory than previous research has suggested and that those institutional contradictions generated new and unexpected kinds of conflicts.[1]

While Piven and Cloward link workfare to the workhouse, Rose (1994, 1995) links workfare to the WPA. She contrasts mandatory, punitive work requirements (workfare) to voluntary public employment programs (what she calls "fair work") in the United States from the 1930s to the present. Her main thesis is that workfare enjoys greater political support than fair work, because workfare is more consistent with the logic of production-for-profit and is less threatening to capitalist class interests. While my book builds on some of Rose's findings, it calls into question her sharp dichotomy between stigmatizing workfare programs and dignified fair work programs. I have instead tried to show that both types of programs positioned workers in ambiguous ways and encouraged struggles over their citizenship status and rights. Moreover, like conflicts over the WPA, conflicts over workfare cannot be understood simply in terms of struggles between classes; they also involved struggles over how classes were defined and formed, where class boundaries were drawn, and how class intersected with citizenship, gender, race, and (via the restriction of aid to immigrants) nation.

## Analytical and Theoretical Contributions

This book has aimed not only to deepen our understanding of particular cases like the Freedmen's Bureau, the WPA, and New York's workfare program but also to gain more general insight about citizenship and the welfare state by means of a comparison of those cases. In the pages that follow, I turn from the book's substantive and empirical contributions to its broader analytical and theoretical contributions. I begin by reviewing the book's comparative research design, what I hoped to accomplish with this design, and the analytical similarities among the cases that were revealed. I then situate the book's theoretical contributions within three broad lines of sociological research on the welfare state: the first examines the welfare state in relation to gender and racial divisions, the second in terms of political institutions, and the third in the context of citizenship struggles. Finally, I end with a brief discussion of the book's normative implications for ongoing debates about the proper balance between the rights and obligations of citizenship.

### Analytical similarities

The cases examined in this book are not simply policies, though policy innovations are an important element of each case. Rather, the cases are episodes of struggle over the civic classification of welfare-state claimants within the history of America's particular welfare-state regime.[2] Of course, these cases are hardly equivalent. As noted in the introduction,

struggles over the classification of Freedmen's Bureau clients, WPA workers, and workfare workers took place under very different conditions,
making those conflicts dissimilar in many respects. However, it would be
a mistake to conclude that each struggle was historically unique and only
capable of being understood in its own terms. Despite the profound differences among the book's cases, these struggles shared fundamental analytical similarities, which I have sought to reveal. In part, the similarities
are rooted in enduring social practices and cultural anxieties that shaped
conflicts over the status and rights of welfare-state claimants in comparable ways for more than a century. For example, in all three cases, social
provision was conditioned on work or public service more broadly. While
this linkage could be and often was used to discipline clients, it also provided clients with a basis for challenging their classification as dependent
paupers and claiming rights that paupers were typically denied. Similarly,
longstanding fears about political patronage were an important element
in all three cases as well. These fears encouraged efforts to curtail the
political rights of Freedmen's Bureau clients during Reconstruction and
of WPA workers during the New Deal. More recently, these fears reinforced conservatives' preference for policy innovations like the EITC,
which relied on existing delivery mechanisms that allowed less scope for
patronage, over policy innovations that required the creation of a new
institutional infrastructure, which could be used (like the Freedmen's Bureau and the WPA) to mobilize welfare-state claimants.

The similarities among the book's primary cases do not end there.
By means of historical comparisons, I have attempted to show that these
cases can be analyzed in terms of analogous causal processes. Following Elster (1989), Stinchcombe (1991), Tilly (1997), and others, these
processes may be understood as social mechanisms or combinations of
mechanisms. Some of these, such as the "hysteresis effect" or the "theory effect," have been derived from the cultural sociology of Pierre
Bourdieu. Others, like criteria shifting, are newly identified. Still other
mechanisms, including social closure, moral entrepreneurship, in-group
purification, and policy competition, were drawn from classical sociological theory (Weber [1922] 1978), symbolic-interactionist theories of deviance (Becker 1963; Goffman 1963), or previous studies of the American welfare state (Cates 1983). This book's aim was not primarily to
discover new mechanisms, though I have tried to show how previously
discovered mechanisms may help to explain phenomena other than those
that they were originally intended to explain. Rather, the book's compar-

isons identify those mechanisms (whether new or previously discovered) that played a crucial and recurrent role in struggles over the classification of welfare-state claimants. These mechanisms do not, of course, add up to a general or invariant model of classification struggles. Like all social mechanisms, they concatenate into different outcomes "depending on the initial conditions, combinations, and sequences" in which they occur (McAdam, Tarrow, and Tilly 2001, 37). Consequently, though the history of American welfare-state development is replete with classification struggles, there is no reason to expect that they have unfolded in precisely the same way. However, it is reasonable to expect that similar mechanisms and processes contributed to their emergence and outcomes.[3]

### Race, gender, and the welfare state

Previous research has shown how the U.S. welfare state reflected and reinforced gender and racial divisions. However, this research has remained largely confined to the twentieth century, focused mainly on the social policies introduced during the Progressive era and the New Deal. This limitation makes sense if one takes as one's object of study a modern welfare state assumed to have emerged in the twentieth century in reaction to (and thus clearly distinguishable from) the relief arrangements that preceded it. In contrast, this study has challenged that assumption. The line that separates traditional poor relief from the modern welfare state, I have argued, is not so bright, because policy innovations frequently provoked struggles over whether to model new policies on or sharply distinguish them from poor relief. This unconventional perspective suggests that the "two-tier" or "two-channel" welfare state that emerged in the twentieth century has deeper historical roots than previously thought, roots that precede the workmen's compensation and mothers' aid policies of the Progressive era by decades. Ultimately, I would argue, it was the sociopolitical division established in the nineteenth century between citizens and paupers, a division that was, from its inception, gendered (insofar as poor relief was regarded as antithetical to manly independence) and racialized (insofar as pauperism was associated with slavery), which set the precedent for the bifurcated welfare state of the twentieth century. Rather than efface that division, the modern welfare state has reproduced it in new forms.

While gender divisions played an important role in the struggles I have examined, the book has mainly foregrounded racial divisions. The finding that welfare-state claimants were more likely to be classed as paupers when their opponents mobilized a racial backlash against them will surprise few readers; the book's most important contributions lie elsewhere. To begin with, I have shown how Bourdieu's constructionist understanding of class can fruitfully be extended to race. Rather than taking racial divisions and racial groups as given, I investigated how and why agents mobilized along racial lines. Symbolic work was essential to this process: Like classes, racial groups are formed through classification struggles and "emerge in reality only if there is symbolic work to form group identity" (Swartz 1997, 186). Just as classification struggles are a hidden but crucial dimension of class struggles, so too are they a crucial dimension of racial conflict. Of course, agents do not create racial divisions *de novo,* but symbolic work is required to render racial divisions explicit, salient, and socially significant, thereby turning potential racial groupings into real, mobilized racial groups. This is especially true when alternative groupings are possible, plausible, and actively promoted. (Racial groupings may be divided, for example, along class, gender, or nativity lines.) Moreover, symbolic work is crucial to race-making and racial mobilization in another way as well. Symbolic work is not only needed to mobilize agents along racial lines in the present; such work is also enabled and constrained by the legacy of past classification struggles. Thus, the book goes beyond the commonplace assertion that racial divisions within the American working class constrained the development of the U.S. welfare state. Racial divisions did indeed contribute to the failure of the classification struggles examined in this book, but those divisions were also, at least in part, a product of earlier classification struggles. When black welfare-state claimants failed to obtain recognition as full citizens, those failures reinforced racial divisions within the working class. Past failures did not make it impossible to overcome racial divisions in the next round of classification struggles, but they did make it more difficult.

This perspective on race and the welfare state improves upon reductionist accounts of racial inequality in several ways. According to one such account, the racial divisions (and, by extension, gender divisions) within the American welfare state are primarily a reflection of segmented labor markets or other preexisting structural inequalities. In contrast, I have argued that racial divisions within the welfare state were the outcome of historically contingent classification struggles. To be sure, preexisting structural inequalities influenced those struggles. However, "symbolic struggles . . . have a *specific logic* which endows them with a real autonomy from the structures in which they are rooted" (Bourdieu 1989, 20–21; original emphasis). Thus, I have attempted to bring agency and praxis into an otherwise overly structuralist account of welfare state development.

Another form of reductionism can be found in accounts that reduce racial politics (and, by extension, gender politics) to class politics. This approach views racial divisions as expressions of a false consciousness among workers that obscures their objective class interests.[4] The problem with this approach is that it is simultaneously too constructionist in some ways and not constructionist enough in others. It is too constructionist about racial categories, which are dismissed as illusory or unreal because they are constructed. At the same time, it is not constructionist enough about classes and class interests, the construction of which it neglects, because it considers them somehow more real or objective than race. Consequently, this approach has a difficult time explaining why white workers have so often pursued "illusory" interests and ignored their "real" interests. My approach avoids these difficulties because it is intersectional rather than reductionist, more consistently constructionist, and does not privilege one kind of social category over others.

Finally, the approach to race and the welfare state developed in this book pushes sociological analysis beyond the false dichotomy of what Manza (2000b, 828–32) calls the symbolic-racism and group-interest models of racial conflict. The symbolic-racism model "emphasizes the deep embeddedness and durability of white racism independent of actual group interests" (829). In contrast, the group-interest model argues that "racial and ethnic groups experience a sense of competition over scarce resources (which has a real, not purely symbolic foundation), and dominant groups generate stereotypes of subordinate groups to justify their dominance" (830). Both models provide an inadequate and distorted understanding of racial conflict, because they each lack important elements found in the other model. Proponents of the symbolic-racism model are wrong to disconnect racism from interests. At the same time, proponents of the group-interest model fail to see that groups have symbolic as well as material interests and that symbolic work is needed to form groups and define group interests in the first place. This study has sought to integrate these competing models, thereby yielding a better understanding of the relationship between race and the welfare state.

*Historical institutionalism and the welfare state*

While seeking to shed new light on the relationship between welfare-state development and racial formation in the United States, this book has also sought to engage historical-institutionalist theories of the welfare state. These theories emerged in part as a reaction to an older "national values" approach, which sought to show how America's liberal political culture limited the growth of the U.S. welfare state (for a critical review of the national-values approach, see Orloff and Skocpol 1984; Weir, Orloff, and Skocpol 1988a, 10–13; Skocpol 1992, 15–23). The development of historical institutionalism in this manner encouraged scholars on both sides of the debate to separate what is, in fact, unified in practice—the material and symbolic dimensions of social life—and to privilege one over the other. I have attempted to integrate institutionalist and culturalist approaches into a more general theoretical framework, one that simultaneously stresses the cultural dimension of institutions and the institutionalization of culture. At the same time, this framework takes neither political culture nor political institutions as givens. In contrast to the national-values approach, which regarded political culture as unitary, static, and consensual, I have emphasized its complex, dynamic, and disputed nature. Following Rogers Smith (1993, 1997), I have argued that American political culture consists of multiple traditions upon which actors can draw, not a single, hegemonic liberal tradition that invariably constrains welfare-state development.[5] The complex, dynamic, and disputed nature of American political culture helps, in turn, to explain institutional change. As agents contest the cultural schemas, principles of division, and classificatory systems that are objectified in institutions, their struggles may transform the institutions and alter their policy feedback effects. The WPA, for instance, initially encouraged the mobilization of its clients as citizen-workers, but later discouraged their mobilization as a result of the anti-Communist reforms introduced in the late 1930s.

The notion of policy feedback effects has been central to historical-institutionalist studies of the welfare state. As noted in chapter 1, these studies typically assess policy feedback in one of two ways: social citizenship theories emphasize the potential of social policies to empower dominated groups, while social control theories stress the regulatory and disciplinary functions of social policy. This study has drawn on both perspectives while trying to move beyond their respective limitations. Those limitations are most clearly evident in the case of the hybrid policies investigated here, which placed their clients in an intermediate position within the welfare field. First, consider the social citizenship perspective. This approach rightly holds that social rights may facilitate the mobilization of dominated groups, but it does not adequately explain how. Proponents of this view usually explain mobilization by pointing to the potential "independence effects" of social policies, that is, how social policies provide resources that may render wage earners less dependent on employers, women less dependent on male breadwinners, and so forth. Social citizenship theories thus see social policies as state interventions into conflicts between already constituted groups (e.g., workers and capitalists) pursuing pre-given interests. From this perspective, policies shape politics by providing incentives and resources for collective action, but they do not enter into or influence the constitution of the groups themselves. Hence, social citizenship arguments presuppose rather than explain the formation of collective actors "able to recognize the opening of political opportunities and to mobilize . . . [new] resources for political purposes" (Polletta and Jasper 2001, 286). In contrast, social control theories explicitly attend to the ways in which social policies constitute recipients of public aid as a group, but they assume that such groups are formed in an inherently stigmatizing and demobilizing way.[6] If social citizenship theories presuppose but do not explain the formation of the groups that social policies are said to empower, then social control theories conflate the formation of groups with their social control. In the preceding chapters, I have drawn upon Bourdieu's cultural sociology, in particular, his concept of classification struggles, to transcend these limitations. Classificatory schemes, I have argued, are constitutive of the groups that struggle over social welfare policy, but those schemes are neither merely imposed from above (by the state or dominant groups) nor inherently demobilizing. Rather, "classificatory systems are . . . the stake of struggles between the groups they characterize and counterpose, who fight over them while striving to turn them to their advantage" (Bourdieu [1979] 1984, 477).

## Citizenship struggles and the welfare state

By relating Bourdieu's ideas about symbolic classification to the welfare state, this study has broadened the concept of classification struggles and extended it in new directions. I have used the concept to explore not just class formation but also how the categories of class, race, gender, and nation have intersected—in changing and contested ways—with the category of citizenship. Indeed, as I noted in chapter 1, this book is not so much a study of class struggles as citizenship struggles, by which I mean struggles over the meaning and boundaries of citizenship, the legal guarantees attached to the status of citizenship, and the material and symbolic profits that the status confers. This is not to deny the importance of class struggle or gender or racial politics in the development of the U.S. welfare state. Rather, it is to suggest that classification struggles were an essential aspect of all such conflicts, and that the significance of these conflicts can only fully be understood in relation to citizenship.

In this approach to the welfare state, I am indebted to T. H. Marshall ([1949] 1964) no less than to Bourdieu. However, the book relies upon an unconventional reading of Marshall's work to raise new questions and yield new insights about the welfare state. As Marshall is typically read, the modern welfare state represents the last stage in a steady development of citizenship over the past three centuries, from civil to political to social rights. This narrative of a cumulative expansion of citizenship rights provided the theoretical framework and research agenda for most subsequent studies of the welfare state. Why, social scientists asked, was the development of social citizenship more advanced in some countries while lagging in others (with the U.S. usually cast in the role of the laggard)? In contrast, my reading of Marshall's work suggests a more complex relationship among civil, political, and social rights. As previous chapters have shown (and as Marshall himself suggested), civil and political rights could be and often were treated as an alternative to social rights rather than a foundation for them. The welfare state was therefore shaped not only by political struggles to acquire new social rights but also by struggles to preserve the civil and political rights of welfare-state claimants. When welfare-state development is viewed in this way, it raises a different set of questions. Why in some cases have newly established social rights been integrated into the status of citizenship while in other cases they were detached from it? From this perspective, political struggles over the welfare state involve more than claims to economic security. They are also struggles about civic inclusion, symbolic classification, and collective identity—in short, what Fraser (1995) and Honneth (1995) call struggles for recognition.

This view of welfare-state development has important implications for the long-running debate between advocates of universal and targeted social welfare policies. Advocates of targeting have argued that it is fairer and more affordable to direct social spending to those who most need and deserve it. In contrast, proponents of universalism have argued that social rights should be linked to citizenship rather than employment (social insurance) or need (public assistance), because targeting generates invidious distinctions, while universalism promotes broad, cross-class solidarity and widespread political support for the welfare state. While I am sympathetic to arguments for universalism, my research suggests that those arguments must be qualified in two ways. First, I found that it is not the presence or absence of specific policy features (such as means testing) that stigmatizes clients, but rather a "family resemblance" between the policy and traditional poor relief. The more features a policy shares with traditional poor relief, I have argued, the more likely it is that clients of the policy will be stigmatized as paupers. Thus, stigmatizing policies can be expected to share many features with traditional poor relief, but each policy may not share the same features. (This explains why the EITC, for example, could be means-tested but nonstigmatizing.) In this regard, I have treated traditional poor relief as an ideal type in the Weberian sense, which subsequent policy innovations may approximate to a greater or lesser extent. Second, my findings challenge the assumption that universalism is always synonymous with citizenship. When we recall that citizenship is at least potentially an instrument of social closure and social stratification; that the relationship between citizenship and other social categories, such as class, gender, and race, is contested and historically variable; that citizenship is a gradated category rather than a uniform status; and that citizenship is always defined in opposition to other categories (traitors, foreigners, aliens, subversives, and the like), then it becomes apparent that the equation of universalism with citizenship is unwarranted. Attaching social rights to citizenship may result in more universalistic social provision, but it does not necessarily do so, for the universalism of such arrangements depends importantly on the scope and boundaries of citizenship itself.

*Beyond the authoritative welfare state:*
*Rethinking the social obligations of citizenship*

Finally, my research findings have normative implications for the ongoing debate about the proper balance between the rights and obligations of citizenship. This debate can be traced back to T. H. Marshall's own observations in 1949. "What is the effect," he asked, "of the marked shift of emphasis from [citizenship] duties to rights?" (71). Rights, he answered, had been "multiplied, and they are precise." In contrast, duties had either become "compulsory," in which case they required no "act of will" or "sentiment of loyalty," or else appeared "vague," "remote," and "unreal." Marshall placed special emphasis on the "duty to work" (117), noting that "it is no easy matter to revive the sense of personal obligation to work in a new form in which it is attached to the status of citizenship" (118). In the 1980s, the New Right revived these concerns and reformulated them along conservative lines, criticizing the welfare state for promoting an excessive emphasis on citizenship rights at the expense of civic obligations. Since the fulfillment of common obligations is no less essential to full membership than equal rights, conservatives argued, the welfare state must go "beyond entitlement" and enforce the social obligations of citizenship in order to fully incorporate the poor as members of the political community (Mead 1986; Kaus 1992). As Kymlicka and Norman (1994, 355–57) note, this was "the idea behind . . . 'workfare' programs, which require welfare recipients to work for their benefits, to reinforce the idea that citizens should be self-supporting."

All parties to this debate agree that social policies influence the habits and mores of citizens and (depending on the institutional design of the policies) may do so in ways that are salutary or harmful to democracy. The disagreements turn on more specific questions, namely, what is meant by good citizenship and which policy features best promote it. What do the findings presented here contribute to this debate? To begin with, this study challenges a key assumption of the New Right's critique: that the welfare state has excessively expanded citizenship rights at the expense of duties. Even when welfare-state claimants gained new social rights, they sometimes experienced a curtailment of civil and political rights. In addition, the steady decline of industrial citizenship in the United States since 1980—manifested not only by corporate and governmental assaults on labor unions and the weakening of labor laws but also by the creation of new categories of workers who are not covered by existing labor laws at all—represents a further erosion of citizenship rights. Thus, the development of the American welfare state is a more complex story in which rights have been lost as well as gained.

Furthermore, my findings question an important implication of the New Right's critique that has been embraced by many centrists and even by some liberals as well. The implication may be stated as follows: if full membership in a political community requires the fulfillment of common obligations as well as equal rights, then the failure to fulfill those obligations—particularly the obligation to work—will stigmatize welfare recipients, preclude their incorporation as full members into the political community, and undermine public support for welfare programs. Most forcefully stated by Kaus (1992), this argument encouraged proposals in the late 1980s and early 1990s to strengthen work requirements for welfare recipients or replace welfare altogether with a "neo-WPA."[7] Contrary to this argument, I found that conditioning social rights upon work or employment did not invariably legitimize them. While OAI and EITC recipients did obtain recognition as independent citizen-workers, WPA workers and workfare workers failed to do so. Thus, work may be necessary to "earn" full and equal citizenship in the United States (Shklar 1991, chap. 2), but it does not appear to be sufficient.

This discussion of work requirements points to yet another flaw in the New Right's critique of social citizenship and the welfare state. Proposals for a more "authoritative" welfare state presume a consensus about the social obligations of citizenship, and they presume that such a welfare state would hold all Americans to the same standards. However, historical evidence reveals these assumptions to be problematic in a number of ways. First, the meaning of good citizenship has changed over time (Schudson 1998) and is frequently contested by policymakers, welfare-state claimants, and other interested groups. The social obligations of citizenship are therefore a matter of political controversy and ideally, in a democratic society, a matter for public debate and deliberation. Disagreements about civic obligations do not make it illegitimate to use public policy to promote good citizenship, but they do require a shift from a conventional to a postconventional view of civic obligations, in which the obligations themselves can be critically and continually examined and reconsidered.[8] Second, an authoritative welfare state that sought to impose the same specific and concrete obligations on all Americans would be unsuitable for a modern, complex society with a highly developed social division of labor. Under such conditions, what T. H. Marshall described as the vagueness of civic duties becomes inevitable. The social obligations of citizenship necessarily become more general and abstract, which allows them to be fulfilled in different ways by different groups.[9] This is evident from the citizenship struggles examined in this book. Americans have claimed rights not only as citizen-workers but as citizen-soldiers and citizen-mothers as well. In each case, new social rights were justified as compensation for public service, suggesting a general obligation to reciprocate or give back to society (Mauss [1925] 1990, chap. 4). However, the nature of the public service varied, suggesting that this obligation may be satisfied in a number of ways: through military service, socially useful labor, or mothering. By focusing narrowly on paid employment, an authoritative welfare state neglects and devalues other ways in which Americans might fulfill their civic duties.[10] Third, while it may be appropriate and necessary for different groups to fulfill their civic obligations in different ways, civic obligations ought not to vary in invidious ways. Yet past experiments with authoritative social policies often led to this result. For African Americans, enforcement of civic obligations typically meant making them better laborers: disciplined, docile, and deferential to whites. For women, enforcement of civic obligations frequently meant making them better wives who would conform to traditional and often inegalitarian gender norms. In both cases, the civic obligations of minority groups were not only defined differently but also in a manner that imposed special burdens or restrictions upon them, disadvantaged them, or reinforced their subordination. Given these precedents, there are good reasons to fear that the revival of authoritative social policies may have similar consequences. The danger of such policies, particularly for Americans who belong to what the courts term a "suspect class," is that civic obligations may be defined and enforced in an illiberal manner that erodes their rights and undermines civil equality.[11] Thus, rather than promoting full membership and social inclusion, as the New Right argues, an authoritative welfare state could well have the opposite consequences.

Lastly, my research suggests that a key element of the New Right's critique, the notion of "welfare dependency," rests upon a kind of historical amnesia. An important aim of the book has been to problematize the independent/dependent dichotomy (and related dichotomies) by revealing how the boundary has been socially and historically constructed, contested, and relocated over time. The line is, in other words, a matter of convention. This is not meant to suggest that dependence itself is a discursive construction, only the division of the social world into the categories of independent and dependent. In a complex society with a highly developed social division of labor, individuals are always mutually interdependent upon one another. Consequently, in order to categorize individuals as independent or dependent, some forms of dependence must be recognized as socially significant while others are not. By treating dependency as a product of our own classifying practices, as something we attribute *to* others rather than an inherent attribute *of* others, I have tried to de-fetishize it, to expose the arbitrariness of the independent/dependent division, and to retrieve the possibility that people could be classed differently. As historical and social conditions change, this kind of reconsideration becomes more pressing. Should we continue to equate employment with economic independence when jobs fail to pay a living wage, provide adequate security, or allow workers some modicum of industrial citizenship? Should we continue to class welfare recipients as dependent paupers when welfare benefits potentially provide them with greater independence from employers and male breadwinners or when the recipients of comparable forms of public aid are classed as independent citizens? By treating the independent/dependent dichotomy as a historically and socially constructed boundary rather than a set of fixed categories, we can begin to raise and debate these kinds of questions. Of course, a more egalitarian and inclusive welfare state cannot be built merely by working upon people's minds. But transforming the categories of perception and evaluation through which we construct the world is the first step toward reconstructing it.

# Notes

## Chapter One

1. The concept of social closure can be traced back to Max Weber ([1922] 1978); see also Parkin (1979) and Murphy (1988). Interestingly, the French Revolution not only invented modern national citizenship (Brubaker 1992, chap. 2) but also distinguished passive and active versions of it, making citizenship a means of internal social closure from the very beginning. On citizenship as a gradational status, see Glenn (2002, 54; emphasis in the original): "At the most general level is the notion of citizenship simply as belonging—membership in the community, sometimes defined as the nation. Within this meaning, however, there are several sub-meanings, including the notion of *standing* (being recognized as a full adult capable of exercising choice and assuming responsibilities); the notion of *nationality* (being identified as part of a people who constitute a nation, whether corresponding to the boundaries of a nation or not); and the notion of *allegiance* (being a loyal member of the community). A given category of people may be excluded from one of these meanings of citizenship but included in other meanings." While focusing on the curtailment of citizenship rights (what Glenn calls standing), I occasionally allude to these other forms civic exclusion as well.

2. Although Marshall's remarks about poor relief and protective labor laws refer to Britain, they are true for the United States as well. On the loss of civil rights through internment in poorhouses and workhouses, see Rothman (1971, chap. 8). On the disfranchisement of paupers, which was not fully abolished until the 1960s, see Steinfeld (1989) and Keyssar (2000, 61–65, 271–72). On protective labor laws for women, see Skocpol (1992, 373–423); Mettler (1998, 34–37); and Glenn (2002, 84–85). As in Britain, American courts struck down protective labor laws for men on the grounds that such laws violated their civil rights—in particular, their constitutionally guaranteed liberty of contract. This interpretation of the Constitution's Fourteenth Amendment (one of the three Reconstruction

amendments) was enshrined in the 1905 Supreme Court decision *Lochner v. New York* and not seriously challenged until the 1930s.

3. As Somers (1993, 590) points out, "Marshall's core conceptions remain the touchstone for much recent scholarly work on citizenship." See, for example, Giddens (1987, chap. 8); Mann (1987); Barbalet (1988); Turner (1990); Somers (1993, 1994); Bulmer and Rees (1996); and Katz (2001). This work is no exception.

4. I use *client* as a generic term to indicate a recipient of state benefits, regardless of what form the benefits take, how eligibility is determined, or how the benefits are financed. I use the term interchangeably with *claimant* (a person who claims state benefits), though the latter term has a more active connotation. While I sometimes employ the language of the people I study rather than my own terms, it must be remembered that their language was itself contested and varied. In contemporary usage, *client* may imply for some the sorts of rights that policymakers often restricted, while for others it indicates a depoliticized role in contrast to citizenship (Habermas 1987, 348–51). Although neither of these meanings are necessarily intended here, this ambiguity underscores the point that the term *client* can be constructed and perceived in different ways.

5. Some groups in United States, most notably African Americans during Reconstruction and women during the Progressive era, lacked full civil or political rights during their struggles for new social rights. Thus, rather than preserve their civil and political rights while acquiring new social rights, they had to struggle for civil, political, and social rights simultaneously. This often led to conflicting strategies and, as Marshall ([1949] 1964) would lead one to expect, an ambivalent or conflicted orientation to the market. During Reconstruction, some African-American leaders opposed state provision of social welfare for former slaves because they feared it would hinder their efforts to acquire full civil and political rights (see chap. 2). Conversely, some women's groups opposed the Equal Rights Amendment, first introduced in Congress in 1923, because they feared it would encourage the courts to strike down protective labor laws for women.

6. If civic rehabilitation brings to mind the "civilizing process" described by Elias (1978), it may be because the notions of civility and citizenship are historically related. The argument that social welfare policies are formative and constitutive rests on a conception of power developed by Michel Foucault (1980). For an argument in favor of "authoritative" social welfare policies, see the classic statement by Mead (1986). While it would be an exaggeration to equate paternalistic or authoritarian social policies with the kind of "totalitarian democracy" described by Talmon ([1952] 1960), there are clearly affinities between them. On different models of citizenship, see Schudson (1998).

7. For an earlier elaboration of the explanatory strategy described by Tilly, see Stinchcombe (1978). On causal mechanisms as an alternative to both general covering laws and historicist accounts that eschew generalization altogether, see

Merton (1968); Elster (1989); Stinchcombe (1991); Tilly (1997); and McAdam, Tarrow, and Tilly (2001).

8. This is especially evident in regard to the WPA, a third and now-missing component of the New Deal welfare state, alongside social insurance and public assistance (Harvey 1989, chap. 1; Amenta 1998; Goldberg 2005). My use of the term liberal closely follows Orren (1991), R. Smith (1993), and Mettler (1998). Social policies are liberal in this sense when they position individuals as rights bearers and purchasing consumers, take on "some of the trappings of civil exchange," and guarantee "secure entitlements . . . by mimicking private contracts" (Fraser 1989, 151–52; Fraser and Gordon 1992, 60).

9. The concept of classification struggles is indebted to the work of Emile Durkheim, who stressed "the independent causal importance of symbolic classification, the pivotal role of the symbolic division between sacred and profane, the social significance of ritual behavior, and the close interrelationship between symbolic classifications, ritual processes, and the formation of social solidarities" (Alexander 1988b, 2; see also Emirbayer 1992, 1996a, 1996b). The concept also has affinities with social-constructionist perspectives, including Schneider and Ingram (1993, 1997, 2005), Schram (1995), and the labeling theory of deviance associated with Becker (1963) and others. Subsequent chapters allude to Becker's concept of moral entrepreneurship, through which people identify deviance, bring it to the attention of others, and create and enforce rules against it. Strictly speaking, Bourdieu's approach is best characterized as constructionist-structuralism, since he argues that the social construction of groups is structurally constrained by the distribution of agents in social space.

10. The reclassification of wage earners as independent initially rested on the assumption, embedded in the free-labor ideology of the mid-nineteenth century, that wage labor was "only a temporary step on the way to self-employment. . . . As a stepping stone wage labor was acceptable, but as a permanent condition it was scandalous." As wage labor became increasingly prevalent and inescapable after the Civil War, the labor movement shifted from a rejection of permanent wage labor to a demand for a "family" or "living" wage, which replaced self-employment as the "benchmark of freedom, independence, and citizenship" (Glickman 1997, 1–7, 12). At this point, one begins to see the emergence of Shklar's (1991, 64) "independent citizen-earner," whose status as a "free remunerated worker" allows him to become a "recognized and active citizen." This shift from a rejection of wage labor to a demand for a living wage was completed by the 1930s, making the WPA's substandard security wage deeply threatening to workers.

11. Like "political and constitutional developments in the states," nineteenth-century reforms of poor relief also "moved to firm up the distinction in condition and status between pauper and wage earner" (Glickstein 2002, 70). In particular, reformers sought to institute the principle of less eligibility, according to which relief must always be less desirable than even the worst employment. In this way,

New York's Association for Improving the Condition of the Poor, "a model for urban reformers elsewhere in the nation," aimed, in the words of an 1850 report, to draw "'a line of distinction between the pauper and the independent laborer'" (Montgomery 1993, 68).

12. Cf. Lamont (1992). Just as twentieth-century middle-class professionals relied on a variety of criteria (economic, moral, and cultural) to draw boundaries between themselves and others, so too Americans have drawn the boundaries of citizenship on the basis of multiple and shifting criteria.

13. Tarrow (1994, 18) defines the political opportunity structure as "consistent—but not necessarily formal, permanent or national—dimensions of the political environment which either encourage or discourage people from using collective action."

14. Cf. Wright's (1978, 62, 88, 106) idea of "contradictory class locations," in which the multiple processes that constitute class relations do not entirely correspond. Consequently, Wright argues, these locations have less "determinate probabilities of being organized into given class formations" and are therefore "characterized by multiple potential mappings into class formations." However, the contradictory locations I have in mind are not between capitalists and proletarians, but rather, between citizens and paupers. Furthermore, this division is not generated by control over economic capital (the means of production, labor power, or investments), but by processes of social closure through which agents monopolize the material and symbolic profits of citizenship while excluding others.

15. To be sure, Bourdieu's attempt to develop a sociology of practices that "combines both material and symbolic dimensions" was "inspired by Marx's first thesis on Feuerbach, which emphasizes the underlying unity of all social life as practical activity" (Swartz 1997, 40). However, Marx's base/superstructure model reproduced the very materialism/idealism dichotomy that he rejected in "Theses on Feuerbach" (Tucker 1978, 143–45). As these remarks suggest, I do not aim to disprove the Marxist perspective or test it against a competing model, but rather, to reconstruct it with the aid of Bourdieu's cultural sociology. Reconstruction in this sense means "taking a theory apart and putting it back together again in a new form in order to attain more fully the goal it has set for itself" (Habermas 1979, 95).

16. Marx himself comes close to adopting this view in *The Eighteenth Brumaire* ([1852] 1963) when he suggests that it was not the real material interests of the French peasantry but rather "historical tradition" that led them to endorse Bonaparte. As Reinhardt (1997, 132–38) points out, this argument subverts a simple base/superstructure model, making cultural traditions "the prevailing forces in the pivotal struggle for control of the [French] state. Marx criticizes the spurious nature of the [Napoleonic] tradition . . . but he does not offer a compelling materialist explanation of this tradition's hold on the populace." To be sure, "the essay does not show us that 'ideas' are 'causally determining,' that politics is merely

a matter of vision and will." However, Marx's "account of popular Bonapartism reveals—if not altogether self-consciously—the discursive constitution of real effects, the political production of the peasantry *as a class*. It is the performative work done by Bonaparte's acts of representation that make this 'non class' into something 'real.' Bonapartism '*constitutes* the very interests it signifies': they were not simply there, prior to this constitution."

17. As Bourdieu and Wacquant (1992, 123) point out, the "narrow, economistic conception of the 'rationality' of practices ignores the individual and collective *history* of agents through which the structures of preference that inhabit them are constituted" (emphasis in the original). Marx criticized utilitarianism on similar grounds for envisioning the individual "not as a historic result, but as history's point of departure" (Tucker 1978, 222).

18. These remarks reveal a tension between the constructionist and structuralist aspects of Bourdieu's thinking. On the one hand, he emphasizes the *social construction* of groups. "The social world may be uttered and constructed in different ways according to different principles of vision and division. . . . [T]he potency of economic and social differences is never so great that one cannot organize agents on the basis of other principles of division—ethnic, religious, or national ones, for instance" (Bourdieu 1989, 19). On the other hand, Bourdieu also argues that group formation is *structurally constrained* by the distribution of agents in social space according to the volume and composition (economic, cultural, social, or symbolic) of the capital they possess. He suggests that groupings of agents who occupy proximate positions in social space will be more stable and durable than groupings of agents who are far apart in social space. "To speak of a social space means that one cannot group just anyone with anyone while ignoring the fundamental differences, particularly economic and cultural ones" (Bourdieu 1985, 726). What I am suggesting here is that classification struggles *influence* and are not merely constrained by the distribution of agents in social space. This point pushes Bourdieu's constructionist structuralism in a more constructionist direction.

19. Cf. Vorspan (1975, 26): "The history of the workhouse system in the later nineteenth century is in large measure a chronicle of the various attempts to abolish the unclassified workhouse and remove the different classes of inmates to specialized institutions." By removing (and thereby constituting) the deserving classes (the sick, children, the aged, etc.) to specialized institutions, reformers aimed to prevent moral contamination by the undeserving classes. A similar logic is apparent decades later in the 1935 Social Security Act, which removed many of the same deserving classes from the general relief population to newly created categorical assistance programs. As this analogy suggests, fears about "moral contamination" (Vorspan 1975, 184–85) or "moral contagion" (Glickstein 2002, 12) provided an important impetus for policy innovation, though the clients of new policies were not always classed as deserving. These examples also demonstrate that culture and institutions are inseparable, since classificatory schemes

are objectified in institutions, and institutions have a cultural aspect or dimension. On the cultural dimension of institutions, see Meyer and Rowan (1991) and Dobbin (1994).

20. Cf. A. Smith (2001, 83): like "ethnic pasts," racialized pasts "help to shape present concerns by providing the cultural frameworks and parameters within and through which the needs and understandings of the present are formed and articulated."

21. "A War on Poverty Subtly Linked to Race," *New York Times,* December 26, 2000.

## Chapter Two

1. When the Thirteenth Amendment was ratified in December 1865, Congress merely intended it to "abolish slavery as chattelism, not to establish equal civil and political rights under congressional guarantee" (Belz 1976, 127). "Neither the amendment's text nor [the Thirty-eighth] Congress's debates made it clear whether the amendment even conferred citizenship on freedmen" (R. Smith 1997, 283). Passage of the 1866 Civil Rights Act and ratification of the Fourteenth Amendment in July 1868 did establish the "rights of freedmen to hold property and to receive impartial treatment in court," but it failed to clarify "other aspects of their place in society" (White 1970, 156; cf. Belz 1976, chap. 8). The Fifteenth Amendment, guaranteeing blacks the right to vote, was not ratified until March 1870.

2. Two different questions were at stake in these competing models of contractual freedom: (1) whether workers had the right to quit before the contract expired and, if not, (2) what civil or criminal sanctions employers could impose on workers to enforce labor contracts. According to Schmidt (1998, 237, 239), the right to quit at any time was not fully established until 1880 (cf. Orren 1991, 85). Steinfeld (2001) argues that the right to quit was still contested into the twentieth century. To further complicate matters, the "competing principles" of Northern jurisprudence "would encounter [during Reconstruction] a southern legal culture that had diluted the sanctity of contract and the right to security without establishing the right to quit" (Schmidt 1998, 7).

3. "The national organization, the managerial hierarchy, and the discipline fostered by the Union Army" were "still relative novelties" in the postbellum civilian world. "Although some [army] volunteers, notably those employed by the railroads, had worked in large, bureaucratically managed corporations before the war, most soldiers encountered organizational life for the first time when they joined the army" (McConnell 1992, 39). Still, the administrative and bureaucratic capacity of the Freedmen's Bureau should not be exaggerated; it was plagued by inadequate manpower and resources, powerless unless sustained by troops, and

dependent on the army for military assistance. Furthermore, relations between the Freedmen's Bureau and the army were not always harmonious. The assistant commissioner for South Carolina complained that "many of the officers in command of troops manifest an aversion to the Bureau, and do not seem disposed to carry out its provisions." He concluded, "The Bureau having been held subordinate to the military, many obstacles have been thrown in the way of performing the duties assigned it. . . . [U]ntil the Bureau has entire and unquestioned control over the affairs entrusted to its charge, its work will necessarily be, to a certain extent, slow and imperfect" (report dated Nov. 1, 1866, Annual Reports of the Assistant Commissioner for South Carolina).

4. Revisionism, as the name suggests, formed as a reaction to an even older and now discredited interpretation known as the Dunning school, named after historian William Dunning. "The fundamental underpinning of this interpretation was the conviction, to quote one member of the Dunning School, of 'negro incapacity.' The childlike blacks, these scholars insisted, were unprepared for freedom and incapable of properly exercising the political rights Northerners had thrust upon them" (Foner 1988, xx). For a review of the Dunning school, revisionism, and post-revisionism, see Foner (1988, xix–xxvii).

5. Of course, as Colby (1985, 229) points out, "segregated services during this era were significantly better than what they replaced—no services for blacks."

6. Although Congress passed the Southern Homestead Act in 1866, which opened federal lands in five Southern states for settlement, it provided lands of inferior quality and failed to furnish the farming equipment or subsistence necessary to homesteaders until they harvested their first crop (see the 1866 annual reports of the Assistant Commissioners for Louisiana and South Carolina). These flaws made it "so defective that few Negroes dared to try to open farms under its terms, and even fewer succeeded" (Bentley 1955, 144–46; cf. Lanza 1990).

7. What O'Connor (1973) describes as the accumulation and legitimation functions of the welfare state roughly correspond to the functions identified by Piven and Cloward ([1971] 1993): disciplining labor and quelling civil disorder. My references to these functions are only meant to suggest an analogy with the modern welfare state, not to suggest that a modern welfare state existed in the nineteenth century. Furthermore, recognition of these functions is not meant to imply a functionalist or capitalist-hegemony view of welfare state development. As noted in chapter 1, social policies may have regulatory functions yet fail to conform to a coherent functionalist logic.

8. In this respect, the Freedmen's Bureau anticipated later social policies: using "tactics reminiscent of the traditional political machine," the Kennedy and Johnson administrations relied on new anti-poverty programs in the 1960s to "cultivate the allegiance of urban black voters," "offering jobs and services to build party loyalty" (Piven and Cloward [1971] 1993, 256–63).

9. Disputes between Radical Republicans and white supremacists can be seen

in part as a conflict between civic and ethnic nationalism. Viewed in this way, Reconstruction invites comparisons to other nations with strong civic nationalist traditions, such as France. Radical Republicans sought to turn black slaves into American citizens in much the same way that the French state sought to turn Jews, peasants, and immigrants into Frenchmen (Hertzberg 1968; E. Weber 1976; Brubaker 1992). These efforts reflected an inclusive stance toward civic outsiders (in contrast to ethnic nationalism), but they also made civic inclusion and equality conditional upon moral and social transformation of outsiders.

10. Though Swayne may also have had federal courts in mind, most of the institutions to which he referred were local or state level. His approach was typical of bureau officials elsewhere.

11. Contemporaries of the commissioner, including the influential Congregational minister Henry Ward Beecher, conceived of the bureau's work in similar terms (McFeely 1968, 87). The United States Christian Commission was formed in November 1861 as "a national agency in which evangelical Christians from various denominations across the North could unify and coordinate their efforts to minister to the Union soldiers in an orderly, methodical way. . . . To carry out those operations, it developed a vast organization, with field superintendents in each army corps supervising the efforts of some 5,000 volunteer delegates—the actual ministers of the Christian Commission—throughout the far-flung Union armies" (Woodworth 2001, 167ff.; see also Shattuck 1987, 24, 26–33). The Christian Commission was not a government agency, but it did operate with government support and encouragement.

12. Just as bureau agents sought to break what they regarded as the cultural legacy of slavery, later reformers would seek to break an alleged culture of poverty among the urban black poor (Katz 1989, 16–23).

13. On Protestantism and social discipline, see also M. Weber (1958) and Thompson (1963), chap. 11.

14. Marshall refers here to Britain's Factory Acts, but the same tendency was evident in the United States, particularly in response to the movement for an eight-hour workday (Montgomery [1967] 1981). For example, when the 1865 Massachusetts Commission on the Hours of Labor and the Condition and Prospects of the Industrial Classes concluded that the Massachusetts legislature should not adopt legislation limiting the workday to eight hours, "it justified its position by asserting that legislation interfering in the contract between laborer and capitalist would violate the right of free contract." In the words of the commission's report, "Children and minors may be properly restrained for their own good. But when the season of pupilage is over, and the goal of manhood reached, then it is for the *man,* and not the *State* to say how many, or how few hours in the day he will use hand or brain for himself or those dear to him." "Take this right from the workingman," *Chicago Tribune* editor Horace White added in 1867, "and he is as completely enslaved as the negro was five years ago" (N. Cohen 2002, 34–35, 40).

15. *Ex parte Milligan,* 4 Wall. 2, 1866.

16. As these remarks suggest, the Freedmen's Bureau posed many of the same dilemmas for Radical Republicanism in the South as the labor reform movement did in the North. These dilemmas stemmed from the Radicals' "reluctance to interfere with freedom of contract," "even for the sake of promoting the moral character and good citizenship of the workers," and "the Radical tenet that the triumph of the nation eradicated class" (Montgomery [1967] 1981, 230–33, 247).

17. Andrew Johnson's hostility to the Freedmen's Bureau stemmed not only from racism but also from competing ties of patronage. His Amnesty Proclamation included "the provision that those excepted from automatic amnesty needed to apply to the President personally for pardon." This provision served as a "system for the dispensing of political patronage throughout the South" (McFeely 1968, 93). Johnson's efforts to direct patronage to Southern whites required restoration rather than redistribution of abandoned and confiscated land.

18. Thus, it was not merely degraded labor that Americans considered morally contagious (Glickstein 2002), but degraded civic practices as well. Like free laborers, free citizens could not elevate slaves; slaves would only debase them. Just as "'undeserving' recipients of relief would demoralize independent laborers and poison the work incentives of the capitalist market" (Glickstein 2002, 12), so, too, would they demoralize independent citizens and poison the virtuous habits on which a republican polity depended.

19. On the ritual degradation of relief recipients, see Piven and Cloward (1977, 41–44) and Piven and Cloward ([1971] 1993, 165–75, 395–97). Cf. Durkheim's discussion of the functions of punishment (Durkheim [1893] 1984, 60–64), Goffman's concept of ritual profanation (Goffman 1967, 85–90), and Foucault's "punitive semiotechnique" (Foucault [1975] 1977, 101, 104).

20. For similar reasons, "the postwar Union army" was even "blacker than the wartime services. At the end of the war, blacks composed about 11 percent of the approximately 1,000,000 Union soldiers, but by the fall of 1865, when the entire army had shrunk to some 227,000 men, blacks made up roughly 36 percent of the total" (Berlin, Reidy, and Rowland 1982, 733). This undoubtedly contributed to the hostility of Southern whites to Northern occupation.

21. As Gramsci (1971, 326) points out, a "conception of the world" is not only articulated intellectually, but may also be implicit in practices or modes of conduct. Cf. Clemens (1996) on the framing function of organizational forms.

22. The Union League may have helped broker this alliance. Women were actively involved in the Ladies' Union League, also known as the Women's Loyal National League; its leadership included feminists like Elizabeth Cady Stanton and Susan B. Anthony (Gibson 1957, 307–11).

23. Aside from traditional poor relief, the other major competitor in the welfare field was the Civil War pension system, which is discussed in the next chapter. However, the military officers who administered the Freedmen's Bureau would

hardly seek to improve and expand their agency at the expense of veterans' pensions. Moreover, while the Freedmen's Bureau was administered by military men, the Pension Bureau was staffed by civilians or ex-soldiers whose jobs depended on the legitimation and expansion of the Civil War pension system. This provided Pension Bureau officials with a much stronger incentive to distinguish pensions from traditional poor relief.

24. The reconstructed Southern states failed to compensate for the loss of the Freedmen's Bureau. Although state legislatures briefly expanded public health, public works, schools, and welfare during Radical Reconstruction, social rights reached their nadir during Redemption. Without social rights, black laborers were vulnerable to economic coercion, which made it harder for them to exercise their civil and political rights effectively and easier for Southern political leaders to control their votes.

## Chapter Three

1. Since many freedmen were also Union veterans, the Freedmen's Bureau and the Pension Bureau served overlapping constituencies. A large degree of overlap would make comparison problematic. However, as noted in this chapter, blacks were underrepresented among pension recipients and marginalized in the main pressure group that represented them; thus, the overlap was considerably reduced.

2. One possible objection to this analogy between the Union League and the GAR is that the former was politically weaker than the latter. Indeed, the Union League was already in decline in the South by 1869, while the GAR didn't reach the zenith of its power until 1890. These differences in political power arguably contributed to the divergent civic classification of freed slaves and veterans. However, this is not so much an alternative explanation as one subsumed by my own. The political power of these pressure groups cannot be understood apart from their relation to elites and other agents in the welfare field, the structure of the policies that encouraged their expansion, or the broader racial politics that shaped their trajectories. In regard to racial politics, it should be borne in mind that the decline of the Union League was mainly due to counter-mobilization by the Ku Klux Klan (Fitzgerald 1989, 2).

3. "Veterans regarded the civil-service reformers as highly inimical to their interests; when the [1883] Pendleton [Civil Service] Act went into force, [President Benjamin] Harrison had to worry about the reaction of his soldier-constituents.... Opposition to the Pendleton Act and the Civil Service Commission which it established became general among Grand Army members.... Officers foresaw that it would hamper their efforts to squeeze former soldiers into government jobs" (Dearing 1952, 284). At the state and federal levels, veterans continued to battle

with civil-service reformers over preference in appointments well into the 1890s (Dearing 1952, 439, 441). As noted in the next chapter, the Pendleton Act later played a role in struggles over the classification of WPA workers.

4. Although Skocpol (1992, 145) concludes that "nothing exact can be said about the proportions of illegitimate pensioners or expenditures," she estimates that "some (undetermined) thousands, or conceivably tens of thousands, of the nearly one-million pensioners in 1910 were bogus." As in the case of the Freedmen's Bureau, allegations of fraud were exaggerated for political purposes, but they had some basis in reality, which made them credible.

5. Dependent pension bills "called for the pensioning of all ex-soldiers who were unable to support themselves because of infirmities, whether those infirmities had anything to do with war service or not; they were, in a sense, extensions of the local and state-level efforts to keep ex-soldiers out of almshouses." Service pension bills "were proposals to pension every honorably discharged soldier who had served a given term (usually sixty or ninety days), regardless of his physical or financial condition" (McConnell 1992, 149–50).

6. An obvious difficulty with business-centered theories, in addition to those noted in this chapter, is that capital was at least temporarily divided along sectional lines, weakening capitalist leadership and authority. Indeed, sectional and (in the case of labor) racial divisions splintered capital and labor alike, constraining class action (Du Bois [1935] 1962, 609). Interestingly, just as classes were fractured along these lines, racial groupings were divided along sectional and class lines. This was true for blacks as well as whites. In contrast to most freedpeople, Southern black leaders during Reconstruction were disproportionately free-born, educated, and relatively wealthier mulattoes or former slaves who had held more favored stations, which frequently led the leaders to take more moderate stands on land and labor than their constituents (Holt 1977, chap. 6, chap. 7; Holt 1982; Hume 1982; Meier 1982, 394–95; Rankin 1982). Southern planters sometimes tried to exploit these class divisions among blacks. A white planter in South Carolina, for example, "declared that whites need not concern themselves with the [1875] Civil Rights Bill, for it would only benefit the educated class among the blacks and would serve to ally them even closer to the upper-class whites" (Holt 1977, 166–67). These competing sources of social division made classification struggles a crucial dimension of class struggles during Reconstruction.

7. For similar reasons, McConnell's explanation for the success of Civil War pensioners is also inadequate. He argues that "veterans' arguments for entitlement [were] persuasive" because they linked "important Victorian values like independence and manliness—the same values that historically had justified only local and intermittent charity—with participation in the war" (McConnell 1992, 162–65). Since similar appeals were made in struggles over the Freedmen's Bureau and its clients, they may have been necessary conditions for success, but they could not have been sufficient.

8. Although Congress initially limited pensions to clients who were deemed unemployable (disabled veterans and widows), the Pension Bureau did not investigate whether applicants had means of supporting themselves other than employment, nor did it restrict pensions to the indigent.

9. Jensen (2003) describes Civil War pensions as an entitlement. I describe them as a quasi-entitlement, because their entitlement status was arguably limited by the discretionary aspects of the program, which allowed politicians to use pensions for patronage purposes.

10. Lack of congressional appropriations during the bureau's first year of operations forced bureau agents to depend on other sources of revenue like the rental or sale of abandoned or confiscated property (Office of the Commissioner, Annual Reports, 1866–68, Boxes 1, 3, 4). This made the bureau's redistributive features even more salient. On the "wages of whiteness," see Du Bois ([1935] 1962, 700): "It must be remembered that the white group of laborers, while they received a low wage, were compensated in part by a sort of public and psychological wage. They were given public deference and titles of courtesy because they were white." Racial equality did not deprive whites of deference, but it did threaten their ability to monopolize it.

11. Northern capitalists could have defined their interests differently. Congressman Thomas Eliot defended his Freedmen's Bureau bill on proto-Keynesian grounds, arguing that the bureau would help "form a new class of consumers for Northern products" after the war (Bentley 1955, 38–39; Du Bois [1935] 1962, 220). Similarly, in 1865, Martin Delaney, a black army officer and Freedmen's Bureau official, published an appeal for a "triple alliance" among capital, land, and labor to reconstruct the South. Redistribution of land to freedmen, he argued, would benefit Northern investors by creating "a great market, . . . a new source of consumption of every commodity in demand in free civilized communities." Freedpeople would become "great consumers" of farm implements, new houses, better food, and "genteel apparel" (quoted in Schmidt 1999, 233). Delaney's plan was greeted with indifference, suggesting that Northern capitalists had difficulty seeing freedpeople as consumers. This difficulty may have reflected the assumption, widespread among Northerners, that freedpeople did not yet have the habits that were necessary and appropriate for a free-labor society. Northern educators sought to inculcate these habits, in part by "expand[ing] the freedmen's material aspirations, the 'wants' that classical economists viewed as the most effective spur to self-directed labor" (Foner 1988, 146–47).

12. Pensions for former slaves might have avoided the political drawbacks associated with redistributive and regulatory policies. In fact, Nebraska congressman William Connell introduced a bill to provide freedmen's pensions in 1890 (Vaughan 1891, 32–33, 38–41). The bill was modeled on Civil War veterans' pensions, which its supporters invoked as a positive policy precedent (Berry 2005, 34, 44). However, the ex-slave pension bill was poorly timed. By 1890, the nega-

tive reaction to Civil War pensions made the creation of new pension programs unlikely. Nevertheless, like promises of land reform during Reconstruction, the ex-slave pension bill was not forgotten. "In 1934, a number of old ex-slaves wrote President Franklin D. Roosevelt, 'Is there any way to consider the old slaves?' One asked specifically, whatever happened to the idea of 'giving us pensions in payment for our long days of servitude?' The government officials replied that no legislation existed" (Berry 2005, 224). On the movement for freedmen's pensions, see Berry (1972, 2005).

13. In contrast to liberal reformers, "the pro-Grant stalwart faction of the Republican party . . . continued to stand by the southern Negroes and to demand that their civil and political rights be protected." Unhampered by concerns about patronage politics, Republican stalwarts sought to maintain a Southern Republican Party with black votes (Stampp 1965, 192).

14. Like the underrepresentation of blacks, the absence of the new immigrant working class in the Civil War pension rolls probably also helped pensioners avoid a racialized political backlash. The new immigrants began to arrive from eastern and southern Europe in the 1880s, too late to participate in the Civil War and gain entitlement to military pensions (Skocpol 1992, 135–38; Orloff 1993b, 137). Of course, there were "old immigrants" (primarily from northern and western Europe) among Union veterans (Vinovskis 1989). However, American attitudes toward immigrants varied depending on how remote they were "in culture and race" (Higham [1955] 1983, 24–27). With the onset of the new wave of immigration, older immigrants were "rendered indelibly white by the presence of populations even more problematic than themselves" (Jacobson 1998, 76).

15. Like the Civil War pension rolls, the GAR was predominantly male and native born; immigrants, Catholics, industrial workers, and women were absent, underrepresented, or relegated to secondary positions within the organization (McConnell 1992, 71, 79, 81, 208–13, 218–20). These patterns of exclusion, like those in the pension system itself, may also have helped insulate Civil War pensioners from a political backlash. In fairness, the GAR's conception of the nation was not based on ascriptive criteria, nor (with the important exception of racial segregation) did it practice active discrimination. Rather, the GAR based membership on participation in a war that "occurred too early for the latecomers and too selectively for women and most blacks. An army mostly native-born and white, in other words, produced a social organization mostly native-born and white, in a nation that was becoming more diverse every year" (McConnell 1992, 71).

16. Like the racial backlash, the anti-patronage backlash was also partly a product of policy structure, which can foster negative reactions of various kinds. Skocpol (1992, 278) suggests that reactions to Civil War pensions varied according to observers' social class: In contrast to "elites and the educated middle class," "many labor leaders . . . regarded the Civil War pensions as an honorable, democratic precedent that should to be extended to new categories of worthy citizens"

(278). I suggest that it is not only the social class of observers but also the race (and perhaps the class and gender) of clients that shapes public reactions to new policies. The postbellum campaign to abolish outdoor relief for the poor provides additional support for this thesis. Like the Freedmen's Bureau in the South, local poor relief in the North was manipulated for patronage purposes and went disproportionately to clients whom reformers deemed racially unfit for self government, namely, the new immigrant working class (Skocpol 1992, 92–100; Lui 1995). As one would expect if the effects of anti-patronage sentiment were mediated by racial politics, "charity reformers were tightening their scrutiny of applications for relief from impoverished working people of largely foreign origins" while the Pension Bureau treated its predominantly white and native-born clients as worthy, rights-bearing citizens (Montgomery 1993, 81).

17. This argument is indebted to Glickstein (2002, 12, 46), who argues that American white workers did not derive their sense of self "with exclusive reference" to black slave labor. "Blacks and economic competition from black labor, be it slave or free, constituted a significant, but only one, form of otherness in antebellum America." However, according to Glickstein (2002, 2–3, 227), "ideological preparation for the [Civil W]ar" encouraged a "simplistic dichotomization of slave versus free labor," marginalizing and eclipsing "concerns over other forms of servile labor and work-degrading processes." In contrast, I suggest that by equating pauperism with slavery, Americans continued to express their anxieties about pauperism in the language of Republican free-labor ideology.

18. Although "getting land sufficient for the four million freed blacks was a major problem," "the problems of land supply should not be exaggerated. From 1862 through 1871, the federal government granted 120 million acres of land to the railroads and conferred another 105 million acres on western homesteaders and the Morrill Act land grant colleges. More than 67 million acres were given the railroads during the three years of the Freedmen's Bureau's existence" (R. Smith 1997, 301). Of course, "land is only one of the scare resources of underdeveloped rural societies; where not accompanied by control of credit and access to markets, land reform can often be a 'hollow victory.'" Nevertheless, "land distribution would have had profound consequences for Southern society, weakening the land-based economic and political power of the old ruling class, offering blacks a measure of choice as to whether, when, and under what circumstances to enter the labor market, and affecting the former slaves' conception of themselves" (Foner 1988, 109).

19. *The Nation,* perhaps with the Paris Commune of 1871 in mind, equated the political empowerment of propertyless blacks with "socialism" (quoted in Sproat 1968, 39). This sort of language anticipated the use of anti-Communism in the late 1930s for similar ends, namely, to curb the political rights of those receiving government assistance, thereby weakening the constituency for such assistance (see chapters 4 and 5).

20. Since the civil rights movement in the mid-twentieth century, Americans have drawn very different conclusions from the history of Reconstruction. As Pierson (1993, 615–16) points out, the lessons we learn from past policy decisions are shaped by preexisting beliefs and often contested. On the reaction against patronage politics and its adverse consequences for new social spending programs, see Orloff and Skocpol (1984); Orloff (1988, 1993b); and Skocpol (1992, 1995a). Opposition to new social spending for blacks is evident from failed bills to enact pensions for ex-slaves (Berry 1972, 2005); failed bills to establish a home for indigent, aged, or infirm freedpeople, probably modeled on the National Home for Disabled Volunteer Soldiers (Taylor 1922, 163–165); and the reluctance of Congress to assist black depositors after the collapse of the Freedman's Savings Bank (Osthaus 1976). Restrictions on black political participation (literacy tests, poll taxes, and the like) took longer to develop. Despite the collapse of Republican regimes in the South in the 1870s, the Redeemer governments did not disfranchise blacks until the advent of Southern populism in the 1890s. On the under-democratization of the South as a key constraint on U.S. welfare state development, see Quadagno (1994) and Amenta (1998).

## Chapter Four

1. During the First New Deal (1933–1934), the Roosevelt administration pursued reform and recovery primarily through the Agricultural Adjustment Act and the National Industrial Recovery Act. The Supreme Court struck down both laws as unconstitutional in 1935, which forced Roosevelt to introduce or support a series of new economic and social measures, collectively known as the Second New Deal. These measures included the WPA, the National Labor Relations Act, and the Social Security Act, all enacted in 1935 and eventually upheld by the Supreme Court.

2. According to Lorence (1994; 1996, 231–35, 274–75, 290), this percentage fell in the movement's final years. As anti-Communist attacks on the Workers Alliance mounted and the Congress of Industrial Organizations (CIO) began to compete with it to recruit WPA workers, he argues that the proportion of the Workers Alliance membership consisting of unemployable persons grew in the early 1940s. Nevertheless, the Workers Alliance continued to speak for and act on behalf of WPA workers.

3. For an analysis of the WPA in relation to racial divisions, see chapter 5. For now, suffice it to say that the national tier of New Deal social and labor policies was not only predominantly masculine but also largely white. In this respect, too, the WPA was ambiguously situated within the bifurcated New Deal welfare state. Although most WPA workers were white, the proportion of black workers grew in the program's final years. This was because blacks, like women, faced greater

difficulty finding private employment and therefore left the WPA rolls more slowly
(D. Howard 1943, 285–98; Brown 1999, 77–79, 89).

4. Home relief was a form of poor relief provided by local or state governments, so called because it did not involve internment in a poorhouse or workhouse. To receive poor relief, an individual was traditionally required to swear that
she was destitute and had lived in the locality for a specified amount of time. Even
after they secured WPA employment, workers were sometimes forced to supplement their wages with direct relief if their WPA wages were not sufficient to support their families (Rose 1994, 98). WPA workers were subjected to other forms
of ritual degradation as well, including fingerprinting by law enforcement officials
(*Work,* April 9, 1938, 3; May 7, 1938, 1; December 17, 1938, 8; January 28, 1939, 5).

5. First Lady Eleanor Roosevelt and secretary of labor Frances Perkins suggested that the federal government should classify WPA workers as employed
for the purpose of measuring and reporting unemployment ("First Lady Talks of
Jobs," *New York Times,* February 1, 1939; "Miss Perkins Sees Upswing in Jobs,"
May 7, 1939). A widely circulated pamphlet entitled *Our Job with the WPA* bluntly
told WPA workers: "You are off relief. You are working" (U.S. Works Progress
Administration 1936, 8).

6. Historically, relief officials often compensated relief work with in-kind assistance rather than cash as a way of "signaling concretely the difference between
ordinary wages and work-relief payments" (V. Zelizer 1994, 132). Congress instituted prevailing wages with the 1936 Emergency Relief Appropriation Act. However, rather than raise the WPA security wage, Congress reduced "the hours of labor until the amounts of the original security wage translated into hourly terms
equaled the prevailing wage" (Macmahon, Millett, and Ogden 1941, 152–56; see
also *Workers Alliance,* August 15, 1935, 1; October 2, 1935, 1; "First July Issue"
[1936], 1; Seymour 1937, 40; Millett 1938, 41–45; Ziskind 1940). In August 1939,
Congress abandoned the prevailing wage policy and set hours uniformly at 130
per month (Rose 1994, 98).

7. The principle of less eligibility holds that relief must be less desirable than
even the worst employment. As WPA workers were demanding pay equal to that
of federal employees, public works employees, and employees in private industry,
CIO president John Lewis was publicly advocating equal pay for women engaged
in "substantially the same work" as men (Mettler 1998, 48, 189). Given the identical language in which these claims were made, it would be hard for WPA workers
to miss the parallel.

8. New Dealers also had to contend with the policy goals of congressional
conservatives. However, their influence is reflected less in the WPA's initial policy
design than in subsequent reforms of the program discussed later in this chapter.

9. Prior to the Nazi regime, the German unemployed movement was the
largest in continental Europe, and German work relief fostered similar struggles over the status and rights of relief workers (Crew 1998, 188–263; Perry 2000,

172, 190–91). For a comparison of German and American public-works policies, see Garraty (1973). In the United States, Senator Robert Wagner, the architect of the National Labor Relations Act, summarized industrial democracy this way: "Democracy cannot work unless it is honored in the factory as well as the polling booth; men cannot be truly free in body and in spirit unless their freedom extends into the places where they earn their daily bread" (NLRB, 9). Proponents of industrial democracy drew upon and reworked older elements in American political culture that can be traced back to working-class republicanism (Wilentz 1984; Tomlins 1985).

10. Poorhouses, it should be noted, had by no means disappeared in the 1930s; such institutions continued to exist and operate during the Great Depression (Piven and Cloward [1971] 1993, 48; Wagner 2005).

11. These debates were never fully settled, and local practices varied (Seymour 1937, 45–46; *Work,* December 3, 1938, 7; November 9, 1939, 3; U.S. Congress. House 1939–40, 69–70). However, despite the adoption of project locals in some places, fraternization continued to occur at higher levels of the Workers Alliance, which was organized along territorial rather than program-specific lines. Locals elected delegates to a countywide or statewide organization, and these various constituent units elected delegates to nation-wide annual conventions (U.S. Congress. House 1939–40, 36).

12. Quoted in "'Demands' Pay Rise for WPA Workers," *New York Times,* August 25, 1936.

13. There is some debate about whether social workers or other types of administrators were more likely to emphasize the work aspects of work relief. Bremer (1975, 641) argues that social workers sought to "maximize work relief's work aspects and to minimize its relief aspects as much as possible." In contrast, Schwartz (1984, viii, 237–238) argues that as engineers, technicians, and management experts replaced social workers as administrators, they ran work relief programs "more like an emergency employment corporation rather than charitable made work." Evidence from the WPA is mixed: Both Harry Hopkins, the social worker who headed the WPA from 1935 to 1939, and Francis Harrington, who was recruited from the U.S. Army Corps of Engineers to replace Hopkins, seem to have emphasized the WPA's work aspects.

14. "WPA Union Seeks C.I.O. Affiliation," *New York Times,* July 14, 1937.

15. The Workers Alliance worked hard to get WPA officials to recognize it as a bona fide labor union (Ziskind 1940; Karsh and Garman 1961, 93), which was not always an easy task. For example, New York City WPA administrator Victor Ridder insisted that the Workers Alliance was an "agitating organization" rather than a "labor organization" ("Alliance Upheld in WPA Bargaining," *New York Times,* June 14, 1936; *Workers Alliance,* "First July Issue" [1936], 2). When Aubrey Williams overruled Ridder in 1936, the Workers Alliance seized upon the ruling as confirmation of its claims, declaring "Recognition Won!" on the front page of its

newspaper ("Alliance Upheld in WPA Bargaining," *New York Times*, June 14, 1936; *Workers Alliance*, "First July Issue" [1936], 1–2). Although the WPA agreed to allow the Workers Alliance to represent those WPA workers who were members (or who designated it as their representative), it did not consider the Workers Alliance to be the representative of all WPA workers, nor did it consider the Alliance to be the exclusive representative of WPA workers.

16. Nine percent of the protest events organized wholly or partly by the Workers Alliance between 1935 and 1941 involved walk-out strikes by WPA workers. The Workers Alliance adopted the sit-down strike even more widely, particularly during the sit-down strike wave among workers in private industry between 1936 and 1937 (Ziskind 1940, 175–76; Babson 1999, 95–103). Adoption of this tactic peaked in 1937, when 41 percent of the protest events organized by the Workers Alliance involved sit-down strikes or occupation of property. Overall, between 1935 and 1941, 23 percent of the protest events organized by the Workers Alliance involved sit-down strikes. These conclusions are based on protest event data gathered by the author from the *New York Times*. For additional data on WPA strikes, see the tables of strikes and lockouts by industry published in the U.S. Department of Labor's *Monthly Labor Review*. On organizational form as frame, see Clemens (1996).

17. "Public Questioned on WPA," *New York Times*, July 19, 1939.

18. There is not enough public opinion data to track changes in the views of WPA workers over time. The average number of persons employed on WPA projects in July 1939 (when the poll was taken) was 2,282,087 (U.S. Federal Works Agency 1946, 28).

19. On the transposition of cultural schemas across institutional settings, see Sewell (1992).

20. "'Demands' Pay Rise for WPA Workers," *New York Times*, August 25, 1936.

21. The WPA did establish a Labor Policies Board, which was meant to be analogous in some respects to the NLRB, but it lacked enforcement provisions (and therefore failed to satisfy the Workers Alliance) and was eventually discontinued (*Work*, August 13, 1938, 7; October 22, 1938, 4, 7).

22. Later scholarship suggests that these fears were not unfounded. According to Piven and Cloward ([1971] 1993, 106), the Workers Alliance was "perhaps the most formidable organization of the able-bodied unemployed in American history." But even if the threat posed by the Workers Alliance was inflated, fear of the movement was real in its consequences, which included the political reaction described later in this chapter.

23. A major cause of Republican gains in the 1938 election was the so-called Roosevelt Recession from late 1937 to 1938, which halted a modest economic recovery in the preceding four years. Conservatives blamed the recession on the "anti-business" policies of the New Deal. Even Amenta (1998, 137), who argues that the 1939 Congress was "far from dominated by conservatives," concedes that

"the pro-spenders lost their majority" after the election. The coalition between Republicans and Southern Democrats was brokered and constructed in part through the discourse of anti-Communism.

24. These congressional investigations were ritualized in several ways. First, this activity was ceremonial in Goffman's (1967, 48–56) sense, that is, a conventionalized means of communicating one's evaluation or assessment of another's status. Second, Bergesen (1984, 13–14) argues that "the modern nation-state manufactures subversives to create a ritual contrast with its set of collective representations. *The function of creating this symbolic contrast with images of collective political purposes is precisely to dramatize and reaffirm the very meaning of these images of the corporate political state*" (original emphasis). Although conservatives did not "manufacture" Communists, moral entrepreneurship served a similar function. Third, these congressional investigations in particular, and, more generally, the Red Scare of the late 1930s, involved the kind of "generalization" that Alexander (1988a, chap. 5; 1989, chap. 6) sees in political rituals like Watergate, through which "social solidarities are reworked" and classificatory systems are transformed. Fourth, committee hearings helped to bring about a convergence of ethos and world view in the manner described by Geertz (1973, 113–14, 119).

25. James Patterson (1967, 293) suggests that Sheppard was "a loyal administration man" despite the critical report issued by his committee. However, Amenta (2001, 274) identifies Sheppard as one of the thirty staunchest opponents of the WPA in the U.S. Senate. Three of the committee's five members (including Sheppard) were Southern Democrats or Republicans, and the Workers Alliance denounced it (along with the House Special Committee on Un-American Activities) as "one of the fronts for reaction" (U.S. Congress. Senate 1939, Part I, 2, 39; *Work,* January 14, 1939, 3; J. Patterson 1967, 246–47).

26. Although Dies generally supported the New Deal before 1937, his fears of radicals and foreigners later led him to demand a congressional investigation into the sit-down strikes of 1937 and to oppose the 1938 Fair Labor Standards Act. Dies "felt strongly about . . . aliens. . . . From his first days in the House Dies championed the view that the solution for the Depression lay in deporting as many foreigners as possible to open jobs for native-born Americans. Allied with this xenophobia was a belief that aliens and radicals dominated the CIO" (J. Patterson 1967, 135, 166–168, 180, 194–95, 243, 245). See below on how anti-Communism was linked to suspicion of foreign-born workers.

27. Woodrum was one of the most conservative Democrats in the House of Representatives; he represented a rural Southern district, tried to restrict relief spending after 1937, and opposed the Roosevelt administration on at least a quarter of key roll-call votes (Patterson 1967, 172, 237, 294, 339–43). Workers Alliance members referred to Woodrum's committee as the "Baby Dies Committee," and they hated Woodrum so much they tried to burn him in effigy at a 1939 demonstration in New York City (*Work,* July 29, 1939, 1; see also *Work,* May 6, 1939).

28. On social insurance and pensions, see Orloff (1993b, chap. 9). She argues that concerns about patronage did not forestall enactment of OAI, because "action on social provision was politically necessary" during the Depression, "and political elites in the Roosevelt administration felt they had to take action or face the passage of 'politically unwise' legislation" (270). An alternative explanation, suggested in chapter 3, is that the reaction against patronage was more effective when it was associated with a racial backlash against the policy's clients. On the racial backlash against the WPA, see chapter 5.

29. "High Relief Aides Seen Helping Reds," *New York Times,* June 8, 1937.

30. The Pendleton Act was the same legislation opposed by the GAR in the 1880s (see chapter 3). In addition to its restrictions, the 1937 Emergency Relief Appropriation Act stipulated that the funds it appropriated could not be "used to pay the salary or expenses of any person who is a candidate for any State, district, county or municipal office. . . in any primary, general or special election, or who is serving as a campaign manager or assistant thereto for any such candidate." In February 1938, the U.S. Comptroller General ruled that this provision applied to WPA project workers as well as administrative and supervisory personnel. Lasser condemned the ruling as "the first step toward disenfranchising the unemployed" (*Work,* April 9, 1938, 1–2). The use of cash relief for political purposes became a contentious issue in the 1930s in part because cash benefits were more difficult for authorities to earmark for activities they approved.

31. See also "WPA Sounds Appeal for Votes," *New York Times,* June 28, 1938; "400,000 in the WPA to Join Vote Fight," July 8, 1938; "Workers Alliance in Political Drive," August 21, 1938.

32. See also "Hopkins Hits Plan of Campaign Fund by WPA Employees," *New York Times,* August 23, 1938; "Play Tour by WPA Faces Fight Here," August 26, 1938; "Roosevelt Denies Rift with Farley," "Sheppard Warns Lasser on Funds," August 27, 1938; "Alliance Ignores Fund-Raising Ban," August 28, 1938; *Work,* October 22, 1938, 6; U.S. Congress. Senate 1939, Part II, 374, 376, 377.

33. The Workers Alliance also invoked the labor-union model of organization to justify its fund-raising activities, representing its members as workers as well as citizens. "Like any other trade union," Alliance leaders explained, "we have to go to our membership for support" ("Hopkins Hits Plan of Campaign Fund by WPA Employees," *New York Times,* August 23, 1938). The implication here was that WPA workers were once again being denied the rights of other workers.

34. "Hopkins Hits Plan of Campaign Fund by WPA Employees," *New York Times,* August 23, 1938; "Play Tour by WPA Faces Fight Here," August 26, 1938; "Roosevelt Denies Rift With Farley," "Sheppard Warns Lasser on Funds," August 27, 1938; "Alliance Ignores Fund-Raising Ban," August 28, 1938.

35. For a more detailed account of anti-Communism and its impact on the Workers Alliance in the late 1930s, see Goldberg (2003).

36. Compare the two modes of representing the social death of slaves. In the extrusive mode, "the dominant image of the slave was that of an insider who . . . ceased to belong and had been expelled from normal participation in the community because of a failure to meet certain minimal legal or socioeconomic norms of behavior. The destitute were included in this group, for while they perhaps had committed no overt crime, their failure to survive on their own was taken as a sign of innate incompetence and of divine disfavor." In contrast, "in the intrusive mode of representing social death the slave was ritually incorporated as the permanent enemy on the inside—the 'domestic enemy,'" who "did not and could not belong because he was the product of a hostile, alien culture" (O. Patterson 1982, 39–41).

37. For a detailed account of these struggles within the Workers Alliance, see Goldberg (2003). There, the struggles are analyzed in terms of in-group purification, a process in which one part of a group "take[s] up in regard to those who are more evidently stigmatized" than themselves "the attitudes the normals take" toward the group as a whole (Goffman 1963, 107–8). In this case, non-Communists increasingly looked upon Communists as an organizational fifth column seeking to control the Workers Alliance, in much the same way conservatives saw the Workers Alliance as a national fifth column seeking to control the WPA. On exit and voice, see Hirschman (1970).

38. "Sharply Changed WPA Planned in Relief Bill," "Workers' Alliance Assailed," *New York Times,* June 18, 1939, "Relief Bill Aimed at WPA Radicals Ready for House," June 13, 1939.

39. On perceptions of Communists, see Karsh and Garman (1961, 103–4) and Bakke (1940a, 59–66). New Dealers opposed special programs and benefits for veterans, preferring instead to meet the needs of veterans through "programs directed at the entire population" (Amenta and Skocpol 1988, 85). Addressing the American Legion in 1933, President Roosevelt declared: "No person, because he wore a uniform, must thereafter be placed in a special class of beneficiaries over and above all other citizens. The fact of wearing a uniform does not mean that he can demand and receive from his Government a benefit which no other citizen receives" (quoted in Mettler 2005, 19). As late as 1942, Roosevelt's National Resources Planning Board envisioned comprehensive expansion of New Deal programs rather than special legislation for veterans following the war. However, the Second World War brought "what the New Deal reformers had hoped to avoid: a special welfare state for a substantial sector of the population [veterans] deemed especially deserving" (Amenta and Skocpol 1988, 93–94).

40. "Relief Bill Aimed at WPA Radicals Ready for House,"*New York Times,* June 13, 1939.

41. See also "Relief Bill Aimed at WPA Radicals Ready for House,"*New York Times,* June 13, 1939; "Sharply Changed WPA Planned in Relief Bill," "Workers' Alliance Assailed," June 18, 1939.

**Chapter Five**

1. OAI was renamed Old Age and Survivors Insurance (OASI) in 1939 and Old Age and Survivors Disability Insurance (OASDI) in 1956. The WPA was renamed the Work Projects Administration in 1939. To avoid confusion, I use the original names throughout the chapter.

2. Since everyone gets old but not everyone becomes unemployed, one might expect that more Americans had a stake in OAI than the WPA. However, as indicated here, these risks were not clearly separated in the 1930s. Furthermore, the risk of unemployment would loom larger in an era of mass unemployment, and because few elderly persons received OAI benefits in the 1930s and 1940s, the population as a whole could not be said to have had a stake in the program then.

3. Although OAI and the WPA both conditioned benefits on work, neither OAI recipients nor WPA workers were homogeneous in terms of their occupational backgrounds. As a result, the clients of both policies possessed varying amounts of economic and cultural capital and were, thus, dispersed in social space. This dispersion likely constrained efforts to mobilize OAI recipients and WPA workers as cohesive groups. (Although there were no efforts to mobilize OAI recipients in the 1930s and 1940s, political parties and senior citizen interest groups began to do so in the 1960s [Campbell 2003, chap. 4].) However, there is no evidence to suggest that occupational diversity was greater among WPA workers than it was among OAI recipients.

4. For annual unemployment rates, see U.S. Department of Commerce (1975, 135). "By 1939 many had come to conclude . . . that millions of jobless would never find jobs again, not even if 'recovery' was finally achieved. . . . As late as 1941, the unemployed still numbered six million, and not until the war year of 1943 did the army of the jobless finally disappear" (Leuchtenburg 1963, 263, 346–47). Roosevelt himself supported a reduction in WPA funding in 1937, but he reversed his stance during the economic recession of 1937–1938. As noted in the previous chapter, retrenchment efforts by Republicans and business organizations began as early as 1936; these efforts became more successful when Republicans formed a conservative coalition with Southern Democrats in the late 1930s.

5. The President's Committee on Economic Security suggested in 1935 that a permanent works program would be necessary even "in normal times . . . to help meet the problems of stranded communities and overmanned or declining industries" (quoted in Harvey 1989, 19). Roosevelt signaled this permanency in 1939, noting in his budget message that "extraordinary expenditures, including funds for the WPA, were to be a permanent part of the budget," and incorporating the WPA "as a permanent bureau in the newly created Federal Works Agency" (Amenta 2001, 264; see also D. Howard 1943, 361–68). As late as 1942, when the WPA was terminated, the National Resources Planning Board called for

an improved and fully nationalized version of the program that would be separated from relief (Amenta 1998, 194–95).

6. Altmeyer was chairman of the SSB or commissioner for Social Security from 1937 to 1953.

7. Despite their initial preference for public assistance, conservatives agreed to expand OAI benefits in 1939 in order to deplete the program's growing reserve fund. Social insurance, it should be added, faced competition not only from other public policies but also from "the growing sphere of private retirement provision," including "union-negotiated [pension] plans" (Hacker 2002, 86, 130–31; cf. Sparrow 1996, 47–52).

8. "Fusion of Jobless and Aged Planned," New York Times, February 12, 1939. The old-age pension movement was also analogous to the GAR. In fact, "the Townsend membership included aged members of the Grand Army of the Republic," and the number of GAR posts per capita in each state was positively associated with the number of Townsend clubs per capita (Amenta and Zylan 1991, 257, 262).

9. An alternative danger was that OAI would itself begin to resemble a flat pension system. According to Hacker (2002, 136), "program executives" worried that a "flattening of [OAI] benefits" in the late 1940s would make the program "more similar to a system of flat-rate assistance" and undermine "the distinction between Social Security and means-tested old-age assistance payments." See later in this chapter on the potential loss of distinction between the two systems.

10. In 1939, Congress authorized supplemental benefits for dependents of retired workers and for surviving dependents in case of death. Congress extended OAI benefits to regularly employed agricultural and domestic workers in 1954 (Mettler 1998, 217–18; Campbell 2003, 85). Disability benefits were added in 1956.

11. Congress increased OAI benefits in 1950 and began automatic adjustments to benefits in 1975.

12. Cf. J. Zelizer (1998, 13–14): "Without these symbolic distinctions, social insurance would not have been as attractive, as generous, or as desirable. One main reason citizens and politicians privileged social insurance was the perception that it was an earned right. As a result, claimed the policymakers, its benefits did not create dependency on the government. This definition of the policy was not inherent to the benefit, but had to be constructed through a complex tax system with its symbols and its rhetoric."

13. Even after the 1950 amendments, policymakers acknowledged that distinctions between old-age insurance and public welfare were still "primarily symbolic." House Ways and Means chairman Wilbur Mills, for example, admitted that "the net effect upon the individual who pays a tax is the same whether it is a social-security tax or an income tax." "Regardless, they continued to encourage the belief that the payroll tax" separated OAI "from other forms of welfare: In their

rhetoric, policymakers did not even call the payroll tax a 'tax,' but referred to it as a 'contribution'" (Zelizer 1998, 77–78). Lieberman (1998) argues that the payroll tax did not merely distinguish OAI from relief, but also created incentives to expand the program: "By linking benefits to contributions, OAI created a perpetual constituency for itself. . . . Those workers who had been paying OAI taxes in 1937 (the first year taxes were collected) had an instant stake in the program and an interest in keeping the payroll tax as low as possible for as long as possible. This objective could be accomplished either by restricting benefits or by finding new sources of revenue, which meant, as long as there were uncovered workers, bringing new workers into the system" (Lieberman 1998, 70, 90–92, 106, 109). In contrast, programs with a non-contributory finance structure (like the WPA) lacked an "expansionary logic" and "generated intense and enduring political and ideological conflicts . . . along class lines" (Lieberman 1998, 121, 123–124). While my own analysis is indebted to and generally consistent with Lieberman's approach, I question whether these specific policy features fully explain the divergent classification of OAI recipients and WPA workers. First, few of OAI's constituents understood how the program's finance structure worked (Schiltz 1970, 31–35, 53, 79–80, 178–180). Second, though financed through general revenues, the WPA also created a constituency for itself, including WPA workers and indirect beneficiaries of the program (Amenta 1998, 220). Third, while OAI's finance structure may have created an expansionary logic, expansion and legitimation of the program still required the consent of Southern Democrats in the 1930s and 1940s (see later in this chapter).

14. Although the Social Security Act left it to the states to define need, the SSB constrained how they did so. According to Altmeyer (1966), the SSB insisted on tighter eligibility standards not only to weaken OAA as a competitor, but also to discourage politicians from distributing OAA benefits as political patronage.

15. On the SSB's institutional autonomy, see Derthick (1979, 34–36). Admittedly, the public was slow to recognize the distinction between social insurance and public assistance that the SSB tried so hard to foster. While public support for old-age programs increased steadily from 1935 to 1944, there was still considerable confusion of OAI with OAA during this period (Schiltz 1970, chap. 2).

16. Additional factors encouraging fiscal conservatives to favor OAI included its shift toward pay-as-you-go financing in 1939 and the belief that its reliance on payroll taxes would limit its expansion. Hacker (2002, 98–104, 108–11, 135–42) argues that business, though initially opposed to OAI, became more supportive because private and public pensions could be integrated. This may explain business support for public pensions in general, but it seems likely that policy competition encouraged business to back OAI over OAA.

17. For a dissenting view that questions the importance of racial considerations in the design of the Social Security Act, see Davies and Derthick (1997). They argue that a host of nonracial factors contributed to the exclusion of agricultural

and domestic workers from social insurance and the elimination of the "decency and health" standard for public assistance. While this claim is undoubtedly correct, their dismissal of racial politics is overstated. An extended response to Davies and Derthick (1997) is beyond the scope of this chapter, but for critical rejoinders see Lieberman (1998, 24, 41–43), who marshals historical and comparative evidence to show that the administrative difficulties of including agricultural and domestic workers were not decisive; Manza (2000a, 309–10), who argues that "the Southern racial order lay behind" arguments about states' rights or administrative capacity; and Brueggemann (2002, 164), who notes that nonracial obstacles to inclusion did "not negate the motives southern planters had to block direct relief to black farm workers." Brueggemann adds that "many of the administrative difficulties were subsequently overcome, suggesting an issue of political will rather than logistical feasibility" (164). Key participants in the development of the Social Security Act attested to Southerners' racial concerns or played down the importance of administrative difficulties (Altmeyer 1966, 35; Perkins 1946, 297–98; Witte 1962, 143–44, 152–54).

18. In contrast, the Townsend Plan provoked opposition from Southern Democrats, because it offered generous pensions to every American citizen, black as well as white, thereby threatening "the South's supply of cheap labor" (Holtzman 1963, 55, 96, 155).

19. A similar contrast can be made to unemployment insurance. The SSB insisted that states pay unemployment insurance benefits through the U.S. Employment Service, not through "poor-relief offices" (Altmeyer 1966, 62). This was yet another way it distinguished social insurance from relief.

20. Even when wages were substandard (that is, below the prevailing wage), the WPA still sometimes released black workers at harvest time. WPA administrator Harry Hopkins ordered the practice halted, but "southern work relief administrators generally ignored this order" (Wolters 1970, 207–8).

21. Brueggemann (2002, 161–63) provides a Marxian explanation for this pattern of selective exclusion, which emphasizes the divergent interests of the dominant planter class in rural areas and the nascent Southern industrial capitalist class in urban areas. This account is plausible so far as it goes, though it omits the crucial symbolic work necessary to form and mobilize classes (or class fractions) and concretely define class interests.

22. Other WPA officials were more cautious. In 1939, WPA administrator F. C. Harrington suggested to Congress that "if wage differentials are to be wiped out in this country . . . [the practice] should apply to everybody and WPA should not be the first one to be operated on in that respect" (D. Howard 1943, 162).

23. This discussion of federal wage standards for WPA workers suggests that the program had a quasi-regulatory aspect that OAI lacked. As noted in chapter 3, regulatory policies tend to be "zero-sum in their consequences," generating sharp opposition from "disfavored groups whose actions are regulated" (Skocpol

1992, 82). Southern hostility to the Workers Alliance and its demands can partly be understood in these terms. In this respect, too, the WPA was analogous to the Freedmen's Bureau.

24. A staunch segregationist, Connor later became notorious for using fire hoses and police dogs against nonviolent civil rights protesters in Birmingham in 1963 (Nunnelly 1991).

25. This last reference was a misnomer; delegates were actually referring to the Southern Conference for Human Welfare (*Work,* December 3, 1938, 9; Krueger 1967).

26. The NNC, which was established in 1936, represented younger and more militant African Americans than the NAACP, and sought to move beyond the NAACP's narrow focus on civil rights by addressing "the need for organized efforts to ease the Negro's difficulties in earning a living and particularly in gaining entrance into labor unions" (Wolters 1970, 353). Although NNC leaders ultimately failed to make it "the major organization of the [black] masses," it "seemed for a while that the National Negro Congress might become the first mass Negro organization since Marcus Garvey's Universal Negro Improvement Association of the 1920s" (362). As in the Workers Alliance, "the Communist party had considerable influence within the National Negro Congress" (371).

27. Compare the reaction against foreign-born persons, which is described in chapter 4. Insofar as the whiteness of many immigrant groups was only recently settled—and was, perhaps, still precarious—in the 1930s (Jacobson 1998), representations of the foreign born as a source of Communist subversion may have drawn upon not only the republican tradition in American political culture, which linked social provision to civic virtue, but also on ascriptive forms of Americanism, which linked fitness for self-government to racial qualifications.

28. A further comparison with ADC is instructive. Like the WPA, ADC included several lines of defense that accommodated Southern interests (Lieberman 1998, chap. 4). Because there was little or no political mobilization around ADC in the 1930s and 1940s and therefore no perceived threat, Southern congressmen tolerated the program. In contrast, mobilization around the WPA led to a perceived threat, which in turn led Southerners to repress the Workers Alliance and dismantle the WPA. The waning electoral influence of the Workers Alliance in the late 1930s probably contributed to its repression. As Piven and Cloward (1977) have shown, mobilization without electoral influence increases the likelihood of repression.

29. The Sixth Comintern Congress in 1928 did in fact call for the establishment of a separate "Negro republic" in those Southern counties that contained a majority of African Americans, but the American Communist Party no longer "pushed this theory" after 1934 (Howe and Coser 1957, 206–8). For a discussion of the idea in relation to Marxist debates about the "national question," see Omi and Winant (1986, 45–47).

30. The law in question was presumably one of the black codes described in chapter 2. This connection to Reconstruction was not lost on contemporaries. In 1935, while Herndon was appealing his case to the U.S. Supreme Court, William Brewton told the Georgia legislature: "The principles of communism cannot live where the principles of the Old South flourish; and the principles of communism are here today solely because the principles for which the Old South stood were put under the heel of the Conqueror" (quoted in Moore 1971, 67).

31. Unfortunately, the U.S. Federal Works Agency (1946) provides no figures on the racial composition of WPA workers prior to 1939, making comparison to the program's early years impossible.

32. On racial disparities in unemployment insurance, see Lieberman (1998, 56–64, 211–13). Aid to Dependent Children will be discussed further in chapter 6.

## Chapter Six

1. "New York Girding for Surge in Workfare Jobs," *New York Times,* August 13, 1996; "Divided They Fall?" *Village Voice,* January 28, 1997.

2. Discussion of the mobilization of workfare workers in the 1990s invites comparison to the National Welfare Rights Organization of the 1960s. Such a comparison is beyond the scope of this chapter, but see Reese and Newcombe (2003), who contrast the movements in terms of collective action frames and organizational ideologies.

3. On workfare organizing in other cities, see Reese (2002), Tait (2005, 170–71), and Krinsky and Reese (2006). The struggles over workfare have broader significance for two reasons. First, classification struggles have become a more prominent aspect of labor conflicts in the late twentieth and early twenty-first century United States. Graduate student teachers, for example, who (like workfare workers) provide a low-cost alternative to more expensive labor, were also involved in struggles to obtain recognition as employees (Lafer 2001, 2003). Second, because social benefits became more tightly linked to employment in the late twentieth century (Katz 2001), the question of who is a worker has assumed greater importance.

4. Work incentives were first introduced into AFDC in 1962, when Congress amended the Social Security Act to encourage the employment of welfare mothers through training and social services. In 1967, Congress created the Work Incentive Program (WIN), which provided welfare recipients with supplementary benefits if they gained full- or part-time work. The 1971 Talmadge amendments (named after Georgia senator Herman Talmadge, whose father was governor of Georgia in the 1930s) stressed job placement rather than training, and the 1988 Family Support Act expanded both job training and placement provisions for welfare recipients (Abramovitz 1996; Katz 1989; Piven and Cloward [1971] 1993; Teles 1998).

5. The Supreme Court's application of federal due process protections to public assistance reflected the emergence of a new rights-based model of citizenship in the 1960s (Schudson 1998). The PRWOA did not explicitly deny due process protections, but it rendered their applicability unclear. On the multiple legal meanings of entitlement, see Jeffrey (2002).

6. The state of New York is constitutionally obligated to provide "aid, care, and support of the needy." Consequently, in New York, TANF recipients who reached their five-year federal time limit were still eligible to apply for aid under the state's Safety Net Assistance (SNA) program as long as they did not refuse a specific job without good cause. When tens of thousands of TANF recipients reached their federal time limit in 2001, New York City's Human Resources Administration (HRA) asked them to do just that ("City Offering Work for Some on Welfare," *New York Times,* November 2, 2001; "Uncertainties Loom as New Yorkers Hit Welfare Time Limit," November 30, 2001).

7. The U.S. Supreme Court forcefully articulated liberty of contract in its 1905 decision *Lochner v. New York.* See chapter 1, note 2.

8. The Schumpeterian workfare state is so called in reference to the economist and sociologist Joseph Schumpeter and in contrast to the Keynesian welfare state, which was associated with the economist John Maynard Keynes.

9. On workfare in New York before Giuliani, see Besharov and Germanis (2004, 53–55). On efforts to organize workfare workers in New York City in the 1970s, see Tait (2005, 88–94). For useful overviews of Giuliani's welfare reforms, see Nissen (1999, 242–47); O'Neill et al. (2001, 27–43); Nightingale et al. (2002); and Besharov and Germanis (2004). For an overview of New York State's 1997 Welfare Reform Act, see O'Neill et al. (2001, 17–20).

10. State governments administered general assistance programs for needy adults who did not qualify for AFDC, usually because they did not have dependent children under the age of eighteen. In New York, general assistance was originally known as Home Relief and was subsequently renamed SNA by the 1997 Welfare Reform Act.

11. New York City's HRA "pays for child care for all public assistance recipients with children under the age of 13 who are employed or engaged in approved work activities" (O'Neill et al. 2001, 36). "Parents are free to choose the type of care they prefer, including center-based care, licensed family day care, or informal care by a friend or relative. Child care specialists or job center workers help find child care for recipients who cannot find it on their own." However, the city's Public Advocate "accused HRA of failing to ensure that children are being cared for in safe, appropriate settings" (Besharov and Germanis 2004, 70).

12. See also "Giuliani to Place Disabled Mothers in Workfare Jobs," *New York Times,* June 8, 1998; "Mayor Wants to Abolish Use of Methadone," July 21, 1998; O'Neill et al. 2001, 33–35.

13. "New York City Plans to Extend Workfare to Homeless Shelters," *New York Times,* February 20, 1999; "Work-for-Shelter Enforcement to Begin Dec. 1,"

November 18, 1999; "Work-for-Shelter Requirement Is Delayed by New York Judges," December 9, 1999; "City Decides to Defer Rules on Shelter," December 11, 1999; "City Rules for Shelters Held Illegal," February 23, 2000.

14. See also "Nonprofit and Religious Groups Vow to Fight Workfare Program," *New York Times,* July 24, 1997; "2 Well-Known Churches Say No to Workfare Jobs," August 4, 1997; "Many Participants in Workfare Take the Place of City Workers," April 13, 1998.

15. See also "Evidence is Scant That Workfare Leads to Full-Time Jobs," *New York Times,* April 12, 1998; "Mothers Poised for Workfare Face Acute Lack of Day Care," April 14, 1998.

16. This point applies not only to previous welfare-to-work reforms, but also to public assistance recipients in New York who combined welfare with private-sector employment. These recipients were able to do so because their jobs paid less than the amount a recipient could earn without losing his or her benefits. On the practice of combining work and welfare in New York, see Besharov and Germanis (2004, 81–84).

17. As Steinfeld (2001) has shown, nineteenth-century wage labor was more "forced" than we are accustomed to think. In both England and the United States, labor agreements were rarely terminable at will, and wage labor was not fully free in the modern sense until the last quarter of the nineteenth century. However, Steinfeld's point is not that nineteenth-century actors failed to distinguish between free and forced labor, but that they defined free labor differently. "Like us, they believed that labor could be divided into free and coerced, but they drew the distinction between the two differently than we normally do. For the most part, they did not view wage workers as unfree laborers, even though criminal sanctions were generally available [in England] to enforce wage work" (Steinfeld 2001, 12). The line between free and coerced labor, he suggests, is thus a "matter of convention."

18. The Giuliani administration initially refused to furnish workfare workers to the MTA, because it did not want to pay workers' compensation costs for them, and it feared they would displace city employees in violation of state law. When the city and the MTA resolved these issues in 1999, Giuliani agreed to provide one thousand workfare workers to the MTA ("Pact Reached on Using Welfare Recipients to Clean Subway," *New York Times,* April 26, 1999).

19. "Transit Union Agrees to Allow Workfare Plan," *New York Times,* September 19, 1996; "A Union Chief Whose Life Led to His Workfare Deal," "Mayor Criticizes Transit Plan," September 20, 1996; "Mayor Criticizes Transit Plan," September 20, 1996; "Objections Aside, Transit Officials Predict Mayoral Support on Workfare," September 21, 1996; "Transit Union Dissidents Feel Pressure," October 15, 1996; "Transit Pact is Approved by Workers," October 23, 1996.

20. The notion that social welfare policies have a gender subtext is borrowed from Fraser (1989). The changes described here eroded but did not eliminate the feminine subtext of public assistance. In 1995, a total of 60 percent of public

assistance recipients in the state of New York (including AFDC and Home Relief recipients) were women (New York State Department of Social Services 1995, 35).

21. Although exacerbated by conflicts over civil rights, conflict between white workers and unemployed blacks also reflected "the legacy of a long history in which blacks were used by employers to depress wages and retard unionization" (Piven and Cloward 1974, 226–27, 237).

22. The blurring of racial divisions between municipal employees and workfare workers reduced the social distance between them, making it easier to challenge the classification of workfare workers as paupers. It may also explain why the struggle over workfare was not more explicitly and forcefully framed as a civil rights issue and why there was relatively little collaboration between workfare workers' organizations and black civil rights groups.

23. "Giuliani Proposes a Rise in Spending in His New Budget," *New York Times,* May 9, 1997; "Evidence is Scant That Workfare Leads to Full-Time Jobs," April 12, 1998; "Many Participants in Workfare Take the Place of City Workers," April 13, 1998.

24. Cf. Foucault ([1961] 1965, 38–64) on the ethical meaning that labor assumed in seventeenth-century houses of confinement. Rhetoric about the rehabilitative function of workfare lapsed at times into grotesque self-parody. Jason Turner, whom Giuliani appointed commissioner of New York City's HRA in February 1998, infamously proclaimed that "work makes you free" during a televised discussion of the city's workfare program. When critics pointed out that the same phrase was inscribed on the gates of Auschwitz, Turner was forced to apologize ("City Official is Sorry for Remark Some Thought Was Anti-Semitic," *New York Times,* June 27, 1998).

25. Mollenkopf (1997) notes that the "severe recession between 1989 and 1993 . . . put great strain on the city's budget" (109). Consequently, when Giuliani was elected, the city faced "a budget crisis almost as severe as that of the mid-1970s" (100).

26. On state court rulings, see "WEP Workers Must Get Safety Equipment," *City Law,* September/October 1997, 114; "Judge Limits Assignments for Workfare," *New York Times,* May 10, 1998; and Tait (1998, 143). According to Mahmoudov (1998, 386), workfare workers' claims have consistently "enjoyed more success in state courts than in federal courts" due to "the lack of a federally recognized right to minimum subsistence," the "paucity of federal health and safety statutory protection," and "the failure of federal courts . . . and the DOL [Department of Labor] to enforce a clearly applicable federal minimum wage statute."

27. The concept of disidentification is borrowed from Goffman (1963). On the dramaturgical function of protest, compare Gramsci's (1971, 326) suggestion that a "conception of the world" may be implicit in practices or modes of conduct. On the framing function of organizational forms, see Clemens (1996).

28. "City's Workfare Employees are to Vote on Forming Union," *New York*

*Times,* October 2, 1997; "Read These Ballots, & WEP," *New York Daily News,* October 21, 1997; "United Stance," *Newsday,* October 24, 1997; ACORN 1997e; Tait 1998, 142–43; 2005, 168.

29. Roughly 94 percent of New York's municipal workers were unionized in the early 1990s. These employees comprised two broad categories, civilian and uniformed. Civilians totaled 81 percent of all full-time employees (about 265,000), of whom approximately 77 percent (about 204,000) were represented by District Council 37 or the United Federation of Teachers (Brecher et al. 1993, 242–43). This chapter focuses on District Council 37 for two reasons: it was New York's largest municipal union, and most WEP workers were assigned to city agencies and departments that employed civilian employees represented by District Council 37.

30. "Public Employees Vote 5-Year Deal in New York City," *New York Times,* February 9, 1996; "Inquiry Is Reported into Contract Votes in Municipal Union," November 20, 1998; "Union Chief Says Votes Were Faked on City Contract," November 24, 1998; "Time for a Union Takeover," November 25, 1998.

31. "New York Girding for Surge in Workfare Jobs," *New York Times,* August 13, 1996; "New York Union Leader Urges Halt to Broadening Workfare," September 23, 1996; "Labor Leader Drops Demand on Workfare," September 28, 1996; AFSCME 1997a.

32. "City Hospital Workers Sue Over Layoffs," *New York Times,* April 18, 1998; "Union Leader Equates Workfare with Slavery," April 19, 1998; "Giuliani Drops Workfare Jobs at the Hospitals," April 24, 1998; "Layoffs Rupture Tie Between Giuliani and Labor Leader," April 25, 1998; "Giuliani and Union Postpone Layoffs at City Hospitals," May 2, 1998.

33. "Takeover Is Ordered at Troubled Union," *New York Times,* November 29, 1998; "What Led to the Takeover of a Union, and What's Next," November 30, 1998; "Union's New Chief Vows to Watch Locals Closely," December 3, 1998; "Union Leader's Easygoing Style Blamed in Part for His Fall," December 4, 1998; "Union Scandal Could Produce a Tougher Negotiating Stance," December 20, 1998; Freeman 2000, 313.

34. "Top Court Says New York Can Continue Minimum Wage for Workfare," *New York Times,* February 23, 2000; *New York Law Journal,* February 23, 2000, 26; February 24, 2000, 4. New York was typical in terms of workfare workers' mixed success in securing employee status. A 1997 AFSCME "survey of sixteen states that had enacted workfare legislation . . . indicated that only two states . . . gave workfare participants legal employee status. However, workfare participants have had overwhelming success in securing coverage under workers' compensation — a right governed exclusively by state law. . . . [S]ix states have explicitly covered workfare participants under their own minimum wage laws. Some states have simply enacted statutes requiring that workfare participants be 'paid' the federal minimum wage (i.e., that weekly benefits, divided by weekly hours worked, must equal the minimum wage). A few have even guaranteed workfare participants

prevailing market wages paid for similar work" (Mahmoudov 1998, 356–57, 368). Diller (1998, 27–28) notes that "most states have declined to provide unemployment insurance coverage to workfare workers, and a number of courts have concluded that benefits paid to welfare recipients engaged in workfare are not 'wages' for such purposes. Social Security coverage and the Earned Income Tax Credit are not available to workfare workers. . . . Moreover, states and localities have sought to avoid the provision of workers' compensation to workfare workers injured or killed in performing their assignments. State courts are split on the issue." On workers' compensation, see also Reese (2000).

35. CETA provided block grants to state and local governments for "public service employment," short-term government jobs created for the unemployed in local government or nonprofit agencies (Mead 1986, 31, 62–63). Whether this experiment with work relief also encouraged classification struggles is beyond the scope of this chapter.

36. "Council's Vote on Three Bills Could Provoke Mayoral Vetoes," *New York Times,* February 16, 2000; "Council Overrides Giuliani on 3 Bills, but He Vows Court Fight," March 30, 2000; "Suit Calls for City to Create Welfare Jobs Established by Council," August 16, 2001; "City Offering Work for Some on Welfare," *New York Times,* November 2, 2001.

### Chapter Seven

1. To avoid misunderstanding, it is important to note that while the EITC positioned its clients as rights-bearing citizen-workers, the employers of EITC recipients did not necessarily do so. On the contrary, since the tax credit targeted the working poor, most EITC recipients probably lacked the kind of industrial citizenship described in previous chapters.

2. As noted in the previous chapter, many workfare workers were single mothers who received benefits under AFDC, and later, under TANF. Likewise, the EITC was only available to families with at least one dependent child until Congress expanded eligibility in 1993.

3. In principle, the finance structures of workfare and the EITC differed in an important respect: the federal EITC was paid for entirely by the federal government, while public assistance benefits were paid for partly (in the case of AFDC) or wholly (in the case of Home Relief) by New York State. This difference would presumably give state officials a financial incentive to class workfare workers, but not EITC recipients, as paupers. In practice, however, the difference was not so clear cut. The expansion of the federal EITC was not cost-free for New York State, because New York provided a state EITC that was based upon and linked to the federal EITC (described later in the chapter). Furthermore, the transformation of AFDC into a fixed block grant generated a financial windfall for New

York and other states when public caseloads declined. Although recognition of workfare workers as rights-bearing citizen-workers would have been costly, the windfall could have partly offset those costs.

4. Because this method of financing also linked state EITCs to conventional public assistance, it could have been used to stigmatize the EITC as a form of welfare. However, the connection was not highly visible, and there was little or no moral entrepreneurship to bring it to the attention of the public.

5. New York's business community was not opposed to all public spending; they selectively supported "increased developmental and allocative spending," including spending that improved public safety, provided useful services, or produced "general economic benefits" (Brecher et al. 1993, 30–31). However, these exceptions would not necessarily have inclined businesses to support workfare workers' demands.

6. In New York, the mayoral administration of David Dinkins (Giuliani's predecessor from 1989 to 1993) arguably represented this kind of pro-spending coalition. Despite a severe recession during his term in office, Dinkins managed to increase public spending for economic development, human investment, and redistributive programs (Weikart 2003). As one would expect, municipal financiers largely supported the pro-spending Dinkins for reelection in 1993, while the real estate industry and "other business sectors" tended to support Giuliani (Feiden 1993).

7. On the use of Great Society antipoverty programs for patronage purposes, see also Piven and Cloward ([1971] 1993, 256–63).

8. Christopher Howard (1997) argues that liberals and conservatives could both support the EITC on the basis of different policy goals they attributed to it. This suggests another parallel to previous cases: Like anti-Communism in the 1930s and 1940s, the EITC was effective at realigning social forces into a new political formation, because diverse groups could rally around the same symbol while attributing different meanings to it. On anti-Communism, see chapters 4 and 5.

9. What is perhaps most useful about urban regime theory is that it avoids false dichotomies "between economic determinism and political machination and between the external or structural determinants and local or social construction" (Lauria 1997a, 1). As Mossberger and Stoker (2001, 830) note, urban regime theory places government institutions in their "social and economic setting" without relying "on a simplistic Marxist-informed analysis that sees the local state as either the instrument of business or structurally required to act in the interests of capital." In this respect, urban regime theory comports well with Bourdieu's efforts to integrate subjectivist and objectivist approaches in the social sciences.

10. "Giuliani Edges Dinkins in Bitter NYC Contest," *USA Today,* November 3, 1993; "Call It Quality-of-Rudy Vote," *New York Daily News,* November 6, 1997; "A Portrait of New York City Voters," *New York Times,* November 9, 1997; Mollenkopf 1997, 100; Barrett 2000, chap. 14; Kirtzman 2000, 67, 219.

11. Conversely, "a sizable minority of white, ethnic, middle-class voters must find it in their interest to vote for resurgent reform if it is to succeed" (Mollenkopf 1988b, 250). The mobilization of white ethnic groups in the 1990s was particularly evident from the Jewish vote. Among Jewish New Yorkers, support for Giuliani rose from 65 percent in 1993 to 76 percent in 1997, which was especially remarkable in light of the fact that the Italian-American mayor ran for reelection against a Jewish opponent ("Giuliani Wins New York Mayoralty," *Jerusalem Post,* November 4, 1993; "Republicans Sweep Off-Year Elections," November 6, 1997).

12. Barrett (2000, 310–11) goes so far as to say that Giuliani "would have been a starkly different mayor" if liberal Democrat Mario Cuomo (whom Giuliani endorsed) had remained Governor or if Democrats had retained control of the House. However, this assessment may underestimate the constraints imposed by Giuliani's electoral and governing coalitions.

13. The racial composition of EITC recipients seems not have changed much in the 1990s. Meyer and Holtz-Eakin (2001, 286) report similar data for eligible EITC taxpayers in 1990, and Hoffman and Seidman (2003, 36) note that the EITC population in 1996 "closely mirror[ed]" the EITC population in 2001. It appears that EITC benefits were also more likely than welfare benefits to go to households that included men. In 1996, about 41 percent of all EITC recipient households consisted of married couples (with or without children), 36 percent were headed by single mothers, 10 percent were headed by single fathers, and 13.5 percent consisted of single men or women with no children (Hoffman and Seidman 2003, 40). The eligibility of married couples and the relatively high proportion of men among EITC recipients may have also facilitated recognition of EITC recipients as rights-bearing citizen-workers.

14. "Clinton Wages a Quiet War Against Poverty," *New York Times,* March 30, 1994; "Euphemisms Mask Fervor in Latest Attack on Poverty," April 17, 1994; "A War on Poverty Subtly Linked to Race," December 26, 2000. In addition to attracting publicity, mobilization of workfare workers probably fueled resentment and indignation among white voters. According to Rieder (1985), New York's white, ethnic, middle-class voters expected deferential gratitude from welfare recipients, and they distinguished themselves from welfare recipients on that basis. In the 1980s, "talk about forming a union of welfare recipients" struck one of Rieder's informants as "arrogant, in contrast to his family's humble deference to the intrusions of a paternalistic state" during his childhood, when his mother received welfare (Rieder 1985, 104).

15. Examination of the *New York Daily News* and the *New York Post,* which catered to less educated, more working-class, and more conservative readers, revealed a similar pattern. The *Daily News* published seven articles with "EITC" or "Earned Income Tax Credit" in the headline or lead paragraphs between 1993 and 2001, and the *Post* only published two.

16. The struggles of the nineteenth century were somewhat different. As noted

in previous chapters, those struggles linked benefits to public (especially military) service rather than employment.

## Chapter Eight

1. Like Piven and Cloward ([1971] 1993), Peck's study of workfare in the United States, Canada, and the United Kingdom (2001) also emphasizes how workfare reshapes labor markets and disciplines workers. Peck's study provides a valuable cross-national comparative perspective, but it sacrifices historical depth since it does not explore the relationship between present-day workfare policies and earlier forms of work relief. Furthermore, though Peck examines resistance to the importation and implementation of workfare, he does not provide a sustained discussion of struggles in New York City, the site of the largest workfare program in the United States; he focuses instead on workfare in Los Angeles. Nor does he explore the implications of the struggles over workfare for the citizenship status and rights of workfare workers. These are contributions I have endeavored to make in chapters 6 and 7.

2. On welfare-state regimes, see Esping-Andersen (1990) and Orloff (1993a). Like McAdam, Tarrow, and Tilly (2001, 5), this book focuses on "episodic, public, collective interaction among makers of claims and their objects when (a) at least one government is a claimant, an object of claims, or a party to the claims, and (b) the claims would, if realized, affect the [material or symbolic] interests of at least one of the claimants." Classification struggles, however, are only a subset of what the authors describe as "contentious politics." While all classification struggles may be subsumed under the heading of contentious politics, not all episodes of political contention involve struggles over classification.

3. McAdam, Tarrow, and Tilly (2001, 24) define causal mechanisms as "a delimited class of events that alter relations among specified sets of elements in identical or closely similar ways over a variety of situations" (cf. Merton 1968 and Hedström and Swedborg 1998). Most of the mechanisms mentioned here are described in more detail in chapter 1. The "hysteresis effect" (Bourdieu [1972] 1977, 78, 83) refers to a lag or mismatch between aspirations (habitus) and changing opportunities (field). On the "theory effect," see Bourdieu (1991, 106): "Social science must include in its theory of the social world a theory of the theory effect which, by helping to impose a more or less authorized way of seeing the social world, helps to construct the reality of that world." Previous chapters have alluded to hysteresis and theory effects without explicitly referring to them as such.

4. The reduction of racial politics to class politics has also been criticized by Omi and Winant (1986, chap. 2) and Valocchi (1994). Turning the reductionist argument on its head, Valocchi suggests that class interests in the United States are "racially constructed" and have a "racial basis."

5. In pointing to liberalism as a constraint upon welfare-state development, the national-values approach had in mind the liberal emphasis on limited government and a competitive market economy. However, as institutionalists have pointed out, liberalism was a flexible tradition that could be reworked to justify new social spending programs. Americans have thus been able to draw upon other elements of the liberal tradition (most notably, the rule of law protecting individual rights) to defend the citizenship status and rights of welfare-state claimants.

6. Piven and Cloward ([1971] 1993) exemplify this approach. From the work-house to the WPA to workfare, they argue that work requirements for relief recipients served to discipline labor and regulate the poor. In fact, their work provides three different versions of this labor-disciplining thesis. The first version, rooted in Durkheim's ([1893] 1984, 60–64) analysis of the functions of punishment, views work requirements as a form of ritual degradation. According to a second version, work requirements help to moderate civil disorder "by once more enmeshing people in the work role, the cornerstone of social control in any society" (Piven and Cloward [1971] 1993, 97). This version of the argument also has Durkheimian roots in "break-down" theories of collective action (see Tilly, Tilly, and Tilly 1975; Tilly 1981; and Piven and Cloward 1991). A third version, made in reference to the WPA, stresses co-optation. According to this version, New Deal work programs "diverted local [unemployed] groups from disruptive tactics and absorbed local leaders [of the unemployed workers' movement] in bureaucratic roles" (Piven and Cloward 1977, 76). While the arguments I set forth in this book are deeply indebted to Piven and Cloward, I found that work requirements were not inherently or invariably demobilizing. It may be true, as Piven and Cloward argue, that there was more protest by relief recipients in the early 1930s, before the introduction of the WPA, and in the 1960s, before the expansion of workfare. However, disruptive protests are not the only form that classification struggles take. While other forms of claim-making may be less disruptive (and therefore less effective, according to Piven and Cloward), that does not necessarily make the claims less contentious. It is also worth noting that in the classification struggles examined here, there was no tight correlation between the presence of disruptive protest and successful outcomes. Indeed, mobilization of welfare-state claimants was notably absent in the cases of OAI and the EITC.

7. Along with Kaus (1992), proponents of a neo-WPA included Harvey (1989) and Wilson (1996). In 2005, former U.S. Senator John Edwards called for a New America Initiative "modeled after the Works Progress Administration" (One America Committee, mass e-mail message, September 9, 2005). In my view, a neo-WPA would likely be more liberal and therefore preferable to existing workfare programs. However, proponents of a neo-WPA would do well to remember the grievances, problems, and conflicts surrounding the original program, which any new policy would also have to address.

8. This point is indebted to Kohlberg (1963), who distinguished preconven-

tional, conventional, and postconventional stages of moral development, and Habermas (1979), who argued that the process of moral development is collective as well as individual. Mead's (1986) authoritative welfare state is strikingly reminiscent of what Kohlberg described as the "law and order" phase of development (part of the conventional stage), characterized by an "orientation toward authority, fixed rules, and the maintenance of the social order." At this stage, "right behavior consists of doing one's duty, showing respect for authority, and maintaining the given social order for its own sake" (Habermas 1979, 80).

9. This point is indebted to Durkheim ([1893] 1984) and Parsons (1977), who described a similar generalization of the "collective consciousness" or values of modern societies. Durkheim suggests that generalization of the collective consciousness goes hand in hand with the postconventional stage of moral development: As rules of conduct become more general, they allow for more individual reflection and dissent.

10. Kaus (1992) comes close to recognizing this problem when he subsumes military service under the heading of work. But if military service may be considered work, why not other activities? Whether one recognizes other forms of public service besides work or stretches the meaning of work to encompass all forms of public service, one arrives at the same result: the need for a more general conception of social obligations.

11. The Supreme Court developed the term "suspect class" in reference to the equal protection clause of the Fourteenth Amendment to the U.S. Constitution. The term refers to categories of individuals (such as racial minorities or women) whom the courts deem deserving of greater judicial protection through stricter scrutiny of legislation.

# Bibliography

## Archival Sources

*The American Federationist,* newspaper of the AFL, published in Washington, DC, from January 1935 (vol. 42, no. 1) through December 1941 (vol. 48, no.12). Wisconsin Historical Society, Madison.

Hopkins, Harry L. Container 35. File: Federal Emergency Relief Administration: Works Progress Administration: Releases, Speeches, etc., 1938–1939. Franklin D. Roosevelt Presidential Library, Hyde Park, NY.

———. Container 80. File: FERA-WPA Legislative and Legal Proceedings: Works Progress Administration Investigation. Franklin D. Roosevelt Presidential Library, Hyde Park, NY.

Jaffe, Eli. 1993. *Oklahoma Odyssey: A Memoir.* Tamiment Library & Robert F. Wagner Labor Archives, Elmer Holmes Bobst Library, New York University.

Lasser, David. 1939. *Old-Age Security: $60 at 60.* Washington, DC: Workers Alliance of America. Reprinted as *The $60 at 60 Pension Plan: Minimum Security for Our Senior Citizens,* "Publications relating to Workers Alliance of America [1936–1975]," Tamiment Library & Robert F. Wagner Labor Archives, Elmer Holmes Bobst Library, New York University.

Office of the Commissioner. Annual Reports of the Assistant Commissioner for Alabama, 1866–68, Box 1. Record Group 105, Records of the Commissioner's Office, National Archives, Washington, DC.

———. Annual Reports of the Assistant Commissioner for Louisiana, 1866–68, Box 3. Record Group 105, Records of the Commissioner's Office, National Archives, Washington, DC.

———. Annual Reports of the Assistant Commissioner for South Carolina, 1866–68, Box 4. Record Group 105, Records of the Commissioner's Office, National Archives, Washington, DC.

———. Letters from the Executive Mansion, Box 19. Record Group 105, Records of the Commissioner's Office, National Archives, Washington, DC.

*The Professional Worker.* 1936–1937. Berkeley: Union of Professional Workers (Workers Alliance affiliate). Tamiment Library & Robert F. Wagner Labor Archives, Elmer Holmes Bobst Library, New York University.

Records of the Commissioner. Correspondence, Synopses of Letters and Reports
    Relating to Conditions of Freedmen and Bureau Activities in the States, Jan.
    1866–Mar. 1869. 3 vols. Record Group 105, Records of the Commissioner's
    Office, National Archives, Washington, DC.
Roosevelt, Franklin D. Papers as President, Official File. File 2366 (Workers Al-
    liance of America, 1935–1942). Franklin D. Roosevelt Presidential Library,
    Hyde Park, NY.
———. President's Personal File. File 6794 (American Security Union). Franklin
    D. Roosevelt Presidential Library, Hyde Park, NY.
———. President's Personal File. File 7649 (Lasser, David). Franklin D. Roosevelt
    Presidential Library, Hyde Park, NY.
U.S. Congress. House. 1939–40. *Hearings before the Subcommittee of the Commit-
    tee on Appropriations, 76th Congress, First Session, Acting Under House Reso-
    lution 130.* Record Group 233, National Archives, Washington, DC.
*Work,* newspaper of the Workers Alliance of America, published in Washington,
    DC, from Apr. 9, 1938 (vol. 1, no. 1) through Nov. 1940 (vol. 3, no. 13). Micro-
    film R1568, Tamiment Library & Robert F. Wagner Labor Archives, Elmer
    Holmes Bobst Library, New York University.
*The Workers Alliance,* newspaper of the Workers Alliance of America, published
    in Milwaukee, WI, from Aug. 15, 1935 (vol. 1, no. 1) through "First Septem-
    ber issue" of 1936 (vol. 1, no. 18). Milwaukee, Wisconsin: Workers Alliance of
    America, 1935–1936. Microfilm R1569, Tamiment Library & Robert F. Wag-
    ner Labor Archives, Elmer Holmes Bobst Library, New York University.
Workers Alliance of America. 1937. *How to Win Work at a Living Wage or a De-
    cent Standard of Relief with the Workers Alliance of America.* Washington, DC:
    Workers Alliance of America. From "Publications relating to Workers Alli-
    ance of America [1936–1975]," Tamiment Library & Robert F. Wagner Labor
    Archives, Elmer Holmes Bobst Library, New York University.

## References

Abbott, Martin. 1967. *The Freedmen's Bureau in South Carolina, 1865–1872.* Cha-
    pel Hill: University of North Carolina Press.
Abramovitz, Mimi. 1996. *Under Attack, Fighting Back: Women and Welfare in the
    United States.* New York: Monthly Review Press.
Ackerman, Bruce. 1991. *We the People: Foundations.* Cambridge, MA: Harvard
    University Press.
ACORN. See Association of Community Organizations for Reform Now.
Adler, Moshe. 2002. "Why Did New York Workers Lose Ground in the 1990s?"
    *Regional Labor Review* 5 (Fall): 31–35.
AFL-CIO Executive Council. See American Federation of Labor–Congress of
    Industrial Organizations Executive Council.
AFSCME. See American Federation of State, County, and Municipal Employees.
Ahern, Wilbert H. 1979. "Laissez Faire vs. Equal Rights: Liberal Republicans and
    Limits to Reconstruction." *Phylon* 40, no. 1: 52–65.

Alexander, Jeffrey C. 1988a. *Action and Its Environments.* New York: Columbia University Press.

———. 1988b. *Durkheimian Sociology: Cultural Studies.* New York: Cambridge University Press.

———. 1989. *Structure and Meaning.* New York: Columbia University Press.

Alexander, Jeffrey C., and Philip Smith. 1993. "The Discourse of American Civil Society: A New Proposal for Cultural Studies." *Theory and Society* 22, no. 2 (Apr.): 151–207.

Alston, Lee J., and Joseph P. Ferrie. 1999. *Southern Paternalism and the American Welfare State: Economics, Politics, and Institutions in the South, 1865–1965.* New York: Cambridge University Press.

Altmeyer, Arthur J. 1966. *The Formative Years of Social Security.* Madison: University of Wisconsin Press.

Amenta, Edwin. 1998. *Bold Relief: Institutional Politics and the Origins of Modern American Social Policy.* Princeton: Princeton University Press.

———. 2001. "Who Voted with Hopkins? Institutional Politics and the WPA." *Journal of Policy History* 13, no. 2: 251–87.

———. 2006. *When Movements Matter: The Townsend Plan and the Rise of Social Security.* Princeton: Princeton University Press.

Amenta, Edwin, Ellen Benoit, Chris Bonastia, Nancy K. Cauthen, and Drew T. Halfmann. 1996. "The Works Progress Administration and the Origins of Welfare Reform: Work and Relief in New Deal Social Policy." Unpublished manuscript, Department of Sociology, New York University.

Amenta, Edwin, Neal Carren, and Sheera Joy Olasky. 2005. "Age for Leisure? Political Mediation and the Impact of the Pension Movement on U.S. Old-Age Policy." *American Sociological Review* 70 (Jun.): 516–38.

Amenta, Edwin, Bruce G. Carruthers, and Yvonne Zylan. 1992. "A Hero for the Aged? The Townsend Movement, the Political Mediation Model, and U.S. Old-Age Policy, 1934–1950." *American Journal of Sociology* 98, no. 2 (Sep.): 308–39.

Amenta, Edwin, and Drew Halfmann. 2000. "Wage Wars: Institutional Politics, WPA Wages, and the Struggle for U.S. Social Policy." *American Sociological Review* 65, no. 4 (Aug.): 506–28.

Amenta, Edwin, Drew Halfmann, and Michael P. Young. 1999. "The Strategies and Contexts of Social Protest: Political Mediation and the Impact of the Townsend Movement in California." *Mobilization* 4, no. 1: 1–23.

Amenta, Edwin, and Theda Skocpol. 1988. "Redefining the New Deal: World War II and the Development of Social Provision in the United States." Chap. 2 in *The Politics of Social Policy in the United States.* Eds. Margaret Weir, Ann Shola Orloff, and Theda Skocpol. Princeton: Princeton University Press.

Amenta, Edwin, and Yvonne Zylan. 1991. "It Happened Here: Political Opportunity, the New Institutionalism, and the Townsend Movement." *American Sociological Review* 56, no. 2 (Apr.): 250–65.

American Federation of Labor–Congress of Industrial Organizations Executive Council. 1997. "Welfare and Workers Rights." http://www.aflcio.org/aboutus/thisistheaflcio/ecouncil/eco2171997a.cfm.

American Federation of State, County, and Municipal Employees. 1997a. Legislative recommendations on welfare reform sent to New York State Senate. Unpublished memorandum, April 16, 1997, Albany, NY

——. 1997b. "Organizing Workfare Workers: AFSCME's Road Map." Unpublished report, Washington, DC.

Anderson, Benedict. 1991. *Imagined Communities: Reflections on the Origin and Spread of Nationalism.* Revised edition. New York: Verso.

Anderson, Nels. 1935. "Are the Unemployed a Caste?" *Survey Graphic* 24, no. 7 (Jul.): 345–47, 365, 367.

Association of Community Organizations for Reform Now. 1997a. ACORN Workfare Organizing Project Update: September 1997. Unpublished report, Brooklyn, NY.

——. 1997b. "WEP Workers Organizing Committee, New York ACORN: YE/ YB Report 1997." Unpublished report, Brooklyn, NY.

——. 1997c. "WWOC [WEP Workers Organizing Committee] Update." Unpublished memorandum, n.d., Brooklyn, NY.

——. 1997d. "WEP Workers Action Committee: Welfare Workers' Protection Act Summary." Unpublished memorandum, n.d., Brooklyn, NY.

——. 1997e. *The ACORN Report.* Newsletter from national office (Nov.), Washington, DC: ACORN.

——. 1997f. *United States of ACORN* 16, no. 2 (Mar./Apr.). New Orleans: ACORN.

——. 1997g. *United States of ACORN* 16, no. 4 (Jul./Aug.). New Orleans: ACORN.

——. 1997h. "ACORN's Response to Welfare 'Reform': Building a Union of Workfare Workers," in *ACORN Campaigns: News From the National Office of the Association of Community Organizations for Reform Now* (Apr.), Washington, DC: ACORN.

Axinn, June, and Herman Levin. 1997. *Social Welfare: A History of the American Response to Need.* 4th ed. White Plains, NY: Longman.

Babson, Steve. 1999. *The Unfinished Struggle: Turning Points in American Labor, 1877–Present.* New York: Rowman & Littlefield.

Bakke, E. Wight. 1940a. *Citizens Without Work.* New Haven: Yale University Press.

——. 1940b. *The Unemployed Worker.* New Haven: Yale University Press.

Barbalet, J. M. 1988. *Citizenship: Rights, Struggle, and Class Inequality.* Minneapolis: University of Minnesota Press.

Barrett, James R., and David Roediger. 1997. "Inbetween Peoples: Race, Nationality and the 'New Immigrant' Working Class." *Journal of American Ethnic History* 16, no. 3 (Spring): 3–44.

Barrett, Wayne. 2000. *Rudy! An Investigative Biography of Rudolph Giuliani.* New York: Basic Books.

Becker, Howard S. 1963. *Outsiders: Studies in the Sociology of Deviance.* New York: The Free Press.

Belz, Herman. 1976. *A New Birth of Freedom: The Republican Party and Freedmen's Rights, 1861 to 1866.* Westport, CT: Greenwood Press.

Bentley, George R. 1955. *A History of the Freedmen's Bureau.* Philadelphia: University of Pennsylvania Press.

Bergesen, Albert. 1984. *The Sacred and the Subversive: Political Witch-Hunts as National Rituals.* Storrs, CT: Society for the Scientific Study of Religion.

Berkowitz, Edward D. 1991. *America's Welfare State: From Roosevelt to Reagan.* Baltimore: Johns Hopkins University Press.

———. 1995. *Mr. Social Security: The Life of Wilbur J. Cohen.* Lawrence: University Press of Kansas.

Berlin, Ira, Joseph P. Reidy, and Leslie S. Rowland, eds. 1982. *Freedom: A Documentary History of Emancipation, 1861–1867.* Series 2, *The Black Military Experience.* New York: Cambridge University Press.

Berlin, Ira, Thavolia Glymph, Steven F. Miller, Joseph P. Reidy, Leslie S. Rowland, and Julie Saville, eds. 1990. *Freedom: A Documentary History of Emancipation, 1861–1867.* Series 1, vol. 3, *The Wartime Genesis of Free Labor: The Lower South.* New York: Cambridge University Press.

Berry, Mary Frances. 1972. "Reparations for Freedmen, 1890–1916: Fraudulent Practices or Justice Deferred?" *The Journal of Negro History* 57, no. 3 (Jul.): 219–30.

———. 2005. *My Face is Black is True: Callie House and the Struggle for Ex-Slave Reparations.* New York: Alfred A. Knopf.

Besharov, Douglas J., and Peter Germanis. 2004. "Full-Engagement Welfare in New York City: Lessons for TANF's Participation Requirements." Unpublished manuscript, School of Public Policy, University of Maryland, College Park, MD.

Bourdieu, Pierre. [1972] 1977. *Outline of a Theory of Practice.* Trans. Richard Nice. New York: Cambridge University Press.

———. [1979] 1984. *Distinction: A Social Critique of the Judgement of Taste.* Trans. Richard Nice. Cambridge, MA: Harvard University Press.

———. 1985. "The Social Space and the Genesis of Groups." *Theory and Society* 14, no. 6 (Nov.): 723–44.

———. 1989. "Social Space and Symbolic Power." *Sociological Theory* 7, no. 1 (Spring): 14–25.

———. 1991 *Language and Symbolic Power.* Ed. John B. Thompson. Trans. Gino Raymond and Matthew Adamson. Cambridge, MA: Harvard University Press.

———. 1994. "Rethinking the State: Genesis and Structure of the Bureaucratic Field." *Sociological Theory* 12, no. 1 (Mar.): 1–18.

Bourdieu, Pierre, and Luc Boltanski. 1981. "The Educational System and the Economy: Titles and Jobs." Chap. 8 in *French Sociology: Rupture and Renewal Since 1968.* Ed. Charles Lemert. New York: Columbia University Press.

Bourdieu, Pierre, and Jean-Claude Passeron. 1977. *Reproduction in Education, Society, and Culture.* London: Sage.

Bourdieu, Pierre, and Loïc J. D. Wacquant. 1992. *An Invitation to Reflexive Sociology.* Chicago: University of Chicago Press.

Brecher, Charles, Raymond D. Horton, Robert A. Cropf, and Dean Michael Mead. 1993. *Power Failure: New York City Politics and Policy since 1960.* New York: Oxford University Press.

Bremer, William W. 1975. "Along the 'American Way': The New Deal's Work

Relief Programs for the Unemployed." *Journal of American History* 62: 636–52.

Bremner, Robert H. 1980. *The Public Good: Philanthropy and Welfare in the Civil War Era.* New York: Alfred A. Knopf.

Brinkley, Alan. 1995. *The End of Reform: New Deal Liberalism in Recession and War.* New York: Alfred A. Knopf.

Briskin, Craig L., and Kimberly A. Thomas. 1998. "The Waging of Welfare: All Work and No Pay?" *Harvard Civil Rights-Civil Liberties Law Review* 33: 559–91.

Brown, Josephine Chapin. 1940. *Public Relief, 1929–1939.* New York: Henry Holt and Company.

Brown, Michael K. 1999. *Race, Money, and the American Welfare State.* Ithaca: Cornell University Press.

Browning, Rufus P., Dale Rogers Marshall, and David H. Tabb, eds. 1997. *Racial Politics in American Cities.* 2nd ed. New York: Longman.

Brubaker, Rogers. 1992. *Citizenship and Nationhood in France and Germany.* Cambridge: Harvard University Press.

Brueggemann, John. 2002. "Racial Considerations and Social Policy in the 1930s." *Social Science History* 26, no. 1 (Spring): 139–77.

Bulmer, Martin, and Anthony M. Rees. 1996. *Citizenship Today: The Contemporary Relevance of T. H. Marshall.* London: UCL Press.

Bunche, Ralph J. 1973. *The Political Status of the Negro in the Age of FDR.* Ed. Dewey W. Grantham. Chicago: University of Chicago Press.

Burrows, Roger, and Brian Loader, eds. 1994. *Towards a Post-Fordist Welfare State?* New York: Routledge.

Calhoun, Craig, ed. 1992. *Habermas and the Public Sphere.* Cambridge: MIT Press.

Campbell, Andrea Louise. 2003. *How Policies Make Citizens: Senior Political Activism and the American Welfare State.* Princeton: Princeton University Press.

Cates, Jerry R. 1983. *Insuring Inequality: Administrative Leadership in Social Security, 1935–1954.* Ann Arbor: University of Michigan Press.

CGO. See New York City Council Committee on Governmental Operations.

CGW/CHE. See New York City Council Committee on General Welfare and Committee on Higher Education.

Cimbala, Paul A. 1997. *Under the Guardianship of the Nation: The Freedmen's Bureau and the Reconstruction of Georgia, 1865–1870.* Athens: University of Georgia Press.

Cimbala, Paul A., and Randall M. Miller, eds. 1999. *The Freedmen's Bureau and Reconstruction: Reconsiderations.* New York: Fordham University Press.

City of New York. 1994. *Mayor's Management Report.* New York: City of New York.

———. 1995. *Mayor's Management Report.* New York: City of New York.

———. 1996. *Mayor's Management Report.* New York: City of New York.

———. 1997. *Mayor's Management Report.* New York: City of New York.

———. 1998. *Mayor's Management Report.* New York: City of New York.

———. 1999. *Mayor's Management Report.* New York: City of New York.

——. 2000. *Mayor's Management Report.* New York: City of New York.

——. 2001. *Mayor's Management Report.* New York: City of New York.

City of New York Independent Budget Office. 2000. *Inside the Budget,* no. 72 (Nov. 1, 2000): 1–4.

——. 2001. *Inside the Budget,* no. 82 (May 4, 2001): 1–3.

——. 2002. *Inside the Budget,* no. 99 (May 22, 2002): 1–3.

Clemens, Elisabeth S. 1996. "Organizational Form as Frame: Collective Identity and Political Strategy in the American Labor Movement, 1880–1920." Chap. 9 in *Comparative Perspectives on Social Movements.* Eds. Doug McAdam, John D. McCarthy, and Mayer N. Zald. New York: Cambridge University Press.

Clemens, Elisabeth S., and James M. Cook. 1999. "Politics and Institutionalism: Explaining Durability and Change." *Annual Review of Sociology* 25: 441–66.

Clinton, William J. Address Before a Joint Session of Congress on Administration Goals. *The American Presidency Project* [online]. Eds. John Woolley and Gerhard Peters. Santa Barbara, CA: University of California (hosted), Gerhard Peters (database). http://www.presidency.ucsb.edu/ws/?pid=47232.

Cohen, Nancy. 2002. *The Reconstruction of American Liberalism, 1865–1914.* Chapel Hill: University of North Carolina Press.

Colby, Ira C. 1985. "The Freedmen's Bureau: From Social Welfare to Segregation." *Phylon* 46, no. 3: 219–30.

Committee on Social Welfare Law. 2001. "Welfare Reform in New York City: The Measure of Success." *The Record of the Association of the Bar of the City of New York* 56 (Summer): 322–56.

Crane, Diana, ed. 1994. *The Sociology of Culture: Emerging Theoretical Perspectives.* Cambridge, MA: Blackwell.

Crew, David F. 1998. *Germans on Welfare: From Weimar to Hitler.* New York: Oxford University Press.

Daly, John Patrick. 2002. *When Slavery Was Called Freedom: Evangelicalism, Proslavery, and the Causes of the Civil War.* Lexington: University Press of Kentucky.

Davies, Gareth, and Martha Derthick. 1997. "Race and Social Welfare Policy: The Social Security Act of 1935." *Political Science Quarterly* 112, no. 2 (Summer): 217–35.

Dearing, Mary R. 1952. *Veterans in Politics: The Story of the G.A.R.* Baton Rouge: Louisiana State University Press.

Delgado, Gary. 1986. *Organizing the Movement: The Roots and Growth of ACORN.* Philadelphia: Temple University Press.

Derber, Milton. 1961. "Growth and Expansion." Chap. 1 in *Labor and the New Deal.* Eds. Milton Derber and Edwin Young. Madison: University of Wisconsin Press.

Derber, Milton, and Edwin Young, eds. 1961. *Labor and the New Deal.* Madison: University of Wisconsin Press.

Derthick, Martha. 1979. *Policymaking for Social Security.* Washington, DC: Brookings Institution.

Dewey, John. 1993. *The Political Writings.* Eds. Debra Morris and Ian Shapiro. Indianapolis: Hackett.

Diller, Matthew. 1998. "Working Without a Job: The Social Messages of the New Workfare." *Stanford Law and Policy Review* 9 (Winter): 19–32.

Dobbin, Frank R. 1994. "Cultural Models of Organization: The Social Construction of Rational Organizing Principles." Chap. 5 in *The Sociology of Culture: Emerging Theoretical Perspectives.* Ed. Diana Crane. Cambridge, MA: Blackwell.

Douglas, Mary. 1966. *Purity and Danger: An Analysis of the Concepts of Pollution and Taboo.* New York: Routledge.

Draut, Tammy. 2002. "New Opportunities? Public Opinion on Poverty, Income Inequality Public Policy: 1996–2002." Unpublished manuscript, Demos: A Network for Ideas and Action, New York, NY.

Dreier, Peter, John Mollenkopf, and Todd Swanstrom. 2001. *Place Matters: Metropolitics for the Twenty-First Century.* Lawrence: University Press of Kansas.

Driver, Felix. 1993. *Power and Pauperism: The Workhouse System, 1834–1884.* New York: Cambridge University Press.

DuBois, Ellen Carol. 1978. *Feminism and Suffrage: The Emergence of an Independent Women's Movement in America, 1848–1869.* Ithaca: Cornell University Press.

Du Bois, W. E. B. [1935] 1962. *Black Reconstruction in America.* New York: Free Press.

Durant, Ruth. 1939. "Home Rule in the WPA." *Survey Midmonthly* 75: 273–75.

Durkheim, Emile. [1893] 1984. *The Division of Labor in Society.* Trans. W. D. Halls. New York: Free Press.

———. [1895] 1982. *The Rules of Sociological Method.* Ed. Steven Lukes. Trans. W. D. Halls. New York: Free Press.

———. [1897] 1951. *Suicide: A Study in Sociology.* Trans. John A. Spaulding and George Simpson. Ed. George Simpson. New York: Free Press.

Edelman, Murray. 1961. "New Deal Sensitivity to Labor Interests." Chap. 5 in *Labor and the New Deal.* Eds. Milton Derber and Edwin Young. Madison: University of Wisconsin Press.

Elias, Norbert. 1978. *The Civilizing Process.* Trans. Edmund Jephcott. New York: Pantheon Books.

Ellis, Nan S. 2003. "Work is Its Own Reward: Are Workfare Participants Employees Entitled to Protection Under the Fair Labor Standards Act?" *Cornell Journal of Law and Public Policy* 13 (Fall): 1–27.

Elster, Jon. 1989. *Nuts and Bolts for the Social Sciences.* New York: Cambridge University Press.

Emirbayer, Mustafa. 1992. "Beyond Structuralism and Voluntarism: The Politics and Discourse of Progressive School Reform, 1890–1930." *Theory and Society* 21, no. 5 (Oct.): 621–64.

———. 1996a. "Durkheim's Contribution to the Sociological Analysis of History." *Sociological Forum* 11, no. 2 (Jun.): 263–84.

———. 1996b. "Useful Durkheim." *Sociological Theory* 14, no. 2 (Jul.): 109–30.

Esping-Andersen, Gøsta. 1990. *The Three Worlds of Welfare Capitalism.* Princeton: Princeton University Press.

———. 1999. *Social Foundations of Postindustrial Economies.* New York: Oxford University Press.

Evans, Peter B., Dietrich Rueschmeyer, and Theda Skocpol, eds. 1985. *Bringing the State Back In.* New York: Cambridge University Press.

Fainstein, Norman I., and Susan S. Fainstein. 1988. "Governing Regimes and the Political Economy of Development in New York City, 1946–1984." Chap. 7 in *Power, Culture, and Place: Essays on New York City.* Ed. John Hull Mollenkopf. New York: Russell Sage Foundation.

Fainstein, Susan S. 1990. "Economics, Politics, and Development Policy: The Convergence of New York and London." *International Journal of Urban and Regional Research* 14, no. 4 (Dec.): 553–75.

Farmer, Mary J. 1999. "'Because They Are Women': Gender and the Virginia Freedmen's Bureau's 'War on Dependency.'" Chap. 8 in *The Freedmen's Bureau and Reconstruction: Reconsiderations.* Eds. Paul A. Cimbala and Randall M. Miller. New York: Fordham University Press.

Feiden, Douglas. 1993. "Candidates Covet Stein Supporters," *Crain's New York Business,* May 24–30, 3.

Fitzgerald, Michael W. 1989. *The Union League Movement in the Deep South: Politics and Agricultural Change During Reconstruction.* Baton Rouge: Louisiana State University Press.

Fix, Michael, and Jeffrey Passel. 2002. "The Scope and Impact of Welfare Reform's Immigrant Provisions." Washington, DC: The Urban Institute.

Flanagan, Richard. 1991. *"Parish-Fed Bastards": A History of the Politics of the Unemployed in Britain, 1884–1939.* New York: Greenwood Press.

Fleming, Walter L., ed. 1905. *Documents Relating to Reconstruction.* Morgantown, West Virginia.

Foley, Neil. 1997. *The White Scourge: Mexicans, Blacks, and Poor Whites in Texas Cotton Culture.* Berkeley: University of California Press.

Folsom, Franklin. 1991. *Impatient Armies of the Poor: The Story of Collective Action of the Unemployed, 1808–1942.* Niwot: University Press of Colorado.

Foner, Eric. [1970] 1995. *Free Soil, Free Labor, Free Men: The Ideology of the Republican Party Before the Civil War.* New York: Oxford University Press.

———. 1988. *Reconstruction, 1863–1877: America's Unfinished Revolution.* New York: Harper & Row.

Foucault, Michel. [1961] 1965. *Madness and Civilization: A History of Insanity in the Age of Reason.* Trans. Richard Howard. New York: Vintage.

———. [1975] 1977. *Discipline and Punish.* Trans. Alan Sheridan. New York: Vintage.

Foucault, Michel. 1980. *Power/Knowledge: Selected Interviews and Other Writings, 1972–1977.* Ed. Colin Gordon. Trans. Colin Gordon, Leo Marshall, John Mepham, and Kate Soper. New York: Pantheon Books.

Fraser, Nancy. 1989. *Unruly Practices: Power, Discourse and Gender in Contemporary Social Theory.* Minneapolis: University of Minnesota Press.

———. 1992. "Rethinking the Public Sphere: A Contribution to the Critique of Actually Existing Democracy." Chap. 5 in *Habermas and the Public Sphere.* Ed. Craig Calhoun. Cambridge: MIT Press.

———. 1995. "From Redistribution to Recognition? Dilemmas of Justice in a 'Post-Socialist' Age." *New Left Review* (Jul./Aug.): 68–93.

Fraser, Nancy, and Linda Gordon. 1992. "Contract versus Charity: Why is There No Social Citizenship in the United States?" *Socialist Review* 22: 45–68.

———. 1994. "A Genealogy of Dependency: Tracing a Keyword of the U.S. Welfare State." *Signs: Journal of Women in Culture and Society* 19: 309–36.

Freeman, Joshua B. 2000. *Working-Class New York: Life and Labor since World War II.* New York: Free Press.

Freund, Rudolf. 1969. "Military Bounty Lands and the Origins of the Public Domain." Chap. 1 in *The Old Northwest: Studies in Regional History, 1787–1910.* Ed. Harry N. Scheiber. Lincoln: University of Nebraska Press.

Fuentes, Annette. 1996. "Slaves of New York." *In These Times* (Dec. 23, 1996): 14–17.

Gallup, Alec M. 1999. *The Gallup Poll Cumulative Index: Public Opinion, 1935–1997.* Wilmington, DE: Scholarly Resources.

Gallup Jr., George. 1996. *The Gallup Poll: Public Opinion 1995.* Wilmington, DE: Scholarly Resources.

———. 1997. *The Gallup Poll: Public Opinion 1996.* Wilmington, DE: Scholarly Resources.

Garraty, John A. 1973. "The New Deal, National Socialism, and the Great Depression." *American Historical Review* 78: 907–44.

Geertz, Clifford. 1973. *The Interpretation of Cultures.* New York: Basic Books.

Gellermann, William. 1944. *Martin Dies.* New York: The John Day Company.

Gerteis, Louis S. 1973. *From Contraband to Freedom: Federal Policy Toward Southern Blacks, 1861–1865.* Westport, CT: Greenwood Press.

Gibson, Guy James. 1957. Lincoln's League: The Union League Movement during the Civil War. PhD diss., University of Illinois.

Giddens, Anthony. 1987. *The Nation-State and Violence.* Vol. 2 of *A Contemporary Critique of Historical Materialism.* Berkeley: University of California Press.

———. 1998. *The Third Way: The Renewal of Social Democracy.* Malden: Blackwell.

Gill, Corrington. 1939. *Wasted Manpower: The Challenge of Unemployment.* New York: W. W. Norton & Company.

———. 1940. "Local Non-WPA Work Relief." *American Federationist* 47, no. 4 (Apr.): 386–88.

Gillespie, Ed, and Bob Schellhas, eds. 1994. *Contract with America.* New York: Times Books.

Giuliani, Rudolph W. 1995. State of the City Address. New York City Council Chamber, Jan. 11, 1995.

———. 1996a. "Mayor Giuliani Praises Achievement of Work Experience Program Participants, Commends DC 37 Local 372 for Their Support of Workfare Initiative." Press Release, Dec. 14, 1996. New York City.

———. 1996b. "Message from the Mayor—Work Experience Program." Radio address, Dec. 15, 1996.

———. 1996c. State of the City Address. New York City Council Chamber, Jan. 11, 1996.

———. 1997a. "The Entrepreneurial City." Speech at the Manhattan Institute, New York City, Dec. 3, 1997.

——. 1997b. State of the City Address. New York City Council Chamber, Jan. 14, 1997.

——. 1998. "The Agenda for Permanent Change." Second inaugural address, City Hall, New York City, Jan. 1, 1998.

Glenn, Evelyn Nakano. 2002. *Unequal Freedom: How Race and Gender Shaped American Citizenship and Labor.* Cambridge: Harvard University Press.

Glickman, Lawrence B. 1997. *A Living Wage: American Workers and the Making of Consumer Society.* Ithaca: Cornell University Press.

Glickstein, Jonathan A. 2002. *American Exceptionalism, American Anxiety: Wages, Competition, and Degraded Labor in the Antebellum United States.* Charlottesville: University of Virginia Press.

Goffman, Erving. 1959. *The Presentation of Self in Everyday Life.* New York: Doubleday.

——. 1961. *Asylums: Essays on the Social Situation of Mental Patients and Other Inmates.* Chicago: Aldine.

——. 1963. *Stigma: Notes on the Management of Spoiled Identity.* Englewood Cliffs, NJ: Prentice Hall.

——. 1967. *Interaction Ritual: Essays in Face-to-Face Behavior.* Chicago: Aldine.

Goldberg, Chad Alan. 2003. "Haunted by the Specter of Communism: Collective Identity and Resource Mobilization in the Demise of the Workers Alliance of America." *Theory and Society* 32: 725–73.

——. 2005. "Contesting the Status of Relief Workers during the New Deal: The Workers Alliance of America and the Works Progress Administration, 1935–1941." *Social Science History* 29, no. 3 (Fall): 337–71.

Goldfield, Michael. 1997. *The Color of Politics: Race and the Mainsprings of American Politics.* New York: New Press.

Goodwyn, Lawrence. 1976. *Democratic Promise: The Populist Movement in America.* New York: Oxford University Press.

Gorski, Philip S. 2003. *The Disciplinary Revolution: Calvinism and the Rise of the State in Early Modern Europe.* Chicago: University of Chicago Press.

Gramsci, Antonio. 1971. *Selections from the Prison Notebooks.* Eds. and trans. Quintin Hoare and Geoffrey Nowell Smith. New York: International Publishers.

Green, James, ed. 1983. *Workers' Struggles, Past and Present: A "Radical America" Reader.* Philadelphia: Temple University Press.

Green, Mark. 1995. "New York City 'WAY' Not Yet the Way: A Preliminary Examination of the New NYC Program to Reduce Home Relief Fraud and Encourage Independence." Report by the Office of the Public Advocate for the City of New York (Jun.). New York City.

——. 1997. "From Welfare to Work: Getting Lost Along the Way." Report by the Office of the Public Advocate for the City of New York (Jul.). New York City.

Habermas, Jürgen. 1975. *Legitimation Crisis.* Trans. Thomas McCarthy. Boston: Beacon Press.

——. 1979. *Communication and the Evolution of Society.* Trans. Thomas McCarthy. Boston: Beacon Press.

——. 1987. *Lifeworld and System: A Critique of Functionalist Reason.* Vol. 2 of

*The Theory of Communicative Action.* Trans. Thomas McCarthy. Boston: Beacon Press.

Hacker, Jacob S. 2002. *The Divided Welfare State: The Battle over Public and Private Social Benefits in the United States.* New York: Cambridge University Press.

Hahn, Steven. 2003. *A Nation Under Our Feet: Black Political Struggles in the Rural South from Slavery to the Great Migration.* Cambridge: Harvard University Press.

Hall, Stuart. 1988. "The Toad in the Garden: Thatcherism Among the Theorists." In *Marxism and the Interpretation of Culture.* Eds. Cary Nelson and Lawrence Grossberg. Urbana: University of Illinois Press.

Halle, David, ed. 2003. *New York & Los Angeles: Politics, Society, and Culture.* Chicago: University of Chicago Press.

Hamilton, Dona Cooper, and Charles V. Hamilton. 1997. *The Dual Agenda: Race and Social Welfare Policies of Civil Rights Organizations.* New York: Columbia University Press.

Hartz, Louis. 1955. *The Liberal Tradition in America.* New York: Harcourt, Brace.

Harvey, Philip. 1989. *Securing the Right to Employment: Social Welfare Policy and the Unemployed in the United States.* Princeton: Princeton University Press.

Hasenfeld, Yeheskel, Jane A. Rafferty, and Mayer N. Zald. 1987. "The Welfare State, Citizenship and Bureaucratic Encounters." *Annual Review of Sociology* 13: 387–415.

Heclo, Hugh. 1974. *Modern Social Politics in Britain and Sweden: From Relief to Income Maintenance.* New Haven: Yale University Press.

Hedström, Peter, and Richard Swedborg, eds. 1998. *Social Mechanisms: An Analytical Approach to Social Theory.* New York: Cambridge University Press.

Herndon, Angelo. 1937. *Let Me Live.* New York: Random House.

Hertzberg, Arthur. 1968. *The French Enlightenment and the Jews: The Origins of Modern Anti-Semitism.* New York: Columbia University Press.

Higham, John. [1955] 1983. *Strangers in the Land: Patterns of American Nativism, 1860–1925.* New Brunswick: Rutgers University Press.

Hirschman, Albert O. 1970. *Exit, Voice, and Loyalty: Responses to Decline in Firms, Organizations, and States.* Cambridge: Harvard University Press.

Hoffman, Saul D., and Laurence S. Seidman. 2003. *Helping Working Families: The Earned Income Tax Credit.* Kalamazoo, MI: W. E. Upjohn Institute for Employment Research.

Holt, Thomas. 1977. *Black over White: Negro Political Leadership in South Carolina during Reconstruction.* Urbana: University of Illinois Press.

———. 1982. "Negro State Legislators in South Carolina during Reconstruction." Chap. 9 in *Southern Black Leaders of the Reconstruction Era.* Ed. Howard N. Rabinowitz. Urbana: University of Illinois Press.

Holtzman, Abraham. 1963. *The Townsend Movement: A Political Study.* New York: Bookman Associates.

Honneth, Axel. 1995. *The Struggle for Recognition: The Moral Grammar of Social Conflicts.* Trans. Joel Anderson. Cambridge: MIT Press.

Hopkins, Harry L. 1936. *Spending to Save: The Complete Story of Relief.* Seattle: University of Washington Press.

Howard, Christopher. 1997. *The Hidden Welfare State: Tax Expenditures and Social Policy in the United States.* Princeton: Princeton University Press.

Howard, Donald S. 1943. *The WPA and Federal Relief Policy.* New York: Russell Sage Foundation.

Howard, Oliver Otis. 1907. *Autobiography of Oliver Otis Howard.* Vol. 2. New York: The Baker & Taylor Company.

Howe, Irving, and Lewis Coser. 1957. *The American Communist Party: A Critical History (1919–1957).* Boston: Beacon Press.

Hume, Richard L. 1982. "Negro Delegates to the State Constitutional Conventions of 1867–69." Chap. 6 in *Southern Black Leaders of the Reconstruction Era.* Ed. Howard N. Rabinowitz. Urbana: University of Illinois Press.

Jacobson, Matthew Frye. 1998. *Whiteness of a Different Color: European Immigrants and the Alchemy of Race.* Cambridge: Harvard University Press.

Jeffrey, Randall S. 2002. "The Importance of Due Process Protections After Welfare Reform: Client Stories from New York City." *Albany Law Review* 66: 123–69.

Jensen, Laura. 2003. *Patriots, Settlers, and the Origins of American Social Policy.* New York: Cambridge University Press.

Jessop, Bob. 1993. "Towards a Schumpeterian Workfare State? Preliminary Remarks on a Post-Fordist Political Economy." *Studies in Political Economy* 40 (Spring): 7–39.

———. 1994. "The Transition to Post-Fordism and the Schumpeterian Workfare State." Chap. 2 in *Towards a Post-Fordist Welfare State?* Eds. Roger Burrows and Brian Loader. New York: Routledge.

Johnson, Nicholas. 2000. "State Low-Income Tax Relief: Recent Trends." *National Tax Journal* 53, no. 3, part 1 (Sept.): 403–16.

———. 2001. "A Hand Up: How State Earned Income Tax Credits Help Working Families Escape Poverty in 2001." Washington, DC: Center on Budget and Policy Priorities.

Judge, David, Gerry Stoker, and Harold Wolman, eds. 1995. *Theories of Urban Politics.* London: Sage.

Karsh, Bernard, and Phillips L. Garman. 1961. "The Impact of the Political Left." Chap. 2 in *Labor and the New Deal.* Eds. Milton Derber and Edwin Young. Madison: University of Wisconsin Press.

Katz, Michael B. 1986. *In the Shadow of the Poorhouse: A Social History of Welfare in America.* New York: Basic Books.

———. 1989. *The Undeserving Poor: From the War on Poverty to the War on Welfare.* New York: Pantheon Books.

———. 2001. *The Price of Citizenship: Redefining the American Welfare State.* New York: Henry Holt and Company.

Katznelson, Ira, Kim Geiger, and Daniel Kryder. 1993. "Limiting Liberalism: The Southern Veto in Congress." *Political Science Quarterly* 108, no. 2: 283–306.

Kaus, Mickey. 1992. *The End of Equality.* New York: Basic Books.

Kean, Nicola. 2004. "The Unprotected Workforce: Why Title VII Must Apply to Workfare Participants." *Texas Journal on Civil Liberties and Civil Rights* 9 (Spring): 159–200.

Kelley, Robin D. G. 1990. *Hammer and Hoe: Alabama Communists during the Great Depression.* Chapel Hill: University of North Carolina Press.

Kelly, Patrick J. 1997. *Creating a National Home: Building the Veterans' Welfare State, 1860–1900.* Cambridge: Harvard University Press.

Kessler-Harris, Alice. 1990. *A Woman's Wage: Historical Meanings and Social Consequences.* Lexington: University Press of Kentucky.

———. 2001. *In Pursuit of Equity: Women, Men, and the Quest for Economic Citizenship in 20th-Century America.* New York: Oxford University Press.

Key Jr., V. O. 1949. *Southern Politics in State and Nation.* New York: Alfred A. Knopf.

Keyssar, Alexander. 2000. *The Right to Vote: The Contested History of Democracy in the United States.* New York: Basic Books.

Kirtzman, Andrew. 2000. *Rudy Giuliani: Emperor of the City.* New York: Harper Collins.

Klatch, Rebecca E. 1987. *Women of the New Right.* Philadelphia: Temple University Press.

Klehr, Harvey. 1984. *The Heyday of American Communism: The Depression Decade.* New York: Basic Books.

Kohlberg, Lawrence. 1963. "The Development of Children's Orientations Toward a Moral Order. I: Sequence in the Development of Moral Thought." *Vita Humana* 6: 11–35.

Kornbluh, Felicia A. 1996. "The New Literature on Gender and the Welfare State: The U.S. Case." *Feminist Studies* 22: 171–97.

Krinsky, John, and Ellen Reese. 2006. "Forging and Sustaining Labor-Community Coalitions: The Workfare Justice Movement in Three Cities." *Sociological Forum* 21, no. 4 (Dec.): 623–58.

Krueger, Thomas A. 1967. *And Promises to Keep: The Southern Conference for Human Welfare, 1938–1948.* Nashville: Vanderbilt University Press.

Kymlicka, Will, and Wayne Norman. 1994. "Return of the Citizen: A Survey of Recent Work on Citizenship Theory." *Ethics* 104 (Jan.): 352–81.

Labor Research Association. 2001. "Unions Have the Resources for Growth in Major Metropolitan Areas" (Sept. 9, 2001). Unpublished report, Labor Research Association, New York, NY.

Lafer, Gordon. 2001. "Graduate Student Unions Fight the Corporate University." *Dissent* 48, no. 4 (Fall): 63–70.

———. 2003. "Graduate Student Unions: Organizing in a Changed Academic Economy." *Labor Studies Journal* 28, no. 2 (Summer): 25–43.

Lamont, Michèle. 1992. *Money, Morals, and Manners: The Culture of the French and American Upper-Middle Class.* Chicago: University of Chicago Press.

Lamont, Michèle, and Virag Molnar. 2002. "The Study of Boundaries in the Social Sciences." *Annual Review of Sociology* 28: 167–95.

Lanza, Michael L. 1990. *Agrarianism and Reconstruction Politics: The Southern Homestead Act.* Baton Rouge: Louisiana State University Press.

Lasser, David. 1938. *Work and Security: A Program for America.* Washington: Workers Alliance of America.

———. 1945. *Private Monopoly: The Enemy at Home.* New York: Harper & Brothers.

Lauria, Mickey. 1997a. "Reconstructing Urban Regime Theory." Chap. 1 in *Reconstructing Urban Regime Theory: Regulating Urban Politics in a Global Economy.* Ed. Mickey Lauria. London: Sage.

———, ed. 1997b. *Reconstructing Urban Regime Theory: Regulating Urban Politics in a Global Economy.* London: Sage.

Lemert, Charles, ed. 1981. *French Sociology: Rupture and Renewal Since 1968.* New York: Columbia University Press.

Lescohier, Don. D. 1939. "The Hybrid WPA." *Survey Midmonthly* 75: 167–69.

Leuchtenburg, William E. 1963. *Franklin D. Roosevelt and the New Deal.* New York: Harper & Row.

Levitan, Mark 2003. "It Did Happen Here: The Rise in Working Poverty in New York City." Chap. 8 in *New York & Los Angeles: Politics, Society, and Culture.* Ed. David Halle. Chicago: University of Chicago Press.

Lieberman, Robert C. 1994. "The Freedmen's Bureau and the Politics of Institutional Structure." *Social Science History* 18, no. 3 (Fall): 405–37.

———. 1998. *Shifting the Color Line: Race and the American Welfare State.* Cambridge: Harvard University Press.

Lincoln, Abraham. 1991. *Great Speeches: Abraham Lincoln.* Ed. Stanley Appelbaum. New York: Dover Publications.

Lipset, Seymour Martin, and Gary Marks. 2000. *It Didn't Happen Here: Why Socialism Failed in the United States.* New York: W. W. Norton & Company.

Litwack, Leon F. 1979. *Been in the Storm So Long: The Aftermath of Slavery.* New York: Alfred A. Knopf.

Lorence, James J. 1994. "Controlling the Reserve Army: The United Automobile Workers and Michigan's Unemployed, 1935–1941." *Labor's Heritage* 5: 18–37.

———. 1996. *Organizing the Unemployed: Community and Union Activists in the Industrial Heartland.* Albany: State University of New York Press.

Lowi, Theodore J. 1972. "Four Systems of Policy, Politics, and Choice." *Public Administration Review* 32, no. 4 (Jul.–Aug.): 298–310.

Luers, Walter M. 1998. "Workfare Wages Under the Fair Labor Standards Act." *Fordham Law Review* 67 (Oct.): 203–38.

Lui, Adonica Y. 1995. "Political and Institutional Constraints of Reform: The Charity Reformers' Failed Campaigns Against Public Outdoor Relief, New York City, 1874–1898." *Journal of Policy History* 7, no. 3: 341–64.

Macmahon, Arthur W., John D. Millett, and Gladys Ogden. 1941. *The Administration of Federal Work Relief.* Chicago: Public Administration Service.

Magdol, Edward. 1977. *A Right to the Land: Essays on the Freedmen's Community.* Westport, CT: Greenwood Press.

Mahmoudov, Vadim. 1998. "Are Workfare Participants 'Employees'? Legal Issues Presented by a Two-Tiered Labor Force." *Annual Survey of American Law:* 349–87.

Mann, Michael. 1987. "Ruling Class Strategies and Citizenship." *Sociology* 21 (Aug.): 339–54.

Mantsios, Gregory, ed.1998. *A New Labor Movement for the New Century*. New York: Monthly Review Press.

Manza, Jeff. 2000a. "Political Sociological Models of the U.S. New Deal." *Annual Review of Sociology* 26: 297–322.

———. 2000b. "Race and the Underdevelopment of the American Welfare State." *Theory and Society* 29: 819–32.

Marshall, T. H. [1949] 1964. "Citizenship and Social Class." Chap. 4 in *Class, Citizenship and Social Development*. Garden City, NY: Doubleday.

Marx, Karl. [1852] 1963. *The Eighteenth Brumaire of Louis Bonaparte*. New York: International Publishers.

Mauss, Marcel. [1925] 1990. *The Gift: The Form and Reason for Exchange in Archaic Societies*. Trans. W. D. Halls. New York: W. W. Norton & Company.

McAdam, Doug. 1982. *Political Process and the Development of Black Insurgency, 1930–1970*. Chicago: University of Chicago Press.

McAdam, Doug, John D. McCarthy, and Mayer N. Zald, eds. 1996. *Comparative Perspectives on Social Movements*. New York: Cambridge University Press.

McAdam, Doug, Sidney Tarrow, and Charles Tilly. 2001. *Dynamics of Contention*. New York: Cambridge University Press.

McConnell, Stuart. 1992. *Glorious Contentment: The Grand Army of the Republic, 1865–1900*. Chapel Hill: University of North Carolina Press.

McFeely, William S. 1968. *Yankee Stepfather: General O. O. Howard and the Freedmen*. New Haven: Yale University Press.

McGerr, Michael E. 1986. *The Decline of Popular Politics: The American North, 1865–1928*. New York: Oxford University Press.

Mead, Lawrence M. 1986. *Beyond Entitlement: The Social Obligations of Citizenship*. New York: Free Press.

Meier, August. 1982. "New Perspectives on the Nature of Black Political Leadership during Reconstruction." Afterword in *Southern Black Leaders of the Reconstruction Era*. Ed. Howard N. Rabinowitz. Urbana: University of Illinois Press.

Meriam, Lewis. 1946. *Relief and Social Security*. Washington, DC: Brookings Institution.

Merton, Robert. 1968. *Social Theory and Social Structure*. 3rd ed. Glencoe, IL: Free Press.

Mettler, Suzanne. 1998. *Dividing Citizens: Gender and Federalism in New Deal Public Policy*. Ithaca: Cornell University Press.

———. 2005. *Soldiers to Citizens: The G.I. Bill and the Making of the Greatest Generation*. New York: Oxford University Press.

Mettler, Suzanne, and Joe Soss. 2004. "The Consequences of Public Policy for Democratic Citizenship: Bridging Policy Studies and Mass Politics." *Perspectives on Politics* 2, no. 1 (Mar.): 55–73.

Meyer, Bruce, and Douglas Holtz-Eakin, eds. 2001. *Making Work Pay: The Earned Income Tax Credit and Its Impact on American Families*. New York: Russell Sage Foundation.

Meyer, John W., and Brian Rowan. 1991. "Institutionalized Organizations: Formal Structure as Myth and Ceremony." Chap. 2 in *The New Institutionalism in Organizational Analysis.* Eds. Walter W. Powell and Paul J. DiMaggio. Chicago: University of Chicago Press.

Millett, John D. 1938. *The Works Progress Administration in New York City.* Chicago: Public Administration Service.

Mink, Gwendolyn. 1998. *Welfare's End.* Ithaca: Cornell University Press.

Mitchell, Daniel J. B. 2000. *Pensions, Politics and the Elderly: Historic Social Movements and Their Lessons for Our Aging Society.* Armonk, NY: M. E. Sharpe.

Mollenkopf, John Hull, ed. 1988a. *Power, Culture, and Place: Essays on New York City.* New York: Russell Sage Foundation.

———. 1988b. "The Postindustrial Transformation of the Political Order in New York." Chap. 9 in *Power, Culture, and Place: Essays on New York City.* Ed. John Hull Mollenkopf. New York: Russell Sage Foundation.

———. 1991. "Political Inequality." Chap. 13 in *Dual City: Restructuring New York.* Eds. John Hull Mollenkopf and Manuel Castells. New York: Russell Sage Foundation.

———. 1992. *A Phoenix in the Ashes: The Rise and Fall of the Koch Coalition in New York City Politics.* Princeton: Princeton University Press.

———. 1997. "New York: The Great Anomaly." Chap. 4 in *Racial Politics in American Cities.* Eds. Rufus P. Browning, Dale Rogers Marshall, and David H. Tabb. 2nd ed. New York: Longman.

Mollenkopf, John Hull, and Manuel Castells, eds. 1991. *Dual City: Restructuring New York.* New York: Russell Sage Foundation.

Montgomery, David. [1967] 1981. *Beyond Equality: Labor and the Radical Republicans, 1862–1872.* Urbana: University of Illinois Press.

———. 1993. *Citizen Worker: The Experience of Workers in the United States with Democracy and the Free Market during the Nineteenth Century.* New York: Cambridge University Press.

Moore, John Hammond. 1971. "The Angelo Herndon Case, 1932–1937." *Phylon* 32, no. 1: 60–71.

Mossberger, Karen, and Gerry Stoker. 2001. "The Evolution of Urban Regime Theory." *Urban Affairs Review* 36, no. 6 (Jul.): 810–35.

Murphy, Raymond. 1988. *Social Closure: The Theory of Monopolization and Exclusion.* Oxford: Clarendon Press.

Myles, John, and Paul Pierson. 1997. "Friedman's Revenge: The Reform of 'Liberal' Welfare States in Canada and the United States." *Politics and Society* 25, no. 4 (Dec.): 443–72.

Myles, John, and Jill Quadagno. 2000. "Envisioning a Third Way: The Welfare State in the Twenty-First Century." *Contemporary Sociology* 29, no. 1 (Jan.): 156–67.

Naison, Mark. 1983. *Communists in Harlem during the Depression.* New York: Grove Press.

National Employment Law Project. 1997. "National Local Groups Rally Clinton Administration to Guarantee Workfare Workplace Protections." Press release issued jointly with the Center for Community Change, May 9, 1997.

National Governors' Association, National Conference of State Legislatures, and American Public Welfare Association. 1997. "Analysis of the Personal Responsibility and Work Opportunity Reconciliation Act of 1996." http://www .ncsl.org/statefed/hr3734.htm.

National Labor Relations Board. *The First Sixty Years: The Story of the National Labor Relations Board, 1935–1995*. http://www.nlrb.gov/nlrb/shared_files/ brochures/60yrs_intro.pdf.

Needleman, Ruth. 1998. "Women Workers: Strategies for Inclusion and Rebuilding Unionism." In *A New Labor Movement for the New Century*. Ed. Gregory Mantsios. New York: Monthly Review Press.

NELP. See National Employment Law Project.

Nelson, Cary, and Lawrence Grossberg, eds. 1988. *Marxism and the Interpretation of Culture*. Urbana: University of Illinois Press.

New York City Council Committee on General Welfare and Committee on Higher Education. 1998. Transcript of joint committee hearing held Oct. 14, 1998, City Hall Council Chambers, New York City.

New York City Council Committee on Governmental Operations. 1998. Transcript of committee hearing, Aug. 5, 1998, City Hall Council Chambers, New York City.

New York Jobs with Justice. 1996. "1996 Report." New York City.

New York State Department of Social Services. 1995. *Statistical Supplement to the Annual Report*. Albany, NY: State of New York.

New York Workers' Rights Board. 1996. "About the Workers' Rights Board and the Hearing on the Work Experience Program," handbill, New York, NY.

———. 1997. Videotape of hearing on workfare held Mar. 11, 1997, Legislative Office Building, Albany, New York.

Newman, Abraham L. 2003. "When Opportunity Knocks: Economic Liberalisation and Stealth Welfare in the United States." *Journal of Social Policy* 32, no. 2 (Apr.): 179–97.

Nieman, Donald G. 1979. *To Set the Law in Motion: The Freedmen's Bureau and the Legal Rights of Blacks, 1865–1868*. Millwood, NY: KTO Press.

Nightingale, Demetra Smith, Nancy Pindus, Fredrica D. Kramer, John Trutko, Kelly Mikelson, and Michael Egner. 2002. "Work and Welfare Reform in New York City During the Giuliani Administration: A Study of Program Implementation." Unpublished manuscript, The Urban Institute Labor and Social Policy Center, Washington, DC.

Nissen, Sylke. 1999. "Control and Marginalization: Federal and Local Welfare Politics in New York City." *Crime, Law, and Social Change* 32: 235–56.

NLRB. See National Labor Relations Board.

Nunnelly, William A. 1991. *Bull Connor*. Tuscaloosa: University of Alabama Press.

NYWRB. See New York Workers' Rights Board.

Oberly, James W. 1990. *Sixty Million Acres: American Veterans and the Public Lands before the Civil War*. Kent, OH: Kent State University Press.

O'Connor, James. 1973. *The Fiscal Crisis of the State*. New York: St. Martin's Press.

Offe, Claus. 1984. *Contradictions of the Welfare State.* Ed. John Keane. Cambridge: MIT Press.

Ogden, August Raymond. 1945. *The Dies Committee: A Study of the Special House Committee for the Investigation of Un-American Activities, 1938–1944.* Washington, DC: The Catholic University of America Press.

Omi, Michael, and Howard Winant. 1986. *Racial Formation in the United States.* New York: Routledge.

O'Neill, Hugh, Kathryn Garcia, Virginie Amerlynck, and Barbara Blum. 2001. "Policies Affecting New York City's Low-Income Families." Unpublished manuscript, National Center for Children in Poverty, Mailman School of Public Health, Columbia University, New York, NY.

Orloff, Ann Shola. 1988. "The Political Origins of America's Belated Welfare State." In *The Politics of Social Policy in the United States.* Eds. Margaret Weir, Ann Shola Orloff, and Theda Skocpol. Princeton: Princeton University Press.

———. 1993a. "Gender and the Social Rights of Citizenship: The Comparative Analysis of Gender Relations and Welfare States." *American Sociological Review* 58 (Jun.): 303–28.

———. 1993b. *The Politics of Pensions: A Comparative Analysis of Britain, Canada, and the United States, 1880–1940.* Madison: University of Wisconsin Press.

———. 2002. "Explaining U.S. Welfare Reform: Power, Gender, Race and the U.S. Policy Legacy." *Critical Social Policy* 22, no. 1: 96–118.

Orloff, Ann Shola, and Theda Skocpol. 1984. "Why Not Equal Protection? Explaining the Politics of Public Social Spending in Britain, 1900–1911, and the United States, 1880s–1920." *American Sociological Review* 49 (Dec.): 726–50.

Orren, Karen. 1991. *Belated Feudalism: Labor, the Law, and Liberal Development in the United States.* New York: Cambridge University Press.

Osthaus, Carl R. 1976. *Freedmen, Philanthropy, and Fraud: A History of the Freedman's Savings Bank.* Urbana: University of Illinois Press.

Oubre, Claude F. 1978. *Forty Acres and a Mule: The Freedmen's Bureau and Black Land Ownership.* Baton Rouge: Louisiana State University Press.

Owens, Susie Lee. 1943. The Union League of America: Political Activities in Tennessee, the Carolinas, and Virginia, 1865–1870. PhD diss., New York University.

Palmer, Phyllis. 1995. "Outside the Law: Agricultural and Domestic Workers Under the Fair Labor Standards Act." *Journal of Policy History* 7, no. 4: 416–40.

Parkin, Frank. 1979. *Marxism and Class Theory: A Bourgeois Critique.* London: Tavistock.

Parsons, Talcott. 1977. *The Evolution of Societies.* Ed. Jackson Toby. Englewood Cliffs, NJ: Prentice Hall.

Patterson, James T. 1967. *Congressional Conservatism and the New Deal: The Growth of the Conservative Coalition in Congress, 1933–1939.* Lexington: University Press of Kentucky.

Patterson, Orlando. 1982. *Slavery and Social Death: A Comparative Study.* Cambridge: Harvard University Press.

Peck, Jamie. 2001. *Workfare States.* New York: The Guilford Press.

Peillon, Michel. 1998. "Bourdieu's Field and the Sociology of Welfare." *Journal of Social Policy* 27, no. 2 (Apr.): 213–29.

——. 2001. *Welfare in Ireland: Actors, Resources, and Strategies.* Westport, CT: Praeger.

Perkins, Frances. 1946. *The Roosevelt I Knew.* New York: Viking Press.

Perry, Matt. 2000. *Bread and Work: Social Policy and the Experience of Unemployment, 1918–39.* London: Pluto Press.

Petracca, Mark P., ed. 1992. *The Politics of Interests: Interest Groups Transformed.* Boulder: Westview Press.

Pierce, Paul Skeels. 1904. *The Freedmen's Bureau: A Chapter in the History of Reconstruction.* Iowa City: University of Iowa.

Pierson, Paul. 1993. "When Effect Becomes Cause: Policy Feedback and Political Change." *World Politics* 45 (Jul.): 595–628.

——. 1994. *Dismantling the Welfare State? Reagan, Thatcher, and the Politics of Retrenchment.* New York: Cambridge University Press.

Piven, Frances Fox, ed. 1991. *Labor Parties in Postindustrial Societies.* New York: Oxford University Press.

Piven, Frances Fox, and Richard A. Cloward. [1971] 1993. *Regulating the Poor: The Functions of Public Welfare.* Updated edition. New York: Vintage Books.

——. 1974. *The Politics of Turmoil: Essays on Poverty, Race, and the Urban Crisis.* New York: Random House.

——. 1977. *Poor People's Movements: Why They Succeed, How They Fail.* New York: Vintage Books.

——. 1991. "Collective Protest: A Critique of Resource Mobilization Theory." *International Journal of Politics, Culture and Society* 4, no. 4: 435–58.

Plotke, David. 1992. "The Political Mobilization of Business." Chap. 8 in *The Politics of Interests: Interest Groups Transformed.* Ed. Mark P. Petracca. Boulder: Westview Press.

——. 1996. *Building a Democratic Political Order: Reshaping American Liberalism in the 1930s and 1940s.* New York: Cambridge University Press.

Polletta, Francesca, and James M. Jasper. 2001. "Collective Identity and Social Movements." *Annual Review of Sociology* 27: 283–305.

Porter, David L. 1980. *Congress and the Waning of the New Deal.* Port Washington, NY: Kennikat Press.

Powell, Lawrence Alfred, Kenneth J. Branco, and John B. Williamson. 1996. *The Senior Rights Movement: Framing the Policy Debate in America.* New York: Simon & Schuster Macmillan.

Powell, Walter W., and Paul J. DiMaggio, eds. 1991. *The New Institutionalism in Organizational Analysis.* Chicago: University of Chicago Press.

Quadagno, Jill. 1987. "Theories of the Welfare State." *Annual Review of Sociology* 13: 109–28.

——. 1988a. "From Old Age Security to Supplemental Security Income: The Political Economy of Relief in the South, 1935–1972." Chap. 6 in *The Politics of Social Policy in the United States.* Eds. Margaret Weir, Ann Shola Orloff, and Theda Skocpol. Princeton: Princeton University Press.

——. 1988b. *The Transformation of Old Age Security: Class and Politics in the American Welfare State.* Chicago: University of Chicago Press.

——. 1994. *The Color of Welfare: How Racism Undermined the War on Poverty.* New York: Oxford University Press.

——. 1999. "Creating a Capital Investment Welfare State: The New American Exceptionalism." *American Sociological Review* 64 (Feb.): 1–11.

Rabinowitz, Howard N., ed. 1982. *Southern Black Leaders of the Reconstruction Era.* Urbana: University of Illinois Press.

Rankin, David C. 1982. "The Origins of Negro Leadership in New Orleans during Reconstruction." Chap. 7 in *Southern Black Leaders of the Reconstruction Era.* Ed. Howard N. Rabinowitz. Urbana: University of Illinois Press.

Rauch, Basil. 1944. *The History of the New Deal, 1933–1938.* New York: Creative Age Press.

Reese, Ellen. 2002. "Resisting the Workfare State: Mobilizing General Relief Recipients in Los Angeles." *Race, Gender & Class* 9, no. 1 (Jan.):72–95.

Reese, Ellen, and Garnett Newcombe. 2003. "Income Rights, Mothers' Rights, or Workers' Rights? Collective Action Frames, Organizational Ideologies, and the American Welfare Rights Movement." *Social Problems* 50, no. 2: 294–318.

Reese, Noelle M. 2000. "Workfare Participants Deserve Employment Protections Under the Fair Labor Standards Act and Workers' Compensation Laws." *Rutgers Law Journal* 31 (Spring): 873–911.

Regosin, Elizabeth. 2002. *Freedom's Promise: Ex-Slave Families and Citizenship in the Age of Emancipation.* Charlottesville: University Press of Virginia.

Reinhardt, Mark. 1997. *The Art of Being Free: Taking Liberties with Tocqueville, Marx, and Arendt.* Ithaca: Cornell University Press.

Richardson, E. Allen. 1999. "Architects of a Benevolent Empire: The Relationship between the American Missionary Association and the Freedmen's Bureau in Virginia, 1865–1872." Chap. 6 in *The Freedmen's Bureau and Reconstruction: Reconsiderations.* Eds. Paul A. Cimbala and Randall M. Miller. New York: Fordham University Press.

Rieder, Jonathan. 1985. *Canarsie: The Jews and Italians of Brooklyn against Liberalism.* Cambridge: Harvard University Press.

Roediger, David R. [1991] 1999. *The Wages of Whiteness: Race and the Making of the American Working Class.* Revised edition. New York: Verso.

Roosevelt, Franklin D. 1938. *The Public Papers and Addresses of Franklin D. Roosevelt.* Vol. 5. Ed. Samuel I. Rosenman. New York: Random House.

Rose, Nancy Ellen. 1994. *Put to Work: Relief Programs in the Great Depression.* New York: Monthly Review Press.

——. 1995. *Workfare or Fair Work: Women, Welfare, and Government Work Programs.* New Brunswick: Rutgers University Press.

Rosenzweig, Roy. 1975. "Radicals and the Jobless: The Musteites and the Unemployed Leagues, 1932–1936." *Labor History* 16, no. 1 (Winter): 52–77.

——. 1979. "'Socialism in Our Time': The Socialist Party and the Unemployed, 1929–1936." *Labor History* 20, no. 4 (Fall): 485–509.

——. 1983. "Organizing the Unemployed: The Early Years of the Great Depression, 1929–1933." Chap. 8 in *Workers' Struggles, Past and Present: A "Radical America" Reader*. Ed. James Green. Philadelphia: Temple University Press.

Rothman, David J. 1971. *The Discovery of the Asylum: Social Order and Disorder in the New Republic*. Boston: Little, Brown.

Salmond, John A. 1967. *The Civilian Conservation Corps, 1933–1942: A New Deal Case Study*. Durham, NC: Duke University Press.

Sautter, Udo. 1991. *Three Cheers for the Unemployed: Government and Unemployment before the New Deal*. New York: Cambridge University Press.

Saxton, Alexander. 1990. *The Rise and Fall of the White Republic: Class Politics and Mass Culture in Nineteenth-Century America*. New York: Verso.

Schattschneider, E. E. [1960] 1983. *The Semisovereign People: A Realist's View of Democracy in America*. Chicago: Holt, Rinehart and Winston.

Scheiber, Harry N., ed. 1969. *The Old Northwest: Studies in Regional History, 1787–1910*. Lincoln: University of Nebraska Press.

Schiltz, Michael E. 1970. *Public Attitudes Toward Social Security, 1935–1965*. Washington, DC: U.S. Government Printing Office.

Schmidt, James D. 1998. *Free to Work: Labor Law, Emancipation, and Reconstruction, 1815–1880*. Athens: University of Georgia Press.

——. 1999. "'A Full-Fledged Government of Men': Freedmen's Bureau Labor Policy in South Carolina, 1865–1868." Chap. 10 in *The Freedmen's Bureau and Reconstruction: Reconsiderations*. Eds. Paul A. Cimbala and Randall M. Miller. New York: Fordham University Press.

Schneider, Anne, and Helen Ingram. 1993. "Social Construction of Target Populations: Implications for Politics and Policy." *American Political Science Review* 87, no. 2 (Jun.): 334–47.

——. 1997. *Policy Design for Democracy*. Lawrence: University Press of Kansas.

——, eds. 2005. *Deserving and Entitled: Social Constructions and Public Policy*. Albany: State University of New York Press.

Schram, Sanford F. 1995. *Words of Welfare: The Poverty of Social Science and the Social Science of Poverty*. Minneapolis: University of Minnesota Press.

——. 2000. *After Welfare: The Culture of Postindustrial Social Policy*. New York: New York University Press.

Schudson, Michael. 1998. *The Good Citizen: A History of American Civic Life*. Cambridge: Harvard University Press.

Schwalm, Leslie A. 1997. *A Hard Fight for We: Women's Transition from Slavery to Freedom in South Carolina*. Urbana: University of Illinois Press.

Schwartz, Bonnie Fox. 1984. *The Civil Works Administration, 1933–1934: The Business of Emergency Employment in the New Deal*. Princeton: Princeton University Press.

Sewell Jr., William H. 1992. "A Theory of Structure: Duality, Agency, and Transformation." *American Journal of Sociology* 98: 1–29.

Sexton, Patricia Cayo. 1991. *The War on Labor and the Left: Understanding America's Unique Conservatism*. Boulder, CO: Westview Press.

Seymour, Helen. 1937. The Organized Unemployed. PhD diss., University of Chicago, Chicago, IL.

Shattuck Jr., Gardiner H. 1987. *A Shield and Hiding Place: The Religious Life of the Civil War Armies.* Macon, GA: Mercer University Press.

Shklar, Judith N. 1991. *American Citizenship: The Quest for Inclusion.* Cambridge: Harvard University Press.

Skocpol, Theda. 1980. "Political Response to Capitalist Crisis: Neo-Marxist Theories of the State and the Case of the New Deal." *Politics and Society* 10: 155–201.

———. 1985. "Bringing the State Back In." Chap. 1 in *Bringing the State Back In.* Eds. Peter B. Evans, Dietrich Rueschmeyer, and Theda Skocpol. New York: Cambridge University Press.

———. 1992. *Protecting Soldiers and Mothers: The Political Origins of Social Policy in the United States.* Cambridge: Harvard University Press.

———. 1995a. "America's First Social Security System: The Expansion of Benefits for Civil War Veterans." Chap. 2 in Theda Skocpol, *Social Policy in the United States: Future Possibilities in Historical Perspective.* Princeton: Princeton University Press.

———. 1995b. "Targeting Within Universalism: Politically Viable Policies to Combat Poverty in the United States." Chap. 8 in Theda Skocpol, *Social Policy in the United States: Future Possibilities in Historical Perspective.* Princeton: Princeton University Press.

———. 1995c. *Social Policy in the United States: Future Possibilities in Historical Perspective.* Princeton: Princeton University Press.

Skocpol, Theda, and Edwin Amenta. 1986. "States and Social Policies." *Annual Review of Sociology* 12: 131–57.

Skowronek, Stephen. 1982. *Building a New American State: The Expansion of National Administrative Capacities, 1877–1920.* New York: Cambridge University Press.

Smith, Anthony D. 2001. *Nationalism: Theory, Ideology, History.* Malden, MA: Polity Press.

Smith, Rogers M. 1993. "Beyond Tocqueville, Myrdal, and Hartz: The Multiple Traditions in America." *American Political Science Review* 87: 549–66.

———. 1997. *Civic Ideals: Conflicting Visions of Citizenship in U.S. History.* New Haven: Yale University Press.

Smith, Timothy L. 1957. *Revivalism and Social Reform in Mid-Nineteenth-Century America.* New York: Abingdon Press.

Snow, David A., and Robert D. Benford. 1988. "Ideology, Frame Resonance, and Participant Mobilization." *International Social Movement Research* 1: 197–217.

Somers, Margaret R. 1993. "Citizenship and the Place of the Public Sphere: Law, Community, and Political Culture in the Transition to Democracy." *American Sociological Review* 58 (Oct.): 587–620.

———. 1994. "Rights, Relationality, and Membership: Rethinking the Making and Meaning of Citizenship." *Law & Social Inquiry* 19 (Winter): 63–112.

Soss, Joe. 1999. "Lessons of Welfare: Policy Design, Political Learning, and Political Action." *American Political Science Review* 93: 363–80.

——. 2002. *Unwanted Claims: The Politics of Participation in the U.S. Welfare System*. Ann Arbor: University of Michigan Press.

Sparrow, Bartholomew H. 1996. *From the Outside In: World War II and the American State*. Princeton: Princeton University Press.

Sproat, John G. 1968. *"The Best Men": Liberal Reformers in the Gilded Age*. New York: Oxford University Press.

Stack, Carol B. 1974. *All Our Kin: Strategies for Survival in a Black Community*. New York: Harper & Row.

Stampp, Kenneth M. 1965. *The Era of Reconstruction, 1865–1877*. New York: Alfred A. Knopf.

Stanley, Amy Dru. 1992. "Beggars Can't Be Choosers: Compulsion and Contract in Postbellum America." *Journal of American History* 78, no. 4 (Mar.): 1265–93.

Steinfeld, Robert J. 1989. "Property and Suffrage in the Early American Republic." *Stanford Law Review* 41: 335–76.

——. 2001. *Coercion, Contract, and Free Labor in the Nineteenth Century*. New York: Cambridge University Press.

Steinmo, Sven, Kathleen Thelen, and Frank Longstreth, eds. 1992. *Structuring Politics: Historical Institutionalism in Comparative Analysis*. New York: Cambridge University Press.

Stepan-Norris, Judith, and Maurice Zeitlin. 2003. *Left Out: Reds and America's Industrial Unions*. New York: Cambridge University Press.

Stettner, Andrew. 1999. "A Dubious Future: The Challenge of Welfare Reform in New York City." *Georgetown Public Policy Review* 73 (Fall): 73–91.

Stinchcombe, Arthur L. 1978. *Theoretical Methods in Social History*. New York: Academic Press.

——. 1991. "The Conditions of Fruitfulness of Theorizing About Mechanisms in Social Science." *Philosophy of the Social Sciences* 21: 367–88.

Stoker, Gerry. 1995. "Regime Theory and Urban Politics." Chap. 4 in *Theories of Urban Politics*. Eds. David Judge, Gerry Stoker, and Harold Wolman. London: Sage.

Stoltzfus, Emilie. 1999. "'We Are Contributors to Our Society': Productive Citizenship and the Post-World-War-II Call for Child Care as a Social Wage in California." Unpublished manuscript, Claremont Graduate University, Claremont, CA.

——. 2003. *Citizen, Mother, Worker: Debating Public Responsibility for Child Care After the Second World War*. Chapel Hill: University of North Carolina Press.

Stone, Clarence N. 1993. "Urban Regimes and the Capacity to Govern: A Political Economy Approach." *Journal of Urban Affairs* 15, no. 1: 1–28.

Sullivan, Patricia. 1996. *Days of Hope: Race and Democracy in the New Deal Era*. Chapel Hill: University of North Carolina Press.

Swartz, David. 1997. *Culture and Power: The Sociology of Pierre Bourdieu*. Chicago: University of Chicago Press.

Tait, Vanessa. 1998. "Knocking at Labor's Door: Workfare Workers Organize." *New Labor Forum* 3 (Fall/Winter): 139–50.

———. 2005. *Poor Workers' Unions: Rebuilding Labor from Below.* Cambridge, MA: South End Press.

Talmon, Jacob Leib. [1952] 1960. *The Origins of Totalitarian Democracy.* New York: Frederick A. Praeger.

Tarrow, Sidney. 1994. *Power in Movement: Social Movements, Collective Action and Politics.* New York: Cambridge University Press.

Taylor, Alrutheus A. 1922. "Negro Congressmen a Generation After." *The Journal of Negro History* 7, no. 2 (Apr.): 127–71.

Teles, Steven M. 1998. *Whose Welfare? AFDC and Elite Politics.* Lawrence: University Press of Kansas.

Thompson, E. P. 1963. *The Making of the English Working Class.* New York: Pantheon Books.

Tilly, Charles. 1981. "Useless Durkheim." Chap. 4 in *As Sociology Meets History.* New York: Academic Press.

———. 1995. "To Explain Political Processes." *American Journal of Sociology* 100, no. 6 (May): 1594–610.

———. 1997. "Means and Ends of Comparison in Macrosociology." *Comparative Social Research* 16: 47–57.

Tilly, Charles, Louise Tilly, and Richard Tilly. 1975. *The Rebellious Century, 1830–1930.* Cambridge: Harvard University Press.

Tilly, Chris. 1996. "Workfare's Impact on the New York City Labor Market: Lower Wages and Worker Displacement." Working Paper #92. New York: Russell Sage Foundation.

Tocqueville, Alexis de. [1835] 1972. *Democracy in America.* Vol. 1. Ed. Phillips Bradley. New York: Random House.

———. [1840] 1972. *Democracy in America.* Vol. 2. Ed. Phillips Bradley. New York: Random House.

Tomlins, Christopher L. 1985. *The State and the Unions: Labor Relations, Law, and the Organized Labor Movement in America, 1880–1960.* New York: Cambridge University Press.

Trattner, Walter I. 1984. *From Poor Law to Welfare State.* New York: Free Press.

Tucker, Robert C., ed. 1978. *The Marx-Engels Reader.* 2nd ed. New York: W. W. Norton & Company.

Turner, Bryan S. 1990. "Outline of a Theory of Citizenship." *Sociology* 24 (May): 189–217.

Tynes, Sheryl R. 1996. *Turning Points in Social Security: From "Cruel Hoax" to "Sacred Entitlement."* Stanford: Stanford University Press.

Urban Justice Center. 1996. "Principles of Unity," Dec. 1, 1996, New York City.

U.S. Congress. 1939. *Congressional Record.* 76th Cong., 1st sess. Vol. 84, pt. 13, appendix. Washington, DC: U.S. Government Printing Office.

U.S. Congress. House. 1938. *Hearings Before a Special Committee on Un-American Activities, 75th Congress, Third Session, on H. Res. 282.* Vols. 1 and 2. Washington, DC: U.S. Government Printing Office.

U.S. Congress. Senate. 1939. *Investigation of Senatorial Campaign Expenditures and Use of Governmental Funds. Report of the Special Committee to Investigate Senatorial Campaign Expenditures and Use of Governmental Funds in 1938, Pursuant to Senate Resolution No. 283 (Seventy-fifth Congress) and Senate Resolution No. 290 (Seventy-fifth Congress).* Parts I and II. Washington, DC: U.S. Government Printing Office.

U.S. Council of Economic Advisors. 1997. "Explaining the Decline in Welfare Receipt, 1993–1996." U.S. Council of Economic Advisors, Executive Office of the President, Washington, DC. Report dated May 9, 1997. http://clinton4.nara.gov/WH/EOP/CEA/Welfare/.

U.S. Court of Appeals for the Tenth Circuit. 57 F.3d 1544; 1995 U.S. App. LEXIS 15164; 130 Lab. Cas. (CCH) P33,272.

U.S. Department of Commerce, Bureau of the Census. 1975. *Historical Statistics of the United States: Colonial Times to 1970.* Part 1. Washington, DC: U.S. Government Printing Office.

U.S. Department of Labor, Bureau of Labor Statistics. 1940. "Negroes Under WPA, 1939." *Monthly Labor Review* 50 (Mar.): 636–38.

U.S. Federal Works Agency. 1946. *Final Report on the WPA Program, 1935–43.* Washington, DC: U.S. Government Printing Office.

U.S. Works Progress Administration. 1936. *Our Job with the WPA.* Washington, DC: U.S. Government Printing Office.

U.S. Work Projects Administration, New York (City). 1940. *Work Project Office Manual.* Mar. 31, 1940. New York: Work Projects Administration for the City of New York.

U.S. Work Projects Administration. 1941. *Public Work Reserve Manual of Procedures for the Field Staff.* Washington, DC: Work Projects Administration.

U.S. Work Projects Administration. 1942. *Manual of Rules and Regulations.* Vols. 1–4. Washington, DC: Work Projects Administration.

Valocchi, Steve. 1994. "The Racial Basis of Capitalism and the State, and the Impact of the New Deal on African Americans." *Social Problems* 41, no. 3 (Aug.): 347–62.

Vaughan, Walter. 1891. *Vaughan's "Freedmen's Pension Bill."* Chicago: W. R. Vaughan.

Ventry Jr., Dennis J. 2001. "The Collision of Tax and Welfare Politics: The Political History of the Earned Income Tax Credit." Chap. 1 in *Making Work Pay: The Earned Income Tax Credit and Its Impact on America's Families.* Eds. Bruce D. Meyer and Douglas Holtz-Eakin. New York: Russell Sage Foundation.

Vila, Daniel. 1997. "N.Y. Workfare Participants Demand a Union." Report posted Feb. 1997 on SOCNET, http://socnet.net/.

Vinovskis, Maris A. 1989. "Have Social Historians Lost the Civil War? Some Preliminary Demographic Speculations." *Journal of American History* 76, no. 1 (Jun.): 34–58.

Vorspan, Rachel. 1975. The Battle over the Workhouse: English Society and the New Poor Law. PhD diss., Columbia University, New York.

Wagner, David. 2005. *The Poorhouse: America's Forgotten Institution.* Lanham, MD: Rowman & Littlefield.

Weber, Eugen. 1976. *Peasants into Frenchmen: The Modernization of Rural France, 1870–1914.* Stanford: Stanford University Press.

Weber, Max. [1922] 1978. *Economy and Society: An Outline of Interpretive Sociology.* Eds. Guenther Roth and Claus Wittich. Berkeley: University of California Press.

———. 1946. *From Max Weber: Essays in Sociology.* Trans. and ed. H. H. Gerth and C. Wright Mills. New York: Oxford University Press.

———. 1958. *The Protestant Ethic and the Spirit of Capitalism.* Trans. Talcott Parsons. New York: Charles Scribner's Sons.

Webster, Laura Josephine. [1916] 1970. *The Operation of the Freedmen's Bureau in South Carolina.* New York: Russell & Russell.

Weikart, Lynne A. 2003. "Follow the Money: Mayoral Choice and Expenditure Policy." *American Review of Public Administration* 33, no. 2 (Jun.): 209–32.

Weir, Margaret. 1992. *Politics and Jobs: The Boundaries of Employment Policy in the United States.* Princeton: Princeton University Press.

Weir, Margaret, Ann Shola Orloff, and Theda Skocpol. 1988a. "Understanding American Social Politics." Introduction to *The Politics of Social Policy in the United States.* Eds. Margaret Weir, Ann Shola Orloff, and Theda Skocpol. Princeton: Princeton University Press.

———, eds. 1988b. *The Politics of Social Policy in the United States.* Princeton: Princeton University Press.

White, Howard A. 1970. *The Freedmen's Bureau in Louisiana.* Baton Rouge: Louisiana State University Press.

Wilentz, Sean. 1984. *Chants Democratic: New York City and the Rise of the American Working Class, 1788–1850.* New York: Oxford University Press.

Williams, Linda Faye. 2003. *The Constraint of Race: Legacies of White Skin Privilege in America.* University Park: Pennsylvania State University Press.

Wilson, William Julius. 1996. *When Work Disappears: The World of the New Urban Poor.* New York: Alfred A. Knopf.

Windhoff-Heritier, Adrienne. 1992. *City of the Poor, City of the Rich: Politics and Policy in New York City.* New York: Walter de Gruyter.

Wise, Daniel. 1997. "Use of Prevailing Wage Required for Workfare." *New York Law Journal* 226 (May 13, 1997): 1.

Witte, Edwin E. 1962. *The Development of the Social Security Act.* Madison: University of Wisconsin Press.

Wolters, Raymond. 1970. *Negroes and the Great Depression: The Problem of Economic Recovery.* Westport, CT: Greenwood.

Woodward, C. Vann. 1957. "The Political Legacy of Reconstruction." *Journal of Negro Education* 26, no. 3 (Summer): 231–40.

Woodworth, Steven E. 2001. *While God is Marching On: The Religious World of Civil War Soldiers.* Lawrence: University Press of Kansas.

Wright, Erik Olin. 1978. *Class, Crisis, and the State.* London: New Left Books.

Zelizer, Julian E. 1998. *Taxing America: Wilbur D. Mills, Congress, and the State, 1945–1975.* New York: Cambridge University Press.

Zelizer, Viviana A. 1994. *The Social Meaning of Money.* New York: Basic Books.

Zimmermann, Wendy, and Karen C. Tumlin. 1999. "Patchwork Policies: State

Assistance for Immigrants under Welfare Reform." Washington, DC: The Urban Institute. http://www.urban.org/url.cfm?ID=309007.

Ziskind, David. 1940. "Strikes on Public Employment Projects." Chap. 10 in *One
Thousand Strikes of Government Employees*. New York: Columbia University
Press.

# Index